Catholicism and the Shaping of Nineteenth-Century America

Catholicism and the Shaping of Nineteenth-Century America offers a series of fresh perspectives on one of the most familiar themes – the nation's encounter with Catholicism – in nineteenth-century American history. While religious and immigration historians have construed this history in univocal terms, Jon Gjerde bridges sectarian divides by presenting Protestants and Catholics in conversation with each other. In so doing, Gjerde reveals the ways in which America's encounter with Catholicism was much more than a story about American nativism. Nineteenth-century religious debates raised questions about the fundamental underpinnings of the American state and society: the shape of the antebellum market economy, the transformation of gender roles in the American family, and the existence of slavery in an ostensibly democratic polity were only a few of the issues engaged by Protestants and Catholics in a lively and enduring dialectic. While the question of the place of Catholics in America was left unresolved, the very debates surrounding this question generated multiple conceptions of American pluralism and American national identity.

Jon Gjerde (February 25, 1953–October 26, 2008) was an American historian and the Alexander F. and May T. Morrison Professor of American History and American Citizenship at the University of California, Berkeley. At Berkeley, he also served as chair of the Department of History and dean of the Division of Social Sciences in the College of Letters and Science. He is the author of the award-winning *From Peasants to Farmers: The Migration from Balestrand, Norway, to the Upper Middle West* and *The Minds of the West: Ethnocultural Evolution in the Rural Middle West, 1830–1917*.

S. Deborah Kang is an assistant professor in the Department of History at California State University, San Marcos, and a former postdoctoral scholar in the Department of History at the University of California, Berkeley. She is a specialist in the areas of American legal, western, and immigration history and the author of *The Legal Construction of the Borderlands: The INS, Immigration Law, and Immigrant Rights on the U.S.-Mexico Border*, which will be published in 2012.

Catholicism and the Shaping of Nineteenth-Century America

JON GJERDE

Edited by
S. DEBORAH KANG

CAMBRIDGE
UNIVERSITY PRESS

CAMBRIDGE UNIVERSITY PRESS
Cambridge, New York, Melbourne, Madrid, Cape Town,
Singapore, São Paulo, Delhi, Tokyo, Mexico City

Cambridge University Press
32 Avenue of the Americas, New York, NY 10013-2473, USA

www.cambridge.org
Information on this title: www.cambridge.org/9780521279666

First published 2012

Printed in the United States of America

A catalog record for this publication is available from the British Library.

Library of Congress Cataloging in Publication data
Gjerde, Jon, 1953–2008.
Catholicism and the shaping of nineteenth-century America / Jon Gjerde ; edited by S. Deborah Kang.
  p. cm.
Includes bibliographical references and index.
ISBN 978-1-107-01024-6 (hardback) – ISBN 978-0-521-27966-6 (paperback)
  1. United States – Church history – 19th century. 2. Christianity – United States –
Influence. 3. United States – History – 19th century. 4. Catholic Church – United States –
History – 19th century. 5. Catholic Church – Relations – Protestant churches. 6. Protestant
churches – Relations – Catholic Church. I. Kang, S. Deborah, 1970– II. Title.
BR525.G47 2011
277.3'07–dc22
                                                              2011009194

ISBN 978-1-107-01024-6 Hardback
ISBN 978-0-521-27966-6 Paperback

Contents

Illustrations

Editor's Preface

Jon Gjerde planned to both begin and end his manuscript for *Catholicism and the Shaping of Nineteenth-Century America* with an account of the 1844 anti-Catholic riots in Philadelphia.[1] As a signal moment in the history of anti-Catholicism in the United States, the Philadelphia riots, as well as the violence that suffused the relationship between the nation's Protestants and Catholics, figure prominently in historical accounts of American nativism.[2] Gjerde recognized that he was treading on well-worn historical ground when he chose to remind his readers of the Philadelphia riots. But he did so in order to offer his own broad reinterpretation of the relationship between America's Protestants and Catholics, arguing that an emphasis on the violence was "not wrong, but ... must be clarified, enlarged, and probed further."[3] In Gjerde's rendering, anti-Catholicism found expression in a less-violent register – in an enduring and frequently charged conversation between Protestants and Catholics about the fundamental underpinnings of the American state and society. This conversation, moreover, bore lasting consequences for the nation-building project in the nineteenth century and beyond. In *Catholicism and the Shaping of Nineteenth-Century America*, religious conflict did not serve only as a proxy for violence; in Gjerde's words, it also reshaped "American religious and political life for years to come."[4]

Jon Gjerde, who was dean in the College of Letters and Science and the Alexander F. and May T. Morrison Professor of American History and American Citizenship at the University of California, Berkeley, unexpectedly passed away in October 2008, at the age of fifty-five. Earlier that year, he had

---

[1] Jon Gjerde, *Catholicism and the Shaping of Nineteenth-Century America* (New York: Cambridge University Press, 2012), Chapter 1; Jon Gjerde, "Chapter 7, Riotous Politics: Political Developments before and after the Civil War" (unpublished manuscript, n.d.), 1.

[2] See, for example, Ray Allen Billington, *The Protestant Crusade, 1800–1860* (New York: Macmillan, 1938); Dale B. Light, *Rome and the New Republic: Conflict and Community in Philadelphia Catholicism between the Revolution and the Civil War* (Notre Dame, IN: University of Notre Dame Press, 1996); Noel Ignatiev, *How the Irish Became White* (New York: Routledge, 1995).

[3] Gjerde, *Catholicism*, "Introduction."

[4] Gjerde, "Chapter 7, Riotous Politics," 1.

submitted a nearly complete draft of *Catholicism and the Shaping of Nineteenth-Century America* to Cambridge University Press for review. All that remained to be done was the completion of a seventh and final chapter about Catholics, Protestants, and American electoral politics after the Civil War and an epilogue on the implications of the Catholic-Protestant divide for contemporary religious conflicts. Despite the unfinished state of the manuscript, Cambridge decided that the Introduction and Chapters 1 through 6 could stand on their own merits and together constituted a clear and incisive account of relations between Protestants and Catholics in the nineteenth century. Given the polished state of these chapters, only relatively minor changes have been made throughout the text and footnotes. I have kept intact the sections of the manuscript that foreshadow the argument Gjerde planned to make in Chapter 7, which would have illustrated the relationship between religion and politics in nineteenth-century America. I have also retained Gjerde's direct references to Chapter 7 in the Introduction where they assist the reader in understanding the scope and organization of his narrative. An epilogue, drawing on Gjerde's drafts and notes, has been added to suggest the connections between *Catholicism and the Shaping of Nineteenth-Century America* and the religious debates of the present day. Finally, this preface has been written for the benefit of historians of immigration and religion to address the question of why Gjerde, an esteemed immigration historian, chose to write about religious history and to explain how his multidisciplinary perspective illuminated his study of Protestants and Catholics in nineteenth-century America.

In *Catholicism and the Shaping of Nineteenth-Century America*, Jon Gjerde aimed to recapture what he referred to as the "lost moments" in the history of American anti-Catholicism.[5] For Gjerde, the emphasis on the reactionary elements of anti-Catholicism and nativism in nineteenth-century America had drawn scholarly attention away from the breadth and depth of the relationship between Catholics and Protestants during that period. The tensions in that relationship found expression not only in sporadic violence but also in a lasting debate over some of the most pressing issues of the day, including the shape of the antebellum market economy, the transformation of gender roles in the American family, and the place of slavery in an ostensibly democratic polity. For both Catholics and Protestants, the stakes were high; each group believed that the very fate of the nation – its economy, society, and political institutions – rested on the spiritual character of its citizens. In other words, for both Catholics and Protestants, religion constituted a critical factor in the development of the nation in the nineteenth century.

Catholicism and the Shaping of Nineteenth-Century America, then, recasts the history of anti-Catholicism as a broad story about how a religious conflict built a nation. As Gjerde explains, the unprecedented increase in Catholic migration from Europe to the United States compelled the nation to address the

---

[5] Gjerde, "Introduction" (handwritten notes, n.d.), 1.

problem of how to incorporate diverse religious groups into American society.[6] Moreover, the antebellum encounter with Catholicism, or what Gjerde refers to as the "Catholic challenge," would constitute the first of many moments in which the nation would have to come to terms with the presence of sizeable racial and religious minorities, such as freed slaves, Mormons, Jews, Asians, and Muslims.[7] In this first moment, however, Catholics and Protestants initially responded with violence; the growing Catholic population triggered deadly riots in Boston, New York, and Philadelphia. Yet Protestants and Catholics quickly realized that such riots solved little. As a result, both groups explored alternative approaches; Protestants, for instance, sought to convert Catholics through missionary campaigns and religious education in the public schools. Meanwhile, Catholics adopted what Gjerde refers to as a "pillorized strategy" that "aimed at providing an integration in state and society at the same time that it developed an institutional structure that shielded its adherents from excessive interaction with the unwashed."[8] Parochial schools, convents, and theological seminaries were the primary institutions designed to maintain and expand Catholicism in America.

The conflict between Protestants and Catholics redefined not only social relations but also the relationship between church and state. As Gjerde points out, in their struggles to come to terms with the rapid diversification of American society, Protestants and Catholics articulated distinct views on the relationship between church and state – views that blurred the line separating religion and government. Thus, although, in Gjerde's words, the "formulaic narrative" surrounding the relationship between church and state describes a complete separation, enabling religious liberty and, in turn, religious diversity, antebellum Americans construed that relationship as less clear-cut.[9] For Protestants, the arrival of large numbers of Catholic immigrants exposed contradictions between, on the one hand, their long-standing presumptions about the Protestant underpinnings of the American state (and the concomitant cultural homogeneity of American society) and, on the other hand, their express commitment to religious freedom. In a similar vein, Catholics struggled to reconcile their appreciation for the political freedoms that facilitated the growth of their churches in the United States with their own particularist view of Catholicism

---

[6] As Gjerde and others have explained, the sense of urgency underlying the Protestant and Catholic race for ascendancy resulted from the unprecedented increase in the migration of Catholic adherents from Europe to the United States. As Mark Noll reports, "At the time of the nation's founding in 1776, there were only 25,000 Catholics (1 percent of the population) served by only 23 priests. The religious census of 1906 found that 130 years later the number of communicant Catholics stood at over 12 million (14% of the population) served by over 15,000 clergy in nearly 12,000 church buildings." Mark A. Noll, *The Old Religion in a New World* (Grand Rapids, MI: Wm. B. Eerdmans, 2002), 121. See also Jon Gjerde, *The Minds of the West: Ethnocultural Evolution in the Rural Middle West, 1830–1917* (Chapel Hill: University of North Carolina Press, 1997), 5.

[7] Gjerde, *Catholicism*, "Introduction."

[8] Ibid.

[9] Ibid.

as the one true faith.[10] In summary, both Protestants and Catholics sought to balance their commitments to religious freedom with their convictions that religion was vital to the state and the nation.

In *Catholicism and the Shaping of Nineteenth-Century America*, Gjerde offers no easy resolution to the political conundrums and social conflicts faced by Protestants and Catholics. By the end of the nineteenth century, neither group could claim to have reconstructed a more Catholic or more Protestant society despite their wide-ranging efforts. Instead, Gjerde argues that these religious conflicts produced only a more pluralistic, rather than more homogeneous, society. For example, Protestants hoped that the religious freedoms afforded by America would provide them with a propitious environment in which to convert Catholics, many of whom had lived without an analogous set of religious freedoms in their European homelands. Yet, ultimately, these very freedoms resulted in the creation of new Protestant denominations and in the segregation and growth of Catholic communities. The debates over religious education in the schools also produced a set of unintended consequences for both Protestants and Catholics; for example, public schools introduced secular approaches to education, and Catholics established their own sectarian schools. As Gjerde explains, Catholics and Protestants forged divergent, competing accounts of the nation's economy, society, and even history. In short, both groups came to construe the nation, its present and its future, in their own distinctive terms.

Catholicism and the Shaping of Nineteenth-Century America is a natural extension of Jon Gjerde's earlier work. Drawing on his training in philosophy, religion, and history as an undergraduate at the University of Northern Iowa and in immigration history and demography as a graduate student at the University of Minnesota, Gjerde consistently focuses on cultural conflicts and their influence on the formation of ethnic, racial, religious, and national identities in the United States. His early work, including his first monograph, *From Peasants to Farmers: The Migration from Balestrand, Norway, to the Upper Middle West*, demonstrates how religious conflicts contributed to the formation of a Norwegian American church and, more broadly, a Norwegian American ethnic identity.[11] His second monograph, *The Minds of the West: Ethnocultural Evolution in the Rural Middle West, 1830–1917*, expands this analysis by tracing how theological disputes between and even within the numerous immigrant groups in the West (Norwegian Lutherans, Irish and German Roman Catholics, and East Coast Protestants, among others) served as "expressions of developing ethnic identification[s]."[12]

---

[10] Ibid.

[11] Jon Gjerde, *From Peasants to Farmers: The Migration from Balestrand, Norway, to the Upper Middle West* (New York: Cambridge University Press, 1985); Jon Gjerde, "Conflict and Community: A Case Study of the Immigrant Church in the United States," *Journal of Social History* 19 (1986): 681–97.

[12] Indeed, religious dissent was so common between and within immigrant settlements that "[c]hurch members passionately discussed the theological questions ... 'on the streets and in the

By focusing on the discord within and between immigrant communities, Gjerde underscores the complexities of identity formation in the United States. In this respect, Gjerde's work serves as an explicit rejoinder to an older historiographical tradition that suggests that intra- and intercommunity conflicts ultimately found resolution in the assimilation of disparate migrants into a homogeneous national identity.[13] At the same time, Gjerde exhorts a newer generation of immigration historians, particularly those who reject theories of assimilation in favor of notions of ethnic persistence, to avoid facile assumptions about the existence of consensus in immigrant and ethnic communities.[14] Thus, in one of his most important contributions to immigration history, Gjerde argues that immigrants in the Midwest developed a "complementary identity," that is, a sense of dual identification with both an ethnic group and the nation whereby their identification with the former only reinforced the latter. As Gjerde explains:

> In a very real sense, then, allegiance to the American nation and to cultural traditions carried across the sea could coexist. Indeed, they could be mutually supportive and self-reinforcing. Immigrants celebrated life in the United States because it enabled them to retain beliefs that originated outside of it. They thus could develop a "complementary identity" that pledged allegiance to both American citizenship and ethnic adherence.[15]

Gjerde emphasizes that the complementary identity was not simply a condition of dual consciousness; instead, given the freedom to develop and maintain their ethnic identities in the West, European immigrants, in a paradoxical fashion, also came to identify with the American nation.[16]

---

alleys, in stores and in saloons, and through a continuous flow of agitating articles [in newspapers and periodicals].'" Gjerde, *Minds of the West*, 118.

[13] The work of Frederick Jackson Turner and Oscar Handlin are often cited as two classic examples of an assimilationist approach to immigration history. Frederick Jackson Turner, *The Frontier in American History* (New York: Holt, 1921); Oscar Handlin, *The Uprooted* (Boston: Little, Brown, 1951). On the history of assimilation theory, see Donna Gabaccia, "Is Everywhere Nowhere? Nomads, Nations, and the Immigrant Paradigm of United States History," *Journal of American History* 86, no. 3 (1999): 1115–34; Jon Gjerde, "Rudolph J. Vecoli and the New Social History: An Appreciation," *Journal of American Ethnic History* 28, no. 2 (2009): 14–17; Ewa Morawska, "The Sociology and Historiography of Immigration," in *Immigration Reconsidered: History, Sociology, and Politics*, ed. Virginia Yans-McLaughlin, 187–241 (New York: Oxford University Press, 1990).

[14] A few examples of the key works to challenge Handlin's thesis through an emphasis on ethnic persistence include John Bodnar, *The Transplanted: A History of Immigrants in Urban America* (Bloomington: Indiana University Press, 1985); Kathleen Neils Conzen, *Making Their Own America: Assimilation Theory and the German Peasant Pioneer* (Providence, RI: Berg, 1990); Robert C. Ostergren, *A Community Transplanted: The Trans-Atlantic Experience of a Swedish Immigrant Settlement in the Upper Middle West, 1835–1915* (Madison: University of Wisconsin Press, 1988); Rudolph J. Vecoli, "*Contadini* in Chicago: A Critique of *The Uprooted*," *Journal of American History* 51, no. 3 (1964): 404–17.

[15] Gjerde, *Minds of the West*, 8.

[16] It is also important to note that, for Gjerde, the complementary identity was only one of several outcomes of the theological disputes described in *Minds of the West*. While the complementary

While Gjerde's earlier work examines the processes of identity formation at the local and regional levels, in *Catholicism and the Shaping of Nineteenth-Century America* Gjerde explores this issue on a national scale. Indeed, Gjerde avers that, in the nineteenth century, religion played as much a central role as did ethnicity and race in defining one's attitudes toward one's community and nation. This was not only an American phenomenon but also a global one; that is, religious conflicts, especially those between Catholics and Protestants, shaped the larger debates about nation building and nationalism in Europe during the long nineteenth century.[17] Thus, although new European immigrants, as provisional outsiders in nineteenth-century America, initially sought social and political inclusion on racial grounds, they quickly discovered that religious affiliation constituted an enduring dividing line among self-proclaimed white Americans.[18] In other words, shared claims to a common white identity failed to quell the debates – between new European immigrants and native-born Americans – over their spiritual differences. These religious divides, then, fractured the racial consensus among Americans of European descent and, more broadly, created two divergent views of the American nation.[19]

Gjerde's claims about the relationship between religion and national identity address not only major questions in the field of immigration history but also major problems in American religious history. By examining the role of the Protestant-Catholic dialectic in the development of the nation, Gjerde's last monograph makes a substantial contribution to recent efforts to integrate the

identity enabled immigrants to form allegiances to the nation, religious conflicts generated multiple and even overlapping ethnic affiliations between and, particularly, *within* migrant communities. In a fascinating and nuanced analysis, Gjerde, for example, recounts how a feud between Norwegian American immigrant groups over the predestination doctrine reinforced "cultural variations carried from Norway as well as differences in wealth created in the United States." Gjerde, *Minds of the West*, 119.

[17] On this point, Gjerde's work was deeply informed by the work of European historians such as Linda Colley and Helmut Walser Smith, as well as colleagues in the Department of History at the University of California, Berkeley. See Linda Colley, *Britons: Forging the Nation, 1707–1837* (New Haven, CT: Yale University Press, 1992); Helmut Walser Smith, *German Nationalism and Religious Conflict: Culture, Ideology, and Politics, 1870–1914* (Princeton, NJ: Princeton University Press, 1995); Gjerde, "Notes on the Geopolitics of Religion" (handwritten notes, n.d.).

[18] Gjerde observed that constructions of "whiteness" were particularly important in a "multiracial society with a subject indigenous population and a thriving system of racial slavery." More specifically, he emphasized the ways in which Americans deployed concepts of race so as to rationalize the social, legal, and political dispossession of Native Americans, freed blacks, and slaves. At the same time, new European immigrants sought social acceptance and political integration on racial grounds. Indeed, given that naturalization was predicated on race, the assumption of a "white" racial identity was critical to new immigrants' social and political incorporation into the nation. Gjerde, *Catholicism*, "Introduction."

[19] It is important to note that Gjerde recognized that these religious debates continued to instantiate conceptions of race. Indeed, notions of racial difference were often used to reinforce religious divides. As a result, Gjerde writes, "From this perspective, we profit from viewing the development of an American nation as a process that triangulated race and religion so that Americans were superior racially (in the context of non-Europeans) and religiously (as European but freed of the European Papacy and the Old World)." Gjerde, *Catholicism*, "Introduction."

study of religion into the study of American history as a whole. In so doing, the work departs from a historiographical tradition that construes religious history from either a theological or a sectarian perspective.[20] In addition, Gjerde's dialectical narrative – his consideration of Catholic history and Protestant history in juxtaposition – bridges the sectarian divides that characterized the field for much of the twentieth century. Finally, rejecting the assumptions of historians who link a triumphant narrative about the American past to the nation's Protestant inheritance,[21] Gjerde, like his contemporaries, highlights the plural and even fragmented nature of religious practice in the nation from its founding to the present.[22] Whereas early twentieth-century historians may have drawn easy connections between Protestantism and the American state, nineteenth-century Americans did not. Instead, the question of the nation's religious character was hotly contested between Protestants and Catholics themselves.

At the same time that Gjerde's monograph reflects and advances these methodological developments in the field of religious history, it also offers new insights into key substantive issues, including the history of anti-Catholicism, the separation of church and state, and the relationship between religion and pluralism in nineteenth-century America. As noted earlier, *Catholicism and the*

---

[20] On this historiographical development, see Jon Butler, "Jack-in-the-Box Faith: The Religion Problem in Modern American History," *Journal of American History* 90, no. 4 (2004): 1357–78; Kevin M. Schultz and Paul Harvey, "Everywhere and Nowhere: Recent Trends in American Religious History and Historiography," *Journal of the American Academy of Religion* 78, no. 1 (2010): 129–62.

[21] Published in 1930, William Warren Sweet's *The Story of Religions in America* is often referred to as the culmination of the Protestant synthesis or of a long line of historical studies that since the nineteenth century linked the nation's history to its alleged Protestant origins. William Warren Sweet, *The Story of Religions in America* (New York: Harper and Brothers, 1930). For an overview of the Protestant synthesis, see Sidney E. Ahlstrom, "The Problem of the History of Religion in America," *Church History* 57 (1988): 127–38.

[22] By the 1960s, historians began to underscore the diversity of religious practices from the colonial period to the present. What emerged were studies of African American, Jewish, and Mormon religious practices. In addition, scholars responded to the traditional focus on institutions and theology by examining popular or lay practices. More recently, scholars have explored the spiritual practices, including Hinduism, Buddhism, and Islam, of the nation's most recent immigrants. For overviews of the historical literature on non-Christian and popular religious practices, see Ahlstrom, "The Problem of the History of Religion in America," 127–38; Butler, "Jack-in-the-Box Faith," 1357–78; Leigh E. Schmidt, "A History of All Religions," *Journal of the Early Republic* 24 (Summer 2004): 327–34. On religious pluralism in America, see, for example, William R. Hutchinson, *Religious Pluralism in America: The Contentious History of a Founding Ideal* (New Haven, CT: Yale University Press, 2003); R. Laurence Moore, *Religious Outsiders and the Making of Americans* (New York: Oxford University Press, 1986); Martin E. Marty, *Religion and Republic: The American Circumstance* (Boston: Beacon Press, 1987). A recent issue of the *Annals of the American Academy of Political and Social Science* offers a comprehensive and insightful overview of the state of religious pluralism in the late twentieth and early twenty-first centuries. *Annals of the American Academy of Political and Social Science* 612 (July 2007): 6–252 (special issue on religious pluralism and civil society). Professor Diana L. Eck's Pluralism Project at Harvard University is a particularly valuable resource for tracking the most recent developments with respect to religion, diversity, and discrimination in contemporary America (see http://pluralism.org).

Shaping of Nineteenth-Century America departs from the voluminous scholarship on anti-Catholicism by construing the debates between Protestants and Catholics not simply as an anti-immigrant or reactionary movement but as a conversation, and at times a bitter dialogue, between the two groups about the condition of religion, society, and the state in America. Moreover, Gjerde's decision to consider the history of anti-Catholicism from the perspectives of both Protestants and Catholics adds to a literature that has tended to consider this history from a univocal perspective.[23]

What results from Gjerde's dual focus on Protestant history and Catholic history is a fresh interpretation of pluralism in nineteenth-century America. Gjerde's work reveals that the mere existence of diverse religious groups in the United States did not automatically instantiate a pluralist society. Indeed, the peculiarly nineteenth-century American version of pluralism that emerges in Gjerde's narrative is far less sanguine than those theories of American pluralism that appeared in the twentieth century.[24] More specifically, nineteenth-century

---

[23] On the history of anti-Catholicism, see, for example: Billington, *The Protestant Crusade*; Jenny Franchot, *Roads to Rome: The Antebellum Protestant Encounter with Catholicism* (Berkeley: University of California Press, 1994); Patrick Allitt, *Catholic Converts: British and American Intellectuals Turn to Rome* (Ithaca, NY: Cornell University Press, 1997); Light, *Rome and the New Republic*; Ignatiev, *How the Irish Became White*; Tyler Anbinder, *Nativism and Slavery: The Northern Know Nothings and the Politics of the 1850s* (New York: Oxford University Press, 1992); David H. Bennett, *Party of Fear: From Nativist Movements to the New Right in American History* (Chapel Hill: University of North Carolina Press, 1988); Dale T. Knobel, *Paddy and the Republic: Ethnicity and Nationality in Antebellum America* (Middletown, CT: Wesleyan University Press, 1986); Vincent P. Lannie, *Public Money and Parochial Education: Bishop Hughes, Governor Seward and the New York School Controversy* (Cleveland, OH: Press of Case Western Reserve University, 1968).

[24] By the twentieth century, conceptions of pluralism had come to be more inclusive and tolerant. As a critical response to notions of the "melting pot" and, in turn, an affirmation of immigrant and ethnic contributions to the United States, Horace Kallen, in 1915, began developing the notion of what he, in 1924, would coin "cultural pluralism"; the idea was further reinforced and developed by Kallen's contemporary Randolph Bourne. World War II marked a watershed moment for theories of pluralism in the United States; the horrors inflicted upon the Jews by Nazi Germany informed the reimagination of the national community in Judeo-Christian terms as well as a revival and expansion of Kallen's conception of cultural pluralism. The desegregation campaigns of the 1950s and the civil rights movement of the 1960s famously inspired the development of notions of multiculturalism. More recently, scholars such as David Hollinger, in search of a more capacious discourse by which multiculturalists might achieve their programmatic goals in the public sphere, have articulated the idea of a "postethnic America." Scholarly treatment of pluralism also changed over the course of the twentieth century; after the 1960s, references to the term "pluralism" took on a more normative, rather than descriptive, dimension in multiple disciplines, including history, political science, and sociology. For a history of pluralism in America, see David Hollinger, *Postethnic America: Beyond Multiculturalism* (New York: Basic Books, 1995); Philip Gleason, *Speaking of Diversity: Language and Ethnicity in Twentieth Century America* (Baltimore, MD: Johns Hopkins University Press, 1992); John Higham, *Send These to Me: Immigrants in Urban America* (Baltimore, MD: Johns Hopkins University Press, 1975); Lawrence H. Fuchs, *The American Kaleidoscope: Race, Ethnicity, and the Civic Culture* (Middletown, CT: Wesleyan University Press, 1990). While many have written about Horace Kallen, Daniel Greene's recent essay offers a highly insightful and readable analysis of how

American pluralism, Gjerde argues, was the product of conflict between dispa-rate religious groups rather than of peaceful coexistence; as Gjerde writes, "Paradoxically, I believe that the growth of pluralism in the United States was fostered by efforts to create a homogeneous nation."[25] In *Catholicism and the Shaping of Nineteenth-Century America*, Gjerde demonstrates that pluralism, in its nineteenth-century incarnation, emerged only after Protestants and Catholics had carved out distinct public and private spaces that enabled their tenuous coexistence in America.

Perhaps of greatest interest to Gjerde was the question of how the disparate conceptions of national identity forged by Protestants and Catholics raised challenges for the separation of church and state. In addressing this question from the perspectives of Protestants and Catholics themselves, Gjerde's narrative departs from the political focus of much of the literature on the separation of church and state and instead reveals how social actors, as well as political elites, played a profound role in shifting (and reshifting) the line of separation. In short, Gjerde asks his readers to construe the notion of the separation of church and state as a cultural construction as well as a political and legal one.[26] Gjerde's narrative reveals how the everyday concerns of Catholics and Protestants – concerns about the education of their children, about the changing role of women in the family, and about their own economic well-being in a rapidly modernizing society – informed their opinions about the appropriate relation-ship between religion and government. And this social discontent occasionally

Kallen's development of the notion of cultural pluralism intersected with his own personal and intellectual struggles as a Jewish American. Daniel Greene, "A Chosen People in a Pluralist Nation: Horace Kallen and the Jewish-American Experience," *Religion and American Culture* 16, no. 2 (2006): 161–93. For interpretations of the Judeo-Christian tradition, see Will Herberg, *Protestant, Catholic, Jew: An Essay in American Religious Sociology* (Garden City, NY: Doubleday, 1955); Martin E. Marty, "A Judeo-Christian Looks at the Judeo-Christian Tradition," *Christian Century* 103, no. 29 (1986): 858–60; Mark Silk, "Notes on the Judeo-Christian Tradition, " *American Quarterly* 36, no. 1 (1984): 65–85; Deborah Dash Moore, *GI Jews: How World War II Changed a Generation* (Cambridge, MA: Harvard University Press, 2004); David Hollinger, "Jewish Intellectuals and the De-Christianization of American Public Culture in the Twentieth Century," in *Science, Jews, and Secular Culture: Studies in Mid-Twentieth Century American Intellectual History* (Princeton, NJ: Princeton University Press, 1996); Katherine Healan Gaston, "The Genesis of America's Judeo-Christian Moment: Secularism, Totalitarianism, and the Redefinition of Democracy" (Ph.D. diss., University of California, Berkeley, 2008).

[25] Gjerde, *Catholicism*, "Introduction."

[26] In this respect, Gjerde's work serves as response to Philip Hamburger's call to construct cultural and social accounts of the separation of church and state. As Hamburger writes, "[The] separation of church and state cannot be understood simply as the product of great men, whether Roger Williams, Thomas Jefferson, or Hugo Black. Nor can it be understood merely as an institutional development, whether in the documents of the U.S. Constitution or in the opinions of the Supreme Court. Instead, the redefinition of American religious liberty as a separation of church and state needs to be considered within the context of America's broader ideas, culture, and society. Amid these wider circumstances, including changing popular perceptions and fears, Americans gradu-ally transformed their understanding of religious liberty." Philip Hamburger, *Separation of Church and State* (Cambridge, MA: Harvard University Press, 2002), 17.

inspired Protestants and Catholics alike to seek redress in the public sphere, pursuing political solutions to perceived religious crises. The New York school controversy that Gjerde relates marked one of the most prominent instances in which religious groups sought state support for religious mandates. As Gjerde planned to argue in a final chapter, when that school reform effort failed, both Protestants and Catholics sought public power through active participation in electoral politics.[27]

In the tradition of his earlier work, Gjerde's final study reflects his long-standing commitment to producing scholarship that conveys the complexities of the past. As he often reminded his readers and students, "History indeed is messy, and master narratives create only a false clarity of a national whole that not coincidentally often is willing to exclude many of its subjects. In an era when we are fed monochromatic tales about the end of history and the unilateral march of freedom, we profit from understanding the multifarious directions of historical development.[28] As a result, through his own scholarship Gjerde routinely spoke to multiple audiences, including historians of immigration, the West, and religion. Gjerde's approach in *Catholicism and the Shaping of Nineteenth-Century America* is no different, traversing the fields of immigration and religious history to produce a highly nuanced and insightful account of how a religious conflict shaped a nation.

Words cannot express the profundity of the loss felt by the campus of the University of California, Berkeley, on the day we received news of Jon Gjerde's death. A scholar who frequently wrote about ethnic and cultural conflicts, Gjerde was known on campus and in the historical profession as a man who was unfailingly calm, kind, and generous. He brought a sense of intelligent and steady leadership to his roles as the dean of the Division of Social Sciences in the College of Letters and Science and the former chair of the Department of History. His undergraduate and graduate classes in immigration history were among the most popular on campus, especially because he had earned a reputation as a professor who was always accessible to his students and highly supportive of their intellectual endeavors. Despite having won numerous awards for his scholarly work and his national standing as a leading immigration historian, Jon never wore his accolades on his sleeve. Instead, he was, as his colleague and friend Yuri Slezkine memorialized, "unaffectedly self-effacing but utterly secure in his sense of dignity and belonging." On a daily basis, his presence is palpably missed in the Department of History and on the University of California, Berkeley, campus.

---

[27] As Gjerde writes: "... if the puzzle of the Roman Catholic presence in the United States could not be solved by private religious conversion or by public institutional structures, perhaps it could be addressed by public discourse, most salubriously in the form of electoral politics." Gjerde, "Chapter 7, Riotous Politics," 1.

[28] Jon Gjerde, "Rudolph J. Vecoli and the New Social History," 6–21.

Given the difficult circumstances surrounding the publication of this book, I could not have proceeded without the generous support of Jon Gjerde's colleagues, friends, and family. Chair Mary Elizabeth Berry, Vice Chair James Vernon, and Marianne Bartholomew-Couts in the Department of History made it possible for me to remain at the University of California, Berkeley, for the two years it took to bring this book to completion. During that time, I had the honor and pleasure of interviewing Jon's colleagues about the manuscript; on the Berkeley campus, I owe many thanks to Margaret Anderson, Andrew Barshay, John Connelly, Jan deVries, John Efron, Kerwin Klein, and Peter Zinoman. James Sheehan in the Department of History at Stanford University and Erika Lee in the Department of History at the University of Minnesota provided extremely helpful suggestions and advice. I am deeply grateful to Mary Elizabeth Berry, Margaret Chowning, Robin Einhorn, David Hollinger, Mark Peterson, Yuri Slezkine, and James Vernon for meeting with me to discuss the book and taking the time to read and comment on a draft of the manuscript. A colleague and friend of Jon's in the Dean's Office, Janet Broughton, vice provost for academic affairs and faculty welfare, graciously provided me with intellectual and moral support on numerous occasions. In the early stages of the project, Jon Butler, dean of the Graduate School of Arts and Sciences at Yale University, offered invaluable guidance and encouragement that sustained me through this entire process.

At Cambridge University Press, Lewis Bateman has been the model editor. His unparalleled professionalism; his support of Jon and his work, both in life and after Jon's passing; his graciousness toward Ruth Gjerde, Jon's widow; and his support of my efforts were critical to the completion of this book. I would also like to express my thanks to Anne Lovering Rounds, senior editorial assistant in history and politics, who patiently and kindly addressed my many logistical questions. Mark Fox, production controller, and Camilla Knapp, production editor, provided their invaluable expertise during the production of the manuscript. I could not have asked for a better copy editor than Susan Greenberg; I am deeply grateful to her for her precise and comprehensive review of the manuscript. Allan Ayers generously offered his time and expertise in retouching several of the illustrations for the book. Many thanks are also due Diana Witt, who prepared the index for the book.

I am sure that Jon would have wanted to thank his graduate research assistants for their dedicated and enthusiastic efforts on his behalf. Hannah Farber, Annie Kwon, Chris Shaw, and Phil Wolgin spent years assisting Jon with numerous aspects of the manuscript. I am especially grateful to them for continuing to support this project by answering my many questions these past few years. I am also indebted to Andrew Keating, whose dual talents as a computing consultant and historian were essential as we recovered the files related to this book from Jon's work and home computers.

In Ruth Gjerde, I have had the ideal collaborator. It is a privilege and honor to know and work with Ruth, whose gentle and kind spirit always remind me of everything that is good and positive in life. She found the images for the book and obtained the appropriate permissions. She also assisted with the editing of the final manuscript, reviewed drafts of my preface and epilogue, and identified potential indexers for the project. I know I could not have finished the book without her. Finally, Ruth arranged for me to meet Peter Franson, one of Jon's colleagues and a close friend from graduate school, whose personal insights about Jon and the manuscript provided me with much-needed inspiration at a crucial juncture in my drafting of the book's preface and epilogue.

Kevin Adams at Kent State University and the religious historian Susan Haskell, two of Jon's former students, read and commented on drafts of the Preface and the Epilogue. I am also deeply indebted to Kevin for the tremendous moral support he has given me and this project.

Unknown to me are the many others whom Jon himself would have wanted to thank for their contributions and support. I deeply regret the omissions. But I am certain that Jon would have closed his acknowledgments by thanking his family – his wife, Ruth, and his daughters, Christine and Kari, most of all.

S. Deborah Kang
Berkeley, California

Introduction

How odd that "the City of Brotherly Love," observed the *New Englander and Yale Review* in 1844, was the site of violence and bloodshed, "the scene of action, as a burlesque upon the name." Although nearly every major city in the United States had been disgraced by riots of one form or another in the 1830s and 1840s, Philadelphia had been in a league of its own. Riots against abolitionists in 1834 were followed by periodic violence aimed at the African American community in the 1830s and 1840s that drove many black families out of the city and made the situation for those black residents who remained increasingly unpredictable. Philadelphia was the scene of violence again, in 1840, when the Philadelphia and Trenton Railroad intruded into a residential community and was destroyed, and, four years later, when a weavers' strike turned violent. Philadelphia by the early 1840s clearly had gained "the unenviable distinction" as "the theatre of popular tumults."[1]

Yet the residents of the City of Brotherly Love outdid themselves in May and July of 1844, when Catholics and Protestants squared off for three days of violence, mayhem, and murder that both scarred the city and provoked reflection about the state of affairs in the polyglot cities of the American Northeast (see Fig. 1).[2] The air was tense in Philadelphia in the weeks leading up to the riots. The region had been recently plagued by controversies concerning the role of religion in the public schools in the early 1840s. The recent electoral successes in New York of a nativist political party, dubbed the Native American Party, further inflamed native-born Philadelphians, who on April 15, 1844, resolved both to emulate their counterparts in New York and, more ominously, to gather again in the largely Irish Third Ward

---

[1] "The Philadelphia Riots," *New Englander and Yale Review* 2 (1844): 470.
[2] The account of the Philadelphia riots is amply documented in Ray Allen Billington, *The Protestant Crusade, 1800–1860* (New York: Macmillan, 1938). Although Billington was critical of the American nativists in the riots, he nonetheless used their newspapers as sources. I provide different shadings of his account because I have augmented it with sources from abolitionists and Catholics. See also Dale B. Light, *Rome and the New Republic: Conflict and Community in Philadelphia Catholicism between the Revolution and the Civil War* (Notre Dame, IN: University of Notre Dame Press, 1996); Noel Ignatiev, *How the Irish Became White* (New York: Routledge, 1995).

RIOT IN PHILADELPHIA

FIGURE 1. Controversies over the role of religion in the public schools triggered riots in Philadelphia in May and July of 1844. In response to the mob violence, city officials called upon the state militia to restore order. (Lithograph by H. Bucholzer. *Riot in Philadelphia, June [i.e. July] 7, 1844* [New York and Massachusetts, 1844]). (Popular Graphics Arts Collection, Prints and Photographs Division, Library of Congress, LC-USZ62-3536)

of Philadelphia's Kensington suburb in early May. Ostensibly, the demonstration was focused on Kensington because it had been the site of outrages that had previously disgraced the city. The more probable reason for the invasion was simply to inflame the tensions raging between the Native American Party supporters and their Irish opponents.

In the weeks prior to the meeting to be held in Kensington on May 3, the fledgling nativist organization intensified the disquiet in the city. When the meeting was held on a vacant lot near a public school, moreover, the forewarned Irish – both men and women – drove them from their neighborhood. According to one report, the Irish mob demolished the speaker's platform and forced the "native Americans ... to flee under a shower of missiles, accompanied with shouts, oaths, hisses and groans."[3] When the nativists reassembled at a safe haven, they solemnly protested "this flagrant violation of the rights of American citizens" and "this outbreak of a vindictive, anti-republican spirit" displayed by "the alien population" and passed a series of resolutions, including the promise that they would reassemble again at the same location three days hence.[4] The gauntlet had been thrown down.

[3] "The Philadelphia Riots," 475.
[4] *Native American*, 4 May 1844, cited in Billington, *Protestant Crusade*, 222–23.

On May 6, a crowd of several thousand, some of whom had been mobilized by the nativist publicity following the first meeting and who undoubtedly were looking for trouble, gathered again at the vacant lot. The American flag was raised over the speaker's dais, and a few speeches were presented before a downpour interrupted the meeting and drove the participants to march to a nearby market house. What happened next is not clear, but it is certain that shortly after the next speaker took the stage, a commotion occurred, clubs were swung, stones were thrown, and a pistol was fired in the melee that struck and mortally wounded George Shiffler, one of the Protestant marchers. Amid the confusion that ensued, a crowd of Irish, many of them armed, rushed into the fray. With guns blazing, they drove out the nativists, who momentarily rallied "around the remnants of their flag, which the Irish had torn to shreds."[5]

Although sporadic violence punctuated the night, the next day promised to be even more violent. Crowds throughout the city were harangued by impromptu speakers on the evils of Catholicism. The nativist newspaper, the *Native American*, declared that "another St. Bartholomew's day is begun on the streets of Philadelphia" and that "the bloody hand of the Pope has stretched itself forth to our destruction." The best recourse, the *Native American* concluded, was to arm. Amid this disquiet, yet another meeting commenced in the early afternoon at Independence Square. Despite calls for forbearance and respect for the law, members of the crowd resolved to invade Kensington yet again. As the mob marched through the Irish neighborhood, it carried their tattered flag and a banner that advised, "this is the flag which was trampled under foot by the Irish Papists."[6] Not unexpectedly, the demonstration turned to violence. The building of the Hibernia Hose Company, an Irish fire company, was stormed and destroyed. Irish snipers apparently shot at the marchers, who responded by torching the buildings that housed them. By midnight, when a military detachment finally restored some semblance of order, some thirty homes of Irish families had been burned to the ground.[7]

The violence in Irish neighborhoods continued the following day. The nativist mob now held the balance of power, and the Irish apparently offered little resistance and "fled in terror to save themselves and families."[8] The mobs continued to

[5] The depiction of heroic defenders of the flag that had been defiled by the Irish is found in "The Philadelphia Riots," 476, which is clearly sympathetic to the Protestant side.

[6] This observation comes again from "The Philadelphia Riots," 476. It continued, "[N]othing could exasperate the inflammable portion of American citizens more than the sight of their dishonored flag."

[7] Those sympathetic to the American born nonetheless admitted that innocents might have been victims during this second night of rioting. "Probably some of the Irish were consumed in their dwellings; others were shot down in attempting to escape. Families were driven from their flaming houses, they knew not whither, exposed to the insults of a mob, whose fury had already made them mourners for a husband, a father, a brother, a son. The Native Americans felt that they had done enough. Revenge herself stood appalled and sickened at her own dreadful work." Cited in "The Philadelphia Riots," 477.

[8] Ibid., 478.

burn homes, sparing only those that had signs placed on them with the notice "Native American." And then the mob turned its attention to the Irish Catholic churches. St. Michael's Church, including its rectory and convent, was burned to the ground, in part because of rumors that it concealed weapons for an Irish Catholic army and despite the presence of the militia charged with its protection. As the parish priest fled in disguise, members of the militia became the victims of insults and dung thrown at them by the mob. Next, the mob moved toward St. Augustine's Church, where Philadelphia's mayor harangued the crowd with assurances that it contained no weapons. The mob ignored his plea, and he was rewarded with a blow to the head from a stone thrown by a member of the crowd, which then rushed past him and set the church afire. At the peak of the violence, sections of Philadelphia were in flames and many among the Irish population had fled in fear.

The disorder of mob rule finally began to ebb at the beginning of the fourth day of the riot. Philadelphia's mayor and sheriff, at the urging of many of the city's residents, called for a curfew that would be enforced by the state militia. A meeting called by the mayor resolved to appoint ad hoc special police who would patrol the streets of Kensington. The governor, sobered by the unprecedented violence, arrived in the city and worked out plans for martial law, including the allocation of thousands of dollars to finance a return to order. Perhaps most importantly, many Philadelphians had decided that enough was enough. The riots had set the city in the worst light across the nation. "Who would not give worlds," asked the editor of the *Spirit of the Times* rhetorically, "to wipe off the foul blot from the disgraced name of our city?"[9]

In many respects, however, the calm was deceiving. Hard feelings simmered below the surface, and, even though Bishop Francis Patrick Fenrick suspended public worship in the Catholic churches of the city, violence continued to be aimed at these symbols of Catholic life. Rumors of Catholic plots swirled about the city. Advertisements posted for the theater presentation of *Fortunio and His Seven Gifted Servants* led some anxious Philadelphians to conclude that the signs were a coded exhortation by which the pope urged the city's Catholics to arm themselves.[10] American nativists, moreover, strove to keep the memory of the riot alive. On Independence Day, a few weeks following the riot, some seventy thousand people marched in a procession through Philadelphia following carriages bearing the widows and orphans of American martyrs.[11]

The procession again triggered anti-Catholic sentiments, this time in the suburb of Southward rather than Kensington. When the priest of the Church of Saint Philip de Neri got word that nativists were intent on torching his church, he gathered a cache of arms to protect it. And when rumors of the hidden weaponry spread among nativists, a crowd began to mill about the church. The militia was

[9] "The Riots: Thoughts for the People," *Philadelphia Spirit of the Times*, 25 May 1844, cited in Billington, *Protestant Crusade*, 226.

[10] *New York American Republican*, 13 May 1844, cited in Billington, *Protestant Crusade*, 227.

[11] *Native American*, 6 July 1844, cited in Billington, *Protestant Crusade*, 226.

called and successfully dispersed the crowd on July 5, but it fired on a growing mob the following day. The scene was complicated by the presence of the Hibernia Greens, an Irish voluntary militia, which had congregated to protect the church and which held a prominent American, either as hostage or for his own protection depending on the source, in the church. When the nativist mob succeeded in breaking down the church doors, they freed the American and demanded that the Hibernia Greens leave the church or it would be burned. As the Irish militia-men left the church, they were attacked by the mob, which killed at least one Irishman. When calls for peace were ignored, city officials summoned a larger military company, which in confusion fired again on the nativist crowd, killing seven. An incensed mob in turn attacked the military company, until the latter finally gained control of the situation. Another riot, less than one month after the Kensington riots, ended in more than a dozen dead, scores wounded, and thousands of Irish families fleeing their homes in panic. Peace was a rare commodity in the City of Brotherly Love in the mid-1840s.

In the aftermath of the riots, most commentators publicly regretted the violence and mourned the dead, just as they differed on who was to blame.[12] The city's elite, horrified by the riots, could express unity across religious lines and remonstrate against all violence.[13] Yet the grand jury that was charged with inquiring into the causes of the riots focused on the Irish who precipitated the violence by obstructing the initial peaceful demonstration of the American marchers. The origins of the riots, it concluded, lay in long-standing weaknesses in law enforcement so that "crime having met with little rebuke and scarcely any punishment" emboldened "the abandoned and vicious . . . to hold the law in contempt." When a political movement of native Americans evolved, its meetings "were rudely disturbed and fired upon by a band of lawless irresponsible men, some of whom had resided in our country only for a short period." One outrage led to retaliation, which in turn was followed by additional acts of aggression. The *New Englander and Yale Review* concurred with this conclusion. Alarmed at the political success of Americans who objected to their faith, "they resolved to accomplish by brute force as *Irishmen* and as *Roman Catholics*, that which they could not accomplish peacefully as American citizens." Some of the problems, then, were systemic and could be addressed with better enforcement of the laws. Yet there were other dilemmas based solely on the character of the immigrant population that were less simple to resolve.[14]

Other observers laid the blame at the door of the Americans who engaged in nativist activities and who had coalesced as part of an anti-Catholic political

---

[12] Not everyone allegedly rued the riots in private. A Catholic in Philadelphia noted that his Quaker employers had remarked that "the Papists deserve all this and much more," and that "it were well if every Popish church in the world were leveled to the ground." Cited in "The Anti-Catholic Riots of 1844 in Philadelphia," *American Catholic Historical Researches* 7 (1911): 51, cited in Billington, *Protestant Crusade, 1800–1860*, 230.

[13] This argument is made by Light, *Rome and the New Republic*, 292–93.

[14] Both the findings of the grand jury and the editorial comments on it are found in "The Philadelphia Riots," 479–80.

party. George S. Roberts, who observed the July riots, called the American rioters "the worst class of mankind, the very dregs of the canaille of a large city" who were urged on by "a numerous class of Bible-canting scoundrels, themselves the off-spring of a base hireling ministry."[15] The *Pennsylvania Freeman*, an abolitionist paper, also blamed the nativists and specifically pointed to the formation of the Native American Party, "a party which should be discountenanced by every friend of human brotherhood, which is animated by a spirit hostile to our race, which is anti-republican and tyrannical in its purposes, which makes hatred of one particular class of our fellow countrymen an act of patriotism, and which occupies a position that, sooner or later, if it be not abandoned, will assuredly spread a civil war throughout the country, and lead to scenes of desolation and horror too awful even for the imagination to contemplate."[16]

If commentators disagreed about whom to blame for the violence, they also learned a variety of lessons from the Kensington and Southwark riots. For some observers, the riots illustrated the weaknesses of city governance in Philadelphia and justified changes to prevent them from occurring again. Because Kensington and Southwark, as well as other suburbs inhabited largely by immigrants, were not under the jurisdiction of the city of Philadelphia, the authority of the mayor to suppress them was nonexistent.[17] Attempts had to be made to consolidate the city's government and professionalize its authorities.[18]

For abolitionists, the moral was that inequality was detrimental to Catholics just as it was to blacks and that the actions of the Native American Party were akin to those of Southern slaveholders. "The primary cause [of the riots]," the editor of the *Pennsylvania Freeman* argued, "has been the selfish and anti-christian spirit ... which arrogates to one portion of mankind a superior right over another portion, either as to freedom of opinion religious or political. ... It is a spirit opposed to the great Christian rule of doing as we would be done by, of which spirit, robbery, slavery, political proscription, and religious persecution are only different manifestations."[19] Despite the blame placed on the Irish, moreover, the *Pennsylvania Freeman* identified the root of the conflict to be slavery, "which fosters the spirit of caste, tramples all law and order under foot, and revels in human blood." It was in Louisiana, after all, where the Native American Party originated, and its creation stemmed from the fear that Irish Americans, under the leadership of the Irish nationalist Daniel O'Connell, would join the abolitionists to overthrow slavery. Unfortunately, the paper concluded, "the Irish have disregarded the noble entreaties of their countrymen at home, and instead of aiding the anti-slavery movement, have basely turned their backs upon it." The brutality of the riots was the Irishmen's heavenly

[15] "The Southwark Riots," *Public Ledger*, 23 July 1844.
[16] "Pennsylvania Hall," *Pennsylvania Freeman*, 18 July 1844.
[17] This point was made explicitly in "The Philadelphia Riots," 470–72.
[18] See Ignatiev, *How the Irish Became White*, 150–54.
[19] "The Riots," *Pennsylvania Freeman*, 18 July 1844.

reward for their disavowal of this Christian obligation.[20] Despite these varying perspectives, however, no observer denied that the central role of Roman Catholicism and its place in American society lay at the heart of the riots.

I begin with this extended discussion of the Philadelphia riots to frame the story of antebellum anti-Catholicism that is both well-known and understudied.[21] We know this story well from its public face. An anti-Catholicism in the United States that was already well established in the colonial era became increasingly fierce in the nineteenth century as thousands of immigrants, many of them Roman Catholic, landed on American shores. At the same time, Protestant Americans increasingly saw their nation as an escape from and improvement on the tired systems of Europe, which included monarchical forms of government and authoritarian arrangements of religion. Raucous debate engendered bloody violence in American cities, such as Philadelphia, and in the American countryside. In response, many American nativists formed incipient political movements that evolved into a formidable political organization in the 1850s, known as the American (Know Nothing) Party. The Know Nothings both rose and fell precipitously as the slavery question took center stage and the Civil War forever changed the United States. Anti-Catholicism would not vanish, but it would never again have the coinage that it did in antebellum America.

This narrative is not wrong, but I believe that it must be clarified, enlarged, and probed further. In this book, I will explore the quandaries created for Americans of many stripes who wished to celebrate a developing national tradition that offered rights encoded in American law but who also recognized the religious and cultural diversity of American society. To do so, I will consider a conversation between Protestant America, many of whom were virulently anti-Catholic, and its Roman Catholic counterparts in an era that could produce the Philadelphia riots. The Catholic challenge that became increasingly intense in the 1830s, I will argue, is the first critical moment in working through these quandaries. This debate is instructive both as an important moment in and of itself and as a case study of the larger question of religious diversity in the United States and the ways in which Americans grappled with it. As such, it is an account of nation building and political difference, of social movements and cultural change. It is a story with many actors who actively conversed with one another about their beliefs and the ways in which these beliefs were essential to the future of the nation. In so doing, they contributed to an episode in American history that tells us much about the state of the nation in the nineteenth century and the nation that we have become today. In sum, the importance of this topic, which is often hidden behind the riotous disorder and raucous politics, is one that speaks to the present as well as to the past.

---

[20] "Pennsylvania Hall," *Pennsylvania Freeman*, 18 July 1844.
[21] It is telling that Billington's *The Protestant Crusade*, published some seventy years ago, remains one of the most-cited volumes on the problem of antebellum anti-Catholicism.

This topic resonates first of all with many questions that still plague or fascinate Americans today. At base is the question of the separation of church and state, a structure that remains of great moment in the American present as in the past.[22] The formulaic narrative of church and religion in United States history is centered on the crucial importance of religious choice for Americans, which has allowed the nation's residents to select private belief and has forced church bodies to compete for adherents. The result is a singular religious freedom that actually enabled religious groups in the United States to thrive because of – not despite – the absence of a state church. The genius of this arrangement, the narrative continues, is a freedom of religion that strengthened religious bodies, enabled people to worship (or not worship) according to their individual beliefs, and addressed disconcerting questions of integrating a heterogeneous people into a national whole.[23] Separating the church from the state ironically has created one of the most religious and church-going nations in the developed world.

Yet we are confronted almost daily with realities that show that this story is more ambiguous than it might seem. For one thing, this narrative diminishes the ambiguities of the lines between the church and the state, which have for decades remained indistinct and which have in turn fostered intense debates about church-state interrelationships. As we shall see in the pages that follow, many Americans in the antebellum era believed that the United States was a Christian nation founded on Protestant values and beliefs while, at the same time, they grappled with the meaning of disestablishment. Although the First Amendment did not immediately abjure state support for religion because it did not apply to state governments, disestablishment nonetheless did proceed apace on the local level, a development that at first troubled many Protestant leaders. They had to fuse the conviction of a Protestant national foundation with the mounting reality of disestablishment.

Many Americans today continue to find ambiguities in the boundaries between church and state. And their numbers currently are considerable. Despite the presence of Americans of diverse faiths, the Christian faith continues to dominate in the United States. More than four-fifths of Americans informed interviewers in a 2007 Gallup poll that they identified with a Christian religion. Of those who identified with any religious faith, moreover, well over 90% are Christian. Those who expect that the residents in modern America have rejected mysterious and arcane religious elements, moreover, are sadly mistaken. Among Americans as a whole, 86% of them in the recent Gallup poll affirmed that they believed in God; 70% in the devil; 75% in angels; 81% in heaven; and 69% in hell.[24]

---

[22] See, for example, Jon Meacham, *American Gospel: God, the Founding Father, and the Making of a Nation* (New York: Random House, 2006).

[23] In this bracing environment in antebellum America, pietistic and evangelical Christians were especially successful. Methodism and Baptism, two exemplars of this religious perspective, grew from 19% to 55% of American Christians between 1776 and 1850. Roger Finke and Rodney Stark, *The Churching of America, 1776–2005: Winners and Losers in Our Religious Economy* (Piscataway, NJ: Rutgers University Press, 2005), 56.

[24] See http://www.gallup.com/poll/1690/religion.aspx.

Evangelical Christians and those allied with the Christian Right argue not only that the American nation was based on Christianity at the outset but also that it should remain so today or else face the inevitable decline endured by secular societies. Other surveys, moreover, suggest that these beliefs are shared by the majority of Americans. A survey by the First Amendment Center, for example, discovered that 55% of Americans believed that the Constitution established a "Christian nation."[25] Likewise, a survey conducted by the Pew Research Center in 2002 revealed that 67% of Americans affirmed that the United States was "a Christian nation." Nearly half of the respondents, moreover, believed that the United States has had special protection from God for most of its history, a proportion that rose to 71% among white evangelicals and 58% among African Americans. (Roman Catholics at 39% were the least likely to agree with this proposition.) Conversely, 58% thought that the strength of the United States was based on its people's religious faith.[26] Results from the surveys of the First Amendment Center indicated that fully half of the respondents believed that schools should teach the Bible as "a factual text in history class" and that 58% said teachers in public schools should be allowed to lead prayers in class.[27]

This perspective is shared by some academics who lament the increasing pluralism in the United States stemming from what they consider to have been the culture wars of the late twentieth century. Samuel P. Huntington and Alan Wolfe, for example, argue that "the Anglo-Protestant culture of the founding settlers" has been central to the American identity from the beginning. The key elements of this Anglo-Protestantism include, among other traits, Christianity; the dissenting Protestant values of individualism; and "the belief that humans have the ability and the duty to try to create a heaven on earth, a 'city on a hill.'" It is true, Huntington and Wolfe conclude, that this culture has been amended by the contributions of subsequent immigrants, but it is equally true that the essentials remain intact.[28] The waves of immigrants added to American culture, but they did not fundamentally alter the American core.

Other Americans disagree, public opinion polls notwithstanding. Although they too focus on decisions made in the forging of the early American nation, they conclude that the United States is a multicultural nation state that must not privilege Christianity. For them, the genius of the American religious tradition was the ways in which it could integrate those of diverse religious beliefs into membership in the American nation, an integration that was enabled by the maintenance of a strict separation of churchly matters from all activities of the state and its institutions. Indeed, many of these advocates have advanced

[25] See http://www.christianpost.com/pages/print.htm?aid=29297.

[26] "Americans' Struggles with Religion's Role at Home and Abroad," *The Pew Research Center for the People and the Press and The Pew Forum on Religion and Public Life*, press release, 20 March 2002.

[27] See http://www.christianpost.com/pages/print.htm?aid=29297.

[28] Samuel P. Huntington and Alan Wolfe, "Getting Me Wrong," *Foreign Affairs* 83, no. 5 (2004): 156.

the belief that the United States neither is a Christian nation today, nor was it so at its founding. Founding Fathers such as Thomas Jefferson were skeptics, they argue, men who were touched by the Enlightenment and were expectant more of the decline of organized religion than of the millennium. Garry Wills, for example, has recently cited the role of the Enlightenment in not only fostering the "mind" in American religion but also laying the framework for the growth of religion in the United States by virtue of the First Amendment. The free exercise clause, he argues, not only inscribed Enlightenment belief onto American religious traditions but also fostered the growth of religious belief because people could come to their faith on their own terms. In so doing, it enabled people of a variety of beliefs to find a home in the United States and in effect laid the foundation for a pluralist religious tradition.[29] Thomas Jefferson, who reputedly believed religion would die out in the United States as people learned to reason, inadvertently provided the basis for an intensification of religious belief and the increase in churches throughout the United States.[30]

The degree to which the United States is or is not a Christian nation is related to a second obverse question: to what degree can the state intervene in private belief? We are deluged with almost daily reports of religious practices that seemingly violate social norms and demand state action. The religious sanctioning of marriage of underage girls, the seeming torture of animals or the use of illicit drugs in religious ritual, questions of gay marriage, and the ethics and efficacy of home schooling and sectarian schools, among other issues, are tried in the court of public opinion on cable news networks until they typically find their way into a court of law. As we shall see, these debates are not new. The practices among Roman Catholics with regard to family and the role of women were the subject of Protestant condemnation in the nineteenth century just as Catholics simultaneously condemned Protestant American customs. The debates about justice and liberty in the American economy were yet additional points of contention. Conversely, as we consider the degree to which the state may intercede with religious practice today, we also puzzle over the intrinsic value of religious traditions and the extent to which they sustain the state and society. Does the public square need a religious or specifically Christian foundation for the society to sustain itself, as some contend?[31] Or is the belief in God a delusion that is

---

[29] Garry Wills, *Head and Heart: American Christianities* (New York: Penguin Press, 2007).

[30] See also David L. Holmes, *The Faiths of the Founding Fathers* (New York: Oxford University Press, 2006); Steven Waldman, *Founding Faith: Providence, Politics, and the Birth of Religious Freedom in America* (New York: Random House, 2008); Frank Lambert, *The Founding Fathers and the Place of Religion in America* (Princeton, NJ: Princeton University Press, 2003); Lenni Brenner, *Jefferson and Madison on the Separation of Church and State* (Fort Lee, NJ: Barricade Books, 2004); Daniel Dreisbach, *Thomas Jefferson and the Wall of Separation Between Church and State* (New York: NYU Press, 2003); Philip Hamburger, *Separation of Church and State* (Cambridge, MA: Harvard University Press, 2002); Isaac Kramnick and R. Laurence Moore, *The Godless Constitution: A Moral Defense of the Secular State* (New York: W. W. Norton, 2005).

[31] Richard John Neuhaus, *The Naked Public Square: Religion and Democracy in America* (Grand Rapids, MI: Wm. B. Eerdmans; 2nd edition 1986).

detrimental to state and society, as others insist?[32] Debates such as these – with fewer avowed atheists, to be sure – were long-standing disputes that were part and parcel of the conversation between Protestants and Catholics in the nineteenth century.

The antebellum religious debate about Roman Catholicism not only resonates and informs contemporary concerns, it also speaks to a set of issues located in a particular moment in American history. In the half century that followed the Philadelphia riot, the Roman Catholic presence would be one of great import and it would create quandaries in many arenas of American life. If it has currency in modern-day debates, the rise of Roman Catholicism in antebellum America tells us much about the conception of nation and the ways in which Catholicism was denominationalized in the nineteenth-century United States. Those who feared the Roman Catholic Church saw its very presence – in conjunction with guarantees of religious freedom – as offering enormous challenges for the nation. The growth of Roman Catholicism through conversion and especially through immigration forced American-born Protestants to put their ideas about the relationships between the church and the state to a severe test. What could be done to incorporate those who maintained faiths that seemed to reject core values of the nation itself? Some Protestants were optimistic. "It is often said," wrote the editors of the *New Englander and Yale Review* in 1852, "that a system of religion [such as Roman Catholicism] so superstitious, absurd, and despotic, cannot long exist amid the growing light and progressive freedom of the present age."[33] Yet in the same breath, these writers conveyed a growing fear that Roman Catholicism could win the war for the hearts and minds of Americans. If many Americans felt that Catholics would forsake their archaic beliefs, they begged the question of what to do if Catholics failed to do so. If others concluded that the conversion and integration of Catholics was hopeless, they begged the question of what do with an indigestible mass in the body politic.

Many Protestant believers in the nineteenth-century United States were confident that their religion would remain the dominant faith in the nation. Yet even as it did so, Protestants had to confront a series of other difficult questions. If homogeneity was a virtue – and many Protestants believed that it was – could a religiously heterogeneous nation survive? Amid this heterogeneity, how were non-Protestants to be integrated into the polity and society? And what if Protestants themselves were forced to sacrifice their core values to incorporate these disparate elements? The choices made by Americans of various faiths in answering these questions tell us much about the direction that American society would go in the nineteenth century and beyond.

---

[32] Richard Dawkins, *The God Delusion* (Boston: Mariner Books 2006); Christopher Hitchens, *God Is Not Great: How Religion Poisons Everything* (New York: Twelve Books, 2007); Sam Harris, *Letter to a Christian Nation* (New York: Vintage, 2006).

[33] "Vicarious Religion," *New Englander and Yale Review* 10 (1852): 519.

Catholics faced a different challenge: to what degree would they be able to integrate their faith into a national whole? If Protestant American periodicals could boldly condemn Roman Catholicism as "superstitious, absurd, and despotic," how could the Roman Catholic Church find acceptance in American society? Certainly, the liberty to enjoy the free exercise of religion was a gift, but what did it mean to those who were members of a minority faith? As largely an immigrant church, Roman Catholics tended to celebrate the potential of a plural society that ought to welcome disparate elements to its shores. Yet even this recognition created its own quandaries for Roman Catholics, many of whom believed that theirs was the one true faith. How could a pluralist perspective that welcomed a variety of beliefs be integrated into these particularist beliefs?

In addition to grappling with the specific question of antebellum anti-Catholicism and its effects on Catholics and non-Catholics alike, then, this study also touches on the overarching question of religious diversity in the United States. As any schoolchild knows, the United States offered freedom of religion to its residents. The First Amendment's establishment clause specifically forbade an established church. And its free exercise clause prohibited restricting the free exercise of religious belief. As we shall observe, these momentous enactments created vast challenges for church and state alike. Many honored the opportunity for the church freed from the constraints of the state. The general belief was that the church was stronger where it was most free. Others, however, would ponder whether the church could remain independent and true to itself if it was dependent on and lived under the aegis of a state that promised freedom of religion. Put differently, what concessions would church leaders have to make in religious doctrine, in a marketplace of belief, to broaden its appeal to potential members? Conversely, could a state endure without the moral underpinnings that were provided by specific religious systems? Would the acids of modernity create a secular society that would erode the cultural core? If so, which set of religious tenets had to be privileged to undergird the state?

As mentioned earlier, these questions would endure to the present. New religious and racial minorities would challenge the constituency of national membership. After Roman Catholics, African American freedpeople in the Reconstruction era, Mormons in the late nineteenth century, Jews in the mid-twentieth century, and Muslims in the late twentieth century (to name only a few notable examples) would face their own challenges and in turn challenge the American nation to integrate them. And as these culture wars were fought, Americans, who perceived themselves to be at the core of the nation, contested and rued the deterioration of the national whole. The Catholic challenge to the American nation, then, was only one of many moments in American history when a religious or ethnoracial subgroup challenged the normative ideas that constituted the nation. But this is the point: Roman Catholics were indeed the first enormous test, and the ways in which differences were – and were not – resolved had important implications for the groups that followed, and for a number of central questions in American religious history.

The first problem, a problem that continues to plague American society, was the degree to which the United States was a homogeneous Christian nation and how religious minorities were to be integrated into it. I will argue that the story is more complicated than many Americans might wish it to be. If some Protestant Americans clearly believed that the fate of the United States was coupled with a (Protestant) Christian destiny in the early national period, they somehow had to incorporate those who did not share their beliefs into the nation. This task was complicated for many celebrated the American nation *because* it accorded people of a variety of faiths the right to worship freely. As we shall see, a broad range of public figures, including clergymen, politicians, jurists, and writers, believed and even furthered the view that the American nation was founded on Christian principles. At the same time, they asserted that these very principles allowed individuals of different faiths to find asylum, social mobility, and political freedom in the United States. Efforts to sustain a great nation founded on Jesus's gospel and simultaneously offer asylum to those who did not share the Christian faith would continue to be a puzzle that perplexed Protestant America throughout the nineteenth century.

The ways in which Protestants solved these puzzles tell us much about how the United States became an increasingly secularized nation. Over time, Americans in the nineteenth century came to revere the free exercise clause and abide by the establishment clause of the First Amendment as forces that separated their nation from Europe and actually strengthened their churches. If many believed that a church freed from the state improved the former, others suggested that a state without religious interference was also enhanced. Other Americans, however, continued to be less sure. Indeed, a significant number of influential Americans believed that state and society were founded on Christian principles and that the historical advances that characterized their nation were based on these very principles. Jettisoning a Protestant Christian base ironically undermined the very distinctiveness of the American experience, which included religious liberty. The Protestant conundrum, as I term it, was the puzzle of how to integrate non-Protestants into a nation that was established on Protestant principles.

It was how this puzzle was solved – or at least addressed – that led the American nation toward a pluralist vision. And it was Roman Catholicism, as the first major challenge of a religious minority to the nation, that was pivotal in allowing it to attend to these questions. Paradoxically, I believe that the growth of pluralism in the United States was fostered by efforts to create a homogeneous nation. Protestant Americans developed a variety of vehicles to promote homogeneity. As described in Chapter 3, they pinned great hopes on individual conversion that might lead Roman Catholics away from the strictures of a church that was attempting to reroot the authoritarianism and despotism of Europe on American soil. Although these dreams failed to come to pass, a new religious structure emerged in part due to these efforts. Denominationalism took root in the American soil, a coalition of Protestant groups that were willing to overlook certain doctrinal differences among themselves as they simultaneously viewed Roman Catholicism as beyond the pale. When the mass conversion of Roman Catholics failed to occur, Protestant Americans endeavored to use state institutions, most notably the public school, to instruct – some might say to indoctrinate – children on the attractions of Protestant belief and behavior. As Chapter 4 shows, the compromises made in the public school debate furthered the movement of these very state institutions toward a perspective that discounted the appropriateness of Protestant teachings in schools enrolling children of many faiths. The next strategy to discipline Roman Catholicism and even to partly disfranchise its adherents was through political movements that grew at midcentury. In their attempts to reestablish Protestant norms in state and society, these efforts failed, as Chapter 7 argues, in part because they were embedded in electoral politics that was by its very nature pluralistic.[34] Efforts to restore an idyllic Protestant world politically were rejected by a coalition of others who did not wish that world to return. Initial efforts to foster homogeneity resulted in the march toward a pluralist society.

A second question in our story plagued Roman Catholics, and, for them, the puzzle was turned on its head. As a minority, whose membership was often poor and whose faith was frequently vilified, Catholics had to find their place in the national story that for many Protestants was premised on a religious past. Their first response was to rewrite the American narrative to include Roman Catholicism as a central element in the past, present, and future of the United States. Roman Catholics had been part of the colonization of the Americas from the beginning; they had contributed mightily to the creation of the United States; and they were central actors in providing the brains and brawn to build the American economy. The rights established in the Constitution, moreover, were a boon to Catholics and non-Catholics alike. Roman Catholics were free to practice their faith in peace in the United States. Indeed, it was the economic opportunities and political freedoms that attracted immigrants, who were Americans *by choice* and not *by chance*, to the United States. In so choosing, they contributed to a pluralist society, a society that was fruitful *because* of its rich diversity and its novel institutions.

If life in the United States benefited Roman Catholics, the narrative continued, those of the Catholic faith enhanced American society and actually would be a critical element in sustaining the United States in the future. American society, for all its virtues, was too fluid, too unsettled. If it were to continue to prosper, the United States would need a solid Catholic population, hewing to the structure of its priesthood and unwavering in its belief, to sustain it. The Catholic convert Orestes Brownson put it simply: the United States was "the future hope

---

[34] As noted in the Preface, Jon Gjerde planned to write a final chapter on the relationship between religion, specifically the Protestant-Catholic divide, and American politics. While I have eliminated Gjerde's references to Chapter 7 in the remainder of the book, I have retained them in this introduction because they elucidate Gjerde's argument and underscore the broad scope of his narrative.

of the world," but Roman Catholicism was "the future hope of our country."[35] If Protestants envisioned that their various denominations were crucial for the American future, Catholics saw conversion to their faith, as we will observe in Chapter 3, as essential for its prospects.

Until a conversion to Roman Catholicism could occur, however, Catholics had to puzzle over how their faith might be integrated into the institutions of the United States. If they believed that they were central actors in developing the American past and in assuring the American future, others obviously disagreed. This difference of opinion, moreover, was founded in a critical belief among Roman Catholics. As Catholic leaders were marveling at the pluralist society that was the United States, they also acceded to a particularism that increasingly characterized Roman Catholic teachings in the nineteenth century. In the largest gathering of American Catholic Church leaders to date, the Second Plenary Council in 1866 decided that the state was bound to recognize the authority of the Roman Catholic Church, but not Protestant sects, as supreme in its moral teaching; in the process, it set the Catholic Church apart from other religious organizations in the United States.

As Roman Catholics were creating a distinctly American church, then, they had to heed papal pronouncements of their distinctiveness and particularity. The chapters that follow illustrate the path taken by Roman Catholics in their debate with the Protestant majority, a path that ended with a curious combination of pluralist rhetoric and particularist principles. From one perspective, they were part of the religious symphony that existed in the United States, a diversity that was enabled by American principles embedded in the First Amendment. For another, however, they were both a religious tribe and the one true faith whose beliefs had to be differentiated from those among them. The outcome was what I term a pillorized strategy that was aimed at providing an integration in state and society at the same time that it developed an institutional structure that shielded its adherents from excessive interaction with the unwashed. This strategy was based on the notion that Catholics were Americans who participated in many aspects of American life, from electoral politics to economic enterprises. Yet they were simultaneously distinct, and this distinctiveness was fostered by an institutional structure of schools and churches that shielded the believers from too much interaction with others. This differentiation was especially expressed in the school debates outlined in Chapter 4. Like many of the religious minority groups that arrived in the United States after them, Roman Catholics had to chart a winding – and occasionally contradictory – path that both sustained their faith and merged those of their church into the nation. For Catholics, the approach was one of pillorization that would endure well into the twentieth century.

A third element in my story involves the disagreements over the nature and direction of American society in a variety of settings. In February 1881, two

---

[35] Orestes Brownson, "The Mission of America," *Brownson's Quarterly Review* (July 1856): 571–72.

score years after the Philadelphia riots, Oliver Wendell Holmes offered a retro-spective view on the state of religion and society in the contemporary world.[36] "The priest is dead for the Protestant world," he observed.[37] "Luther's inkstand did not kill the devil," he continued, "but it killed the priest, at least for us."[38] Holmes believed that this was an event that was not without its costs because humankind lost a great source of happiness when the authority of the priest was diminished. "It was a great comfort to poor helpless human beings," he argued, "to have a tangible personality of like nature with themselves as a mediator between them and the heavenly powers."[39] As Roman Catholic authority endured, what Holmes called the "long and gradual process to thoroughly repub-licanize the American Protestant descendent of the ancient priesthood" was trans-forming other religious forms.[40] "Republicanism," he averred, "levels in religion as in everything."[41] Lacking Catholic authority, Protestant ministers competed for followers in a marketplace of belief and labored "to preach to hearers who do not believe, or only half believe, what he preaches."[42] Worse still was the depress-ing spectacle of "pews without heads."[43] In a post-Darwinian setting, religious belief was increasingly fluid. "The pulpit has long helped the world," Holmes concluded, "and is still one of the chief defenses against the dangers that threaten society."[44] Many religious tenets, however, "demand revision, and the pews which call for it must be listened to, or the preacher will by and by find himself speaking to a congregation of bodiless echoes."[45] The modern world, in short, had its costs as well as its benefits.

The outcomes wrought by what Walter Lippmann called the acids of mod-ernity, then, were varied in their results. Scholars such as Jenny Franchot and Susan M. Griffin have shown that many antebellum American Protestants maintained a fascination with the trappings and ritual of the Roman Catholic Church even as they disparaged Catholicism.[46] As Patrick Allitt has demonstra-ted, a considerable number, including Sophia Ripley, Orestes Brownson, and Isaac Hecker, found their way to Rome. These notable converts were joined by some sixty thousand others who converted to Roman Catholicism between 1831 and 1860.[47] At the same time, Roman Catholicism in the United States was

---

[36] Oliver Wendell Holmes, "The Pulpit and the Pew," *North American Review* 132 (1881): 117–39.
[37] Ibid., 117.
[38] Ibid.
[39] Ibid., 118.
[40] Ibid.
[41] Ibid., 123.
[42] Ibid., 128.
[43] Ibid.
[44] Ibid., 138.
[45] Ibid.
[46] Jenny Franchot, *Roads to Rome: The Antebellum Protestant Encounter with Catholicism* (Berkeley: University of California Press, 1994); Susan M. Griffin, *Anti-Catholicism and Nineteenth-Century Fiction* (Cambridge: Cambridge University Press, 2004).
[47] Patrick Allitt, *Catholic Converts: British and American Intellectuals Turn to Rome* (Ithaca, NY: Cornell University Press, 1997).

transformed by its encounters with American society. Even those who remained in the fold built a Roman Catholic church where, according to G. K. Chesterton, "in America, even the Catholics are Protestants."[48]

Amid these conversions and this conversation between Roman Catholics and Protestants, even among those who maintained firm convictions in their faith, varying worldviews continued to be expressed. What was the good society? How were domestic relations best maintained? How could the modern world address the increasing inequalities that arose from a developing capitalism? As we shall see, these questions were debated in the context of confessional difference. As myths were written about the good society, religion was central to the story. For Protestants, as we observe in Chapter 1, the American experiment was part and parcel of their religious outlook. The United States was, in fact, based on a Protestant foundation. Moreover, the advancements of humanity were anchored to a Protestant worldview. Not only was this reflected in the development of the United States itself, but it was also mirrored in the current debates that troubled American society. In contrast, Roman Catholics argued, as we have seen (and will observe in greater detail in Chapter 2), that their faith was central to American development in the past and future.

These different perspectives were expressed in a variety of debates about the contemporary state of society. As we will observe in Chapter 5, for example, the state of the family and women's place within it afforded Protestant and Catholic critics the opportunity to stress the advantages of their faith and the weaknesses of the other. The Protestant family, so the criticisms went, exemplified the individualism, materialism, and lack of hierarchy that stood it in bad stead as it attempted to grapple with the modernizing world. The domestic sphere, moreover, was an island unto itself that separated people from a larger community and that encouraged many of the evils of the modern world. In contrast, the Catholic family, according to its Protestant critics, was a reflection of all that was wrong with Romanism. It was one of many institutions that systematically fostered the unfreedom and despotism that characterized the Roman Catholic faith. Women were victims of repression not only within the home but also in relation to their clergy, which literally enslaved some of them. Men, moreover, were disadvantaged in maintaining a patriarchy, as they faced competition with the priesthood. The perversion of the home was yet another serious shortcoming of the Catholic world, because it was the home, these critics concluded, that served as a haven to protect religious belief from the excesses of society.

The feverish changes in the American economy in the antebellum era also elicited varied responses, as we will see in Chapter 6, which complemented the conversation regarding women and the family. Many Protestant voices viewed Roman Catholicism as a force that impeded economic growth and innovation. Indeed, some believed in the possibility of the market to bring about moral and religious change and economic betterment. Although they were careful to criticize

---

[48] Robert N. Bellah, "Is There a Common American Culture?" *Journal of the American Academy of Religion* 66, no. 3 (1998): 622 (citing Chesterton).

the acquisition of wealth for its own sake, they tended not to question the economic system as it was developing in antebellum America. In contrast, many leading Catholic spokesmen wrote an insightful critique of the economic changes in the decades prior to the Civil War. This critique was based on a corporatism that was both sympathetic with those termed "wage slaves" in the new economy and profoundly conservative in offering responses to ameliorate the problem.

Not surprisingly, this dialogue influenced the slavery debate that plagued antebellum American society. Scholars in recent years have underscored the racist outlooks of many of the antebellum white immigrants and ethnics that were instrumental in shaping a white racial identity in antebellum America. Schooled by the Democratic Party, immigrants and ethnics learned about the purchase of whiteness while the party's competitors showed little sympathy for the recent Catholic immigrants. Although this is a powerful explanatory framework to understand how the slavery question was understood by many ethnic groups in antebellum America, it is complemented by a discourse about the nature of economic relationships. For many among the Catholic leadership, slavery was a natural condition that could be explained as part of a symbiotic relationship between those who were inherently unequal. A worldview that conformed nicely to that of the proslavery Southern elite, this belief would sustain a proslavery view among many Roman Catholics in North and South alike.

The political debate in the middle decades of the nineteenth century drew upon these questions – the growing influence of an allegedly despotic Roman Catholicism, the increasingly fractious question of the virtues of free and slave labor, the sense of greater insecurity of the place of labor – and political movements came forth that expressly grappled with the place of Roman Catholicism in American society. Chapter 7 explores these questions. The nativist movement prior to the Civil War coalesced into a faction that became increasingly powerful in the 1850s. Although it was overshadowed by the ever-increasing importance of the slavery question in the years leading up to the Civil War, it illustrated one of the first strictly anti-immigrant movements, movements that we continue to see in the modern era. The Civil War changed everything. The relationship between the church and the state was transformed by the aftermath of the Civil War, just as many Roman Catholics demonstrated their loyalty to the American nation by the shedding of blood. Yet as this chapter will illustrate, anti-Catholicism survived. Debates in the 1870s, which conclude the book, indicate how the question of the division of church and state and the place of Roman Catholics within it would endure.

The Philadelphia riot was just one instance in the peculiar American history with regard to religion and the state. Protestants and Catholics in 1844 literally went to war over questions of whether an independent Roman Catholicism could be integrated into American society and government. They killed each other in disputes over whether Roman Catholicism was an authoritarian wolf in sheep's clothing that would destroy the singular American republican experiment or whether that very republican experiment was tainted by intolerance against religious minorities. And they struggled over specific issues such as whether the Protestant King James or Catholic Douay Bible should be utilized in the schools. America was one of the first nation-states to create a separation of church and state, in both the establishment and the free exercise clauses of the First Amendment, and its peculiar history fostered these episodes of mayhem as it set in motion distinctive developments in American religion. The United States now hosts a varied array of churches stemming from both the simple fact that immigration has created a pluralist society over the course of its history *and* the less explainable fact that it has been a site of religious innovation and invention. A diversity of religious faiths have been transplanted in the United States and originated here. It is now seen to be one of the most religious – and most fundamentalist – nations with a modern and developed economy. Whereas church attendance has dwindled in Europe, the people of the United States have freely sustained their churches and maintained beliefs fostered by them that others see as antimodernist and detrimental to state and society.

All of these factors are interrelated. The free exercise clause created the opportunity for Americans to practice and, on occasion, to invent their faith. The establishment clause prohibited the state from privileging one faith over another. Religious debate was thus part and parcel of civil society, and clergy and laity fought wars for the hearts and minds of potential adherents. The religious marketplace created devoted believers who strove to increase the numbers of those who shared their religious position and were willing to contribute resources toward that end. It also fostered an allegiance to nation because of the religious privileges permitted in the United States. In short, a religious marketplace creates a fluidity that makes religion so meaningful in American society.

All of this, however, came and continues to come at a great potential price. If the *wrong* religion however defined won or wins the contest between religious faiths, the direction – indeed, the destiny – of the nation is at risk. Many Americans today express fears that fundamentalism in contemporary America, with its antimodernist perspectives, might lead political leaders to act on principles that are detrimental to the nation's place in the world economy. Protestant Americans in the nineteenth century had similar fears. If Roman Catholicism led the nation down a path that was contrary to its founding principles and subverted America's singular destiny, the celebrated advances of the American republic were in fact a trap. From the perspective of Roman Catholics, if they were not accorded the purported freedoms in a nation that they chose to join, these advances were a sham. The conversation between Catholics and Protestants in the middle of the nineteenth century, at times civil and at times ferocious, was an attempt to adjudicate these claims, a conversation between citizens and religious believers that would continue in a variety of forms to the present day.

I

The Protestant Conundrum

> The ideas of Christianity and liberty are so completely mingled that it is almost impossible to get [Americans] to conceive of the one without the other.
>
> Alexis de Tocqueville, 1835[1]

Supreme Court Justice Joseph Story would have agreed with Alexis de Tocqueville that nineteenth-century Americans commonly associated their political freedoms with the Christian religion. Story, whose tenure on the Court spanned thirty-some years, had a wide-ranging legal career (see Fig. 2). A longtime opponent of slavery, he wrote the majority decision in the celebrated Amistad case in 1841. Beginning in 1832, he played an active role in fostering the School of Law at Harvard College, one of the first professional law schools in the United States. He is perhaps best known, however, for his multivolume commentary on the United States Constitution in 1833, which aptly illustrates what we might label "Story's Dilemma," a tension in antebellum American society that arguably has not been resolved entirely even today. On the one hand, Story celebrated the clause in Article VI that declares that "no religious test shall ever be required as a qualification to any office or public trust under the United States." This clause, Story argued, was not "introduced merely for the purpose of satisfying the scruples of many respectable persons who feel an invincible repugnance to any religious test or affirmation." Rather, it also had "a higher object, – to cut off forever every pretence of any alliance between church and state in the national government."[2] Story also lauded the First Amendment, which proscribed Congress from enacting any law that established religion or prohibited its free exercise, because rights of conscience were "beyond the just reach of any human power;" there were rights "given by God, and cannot be encroached upon by human authority

[1] Alexis de Tocqueville, *Democracy in America*, ed. J. P. Mayer (New York: Anchor Books, 1969), 293.

[2] Joseph Story, *Commentaries on the Constitution of the United States: With a Preliminary Review of the Constitutional History of the Colonies and States Before the Adoption of the Constitution* (Boston: Hilliard, Gray, 1833), § 1847.

FIGURE 2. Like many Americans, Supreme Court Justice Joseph Story affirmed the freedoms of belief afforded by the Constitution yet also believed that Christianity, particularly Protestant Christianity, was foundational of the American republic. (Daguerreotype Collection, Prints and Photographs Division, Library of Congress, LC-USZ62-110196)

without a criminal disobedience of the precepts of natural as well as revealed religion."[3] Like many Americans, Story marveled at the advances of his young nation in avoiding religious proscription, fostering freedom of belief, and

[3] Ibid., § 1876.

enabling the rights of conscience, which he deemed essential not only for proper religious observance but also for appropriate behavior in the state and society.

Yet in the same breath, Story also wrote that "there will probably be found few persons in this or any other Christian country who would deliberately contend that it was unreasonable or unjust to foster and encourage the Christian religion generally as a matter of sound policy as well as of revealed truth." Indeed, the British American colonies and some states in the federal union retained Christian foundations "without the slightest suspicion that it was against the principles of public law or republican liberty."[4] Significantly, he maintained that "in a republic, there would seem to be a peculiar propriety in viewing the Christian religion as the great basis on which it must rest for its support and permanence." Citing Montesquieu approvingly, he argued that the "Christian religion is a stranger to mere despotic power" and, importantly for our purposes, that "the Protestant religion is far more congenial with the true spirit of political freedom than the Catholic." As Montesquieu wrote, "[T]he people of the north [meaning Protestant Northern Europe] have, and will ever have, a spirit of liberty and independence which the people of the south have not."[5] Story concurred.

In this context, Story's pressing dilemma was the role that Christianity played in sustaining the state at the same time that the federal state established no religion and guaranteed religious freedom. "The right of a society or government to interfere in matters of religion," he argued,

will hardly be contested by any persons who believe that piety, religion, and morality are intimately connected with the well-being of the state, and indispensable to the administration of civil justice. The promulgation of the great doctrines of religion, the being, and attributes, and providence of one Almighty God; the responsibility to him for all our actions, founded upon moral freedom and accountability; a future state of rewards and punishments; the cultivation of all the personal, social, and benevolent virtues, – these never can be a matter of indifference in any well-ordered community.

In the end, Story found it difficult to conceive how "any civilized society" could endure without doctrines of religion that fostered piety and morality.[6]

Story, writing in the year of religious disestablishment in Massachusetts, perceived his to be a brave new world. Although he believed that the state ought not encourage the establishment of Christianity if this practice inhibited the freedom of religion, he argued that to be indifferent to religion – and especially Protestant Christianity – would create "universal disapprobation, if not universal indignation." The pressing question of whether a free government could permanently sustain itself when "the public worship of God and the

---

[4] Ibid., § 1873.
[5] Ibid.
[6] Ibid., § 1871.

support of religion constitute no part of the policy or duty of the state" was one that would be settled, Story concluded, in the American future.[7]

Story was not alone in making this argument.[8] As we will see in this chapter, many Americans viewed affirmations of freedom of belief and proscriptions against an established religion as hallmarks of American society at the same time that they believed that Christianity – and here they usually meant Protestant Christianity – was foundational of the American republic.[9] Indeed, many agreed with Story (and Montesquieu) that Protestant Christianity fostered a celebration of freedom of conscience that in turn underlay the adoption of the very clauses that guaranteed freedoms that would not restrain the practice of non-Protestant faiths. The American challenge was how to foster a Protestantism that maintained republican liberty without hindering the liberty of non-Protestants of their religious beliefs.

Historians today assert a variety of views about the enormity of Story's Dilemma, and their judgments often are twinned with contemporary debates about the influence of religious forces in modern American society. Some historians, such as Isaac Kramnick and R. Laurence Moore, for example, stress the secular elements of the Constitution and focus on the intellectual legacy from which this secularism stemmed. The English liberal tradition, the deism of Thomas Jefferson, the separation of church and state advocated by Roger Williams were all ingredients in a Constitution, written amid the Enlightenment and in a new nation stamped by its religious heterogeneity, that created a "godless document."[10]

Other scholars, who recognize the tension in Story's views, nonetheless stress its pluralist elements that led to a hopeful outlook on American development. John Higham argues that in the early nineteenth century a "Protestant ideology" developed that he believes was forged on two levels of belief. On the one hand, Protestant Americans maintained specific denominational creeds that were in competition with one another. Yet on the other hand, they shared an inclusive truth that fostered unifying ideals.[11] The tenets of this inclusive ideal, according

---

[7] Ibid., § 1875.

[8] Chancellor James Kent, for example, contended that religious liberty was an absolute right and believed that it was intricately related to civil liberty. Nonetheless, he joined others (Vice President Daniel Tomkins, New York Chief Justice Spencer, and Rufus King) during the 1821 debate over the revision of New York's constitution in defending the recognition of Christianity as part of the state's common law and in rejecting a proposed amendment that "no particular religion shall ever be declared or adjudged to be the law of the land." James Kent, *Commentaries on American Law*, ed. O. W. Holmes, Jr., 12th ed. (Boston: Little, Brown, 1873), 2:34–35. See also, B. F. Morris, *Christian Life and the Character of the Civil Institutions of the United States, Developed in the Official and Historical Annals of the Republic* (Philadelphia: George W. Childs, 1864), 657.

[9] Scholars contend that this tension has endured. See, for example, Robert Bellah, "Civil Religion in America," *Daedalus* 96 (1967): 1–21. Bellah's seminal article explores the fact that "the separation of church and state has not denied the political realm a religious dimension" (quotation is from 3).

[10] See Isaac Kramnick and R. Laurence Moore, *The Godless Constitution: A Moral Defense of the Secular State* (New York: W. W. Norton, 2005).

[11] John Higham, "Hanging Together: Divergent Unities in American History," *Journal of American History* 61 (1974): 13. See also Robert T. Handy, *A Christian America: Protestant Hopes and*

to Higham, were simple: religious belief was a private and voluntary act, and the national mission was redemptive. The conflation of religious belief and national belief reinforced each other. An apparently secularizing setting was in fact steeped in a "pan-Protestant ideology that claimed to be civic and universal." Americans could be sustained by a millennial belief that stressed the sacred character of their nation's destiny. The complementarity of the Protestant and the national identity was so striking, according to Higham, that they "eventually overlapped and reinforced one another to the point almost of complete agreement" and "forged the strongest bonds that united the American people during the nineteenth century."[12]

Other historians have echoed Higham's emphasis on the ways in which religious belief buttressed nation. In the early national period, religion and republicanism, writes Gordon Wood, worked hand in hand to foster a nation of civic and religious virtue.[13] Mark A. Noll argues that this integration of religious and political goals endured well into the nineteenth century. He notes that although the vast majority – some five-sixths – of American congregations in 1860 were evangelical, they were not homogeneous.[14] More importantly for our present purposes, Noll, like Higham, perceives an overarching common core of belief above sectarian difference in which evangelical Christianity was central in making the American experiment operative. The "moral goods" promoted by evangelical churches coincided with the moral calculus of republicanism, which, as we shall see, placed a premium on virtue. Although he argues that civic humanism gave way to liberalism and individualism over the course of the early nineteenth century, Noll nonetheless stresses both that evangelical Protestantism buttressed the American republic and that evangelicals discerned the benefits of the republican calculus. The "embrace" between politics and evangelical religion, he concludes, was mutually beneficial.[15]

The implications of these arguments are many. They explain how evangelical religion made the nation safe for democracy because of the moral order that sustained the republican experiment.[16] They show how evangelical Christianity could contribute to a democratization of the United States.[17] Yet they tend to beg the question of the status of non-Protestants in this calculus. The transcendent ideology that joined Protestants, after all, also enabled them to form a powerful

---

Historical Realities (New York: Oxford University Press, 1971); Mark A. Noll, *America's God: From Jonathan Edwards to Abraham Lincoln* (New York: Oxford University Press, 2002), esp. 17; and Nathan Hatch, *The Democratization of Christianity* (New Haven, CT: Yale University Press, 1989).

[12] Higham, "Hanging Together," 13–15 (quotations are from 14 and 15).

[13] Gordon S. Wood, *The Creation of the American Republic, 1776–1787* (Chapel Hill: University of North Carolina Press, 1969), 114–18.

[14] Noll, *America's God*, 170. One assumes that Noll is not including non-Protestant churches in this figure.

[15] Ibid., 192–213 (quotation from 205). See also Rogers M. Smith, *Civic Ideals: Conflicting Visions of Citizenship in U. S. History* (New Haven, CT: Yale University Press, 1997), 84–85.

[16] Handy, *Christian America*, 30–42.

[17] Hatch, *Democratization of Christianity*.

religious unity that could differentiate itself from other faiths. Higham, for his part, argues that the Protestant ideology ultimately was assimilative. Freed from any religious test and guaranteed freedom of belief, Jews and Catholics could embrace this vague but universal creed. At the same time, it energized a Protestant majority with "a unifying purpose" of upholding their ideology that in fact was responsible for society as a whole.

Assimilationist arguments such as these offer a rather harmonious view of the challenges to the American republic and the perceived dangers of the Roman Catholic Church. On the one hand, they explain the coalescence of American society around a religious morality that undergirded the state and enabled a vibrant society that had just embarked on an exceptional governmental experiment to survive. On the other hand, they view the Protestant faith as one that provided an ideology that not only offered an ideal for American society but also was welcoming enough to allow other religious groups to incorporate their ideals without compromising their own systems of belief. In his exploration of the development of religious pluralism in the United States, William R. Hutchinson argues that society in the early national period certainly lacked the sense of pluralism amid religious diversity that Americans enjoy today. Yet in addition to a xenophobic resistance to diversity, Hutchinson detects a "unitive impulse" that resisted diversity and sought to engender unity and social coherence. The outcome of this impulse, which was based on a "desperate, yet perhaps understandable, desire" to re-create an erstwhile homogeneity, was an offer of concessions to outsiders that set in motion a process of successful religious assimilation.[18] Like Higham's Protestant ideology, Hutchinson's unitive impulse contains a faith, perhaps implicit, in an American creed of inclusion.

Such hopeful outcomes, moreover, are based on the assumption that Catholics, who might have appreciated religious rights denied to them in Europe, would have acceded to a putatively Protestant ideology. And they assume that Protestants were comfortable with the motives behind the Catholics' acquiescence to that ideology. As we shall see in later chapters, and especially in Chapter 2, many Catholic immigrants, including powerful authorities within the Church, did indeed appreciate the simple requirements of national membership that had been denied them in Europe. At the same time, they disparaged aspects of a Protestant identity that was in and of itself prejudicial and that, despite claims to the contrary, was particularistic in its promotion of Protestant scripture and belief. Whereas Catholics could celebrate freedom of belief in a state without an established religion, they would dispute that the state was based on a Protestant foundation.

---

[18] William R. Hutchinson, *Religious Pluralism in America: The Contentious History of a Founding Ideal* (New Haven, CT: Yale University Press, 2003), 8. Smith echoes this view by writing that "it was particularly important that the dominant forms of religiosity in a state reinforced republicanism, as Protestantism was thought to do, rather than undermine it as many believed Catholicism did." Smith, *Civic Ideals*, 84. The question that I will pose in the following pages is how Catholicism, given these perceptions, could be integrated into the American republic.

In this chapter, I will consider the Protestant problem vis-à-vis the growing presence of the Catholic Church in the first half of the nineteenth century. In so doing, I complicate the sanguine views of many historians and suggest that the challenges posed by Story's Dilemma were not easily solved and, equally important, that an increasingly powerful Roman Catholicism was pivotal in forcing Americans to come to grips with his quandary.[19] I will argue that a suspicion of Roman Catholicism was not a new phenomenon in the early national period; indeed, it had deep roots in the British and American colonial past. These sentiments found expression in state and federal law and practice well into the nineteenth century. Legal anti-Catholicism, I will argue, was overlaid with a discourse about the American nation and membership within it in the early decades of the nineteenth century that further complicated the place of Catholics and the Church in American society. Americans found themselves amid a nation-building project precisely during an era when a Catholic migration swelled. Protestant belief and the Protestant past were constituent parts of a developing concept of national membership that made Catholic membership in it problematic and articulated a national character that linked American distinctiveness to Protestant attributes. This latter fact, the celebration of Protestant attributes as crucial elements in enabling a republican experiment, imperiled either the American experiment or the Catholic Church's participation in it. In the end, some Americans cherished their nation's commitment to liberty but found that it could work only if those who were tolerated subscribed to an autonomy of conscience. Because the Constitution proscribed religious tests, these Americans expected their neighbors to maintain voluntarily this independence of mind, so central to a proper functioning of both state and society. The fear that Catholics had neither the capacity nor the inclination to sustain this freedom of conscience created a dilemma – what I call the Protestant conundrum – that made it difficult to believe that Roman Catholicism could be adequately integrated into the American nation.

The Protestant conundrum was dependent on notions of American liberty, which many Americans, notwithstanding a flourishing chattel slavery in the United States, perceived to be a hallmark of their nation. Yet as they celebrated these freedoms, some Americans came to express doubts about the degree to which the freedoms inherent in the ideology should be given without restraint. Put simply, were freedoms that were the bedrock of the American nation in danger if they were accorded to all the residents of the United States? If these freedoms were not accorded to everyone, how could Americans continue to argue that freedom was a hallmark of their nation? In sum, many nineteenth-century Americans feared the results of an increasingly heterogeneous society, because they believed that their Protestant core served as the basis for the rights

---

[19] In this way, I am concurring with scholars such as Philip Hamburger, *Separation of Church and State* (Cambridge, MA: Harvard University Press, 2002); and Elwyn A. Smith, *Religious Liberty in the United States: The Development of Church-State Thought Since the Revolutionary Era* (Philadelphia: Fortress Press, 1973).

and possibilities in the new American nation. These concerns became more urgent with the arrival of a Catholic population that reinvigorated the Roman Catholic Church in the United States, a Catholic revival that posed the first real challenge to a homogeneous Protestant American state and society. In the end, the course of American development by the mid-nineteenth century was one wrought as much from religious conflict and contention as from inclusion and assimilation.

The Colonial Inheritance: Catholicism and the State

Two Giants, Pope and Pagan, dwelt in old time; by whose power and tyranny the men whose bones, blood, ashes, & c. lay there, were cruelly put to death. But ... I have learnt since, that Pagan has been dead many a day; and as for the other, though he be yet alive, he is by reason of age ... grown so crazy, and stiff in his joints, that he can now do little more than sit in his Cave's mouth, grinning at Pilgrims as they go by. John Bunyan, 1678[20]

Anti-Catholicism was not an invention of the nineteenth century; it had deep roots in the Anglo-American world. As Linda Colley has persuasively argued, a Protestant identity was created by the diverse peoples of Scotland, England, and Wales in the early eighteenth century giving them a sense of history and of worth that forged them into Britons. Similarly, it was the fear of Catholicism, represented by the inherent threat of Catholic Europe, that provided Britons with the counterexample of their protean nation and a sense that the wars stemming from the Reformation had not ended.[21] John Foxe's *Book of Martyrs*, published first in 1563 and even more widely in the early eighteenth century, starkly portrayed a religious persecution that was integral to Roman Catholicism.[22] Likewise, John Bunyan's *The Pilgrim's Progress*, published in 1678, recounts the journeys of Christians in search of the Heavenly City, a search complicated by Catholics.

British American colonists, like their counterparts in Great Britain, read Foxe and Bunyan. Like Britons, they were able to recount the Protestant martyrdom in the Smithfield fires of 1553 and 1558, when more than three hundred were burned to death. They were able to describe the horrors of the St. Bartholomew's Day massacre of 1572. They knew of the depredations of Guy Fawkes and his conspirators, who in 1605 attempted to blow up the Houses of Parliament. Many believed that Roman Catholics had lit the Great Fire of London in 1666.

Laws in various British American colonies reflected this antagonism to Roman Catholicism. Connecticut law in the seventeenth century, for example, decreed that "no priest shall abide in this dominion: he shall be banished and

---

[20] John Bunyan, *The Pilgrim's Progress from this World to That Which is to Come*, ed. J. B. Wharey and R. Sharrock (Oxford: Oxford University Press, 1960), 65.

[21] Linda Colley, *Britons: Forging the Nation, 1707–1837* (New Haven, CT: Yale University Press, 1992).

[22] The full title is *Book of Martyrs, containing an account of the sufferings and death of the Protestants in the reign of Queen Mary.*

suffer death on his return." These priests, moreover, could be "seized by any one without a warrant."[23] In New York, a law in effect in the eighteenth century stipulated that "every Jesuit and popish priest, who should continue in the colony after a given day, should be condemned to perpetual imprisonment; and if he broke prison and escaped, and was retaken, he should be put to death." A Catholic priest in colonial New York was reportedly hanged publicly because of his religious belief.[24] Although some colonies provided rights of naturalization, citizenship, and religious freedom for Catholics early on, these rights became increasingly restricted following the Restoration in 1689. Maryland's assembly sanctioned the Church of England as the established religion of the colony in 1692. New York colony passed a law in 1691 that provided Christians free exercise of religion excepting those "persons of the Romish religion." It required those naturalized to abjure allegiance to all foreign ecclesiastical and civil powers, which in effect excluded Catholics. By 1740, a parliamentary statute systematically excluded Catholics by imposing a sacramental test.[25]

These examples of anti-Catholicism were reinforced by the mutual dependence of church and state that was firmly rooted in the American colonial experience. As Philip Hamburger has convincingly demonstrated, colonial Americans expressed little inclination to separate church and state or religion and government. Even in the early national period and even among dissenters, Hamburger maintains, Americans remained leery of state and society adrift without the mooring of a religiously based morality.[26]

If a commitment to maintaining ties of church and state created broad challenges for the creation of a multiconfessional society, the significance of conscience in state and society triggered a particular challenge for Roman Catholicism in America. Protestant Americans, beginning in the colonial era, developed a concept of freedom that depended on the independence of conscience.[27] Conscience was comprehended as a distinct facility of moral intuition conceived by God. Humans had to be granted legal immunity from conscience; otherwise, the state seized the place of God in human life. If that conscience – the

---

[23] *The Blue Laws of New Haven Colony, usually called the Blue Laws of Connecticut; Quaker Laws of Plymouth and Massachusetts; Blue Laws of New York, Maryland, Virginia, and South Carolina. First Record of Connecticut; interesting extracts from Connecticut Records; cases of Salem witchcraft; charges and banishment of Rev. Roger Williams, &c., and other interesting and instructive antiquities* (Hartford, CT: Case, Tiffany, 1838), 121, cited in M. J. Spalding, *Miscellanea: Comprising Reviews, Lectures, and Essays on Historical, Theological, and Miscellaneous Subjects*, 4th ed. (Baltimore: John Murphy, 1866), 362.

[24] James Kent, *Commentaries on American Law* (New York, 1827), 2:62–63, cited in Spalding, *Miscellanea*, 362.

[25] James H. Kettner, *The Development of American Citizenship, 1608–1870* (Chapel Hill: University of North Carolina Press, 1978), 113–14; Kent, *Commentaries on American Law*, 2:62–63. See also the *Pilot*, 30 May 1840 and 16 January 1841.

[26] Hamburger, *Separation of Church and State*, 19–107.

[27] This and the following paragraphs borrow from Smith's excellent summary. Elwyn Smith, *Religious Liberty in the United States*, 100–6.

benchmark of freedom – was usurped by coercive authority of a variety of forms, freedom was imperiled. For some, the foundation of civilization was the Bible, which liberated the conscience. For others, who objected to biblical orthodoxy, humankind's conscience was a facility given to it by God. In both cases, a system that would imprison or weaken the conscience was anathema with reference to both church (and religious belief) and state (and membership in a polity).

Anti-Catholicism, from this perspective, was not a simple negative reference toward the Church, but an abiding fear that Catholicism held conscience in captivity, a captivity that had profound implications for religion, state, and society. Catholicism was accused of this captivity of conscience in a variety of forms. Most obviously, the papacy and priesthood held their believers in chains because they explained doctrine, by interpreting the Bible for their laity, and dispensed penance, by hearing the confessions of their flock. This extraordinary power, which imperiled freedom, had implications in a range of settings. If an authoritarian force eliminated conscience in the political realm, the future of freedom within the polity was imperiled. A marital relationship was jeopardized when the priest was privy to the innermost thoughts of a husband or wife. Critical thought in schools was endangered in those schools where the Bible was prohibited or, at best, only read with accompanying comment from a cleric. Simply put, freedom and conscience, which were pillars of society in the evolving American republic, were put at risk by a growing Roman Catholic church.

The era of revolution, deeply influenced by the Enlightenment, was reflected in the disestablishment of religion in many states and, most famously, in the disestablishment clause of the Constitution in Article VI as well as the affirmation of the freedom of religion in the First Amendment. As many scholars have argued, these principles, which were very much an acknowledgment of the reality of religious diversity in American society that precluded the establishment of a single faith, were of singular importance in encoding religious freedom in American federal law. For our purposes, however, two other factors bear emphasis. First, a religious element in state and society, notwithstanding the ratification of the Constitution, remained fundamental to the new nation. As we will see, this dimension was expressed in state constitutions and customary practice. Stephen Botein has gone so far as to suggest that because the federal state was so distant from the citizenry and because its powers were so circumscribed, the framers were motivated less by separation than by the fact "that there was no federal state to be kept separate [from the church]."[28] Second, anti-Catholicism in relation to a religious dimension of American life endured as well. If Protestant Americans were no longer attached to the British Empire, with its close church-state ties, many of them continued to hew to myths of the Catholic Beast told by Britons and colonial Americans alike. More importantly, they

---

[28] Stephen Botein, "Religious Dimensions of the Early American State," in *Beyond Confederation: Origins of the Constitution and American National Identity*, ed. Richard Beeman, Stephen Botein, and Edward C. Carter II (Chapel Hill: University of North Carolina Press, 1987), 315–32 (quote is from 322).

apprehended even more urgently in their new republic that the reality of freedom rested on the independence of conscience, an independence that Roman Catholicism appeared to threaten.[29]

Even if the federal government established no church, then, we must bear in mind three elements. First, many Americans continued to believe that religious faith had to remain as a moral underpinning of society, a belief that became even more salient because the United States was not based on a republican form of government that demanded great responsibility of its citizenry. Second, the myth developed that the United States bore a special burden because of its singular destiny, a destiny that distinguished the United States from Europe and ushered in a new order of the ages. Third, this destiny was connected with an American Protestantism that was differentiated from the authoritarian and despotic regimes of an old world stamped by monarchism and Romanism. Protestantism in the United States became both a necessity for the American republic and a symbol of its distinctiveness.

Following independence, Americans increasingly saw Protestantism as a key element distinguishing them from a benighted Europe. It was true that Protestantism was a European inheritance, but Americans felt that they had reformulated it in their new world and laid the groundwork for a glorious future. The United States and the American people, put simply, were seen to be central actors in a providential story of world liberation. This sense of destiny was a conviction long held by Americans.[30] As early as 1765, for example, John Adams would confide in his diary that "I always consider the settlement of America with Reverence and Wonder – as the Opening of a grand scheme and Design in Providence for the Illumination of the Ignorant and Emancipation of the slavish Part of Mankind all over the Earth."[31]

In stressing the centrality of Protestantism in this historical movement, some went even further than Adams. The War for Independence had encouraged Americans to express an almost messianic position for their newly declared state. Abraham Keteltas, preaching at the First Presbyterian Church in Newburyport, Massachusetts, in 1777, connected the "cause of God" with the "cause of this much injured country." The war, he continued, is "God's own cause," "the grand cause of the whole human race," whose principles if they were adopted "would turn a vale of tears, into a paradise of God."[32] Some

---

[29] Elwyn Smith, *Religious Liberty in the United States*, 101.

[30] See, for example, Ernest Lee Tuveson, *Redeemer Nation: The Idea of America's Millennial Role* (Chicago: University of Chicago Press, 1980); Ruth H. Bloch, *Visionary Republic: Millennial Themes in American Thought, 1756–1800* (New York: Cambridge University Press, 1985); and Conrad Cherry, ed., *God's New Israel: Religious Interpretations of American Destiny*, rev. ed. (Chapel Hill: University of North Carolina Press, 1998).

[31] John Adams, *The Works of John Adams, Second President of the United States*, vol. 1 (Boston: Little, Brown, 1856), 66.

[32] Abraham Keteltas, *God Arising and Pleading His People's Cause; or, The American War in Favor of Liberty, Against the Measures and Arms of Great Britain Shewn To Be The Cause Of God* (Newburyport, MA: John Mycall, 1777).

years later, Ezra Ely Stiles, president of Yale College, portrayed the victorious United States as "God's New Israel, an example of the espousal of a national millennialism that wed Christian liberty with civil liberty."[33] Although Keteltas and Stiles were perhaps immoderate spokesmen, they nonetheless illustrate the marriage of a freedom of religion promised by the founding documents of the United States with a belief that religious morality undergirded the state. Thomas Jefferson's dream of a wall of separation between church and state, in sum, did not mean that religious belief was inconsequential to the American polity. Indeed, without it, the path of the United States was perilous.

In fact, Christianity continued to play a role in the activities of the state well after the ratification of the Constitution. Five states of the union maintained formal denominational establishments when the federal Constitution was adopted; nine of the original thirteen states effectively established Protestantism, and all favored Christianity in some manner. Only Virginia and Rhode Island guaranteed full religious liberty. The most perceptible examples of Protestantism based in law and society not surprisingly were found in northeastern states, where church-state relationships were most clearly entwined in the colonial era. The state constitution of New Hampshire, ratified in 1784, for example, required that the state's chief executive and all members of the New Hampshire Senate and House of Representatives shall be "of the Protestant religion." Article VI of its Bill of Rights authorized towns to support "public Protestant teachers of piety, religion, and morality" through public assessments. Massachusetts' constitution required a test oath for candidates for public office that disavowed any allegiance, temporal or spiritual, to any foreign prince or prelate. Significantly, a fear of Roman Catholicism lay behind the test oath debate. Major Lusk, a delegate to Massachusetts' constitutional convention, who supported the test oath, "shuddered at the idea that Romanists and pagans might be introduced into office, and that Popery and the Inquisition may be established in America."[34] If northern states were most remarkable in establishing Protestantism, those in the South were not immune from the tendency. The South Carolina constitution of 1778, for example, specifically declared that

---

[33] Ezra Stiles, *The United States Elevated to Glory and Honor* (New Haven, CT: Thomas and Samuel Green, 1783). On the connections between Protestant Christianity, millennialism, and a developing civil religion, see Nathan O. Hatch, *The Sacred Cause of Liberty* (New Haven, CT: Yale University Press, 1977).

[34] Although the test oath was established, there was debate and dissent. Rev. Mr. Backus responded to Lusk: "Nothing is more evident, both in reason and the Holy Scriptures, than that religion is ever a matter between God and individuals; and, therefore, no man or men can impose any religious test without invading the essential prerogatives of our Lord Jesus Christ." Backus concluded that "imposing of religious tests has been the greatest engine of tyranny in the world." Major Lusk in Elliott's "Debates," vol. 2, 148, cited in Philip Schaff, *Church and State in the United States; or, The American Idea of Religious Liberty and Its Practical Effects* (New York: G. P. Putnam's Sons, 1888), 26.

"[t]he Christian Protestant religion shall be deemed, and is hereby constituted and declared to be, the established religion of this State."[35]

The very existence of these establishments and test oaths is noteworthy, but even more remarkable is their resiliency. The test oath in New Hampshire was finally eliminated in 1877, and amendments proposing elimination of "Protestant" from the teacher requirement were defeated in five referenda between 1851 and 1902. The Massachusetts test oath was not repealed until 1821. Daniel Webster, engaged in the debate over Massachusetts' revised state constitution the year before, expressed his own concern about the relationship between religion and the state. "I am conscious that we should not strike out of the constitution all recognition of the Christian religion," he said. Rather, he was "desirous, in so solemn a transaction as the establishment of a constitution, that we should keep in it an expression of our respect and attachment to christianity."[36]

Although state governments were most active in fostering church-state relationships, the federal government maintained, or at the very least acceded to, religious custom. Most obviously, the Christian calendar was maintained and a Sunday Sabbath continued to define the American calendar, reflecting a belief held by many that Sunday should be a day of rest. Likewise, other religious traditions were maintained, such as the oath of office that appealed to a God and the appointment of chaplains at public expense in Congress, in the army and navy, and at the military academies. Church property was exempt from taxation. And days of thanksgiving and fasting, which appealed to a deity, were declared by presidents in the early nineteenth century.

Equally telling is that the national state under the auspices of both the Articles of Confederation and the Constitution utilized religious supports to buttress central institutions. Article III of the Northwest Ordinance, which laid out the plan for a territory's admission to the Union, stressed that "religion, morality, and knowledge" were "necessary to good government and the happiness of mankind" and therefore that "schools and the means of education shall forever be encouraged."[37] Ohio's constitution in 1802 is a fascinating reflection both of the legacy of its membership in the Northwest Territory and of Story's Dilemma. Although it provided freedom of religion – "no human authority can control or interfere with the rights of conscience" – it also affirmed, like the Northwest Ordinance, that "religion, morality, and knowledge" were "necessary to good government and the happiness of mankind" so that schools should always be

---

[35] Benjamin P. Poore, *The Federal and State Constitutions, Colonial Laws, and Other Organic Law of the United States* (Washington, DC: U.S. Government Printing Office, 1877), 2:1626–27 (quotation from 1626).

[36] Daniel Webster, *Journal of Debates and Proceedings in the Convention of Delegates, Chosen to Revise the Constitution of Massachusetts* (Boston, 1853), cited in Botein, "Religious Dimensions of the Early American State," 325.

[37] Francis N. Thorpe, ed., *Federal and State Constitutions: Colonial Charters, and Other Organic Laws of the States, Territories, and Colonies, Now or Heretofore Forming the United States of America* (Washington, DC: U.S. Government Printing Office, 1909), 2:961.

encouraged by legislative provision.[38] If children were to be edified in religion and knowledge at the western schools they attended, the families into which they were born would also receive a Christian blessing. Marriages in Massachusetts, for example, could be celebrated only by ordained ministers of an established church or by justices of the peace.[39] All of this supported James Kent's suggestion in 1811 that guarantees of religious freedom were meant to secure the people's "freedom from coercion" but not to "withdraw religion in general, and with it the best sanctions of moral and social obligation from all consideration and notice of the law."[40]

These emblems of the influence of Protestant Christianity were not without opponents. Indeed, national debate became increasingly vociferous as states disestablished religious bodies and as the federal government became increasingly powerful. Perhaps the best example is the debate over Sabbatarianism beginning in the 1820s. On one side of the debate were those who wished to prohibit economic activity, including that by state institutions, on Sunday.[41] On the other side, as Nancy Isenberg notes, critics of Sabbath laws argued that they conditioned people to act according to custom rather than from their own conscience.[42] In so doing, legal protection of religious custom undermined a basis of Protestant belief. Yet dissent did not mean that these symbols became inconsequential. Robert Baird, perhaps the most noted European commentator on the state of American religion, cited an 1844 letter from the American Henry Wheaton, who had observed the connections in laws protecting the Sabbath and church property and in religion's role in regulating marriage and defining blasphemy, to make the point that Christianity was not a rival of the state so much as a "co-worker in the religious and moral instruction of the people."[43]

Nation Building: The Protestant Foundation and the Catholic Threat

Priesthood did not emigrate; by the steadfast attraction of interest; it was retained in the Old World.... Nothing came from Europe but a free people. The people, separating itself from all other elements of previous civilization; the people, self-confiding and industrious; the people, wise by all traditions that favored popular happiness, – the people alone broke

---

[38] Ibid., 5:2910.

[39] John T. Noonan, Jr., *The Lustre of Our Country: The American Experience of Religious Freedom* (Berkeley: University of California Press, 1998), 104.

[40] *The People v. Ruggles*, 8 Johns 545 (Sup. Ct. N.Y. 1811).

[41] See Richard John, *Spreading the News: The American Postal System from Franklin to Morse* (Cambridge, MA: Harvard University Press, 1995); Wayne E. Fuller, *Morality and the Mail in Nineteenth-Century America* (Urbana: University of Illinois Press, 2003); Nancy Isenberg, *Sex and Citizenship in Antebellum America* (Chapel Hill: University of North Carolina Press, 1998), 75–101; and Morton Borden, *Jews, Turks, and Infidels* (Chapel Hill: University of North Carolina Press, 1984), 103–7.

[42] Isenberg, *Sex and Citizenship*, 85.

[43] Robert Baird, *Religion in the United States of America* (Glasgow: Blackie and Son, 1844), 282.

away from European influence, and in the New World laid the foundations of our republic. George Bancroft, 1827[44]

If religious influence on the state endured in the era of disestablishment, Protestant Christianity was also central to American mythmaking and again Catholicism provided a foil for the Protestant ideal. The invention of an American nation was a project of enormous significance in the decades following the American Revolution, but it was an ongoing process that took some time and whose chronology is difficult to define. Whereas one scholar argues that the process did not begin until the 1840s, when Americans were "elaborating a thickening matrix of national institutions and national cultures,"[45] others date the onset of the process much earlier.[46] To identify a conclusion of the process is equally thorny. Although certainly not realized until at least 1865, the invention of the American nation, one might argue, is an ongoing process that endures into the twenty-first century.

The nation-building project itself had a number of components in relation to the fashioning of an American ideology. First, a people that comprised the nation had to be constructed. As scholars have noted repeatedly, moreover, the invention of a people demands in and of itself that those outside the definition of national membership also be delineated. The characteristics of those who are denied national membership clarifies the justifications of those who belong.[47] Second, the myth of nation had to be written. People who belonged to the nation created myths that explained why both their nation and their membership within it were meaningful. Religious belief played a key role in both of these processes.

This undertaking was of course not unique to the United States. Indeed, nation building was fundamental to state building in the Atlantic world in the nineteenth century.[48] If it was a common process in fortifying the nineteenth-century state, however, the contexts of nation differed from place to place. These

---

[44] George Bancroft, *History of the United States from the Discovery of the American Continent*, 25th ed. (Boston: Little Brown, 1874), 2:451.

[45] John Higham, "Instead of a Sequel, or How I Lost My Subject," *Reviews in American History* 28 (2000): 332.

[46] See, for example, Joyce Appleby, *Inheriting the Revolution: The First Generation of Americans* (Cambridge, MA: Harvard University Press, 2000); David Waldstreicher, *In the Midst of Perpetual Fetes: The Making of American Nationalism, 1776–1820* (Chapel Hill: University of North Carolina Press, 1997); and John Murrin, "A Roof without Walls: The Dilemma of American National Identity," in Beeman, Botein, and Carter, *Beyond Confederation*, 333–48.

[47] See Fredrik Barth, ed., *Ethnic Groups and Boundaries: The Social Organization of Culture Difference* (Boston: Little, Brown, 1969). On antebellum America, see David Brion Davis, "Some Themes of Counter-Subversion: An Analysis of Anti-Masonic, Anti-Catholic, and Anti-Mormon Literature," *Mississippi Valley Historical Review* 47 (1960): 205–24, which explores national identity formation in the face of perceived threats from outsiders.

[48] The literature is vast. Ernest Gellner, *Nations and Nationalism* (Ithaca, NY: Cornell University Press, 1983); Benedict Anderson, *Imagined Communities: Reflections on the Origin and Spread of Nationalism* (London: Verso, 1983); Eric Hobsbawm, *Nations and Nationalism since 1780: Programme, Myth, Reality* (Cambridge: Cambridge University Press, 1990). See especially the

varying circumstances provided dissimilar building blocks that would be utilized by actors to define both who belonged to the nation and who did not.

Scholars have identified a number of models that describe how nations were constructed and on what characteristics they were based. Fundamentally, they have debated whether the webs of affiliation among people created a sense of common belonging that was primordial or constructed. To what degree, they have asked, do people maintain characteristics that were ascribed from a long time past? To what degree, in contrast, were these traditions on which people-hood and nationhood were based recent innovations manipulated to foster a sense of common past and common destiny? Most scholars today accept the latter argument that people invented traditions to create imagined communities.

A further issue is the basis that humans use to construct their sense of nation or peoplehood. One variant – "ethnic nationalism" – attributes national membership to racial characteristics that are seemingly immutable. The essence of the nation is located in the people, a conception of a group that is as timeless as it is distinct. Stemming from romantic thought in early nineteenth-century Europe, ethnic nationalism and membership within an ethnic nation was unambiguous; people, because of their past, either belonged or did not. Another model, labeled "civic nationalism," focuses on the political act that creates a sense of people-hood by virtue of membership in a polity. As individuals come together to create a national community, they subscribe to its systems of belief and its myths and in turn are accorded rights irrespective of their varied pasts. The distinctions between ethnic and civic nationalism are clear. One is based on organic relation-ships of "blood," "folk," or "volk," whereas the other is an aggregation of individual citizens. One creates a state out of a nation; the other defines national membership as deriving from allegiance to a state. One is organic in its orienta-tion; the other is liberal. One is particularist; the other is inclusive.

In many ways, religion in general (and Catholicism in particular) is a compli-cating factor in our understanding of these models of nation and in the nation-building project itself. First, it confounds the differentiation between civic and ethnic nationalisms. On the one hand, because religious adherents can convert from their faith, the ascription of religion is not correlative with the immutability of race. If we think of religious faith as an individual choice and membership in a church as a voluntary decision, we can see parallels between voluntary member-ship in a church and in a polity and how an individual could make private decisions to convert one's membership in each. On the other hand, however, if church membership is ascribed by past familial association with a faith and if the church leadership maintains intellectual control over its laity, we are less certain that a civic nationalism would be operative. And this is precisely how many

following, which place religion at the core of nation building in a variety of national contexts: Colley, *Britons*, and Helmet Walser Smith, *German Nationalism and Religious Conflict: Culture, Ideology, Politics, 1870–1914* (Princeton, NJ: Princeton University Press, 1995). Nation building in the context of American nativism but without special cognizance of the importance of religion is treated by Dale T. Knobel, *America for the Americans: The Nativist Movement in the United States* (New York: Twayne Publishers, 1996), 1–40.

Protestant Americans viewed Catholicism in the early nineteenth century. Members of a faith controlled by a tyrannical and authoritarian hierarchy centered outside of the United States, Catholics were an organic bloc of people who would not easily be digested by the American body politic. Neither liberal nor inclusive, the Catholic religion made problematic the development of a nation forged on characteristics that betokened a model of civic nationalism.

A second complication that follows from the first is that religious difference between Roman Catholics and a Protestant majority in the United States created quandaries for members of both confessions. National political rituals that emphasized the unity of the American people were fused, as we shall soon see, with narratives of nation that celebrated the homogeneity and purposefulness of the American people. A nation that was Protestant in origin, that coalesced around Protestant beliefs that enabled a republican government, and that celebrated these traits openly in word and deed complicated Catholic membership in the American nation. If Catholics bore the trappings of a European past that belied the American promise, how were they to be integrated into membership in the evolving nation? If they were perceived as members of a "religion without a country," how were they to be naturalized to American ideals?[49] As we will see in the following chapter, Catholic Americans felt it necessary to remind their Protestant counterparts that they too were critical in building the nation. Yet many Protestants nonetheless considered the Catholic faith and its body of believers outside the pale. In contrast, Protestant Americans puzzled over a national narrative that celebrated an American inheritance replete with new-found freedoms and wrestled with Roman Catholicism's place within it. If its members consisted of an alien group rather than of American individuals, how could they be integrated into the nation? More menacing still, what if Catholics *were* included in the polity and they utilized promised freedoms to undermine the American nation and its government?

When viewed by Protestants with regard to membership in the American nation, Catholics possessed a number of awkward attributes. Americans maintained that they were distinctive in many ways, but three factors – the break with Europe, a republican inheritance, and an ethnoracial and religious diversity – certainly were among the more peculiar factors in the formulation of national membership. Although most of the people in power in the American colonies were European descendents, the American Revolution ruptured many of the sentimental bonds with Europe, and in particular with England, that once had been celebrated by white Americans. For this reason, the republican foundation in the United States was especially vital because it enabled Americans to differentiate their nation from the monarchies of Europe. In this republican world, Americans saw themselves as both blessed with liberty and burdened with the responsibility to be vigilant against abuses of power. They honored their

---

[49] See Susan M. Griffin, *Anti-Catholicism and Nineteenth-Century Fiction* (Cambridge: Cambridge University Press, 2004), 4.

newfound freedom, but they were ever watchful for signs of the abuse of power by dark forces from within or without.

As they celebrated their republican independence, then, the American elite was wary of both powers that would subvert state and society and dependents who either lacked the autonomy to act in the interest of the nation or were easily manipulated by their betters. These dependents consisted of those traditionally set in subservient and domestic positions – such as wives, children, servants, the propertyless – as well as those considered racially unfit for citizenship. Although the definitions of dependency were unfixed, the prominence of race hardened during the early nineteenth century. And here the context of a multiracial society with a subject indigenous population and a thriving system of racial slavery became important. As scholars have stressed in recent decades, by the middle of the nineteenth century a premium was placed on "whiteness" because of the cachet it accorded those who possessed it.[50]

Republican independence and whiteness, as identifiers of Americanness, were conflated yet increasingly salient statuses that became all the more perilous in years of economic uncertainty. American-born white males focused on their independence vis-à-vis those who were unfree, which enabled them to celebrate their stature as independent men. They also stressed their American birth and the inheritance of American traditions that distinguished them from Europe. Their homeland, in contrast to the European states, was a land of freedom and liberty. It was an environment where men, freed from the trappings of corrupt monarchy and a venal priesthood, were able to prosper freely and fulfill their potential as people unfettered from Old World constraints.

In these circumstances, the location of European Catholicism was particularly ambiguous. If Catholic immigrants could convert to republicanism and Americanism (which might be the first steps in their conversion to Protestantism), they might be welcomed into the national body. If they maintained their allegiances to the unfreedom of Europe represented by Roman Catholicism, however, they could be both a symbol of un-American dependence dwelling in the United States *and* a force that could potentially undermine the political freedoms that characterized the American nation.

---

[50] The literature on republicanism and "whiteness" is huge. See, as examples of republicanism, Wood, *The Creation of the American Republic*; Gordon S. Wood, *The Radicalism of the American Revolution* (New York: Knopf, 1991); and Sean Wilentz, *Chants Democratic: New York City and the Rise of the American Working Class, 1788–1850* (New York: Oxford University Press, 1984). Notable studies of race in the antebellum era include David R. Roediger, *The Wages of Whiteness: Race and the Making of the American Working Class* (New York: Verso, 1991); and Matthew Frye Jacobson, *Whiteness of a Different Color: European Immigrants and the Alchemy of Race* (Cambridge, MA: Harvard University Press, 1998). Jacobson notes the greater salience of anti-Catholicism than race before the Civil War. Although organized nativism in the 1840s and 1850s was mainly anti-Catholic, he writes, "race was not altogether absent" (69–70), but neither, one assumes, was it the dominant conceptualization. Indeed, in all of Jacobson's examples, it appears that race and religion were conflated, suggesting that the concept of race had not hardened in the antebellum era.

While race *was* significant, then, its importance has overshadowed an appreciation of the ways in which Americans were also differentiating themselves from Europe. In so doing, the relevance of religious difference has also been discounted. In fact, we profit from viewing the conflation of race and religion in the constitution of American peoplehood. Much of the recent literature on whiteness maintains an assimilative focus in that it illustrates the ways in which Europeans acculturated to the United States through their inculcation of racial ideals. The lines drawn between white and nonwhite, despite contentions over the definition of who embodied the former, ultimately enabled the European immigrants and their descendants to become part of white America. Religious difference complicates this story, however, because it differentiated those of European descent according to their religious confession.

This demarcation is nicely illustrated by American reactions to riots that racked antebellum cities in the 1840s. Following the 1844 Philadelphia riots, which we will consider in detail in a later chapter, Representative Lewis C. Levin spoke on the floor of Congress of the "drilled bands of armed foreigners" that was "an imported element – a European weapon – one peculiar only to the feudal institutions of the Old World."[51] Levin, a Pennsylvania nativist, was able in one sentence to merge the foreign and dangerous presence of the alien. Five years later, the Astor Place riot in New York City elicited similar imagery. Sparked by the debate over whether an American or an Englishman ought to play Macbeth at the Astor Place Opera, the riot was finally quelled by police firing into an urban mob, killing thirty and wounding scores. In the aftermath of the bloodshed, one New York City politician deemed the military that fired on the mob to be "the slaves of her Majesty of England." Another compared the militia unfavorably to that of the czar of Russia. Even though the czar held "the lives of people in little better estimation than that of dogs," he required – unlike the American militia – that his military discharge blanks before firing a round of lead into his people.[52] In these riots, both the people and their authorities embodied European dangers.

As a result of these fears, Americans occasionally merged racial and religious characteristics. One way Americans differentiated themselves from Europeans was to identify with Indians. From the Boston Tea Party through the anti-Catholic Know Nothings in the mid-nineteenth century, Americans often utilized Native American dress and trappings to highlight their American provenance.[53]

---

[51] *Congressional Globe*, 29th Cong., 1st sess., Appendix, 49, cited in Ray Allen Billington, *The Protestant Crusade, 1800–1860* (New York: Macmillan, 1938), 233.

[52] Joel Tyler Headley, *The Great Riots of New York, 1712 to 1873; Including a Full and Complete Account of the Four Days' Draft Riot of 1863* (New York: E. B. Treat, 1873), 120; Richard Moody, *The Astor Place Riot* (Bloomington: Indiana University Press, 1958), 130, 189–94. It bears noting that the Astor Place riot was not so much an expression of anti-Catholicism as it was a row that drew on anti-British sentiment and fears that Britain constituted part of an ongoing European threat to the American republic.

[53] Dale T. Knobel, "Know Nothings and Indians: Strange Bedfellows?" *Western Historical Quarterly* 15 (1984): 175–98.

Jill Lepore has illustrated the ways in which Americans "performed Indianness" and thereby imagined themselves as part of a new national identity that was distinct from a European identity and European culture. The stage actor Edwin Forrest exemplified this phenomenon; his decision to accept theater roles playing an Indian solidified his fame and rendered him a symbol of the nation's separation from Europe.[54] Yet Jenny Franchot has pointed out that the Native Americans were not always classified according to their indigenous qualities. Rather, Indians themselves were Catholicized – after all, Catholic missionaries in Canada and Latin America were the most successful missionaries – and thereby associated with what American Protestants considered to be the worst qualities of the Old World. "In the process," she writes, "these white American Protestants could legitimate their subordination of Indian cultures *and* renew their racial connection to English and Continental culture, now conceived as 'white' rather than as 'Catholic.'"[55] Or, as a nativist tract wrote in the 1850s, "the American people are not a Roman Catholic race."[56] From this perspective, we profit from viewing the development of an American nation as a process that triangulated race and religion so that Americans were superior racially (in the context of non-Europeans) and religiously (as European but freed of the European papacy and the Old World).

Obviously, the boundaries that separated members and outcasts of the American nation were both fluid and contested. As mentioned earlier, the propertyless would become politically entitled in many states in the early nineteenth century. Women throughout the nineteenth century would labor for political enfranchisement, and abolitionists – black and white – would advocate successfully for an end to slavery and the beginning of guarantees of suffrage and due process for the ex-slaves. European immigrants certainly were also in a position to be integrated into state and nation. Yet those of a European past and especially those who practiced a Catholic faith faced challenges if they were to be amalgamated into a nation that was considered by many to be the embodiment of Protestantism. Catholics constructed their own stories of nation that centered on their people and celebrated their contributions to the national narrative (see Chapter 2). But they consistently had to confront the fact in antebellum America that they were in a problematic position as perceived threats to the nation, a predicament only exacerbated by myths Americans developed about the evolution of their nation-state.

Writing a myth of nation building complemented the narrative that defined national belonging. On the one hand, those who perceived themselves to be members of the nation allegedly possessed traits that allowed them to be

---

[54] Jill Lepore, *The Name of War: King Philip's War and the Origins of American Identity* (New York: Vintage Books, 1998), 198–202.

[55] Jenny Franchot, *Roads to Rome: The Antebellum Protestant Encounter with Catholicism* (Berkeley: University of California Press, 1994), 135–36.

[56] *Pope, or President? Startling Disclosures of Romanism as Revealed by its Own Writers. Facts for Americans* (New York: R. L. Delisser, 1859), 254.

instrumental in the historical development of the United States, a development that they believed was of singular importance. On the other hand, those outside of the national boundaries were problematic subjects in the movement of history. As in the explanation of notions of peoplehood, race and religion were again crucial markers in national mythmaking. Yet there was also a critical difference. Whereas race and religion tended to be conflated in the writing of the American myth, the quandaries created with regard to religion – *because* of the inherent racism in the United States – were potentially more troubling. White Americans were confident of their superiority over those they defined as nonwhite, but they viewed ominous developments in the Atlantic world that made religious conquest less certain. Whereas nonwhite people were disfranchised, moreover, the European male immigrant after 1790 enjoyed rights of naturalization and citizenship. The fear of an increasingly powerful and regressive force, embodied in the Church and in European monarchy, coupled with a large body of potentially unassailable immigrants, beholden to these regressive forces, was a daunting prospect.

These challenges notwithstanding, Protestant Americans, in the decades prior to the Civil War, developed a myth that explained their national distinctiveness in terms that were mindful of variations both over time and across space.[57] Most fundamentally, they developed a teleology of the progress of the ages and America's role within it. Early in the nineteenth century, Americans remained under the influence of the Enlightenment with its sense of the possibilities of human betterment. Enlightenment views, however, were soon combined with the sense that the American experience and experiment was special and providential. As English roots were planted in the rich American soil, so the story went, Protestants viewed the development of their nation as unique in the history of the world.

A westward movement was yoked to the ascension of humankind. As Thomas Hart Benton would argue in a congressional session in 1846, "[T]he White race alone received the divine command, to subdue and replenish the earth!" Benton's story began in western Asia, then Europe, and using "the Sun for their guide," he continued, "they arrived, after many ages, on the shores of the Atlantic, which they lit up with the lights of science and religion, and adorned with the useful and the elegant arts."[58] The creation of the United States, for Benton and the many who shared his views, was only one more stage – albeit a very important one – in a movement of history. Likewise, the United States was inspired not only by providence but also by the growth of liberty and freedom. The Reformation, the Glorious Revolution, and the American Revolution, each in its own way, ushered in a new phase of human liberty.

---

[57] See, for example, Major Wilson, "Time and the Religious Dialogue in Mid-Nineteenth Century America," *Midwest Quarterly* 21 (1980): 175–95. Wilson, who focuses on historylessness and modes of historical thought, perceives some similarities between Protestant and Catholic thinkers.
[58] Thomas Hart Benton, *Congressional Globe*, 29th Cong., 1st sess. (28 May 1846).

Scholars in recent years have focused on the paradox in which the story of race is set in relation to the teleology of progress.[59] While Americans perceived a sense of historical development through time that affirmed a sense of human progress, they also maintained an understanding of space that posited human difference. And as in the definitions of the people of the nation, race in the nineteenth century was a crucial element in American mythmaking. Peoples, as Reginald Horsman among others have pointed out, were classified not only by skin color and physique but also according to their historical, philological, and spatial origins. These characteristics, not insignificantly, were correlated with virtue and sophistication.[60] The explanatory power of science combined with the interaction of peoples in the United States convinced white Americans that those of native and African background had descended from a different and "lower" race. Whereas Europeans too would construct schemes of categorization that justified their place and actions in the world, the United States in many ways was a focal point where racialized ideologies evolved and found their fullest expression.

Again, however, race was not the only scheme of categorization that differentiated by space. Americans were also carving the world into disparate arenas divided by religious confession, Christian and non-Christian alike. Like their classifications of racial difference, American Protestants carefully developed schemes of categorization of religious faith that had clear moral underpinnings. Not only did they rank Protestant Christianity as the only true faith, but they also drew connections between religious systems and the secular worlds that they helped create. Protestant Christianity promised salvation and encouraged a society that was just, free, and progressive. The same could not be said for other religious systems to which the other peoples of the world adhered.[61] Schemes of categorization are illustrated by a literal mapping of the world according to its

---

[59] Reginald Horsman, *Race and Manifest Destiny: The Origins of American Racial Anglo-Saxonism* (Cambridge: Harvard University Press, 1981). Benton, in the same speech cited in note 58 above, continued: "Civilization, or extinction, has been the fate of all people who have found themselves in the track of the advancing Whites, and civilization, always the preference of Whites, has been pressed as an Object, while extinction has followed as a consequence of its resistance." Benton, *Congressional Globe*, 29th Cong., 1st sess. (28 May 1846).

[60] Horsman, *Race and Manifest Destiny*.

[61] Americans who were discovering the possibilities of proselytization in the non-Western world puzzled over religions across the globe. Buddhism was described as "a sort of degenerate Christianity" that was both "an invention of the devil" and a system that "enchained the minds of countless millions throughout eastern Asia." Islam was a "delusion" that "by the arm of civil power, holds the scimitar over [the region's head]." Rev. J. W. Wiley, "The Religions of China, No. III," *The Ladies' Repository: A Monthly Periodical Devoted to Literature, Arts, and Religion* 16 (1856): 727–28; "The Prospects which the Present Age Presents to the Cause of Religious Freedom," *New Englander and Yale Review* 3 (1845): 399. Significantly, these non-Christian faiths were often likened to Catholicism both in the non-Western world and in the United States. After "witnessing the exhibitions of Buddhism in eastern Asia," for example, Wiley concluded that "we can only look upon Romanism, in its ecclesiastical institutions and outward form, as Buddhism baptized with a Christian name."

confessions, which was an ongoing process for Protestant Americans as they engaged in missionary work and military adventures.[62] Significantly, the most perplexing region for these cultural cartographers, aside from their home continent, was Europe. It was no revelation to Americans that Europe was profoundly divided by the varieties of Christian belief. The narrative of a Christian triumph in the late Roman Empire followed by the regression of the church and its regeneration in the Reformation was an account well known in the United States. The religious wars that coursed across the continent in the centuries that followed served as cautionary tales for Americans as well, which no doubt figured in the deliberations regarding the framing of the Constitution. And Americans in the nineteenth century continued to be fascinated and troubled by the enduring geopolitical division in Europe, where the boundaries between Protestantism and Roman Catholicism summoned visions of two very dissimilar worlds. The deeper meaning of these divisions simultaneously confirmed Protestant Americans' sense of Catholic degeneration and posed for them weighty challenges. Americans, many of whom visited Europe, composed travelogues that mapped the various regions of Protestantism and Catholicism. These travel narratives often combined a fascination with the lavish ritual trappings of the Catholic world with clear moral judgments regarding the human costs that such a religious culture produced.

In sum, the Protestant geographies of Europe, written by Europeans as well as Americans, constructed a geopolitics of faith as a common organizing tool to criticize Catholicism. A series of publications, all of which were published in the mid-1850s, illustrate this pattern. In 1855, the Calvinist Napolean Roussell, a Parisian, used three measures – wealth, knowledge, and morality – to map Europe according to confession. By comparing contiguous nations of Protestant and Catholic belief, he argued that the former possessed superiority over Catholic lands. Because Catholicism fostered an inefficient society that was promoted by the ignorance in which the Church kept its laity, the people of Catholic lands such as Austria, Belgium, and Ireland were characterized by poverty and superstition. In contrast, the nations of Prussia, Holland, and Scotland were paragons of knowledge, morality, and wealth.[63] "Kirwan," an Irish American convert to Protestantism, made a strikingly similar observation in his letters to Archbishop John Hughes that same year. "Compare Ireland and Scotland; . . . Compare Spain and England, Italy and Prussia, Rome with Edinburgh, Belfast with Cork," he wrote. Travelers in Europe clearly discerned variations when they crossed

---

[62] The mapping of the world in fact touched many Americans' imaginations. A growing travel literature explored the patterns of life and culture, including the religious practices, of many locales. For a brief sampling, see James Jackson Jarves, "Italian Life and Morals – Effects of Romanism on Society," *Harper's New Monthly Magazine* 10 (1855): 320–34; "Italy," *North American Review* 78 (1854): 449–501; and "Notes from Over Sea," *New Englander and Yale Review* 4 (1846): 159–73.

[63] Rev. Napoleon Roussell, *Catholic and Protestant Nations, Compared, in their threefold Relations to Wealth, Knowledge and Morality* (Boston: J. P. Jewett, 1855), reviewed in *New Englander and Yale Review* 13 (August 1855): 484–85.

boundaries that separated papal from Protestant states. The reason for these conspicuous differences, according to Kirwan, was simple. "The obvious marks of higher civilization declare the transition with almost as much plainness as would a broad river or a chain of mountains. Popery," he concluded with tongue in cheek, "with infallible certainty, degrades man."[64]

If European Catholicism was correlated with social and economic degradation, the geopolitical map of European religion also linked civil liberty with Protestantism. As in North America, space was coupled with time and a defining moment in this account was the Reformation. The principle of "Luther's first act of rebellion," wrote J. H. McIlvaine in 1859, was "that the mind and conscience of the individual are responsible to the truth and to God alone." Inherent within this attitude were the principles of individual liberty and individual responsibility and the belief that "the history of the Protestant nations, from the sixteenth century to the present time, chiefly consists of the progressive development" of these ideas. "Freedom of the press, universal education, and all free institutions," concluded McIlvaine, stemmed from this principle of individual liberty, which he considered the result of certain peoples accepting religious change.[65]

By the mid-nineteenth century, the map had become formulaic. "Look over the face of Christendom," asked the *Ladies' Repository* rhetorically in 1853, "and where do we find civil liberty?" It was "precisely where, and only where the Bible and the Reformation were received by the people." Holland, "after unheard-of sufferings and heroism" under the yoke of Spain, freed itself and established a republic. England "received the Bible" and "the Gospel of civil and religious liberty has gone out from them to all nations." In contrast, Austria, Italy, Spain, and Portugal had "sunk to the depth of sloth and slavery!" Not coincidentally, the nations that continued to adhere to Romanism and that were deprived of the Bible were those that were "yet bound in the fetters of ecclesiastical despotism."[66] Macaulay's criticisms in his *History of England* were still more severe. "Throughout Christendom," he wrote, "whatever advance has been made in knowledge, in freedom, in wealth, in the arts of life, has been made in spite of the Church of Rome, and has every where been in the inverse proportion to her power." Whereas "the loveliest provinces in Europe have, under her rule, been sunk in poverty, in political servitude, and in intellectual torpor," the Protestant countries "once proverbial for their sterility and barbarism, have been turned, by skill and industry, into gardens." In sum, he concluded, "whoever passes, in Germany, from a Roman Catholic to a Protestant principality – in Switzerland, from a Roman Catholic to a Protestant canton – in

[64] Kirwan [pseudonym of Nicholas Murray], *Letters to the Right Rev. John Hughes, Roman Catholic Bishop of New York* (New York: Harper and Brothers, 1855), 71.

[65] J. H. McIlvaine, *A Nation's Right to Worship God. An Address Before the American Whig and Cliosophic Societies of the College of New Jersey* (Trenton: Murphy and Bechtel Printers, 1859), 12–13.

[66] "The Bible and Civil Liberty," *Ladies' Repository: A Monthly Periodical, Devoted to Literature, Arts, and Religion* 13 (January 1853): 624.

Ireland, from a Roman Catholic to a Protestant county, finds that he passes from a lower to a higher grade of civilization."[67]

It bears emphasizing that the Protestant myth in broad brushstrokes was sustained by definite underlying concerns about the role that Catholicism played in society. Put differently, it was a celebration of the enduring advances allegedly generated by the Protestant Reformation. At its base, Protestantism unchained the conscience that in turn fostered a freedom of conscience that was crucial in sustaining a modern society. Although conscience was understood as a human faculty of moral intuition created by God to make his will known to humankind, it had subsidiary benefits for the state, society, and economy. The origin of the "sloth and slavery" of Catholic Europe that was apparent in its diminished levels of scientific knowledge, economic innovation, and human freedom was an "ecclesiastical despotism" that shackled the conscience. In contrast, the people of the Protestant lands had "received the Bible" and were not captive to a dogmatic and authoritarian hierarchy. In the coinage of the day, they were free, or at least as free as was possible in benighted Europe. It fell to Americans to work to nurture the Protestant world, in Europe as well as in the United States, in which freedom of conscience was fostered.

Ultimately, then, the Protestant myth of the United States was based on a perception that a geopolitics of faith divided the world into faith-based cultures and that the United States was the foremost example of the advancement of this division. The myth was spatial because it mapped the world according to religious belief and progress but also temporal because it saw a march of civilization westward through time, a march that set the United States at the pinnacle of world civilization. To be sure, the myth also came in secularized forms. The Democratic propagandist John L. O'Sullivan, in his 1839 essay entitled "The Great Nation of Futurity," combined a sense of mission and destiny. "We must onward," he wrote, "to the fulfillment of our mission – to the entire development of the principle of our organization – freedom of conscience, freedom of person, freedom of trade and business pursuits, universality of freedom and equality." "This is our high destiny," he continued,

and in nature's eternal, inevitable decree of cause and effect we must accomplish it. All this will be our future history, to establish on earth the moral dignity and salvation of man – the immutable truth and beneficence of God. For this blessed mission to the nations of the world, which are shut out from the lifegiving light of truth, has America been chosen; and her high example shall smite unto death the tyranny of kings, hierarchs, and oligarchs and carry the glad tidings of peace and good will where myriads now endure in existence scarcely more enviable than that of beasts of the field. Who, then, can doubt that our country is destined to be the great nation of futurity?[68]

---

[67] Thomas Babington Macaulay, *History of England*, cited in Kirwan [pseudonym of Nicholas Murray], *Romanism at Home. Letters to the Hon. Roger B. Taney, Chief Justice of the United States* (New York: Harper and Brothers, 1852), 237–38.

[68] John L. O'Sullivan, "The Great Nation of Futurity," *United States Magazine and Democratic Review* 6 (1839): 426–30.

Yet a Protestantism often underpinned the American myth. The theologian Lyman Beecher, writing from a Christian perspective four years before O'Sullivan, also saw a hopeful future for the United States. When he first encountered the opinion that the millennium would commence in America, he thought it "chimerical." However, now "all providential developments since, and all the existing signs of the times, lend corroboration to it. What nation is blessed with such experimental knowledge of free institutions," he stated,

with such facilities and resources of communication, obstructed by so few obstacles, as our own? There is not a nation upon earth which, in fifty years, can by all possible reformation place itself in circumstances so favorable as our own for the free unembarrassed application of physical effort and pecuniary and moral power to evangelize the world.[69]

The Christian march would continue through time.

In contrast to O'Sullivan's optimism, however, Beecher also betrayed anxiety about an exceptional American future, and as a result, he focused on the need to remain vigilant. "Are not the continental powers alarmed at the march of liberal opinions," he asked rhetorically, "and associated to put them down? and are they not, with the sickness of hope deferred, waiting for our downfall? It is the light of our republican prosperity, gleaming in upon their dark prison house, which is inspiring hope, and converting chains into arms."[70] The "power of mind," he continued, "roused by our example from the sleep of ages and the apathy of despair" was sending an "earthquake under the foundations of their thrones; and they have no hope of rest and primeval darkness, but by the extinction of our light." Religion in history, Beecher assured his readers, has forever formed humanity's character and has been the mainspring of its actions. "It has been the great agitator or tranquilizer of nations, the orb of darkness or of light to the world – the fountain of purity or pollution – the mighty power of riveting or bursting the chains of men."[71]

Beecher's voice of concern that the Catholic Church was a force that boded ill for the American future was shared by many. To cite one instance, Alexander Campbell, the spiritual leader of what became the Disciples of Christ on the American frontier, celebrated the promise of America's role in the coming millennium just as he expressed a fear that the "silent spectator of the varied, ingenious, persevering, and bold efforts of the Romanists to gain the political ascendancy in this country" would impair a millennial future. Because "the Popish religion is utterly incompatible with freedom in any nation," Campbell foresaw the prospect of a "mental slavery" that destroyed any hope for a political liberty and ultimately for American freedom.[72]

---

[69] Lyman Beecher, *Plea for the West* (Cincinnati: Truman and Smith, 1835), 9–10.
[70] Ibid., 50–51.
[71] Ibid., 73.
[72] Alexander Campbell, "Catholic Controversy," *Millennial Harbinger* (1833): 538; Alexander Campbell, *Popular Lectures and Addresses* (Philadelphia: James Challen and Son, 1866), 174.

Lyman's son, Edward Beecher, who was also no friend theologically of Campbell, reiterated the claims of his father and Campbell some decades later. "The great, the impious, the malignant, the all-comprehending, the heaven-daring, the God-defying life of Romanism," Edward argued, was that the Church violated the conscience of the individual, a violation that had temporal and spiritual meaning. Protestantism allowed the United States to develop the principles of civil and religious liberty. Complementary to this worldly contribution was the liberation of the individual and a truer path to God. "What is God's design in raising up this nation?" he asked. The common answer was "to aid in the work of destroying the despotisms of the old world; and their chief danger is from the Papacy and its connected civil systems."[73] But if the cancer of Romanism metastasized in the United States, it would "gain full control over the people, and it will surely overrule, and subdue, and corrupt all the civil authorities of our country – nay, of the world."[74] The manichean forces of history were portentous, and Protestants, many Americans warned their readers, ignored them at their peril.

In the minds of American Protestants, the outcome of the conflict was of a singular moment for the history of the world. The Glorious Revolution, which was often used to represent a world of political progress, stood in stark contrast to the Inquisition that represented the abuses of despotism. Historical development thus was intimately intertwined with a war between religious worlds. Americans often had difficulty bringing these two visions into conformity with each other. If historical improvement was a given, how could one explain the presence of regressive cultural worlds, let alone the ominous conflict that might occur between them? Yet they were often assured by their leaders that the struggle very likely would occur in the United States, a harbinger of world progress and a future battleground of global importance.

As Protestants awaited a worldwide conversion to their version of Christianity, they encountered escalating challenges at home in the early decades of the nineteenth century. While they strove to differentiate their nation from Europe, Europe – and one of the most regressive institutions that characterized European society – was moving to the United States. Immigrants – and especially Catholic immigrants – symbolized actors in a process in which foreign and unfree elements were infiltrating the American republic. Their immigration and the concomitant migration of their institutions were threats to freedom and republican forms of government, not least because they were accorded rights of citizenship. The seeming inevitability of the progress of freedom embedded in the myths about America and the liberties possessed by its people, in short, were endangered by the Roman Catholic Church, which ominously was becoming an ever more prominent force both in the United States and in Europe. Most

See also L. Edward Hicks, "Republican Religion and Republican Institutions: Alexander Campbell and the Anti-Catholic Movement," *Fides et Historia* 22 (1990): 42–52.

[73] Edward Beecher, *The Papal Conspiracy Exposed, and Protestantism Defended, in the Light of Reason, History, and Scripture* (Boston: Stearns, 1855), 371–73, 397.

[74] Ibid., 387.

troubling of all, the genius of the American republic seemingly provided opportunities for the Church to undermine its most sacred contributions to humankind.

The Protestant Conundrum

These are times in which the friends of Christianity are required to sound the alarm, & to inculcate sound principles. I fear that infidelity is [making] rapid progress under the delusive guise of the freedom of religious opinion & liberty of conscience. Justice Joseph Story, 1833[75]

National mythmaking was a practical as well as a symbolic act. By knitting individuals into a national whole, the state (and the elite who were its most substantial beneficiaries) was made more secure. And by linking individual conscience to Protestant belief, Protestant Americans fostered a conviction that a particular religious perspective undergirded their republic and enabled the freedoms it promised. Put differently, if Protestantism sustained an American state that was itself a singular example of freedom, it followed that Protestantism was crucial in sustaining that freedom. In this context, Catholicism, if it threatened that state, was a perilous element because it jeopardized not only the nation-building project but religious liberty as well. If Catholicism was to be abided in the United States, the Protestant puzzles were both how to integrate Catholicism into the nation and how to incorporate it without endangering religious liberty. These challenges were compounded, as religious tests were prohibited in most jurisdictions and any understanding of the importance of conscience could not be imposed legally but had to be instilled culturally.

Protestant Americans possessed a variety of perspectives in their cultural tool kit to address these challenges. Some Americans perceived the influence of religion on the state, whether Catholic or Protestant, and vice versa to be the problem. As is well known, Thomas Jefferson and James Madison fostered an anticlericalism that distrusted any form of established church in the United States. Significantly, the Roman Catholic Church was the exemplar of the dangers of the established church. Jefferson confided to John Adams in 1817 that the Federalist defeat in Connecticut disclosed "the last retreat of monkish darkness, bigotry, and abhorrence." Likening the Protestant establishment in New England to Catholicism, Jefferson concluded that "a Protestant Popedom is no longer to disgrace the American history and character."[76] Near death ten years later, Jefferson reprised the familiar refrain in the last letter he wrote, when he expressed the hope that the United States would be "the signal of arousing men to burst the chains under which monkish ignorance and superstition had

---

[75] Joseph Story to Rev. Jasper Adams, 14 May 1833, Joseph Story Papers, William L. Clements Library, cited in James McClellan, *Joseph Story and the American Constitution: A Study in Political and Legal Thought* (Norman: University of Oklahoma Press, 1971), 139.

[76] Thomas Jefferson to John Adams, in Liscomb, ed., *Writings of Thomas Jefferson*, 15:1108–9, cited in Hamburger, *Separation of Church and State*, 150.

persuaded them to bind themselves, and to assume the blessings and security of self-government," which enabled "the free right to the unbounded exercise of reason and freedom of opinion."[77] For his part, Madison argued that "Government and Religion are in a manner consolidated" in "the Papal System," a consolidation that was the "worst of Govts." Indeed, Madison observed that government in most of the "old world" legally established a particular religion, with the result that "there are few of the most enlightened judges who will maintain that the system has been favorable either to Religion or to Govt."[78]

From this perspective, the strict separation between religion and the state benefited both the spiritual and secular domains.[79] Those who supported Jefferson during his presidency frequently argued that a fusion of religion and state contaminated both. Early in the nineteenth century, the New Yorker Tunis Wortman argued that a church, when it became directly connected with a state, lost its "heavenly" virtues, which resulted in a "state without liberty and a church without religion."[80] A Christian conscience, in this view, thus was not a critical element for state and society because the spheres of creation (or nature) and redemption (or grace) were distinct from each other. Because the state was a part of nature and was shaped by natural law, it was separate from the sphere of the church.

The view of many other white Americans, particularly those in New England, had developed in a very different environment. As mentioned earlier, an established church and a concomitant antipathy toward Catholicism were maintained in many northern states well into the nineteenth century. The sentiment shared by many was that the church could exist apart from government but that the state would find it difficult to survive without a religious underpinning. As Story himself argued in 1833, "[G]overnment can not long exist without an alliance with religion to some extent; & that Christianity is indispensable to the true interest & solid foundations of all free governments."[81]

Some who held these views expressed a confidence that religion would endure to underpin state and society and, more particularly, that Protestantism in America simply was so powerful that it would defeat the Catholic menace. As we will see in later chapters, many Protestants – dazzled by the teleology of their

[77] Thomas Jefferson to Roger C. Weightman, 24 June 1826, in Philip S. Foner, *Basic Writings of Thomas Jefferson* (New York: Wiley Book Company, 1944), 807.

[78] James Madison to Rev. Jasper Adams, September 1832, in *Writings of James Madison*, ed. Galliard Hunt (New York: G. P. Putnam's Sons, 1900–1910), 9:484–48 (quotation from 485).

[79] On this tradition, see Frank Lambert, *The Founding Fathers and the Place of Religion in America* (Princeton, NJ: Princeton University Press, 2003); and Jon Meacham, *American Gospel: God, the Founding Fathers, and the Making of a Nation* (New York: Random House, 2006).

[80] Tunis Wortman, *A Solemn Address to Christians and Patriots*, anonymously in 1800. See Hamburger, *Separation of Church and State*, 122. Hamburger deftly explores the various demands for separation in the early nineteenth century.

[81] Joseph Story to Rev. Jasper Adams, 14 May 1833, Joseph Story Papers, William L. Clements Library, cited in McClellan, *Joseph Story and the American Constitution*, 139.

nation – expected those of other faiths to convert to build a Protestant future. At the very least, they hoped that the prospects of freedom of religion under the aegis of a Protestant ideology would reassure non-Protestants and cause them to abide by the developing arrangements in polity and society. But what if Catholics were not persuaded by American greatness? What if they had other designs regarding American development? The solution ultimately offered by some was not a solution at all, but an admission that because religious liberty was a Protestant inheritance, Americans might limit the liberty of Catholics in order to maintain liberty itself.

In fact, the quandaries of religious freedom only grew in the decades after the ratification of the Constitution. Not only did the proliferation of religious sects increase religious diversity, but vast changes were occurring in the relationships between church and state. Although the federal Constitution abjured an established church, some state governments, as mentioned before, maintained established churches into the nineteenth century. But disestablishment proceeded apace in the nineteenth century, and Massachusetts finally became the last state to disestablish its state church in 1833.[82] The collapse of these established churches created a predicament for the New England Protestant clergy, which puzzled over the ways to maintain society's morals without an established church. Amid this uncertainty, many professing Christians perceived a growing urgency that the state, *because* of disestablishment, had to be based on Christian belief to function effectively. Heman Humphrey, for example, maintained that "the Bible contains the only code of laws, or rather the elements of the only code, which can sustain our free government or any other like it."[83] Presbyterian pastor Ezra Stiles Ely went even further in justifying his advocacy of a Christian political party. "We are a Christian nation," he affirmed, and "we have a right to demand that all our rulers in their conduct shall conform to Christian morality; and if they do not, it is the duty and privilege of Christian freemen to make a new and better election."[84] And Bela Bates Edwards, a professor of Hebrew at Andover, argued in 1848 that "perfect religious liberty does not imply that the government of the country is not a Christian government." Edwards, moreover, believed that the evidence was "convincing" that a "real, though indirect, connection between the State and Christianity is every year acquiring additional strength."[85] "It occurred to none but Catholics," writes Elwyn A. Smith, "to identify this as a doctrine of religion."[86]

Arguments that privileged Protestant Christianity were not the ravings of a lunatic fringe of Protestant ministers: they also had a deep tradition in judicial

---

[82] See James Fulton Maclear, "'The True American Union' of Church and State: The Reconstruction of the Theocratic Tradition," *Church History* 28 (1959): 41–62.

[83] Heman Humphrey, *Miscellaneous Discourses and Reviews* (Amherst, MA: J. S. and C. Adams, 1834), 135.

[84] Ezra Stiles Ely, *The Duty of Freemen to Elect Christian Rulers* (Philadelphia, 1828), 14.

[85] Bela Bates Edwards, *Writings of B. B. Edwards*, ed. Edwards A. Park, vol. 1 (Andover, MA: W. F. Draper, 1858), 489–90.

[86] Elwyn Smith, *Religious Liberty in the United States*, 116.

decisions on both the state and federal levels.[87] Indeed, although those who professed a liberal position might attack attempts such as Ely's bid for a political movement based on Protestant Christianity, judicial decisions supported a legal basis of Christianity in society and repeatedly evinced Story's Dilemma. Some fifty court decisions in state and federal courts prior to the American Civil War expressly relied on the suppositions that the United States was a Christian nation, and countless others relied implicitly on this assumption or simply cited earlier rulings that affirmed it. The judiciary, like many other aspects of the state and federal government already discussed, was unwilling to discount the value of Christian bases in undergirding American society.

A summary of a few judicial rulings at the state and federal level illustrates this perspective. In 1811, the New York Supreme Court in *People v. Ruggles* held that Christianity was a part of New York common law. Ruggles had been convicted for publicly announcing that *"Jesus Christ* was a bastard, and his mother must be a whore."* In the appeal to the New York Supreme Court, Justice James Kent, who delivered the opinion, conceded that "the free, equal, and undisturbed enjoyment of religious opinion ... and free decent discussions on any religious subject is granted." But "to revile, with malicious and blasphemous contempt, the religion professed by almost the whole community, is an abuse of that right." If the Constitution had discarded religious establishments, it did not break down the barriers of common law against "licentious, wanton, and impious attacks upon christianity itself" that would pervert its very meaning. Significantly, not all faiths were accorded these protections. Attacks "upon the religion of *Mahomet* or of the grand *Lama*" were not so protected because "we are a christian people, and the morality of the country is deeply ingrafted upon christianity." If the Sabbath was held to be special in law and if public oaths utilized the Bible, it followed that "wicked and malicious words, writing and actions which go to vilify those gospels continue, as at common law, to be an offence against the public peace and safety."[88]

---

[87] See, for example, Handy, *Christian America*, 27–64.

[88] *People v. Ruggles*, 8 Johns 545 (Sup. Ct. N.Y. 1811). Judicial decisions affirmed that Christianity buttressed not only the state but also societal institutions such as the family. In *Barnes v. First Parish in Falmouth*, 5 Mass. 400 (1810), Chief Justice Theophilus Parsons wrote that Christianity "as understood by protestants, tending by its effects to making every man submitting to its influence, a better husband, parent, child, neighbor, citizen, and magistrate, was by the people established as a fundamental and essential part of the constitution." Cited in Noonan, *Lustre of Our Country*, 98–99. There are many useful studies and source books on the courts, Christianity, and the law. See Joseph Story, *Commentaries on the Constitution of the United States: With a Preliminary Review of the Constitutional History of the Colonies and the States Before the Adoption of the Constitution* (Boston: Little, Brown 1833); Stephen Colwell, *The Position of Christianity in the United States, in its Relations with our Political Institutions and especially with Reference to Religious Instruction in the Public Schools* (Philadelphia: Lippincott, Grambo, 1854); Schaff, *Church and State in the United States*; and Daniel R. Ernst, "Church-State Issues and the Law: 1607–1870," in *Church and State in America: A Bibliographical Guide. The Colonial and Early National Periods*, ed., John F. Wilson (New York: Greenwood Press, 1986), 331–64. Catholics, of course, are not the only minority faith that faced legal inconvenience

Thirteen years later, the Pennsylvania Supreme Court, in *Updegraph v. the Commonwealth*, agreed that "Christianity is and always has been a part of the common law of Pennsylvania." Abner Updegraph was charged with vilifying the Christian religion when he declared, as a member of a debating association, that scripture was "a mere fable" that "contained a great many lies." His conviction was upheld by the court because if someone such as Updegraph was "maliciously to vilify the Christian religion," he had committed an indictable offense. The court argued that "Christianity, general Christianity, is, and always has been, a part of the common law of Pennsylvania." This "general Christianity" was "Christianity, without the spiritual artillery of European countries." And it was universalist because it was a Christianity not "founded on any particular religious tenets; not Christianity with an established church, and tithes, and spiritual courts, but *Christianity with liberty of conscience to all men.*"

If Christianity enabled liberty of conscience, should not Updegraph's views have been protected? And did not this association between Christianity and liberty, as well as the common law, privilege Christianity as a particular faith in Pennsylvania? The answer to both queries, the court assured its citizens, was no. Updegraph had crossed the line, the court argued, with his "outpouring of an invective so vulgarly shocking and insulting that the lowest grade of civil authority ought not to be subject to it." The court likened his debating association to a "nursery of vice" that would prepare "young men for the gallows, and young women for the brothel." Updegraph's was not a reasoned argument, but an "outpouring of an invective" both shocking and insulting to civil society. And not only had general Christianity been embedded in common law, but the freedoms guaranteed by the Constitution were based on it. This general Christianity, moreover, was a generic faith that contained specific liberties in and of itself; it did not give preference to any particular religious persuasion. Rather, it protected believers – including Jews and Unitarians – and promised them "freedom from the demon of persecution, and the scourge of established churches" that characterized European society. Perhaps profanity and blasphemy were not sins against God, but they were crimes against the good order of society that ultimately was the purview of the court.[89]

In 1861, the New York Supreme Court in *Lindenmüller v. People* reaffirmed its earlier finding.[90] "Christianity is not the legal religion of the State," wrote Justice J. Allen for the majority, "but this is not inconsistent with the idea that it is in fact, and ever has been, the religion of the people." Although it was the religion of the people, moreover, this did not mean "perfect civil and political equality" was not secured to those of other creeds. In a somewhat convoluted explanation of the relationship between Christianity, nation building, and liberty, Allen wrote,

in this regard. On Jews, see Morton Borden, *Jews, Turks, and Infidels* (Chapel Hill: University of North Carolina Press, 1984).

[89] *Updegraph v. The Commonwealth*, 11 S.&R. 384, 401 (1824).

[90] Gustav Lindenmüller had openly violated New York's Sabbath laws.

It would be stranger, that a people, Christian in doctrine and worship, many of whom, or whose forefathers, had sought these shores for the privilege of worshipping God in simplicity and purity of faith, and who regarded religion as the basis of their civil liberty, and the foundation of their rights, should, in their zeal to secure to all the freedom of conscience which they valued so highly, solemnly repudiate and put beyond the pale of the law, the religion which was dear to them as life, and dethrone the God who, they openly and avowedly professed to believe, had been their protector and guide as a people.

The absence of a state church was not meant to abolish the Sabbath but rather to permit Christianity to thrive and the church to remain more pure. In effect, the establishment clause ultimately strengthened Christianity.[91]

The United States Supreme Court also heard cases that dealt with church-state relationships. *Vidal v. Girard's Executors* (1844) concerned Stephen Girard, who made a large bequest in his will to create a college provided that "no ecclesiastic, missionary, or minister of any sect whatsoever, shall ever hold or exercise any station or duty whatever in the said college." The case was celebrated in part because of Daniel Webster's argument that "there is nothing that we look for with more certainty than the general principle that Christianity is part of the law of the land." He cited the vestiges of history – ranging from consecrated cemeteries to church structures – that were mute testimonies to the fact that the nation was wedded to religious belief. All of this proclaimed "that Christianity – general, tolerant Christianity – Christianity independent of sects and parties – that Christianity to which the sword and fagot are unknown – general, tolerant Christianity, is the law of the land." Although the will was upheld, Justice Joseph Story, who wrote the majority decision for the Court, again reflected his dilemma. "Christianity," he wrote, is "part of the common law of this State [Pennsylvania]."[92]

Decisions such as these were often complemented by specific rulings that affirmed the constitutionality of legislative acts such as Sunday laws, temperance enactments, or requirements of Bible reading in the public schools. In 1854, for example, the Maine Supreme Court ruled that the requirement that students read the King James Bible in public schools was "not an infringement of religious freedom," thereby upholding the expulsion of a Catholic teenager for refusing to read the Bible in class. The logic from our perspective was disingenuous: citing the maxim *Salus populi suprema lex* (The health of the people is the supreme law), the court found that compulsory reading of the King James Bible, but not the Douay version, was a beneficial practice that advanced the common good.[93]

Much in these judicial pronouncements, despite their frequent hostility to the beliefs and practices of Roman Catholics, conceivably did not impair the Catholic Church. Certainly a universal Christianity could encompass Catholicism, and perhaps even Judaism as the *Updegraph* decision proclaimed.

---

[91] *Lindenmüller v. People*, 33 Barb. (N.Y.) 548 (1861).
[92] *Vidal v. Girard's Executors*, 2 How. 127 (1844) (U.S. Supreme Court).
[93] *Donohue v. Richard*, 38 Me. 376 (1854).

Yet another, more particularistic principle was increasingly expressed by a number of theologians. It maintained that Christianity not only was the basis for society and polity but also was a gift that both promised *and* safeguarded freedom for those in its circle. Protestants, as we have seen, regarded their nation, among other aspects, as an exemplar of Christian liberty without parallel in world history. Americans did not simply enjoy religious freedom but, more broadly, as the philanthropist Stephen Colwell put it, in the United States "all undue restraint" was removed "from the tongue and the pen."[94] These unrivaled freedoms, however, engendered both tremendous possibilities and immense responsibilities.

But here was the dilemma. The Protestant foundation of the American polity allegedly provided marvelous liberties for its residents, which were threatened if the Protestant core was weakened. And these liberties were endangered in a number of ways. For one, Protestants had been schooled to be tolerant of others lest they betray their belief of toleration. But this attitude could be used against them by Roman Catholics and ultimately by the Protestants themselves to undermine that very tolerance. "The emissaries of the Pope," wrote a Bostonian in 1835, "will laud to the skies our toleration and religious freedom, until they enlist us in *propagating* that form of religion which we ought merely to tolerate, for the plain reason that all history teaches us it is a religion that must destroy *ours* as it has every other free government, the moment it gets ascendancy." Likewise, influential citizens in their zeal to be "liberal" condemned their own religion because they were "bitter against Protestants for alleged intolerance toward a religion that tolerates nothing but itself."[95] A quarter of a century later, a nativist asked: "Who are allies of the crafty Jesuits in our own land?" It was not only "the ignorant and superstitious Romanists merely," he answered, but also "the too-trusting and unsuspecting Protestants, whose love of toleration lead them to regard all sects of religionists as equally good."[96] A religious culture focused on religious toleration ironically prepared the way for the destruction of the state that promised this very religious freedom.

How were good Americans to respond to this dilemma? The solutions varied. Some, as we have seen, stressed a universalist Protestantism that would ensure a devotion to the American experiment, by Protestants and non-Protestants alike. Others, as we will observe in later chapters, envisioned the conversion of non-believers to Protestant belief. A significant number of Protestant spokesmen, however, advocated the restriction of freedoms to those who were a threat to the maintenance of liberty. If the Catholic hierarchy endangered American liberty, the rights of the former could be sacrificed for the good of the whole. After all,

---

[94] Colwell, *Position of Christianity in the United States*, 130.

[95] Committee of Publication, *Supplement to "Six Months in a Convent," Confirming the Narrative of Rebecca Theresa Reed, by the Testimony of More than One Hundred Witnesses, Whose Statements Have Been Given to the Committee* (Boston: Russell, Odiorne, 1835), 10, 16–17, 30, 37.

[96] *Pope, or President?*, 233.

American liberty was based on a Protestant sensibility, and threats to Protestantism represented a risk that liberty would be lost as well. Ultimately, these observers concluded that it was better to restrict the freedoms of Catholics so that freedom itself would not be imperiled. A conundrum of faith led them inexorably to support the notion that the measure of religious freedom had to modulate for religious subgroups to ensure religious freedom writ large.

The Protestant quandaries intensified with the upsurge in the size and influence of Catholic America, and accusations against the Church could become grotesque and overwrought. The Church was indicted as an agent in league with the regressive forces of Europe to overthrow the United States through a complicated plan to people the nation with their minions, who would ultimately elect a Catholic government that would usher in the destruction of the republic. A Jesuit's soliloquy in a novel encapsulates well the indictment. "While Catholicism declines in the Old World, " mused the Jesuit, "'tis rising in the New," and "by immense emigration," he continued,

our strength in the United States is rapidly increasing; and the period may not be remote when, even in this land, so rife with heresy and cursed with Godless liberty, the Inquisition shall stretch forth its vindictive arm, to strike down the proud fabrics of Protestantism, and hurl to the ground the free institutions of this boasted Republic! And with a whip of scorpions scourge heresy to the gates of perdition! Who, then, will dare question the supremacy of the pope, – or deny the infallibility of the holy, apostolic church! The impious tree of liberty shall be scathed by the vengeful lightnings of Rome, and shattered beneath the crushing thunders of the Vatican! What a triumph, to see impious Protestant sects humbled in the dust and made to kiss the ground at our feet![97]

Complex stories of captive nuns and lascivious priests graphically and luridly illustrated the profligate powers of the priesthood. If these allegations could border on the absurd, it bears emphasizing nonetheless that they had theological origins with their focus on the restrictions of the freedom that was inherent in one's conscience.

The perceived danger of Roman Catholicism to the United States was exacerbated by the challenges that the Church was simultaneously facing in Europe. The outcome of revolution and European nationalism repeatedly put the papacy in a defensive position, a position it would maintain for much of the nineteenth century. We might date the beginning of this posture to the 1832 encyclical letter of Pope Gregory XVI, which excoriated liberty of conscience. "From that polluted fountain of indifference flows that absurd and erroneous doctrine, or rather raving, in favor and in defense of 'liberty of conscience,'" he wrote, "for which most pestilential error, the course is opened by the entire and wild liberty of opinion, which is everywhere attempting the overthrow of religious and civil institutions and which the unblemishing impudence of some has held forth as an

---

[97] Isaac Kelso, *Danger in the Dark: A Tale of Intrigue and Priestcraft* (Cincinnati: Moore Anderson, Wilstach and Keys, 1854), 69.

advantage of religion."[98] Never one to mince words, the pope offered another blistering attack four years later. Liberty, he averred, fostered "that worst and never sufficiently to be execrated and detested liberty of the press." If this were not bad enough for Americans who were developing an appreciation of freedoms of conscience and the press, the pope continued, "nor can we augure more consoling consequences to religion and to government from the zeal of some to separate the church from the state and to burst the bond which unites the priesthood from the Empire."[99] If these words only confirmed the worst fears of anti-Catholics in the United States, later papal pronouncements, varying from papal infallibility to a syllabus of errors that condemned the separation of church and state, would continue to trouble Americans who viewed the papacy with unease.

The concerns about the pronouncements of the papacy in the United States were coupled with the arrival of thousands of Catholics who embraced a theology that seemingly contradicted the founding principles of the nation. If there were no established religion and if Roman Catholics could become citizens with full rights of religious freedom, Catholicism could become entrenched and the practices of its faith could endanger the republic. Such were the increasing perils of the modern, hybrid society as it evolved in the United States in the early decades of the nineteenth century.

In response, many Americans not only stressed the centrality of Protestant Christianity in governmental institutions but also argued that Protestant Christianity was the basis for American freedoms and exceptionalism. "The toleration which we have established among ourselves, and extend to all who come among us," Colwell wrote in 1854, "is Christian toleration."[100] Because Christian toleration was based on the Bible, "the manual of Christianity,"[101] it followed that scripture was the bedrock of Christian toleration. Rev. J. H. McIlvaine, a Presbyterian clergyman writing five years later, agreed. "Our national character," he argued, "is no less Protestant than it is Christian." As a result, "our civil and religious liberty, all our free institutions, even our civilization itself" was "an outbirth and growth of Protestant Christianity."[102]

---

[98] Cited in Elwyn Smith, *Religious Liberty in the United States*, 104.

[99] *Studium paternae benevolentiae*, translated "The Encyclical Letter of Pope Gregory XVI," in *Baltimore Literary and Religious Magazine*, May 1836, cited in Elwyn Smith, *Religious Liberty in the United States*, 100.

[100] Colwell, *Position of Christianity in the United States*, 98.

[101] Ibid., 116.

[102] McIlvaine, *Nation's Right to Worship God*, 34. It bears emphasizing that McIlvaine among others saw Catholicism as one threat among many. McIlvaine worried about anarchy that resulted from too much freedom as well as authoritarianism that stemmed from too little. He believed that the American nation faced particular challenges because of its heterogeneity (30) and that it had to remain a Protestant nation as a result (32–34). But he also believed that individual freedoms, carried to their logical extreme, resulted in anarchism (16) and in religious terms to a spiritual solipsism (17). Joseph F. Berg came to a similar conclusion. In a rebuttal to an essay by Abel Thomas, Berg argued that Protestant Christianity was the golden mean between popery and infidelity. See Joseph F. Berg, *Trapezium; or, Law and Liberty versus Despotism and*

Christian scripture in turn informed the scripture of a developing American civil religion: John Henry Hopkins, bishop of the Protestant Episcopal Church, contended in 1857 that the Constitution had a Christian character that all Americans were obliged to consider.[103]

The growing heterogeneity of their nation created challenges for this affirmation of "Christian tolerance." If toleration was to be extended "to those who come among us," how would that affect those who practiced different faiths? The answer of these Protestant observers writing as late as the eve of the Civil War was firm: Christianity had to be privileged if toleration was to be maintained. This meant that Roman Catholicism, among other faiths, had to cede elements of its beliefs in order to enjoy the toleration promised by the Christian nation. To be sure, Colwell pointed out, this nation "invited the people of every country to come to live under [the Constitution]." But this did not mean that it had abdicated its "Christian ascendency [sic] nor proclaim that their institutions were purged of the Christian element."[104] Hopkins was less self-restrained. "I hold it preposterous to suppose that a band of Hindoos could settle in any part of our terrritories, and claim a *right*, under the Constitution, to set up the public worship of Brahma, Vishnu, or Juggernaut."[105] For him, because the Constitution was a Christian-based charter, it provided no right for the public exercise of religion that was not Christian in belief.

In sum, not all faiths were created equal. If Hopkins could sanction no un-Christian religious practice, he was forced to conclude that Roman Catholics under the Constitution had no right to the free practice of their religion "without a serious inconsistency." This was so, Hopkins wrote, because "the papal system demands intolerance and exclusion and is the declared enemy to the free exercise of religion, which the Constitution has made one of the supreme laws of the land." The syllogism of what Hopkins called a "very painful and troublesome dilemma" was clear. A Roman Catholic must either be inconsistent with his church or with the Constitution. If he is true to his church, he cannot remain faithful to religious or political freedom in the United States. Conversely, if he remains loyal to his country, he cannot be true "to the faith of popery."[106] Others, less rigid than Hopkins, were willing to allow non-Protestants to profess their faiths. But because Protestantism was the basis of toleration, they stressed that Protestantism nonetheless had to be privileged. Colwell noted that the founders did "commit the perpetuation of Christianity to the Constitution," but they committed the Constitution to a Christian people as a sacred trust.[107]

Anarchy. A Vindication of Protestantism from Papal Assailants, and Infidel Advocates (Philadelphia: E. S. Jones, 1851).

[103] John Henry Hopkins, *The American Citizen: His Rights and Duties, According to the Spirit of the Constitution of the United States* (New York: Pudney and Russell, 1857), 76.

[104] Colwell, *Position of Christianity in the United States*, 20.

[105] Hopkins, *American Citizen*, 77.

[106] Ibid., 85.

[107] Colwell, *Position of Christianity in the United States*, 22.

These concessions to toleration were made necessary by the character of religious life in the United States. The infidelity of nonbelief was complemented by the structures of authority of such faiths as Roman Catholicism. If Americans "intended to extend a real Christian toleration to all people," Colwell argued, "they did not mean that the idolaters or pagans who might come among us should be regarded in their turn as tolerating Christians." Protestant Christians intended that America should remain "a Christian land" with toleration as one of its hallmarks.[108] McIlvaine agreed when he addressed "the enemies of Christianity." "We did not receive our free institutions," he wrote, "nor any of the priceless blessings which distinguish us above all other nations from you, but from our God, and through the channel of the Christian religion." Whereas these enemies dwelling among the Protestants freely received "whatsoever rights, liberties, and blessings" consistent with this Christian nation, any unreasonable demand "in the name of religious freedom" would "soon bring us to your ground, and make of us an infidel nation." So if the enemies argued for liberties of conscience, "it is time you were given to understand, that we also have a conscience, which bids us by the most sacred of all obligations."[109] The dilemmas were clear: if toleration were extended too far, it might ultimately lead to its own demise and authoritarianism and despotism would return.

Simply put, the separation of church and state did not mean to these critics that there should be a separation of the nation from Protestant Christianity. It would be easy, Stephen Colwell argued, to accept liberal notions that Christianity should not have primacy over other faiths, thereby severing the connection between common law and Christianity and "thus legalizing blasphemy and abolishing our code of morals, the basis of Christian civilization."[110] Yet these thinkers categorically rejected making the Constitution a religious-neutral document because the outcomes would be deleterious to national development. If the Bible was lost, the Sabbath abolished, and religion supplanted by atheism, Hopkins assured his readers, the inevitable consequence would be "a scene of anarchy, and bloody violence, and utter destruction of all the rights of man in honor, liberty, property, or even life!"[111] Given the manifest dangers, these men concluded that certain unalienable rights were in fact alienable from a citizenry that hewed to a seemingly alien faith.[112]

---

[108] Ibid., 21.

[109] McIlvaine, *Nation's Right to Worship God*, 40–41.

[110] Colwell, *Position of Christianity in the United States*, 22.

[111] Hopkins, *American Citizen*, 93.

[112] This perspective would endure past the Civil War. Judge John Welch, writing for the Ohio Supreme Court in 1872, argued, "The only foundation – rather, the only excuse – for the proposition, that Christianity is part of the law of this country, is the fact that it is a Christian country, and that its constitutions and laws are made by a Christian people. And is not the very fact that those laws do not attempt to enforce Christianity, or to place it upon exceptional or vantage ground, itself a strong evidence that they are the laws of a Christian people, and that their religion is the best and purest of religions? It is strong evidence that their religion is indeed a

Conclusion

Most Americans, of course, were not willing to concede so much. Most did not want to destroy religious liberty to save it. But many Protestants in antebellum America nonetheless were plagued by varieties of Story's Dilemma. Although they celebrated the elements in the federal constitution that enabled rights of conscience, they remained leery of religious faiths that might constrain those freedoms to the detriment of state and society. Venerating a nation whose society was a harbinger of a progressive future and a repudiation of the unfreedoms of Europe, they were wary of a growing Catholicism that in their minds both rejected freedoms of conscience and fostered the hierarchy and authoritarianism of Europe. Recognizing that the Constitution prohibited the recognition of a particular religion, they nonetheless believed that its genius stemmed from Protestant Christianity.

And certainly not all Americans acknowledged the Protestant conundrum. Catholic Americans, for example, were quick to reprove its Protestant conceits. Orestes Brownson, ever alert to Protestant hypocrisy, chided nativists in 1854. "To deny to Catholics the free enjoyment of their religion in the name of religious liberty," he wrote, "is a little too glaring a contradiction for these times."[113] Elsewhere he took a swipe at those Calvinists who profess "religious liberty, and its very aim is to deny it to Catholics, who in its view, we suppose are reprobates."[114] Intolerance for the sake of tolerance was for Brownson beyond the pale.

Yet the quandary became increasingly pressing for many Americans before the Civil War and endured beyond it. As late as 1888, the theologian Philip Schaff expressed his esteem for the "American theory" of church and state, which secured full liberty of religious thought, made persecution impossible, and "religious and liberty . . . inseparable." The separation of church and state in the United States, however, was "not a separation of the nation from Christianity." Indeed, the First Amendment "could not have originated in any pagan or Mohammedan country" because it "presupposes Christian civilization and culture."[115] And the impasse of the Protestant conundrum endured.

Shortly after the conclusion of the Civil War, a Presbyterian, Philip Lindsley, wondered if a liberal republican government, by guaranteeing rights of conscience, tacitly allowed religious sects to infringe on these rights. If immigrant Catholics were subjected to a spiritual bondage by their church as soon as they landed on American shores, he continued, did not civil government become an abettor of tyranny? Although he advocated for the fullest possible rights of

religion 'without partiality' and *therefore* a religion without 'hypocrisy.'" *Board of Education of Cincinnati v. Minor* 23 Ohio St. 211 (1872).

[113] Orestes Brownson, "Native Americanism: A Few Words on Native Americanism," *Brownson's Quarterly Review* 3 (July 1854): 348.

[114] Orestes A. Brownson, "Liberalism and Socialism," *Brownson's Quarterly Review* 2 (April 1855): 198.

[115] Schaff, *Church and State in the United States*, 9, 10, 53, 40.

conscience, he continued – in almost an afterthought – that "I suppose we would not allow to Moslems or Mormons ... the practice of polygamy; nor to Hindus the satisfaction of burning widows; nor to idolators of any name the privilege of offering to their deities human sacrifices."[116]

Indeed, disputes such as these about the role of religion in cultural practices as well as about the influence of Protestant Christianity in American state and society have persisted, as outlined in the Introduction, to the present day. Yet the antebellum era is especially noteworthy precisely because many held the belief that some sort of alliance between church and state was salutary, even necessary. And the place of Roman Catholicism at that time was particularly vital because it was the foremost religious competitor in the era, a competitor that was growing increasingly powerful at midcentury. If the solutions offered to address Story's Dilemma were usually less draconian than those advocated by critics who proposed an abridgment of religious rights for minority faiths, they were also rarely based on what we might today label a "cultural pluralist" model. Rather, the Protestants' response tended to affirm a belief in Hutchinson's "unitive impulse," an aspiration to emphasize a homogeneity that allegedly characterized the American past and to bring the heterogeneous elements in contemporary society under the aegis of a Protestant worldview.[117] If the members of the numerous Protestant sects could appreciate their common elements that allowed them to create an overarching Protestantism, many of them hoped that Catholics could also fit their religious beliefs into an American Protestant nation.

This aspiration to encourage cultural homogeneity, as we shall see in future chapters, varied in its focus and was not necessarily coercive. Some Protestants felt that the power of Catholicism would melt away in the warmth of an American environment. "The only hope of success in our attempts to make [the Catholic immigrants] American Protestant in their feelings," wrote the *Living Age* shortly after the 1844 riots in Philadelphia between Protestants and Catholics, "is in treating them *kindly.*" "Give them time to become enlightened," the journal continued. "Give them time to understand our institutions. Let them breathe the air of freedom ... and their hearts will swell and burst the chains of spiritual despotism."[118] As we shall also see, moreover, a number of strategies aimed at fostering homogeneity were employed. Many pinned their hopes on individual conversion of the unwashed to Protestantism (Chapter 3), whereas others aimed at the edification of non-Protestant elements through state institutions and, most notably, the public school (Chapter 4). They dreamt of a conversion and assimilation that would unravel the problems about Catholicism that so plagued them. In so doing, they hoped for solutions to the problems

---

[116] LeRoy J. Halsey, ed., *The Works of Philip Lindsley, D.D.*, vol. 3, *Miscellaneous Discourses and Essays* (Philadelphia: J. B. Lippincott, 1866), 424–26.

[117] See also Robert T. Handy, "The Protestant Quest for a Christian America," *Church History* 22 (1953): 8–20, which makes a similar argument.

[118] "The Philadelphia Riots," *Living Age* 23 (1849): 483.

posed by a multiconfessional society that would not compromise their ability to privilege beliefs that they held so dear.

Yet amid a growing and increasingly shrill anti-Catholicism, the Protestant conundrum would not be solved and a unitive impulse could only be a short-term approach. To be sure, some remained less troubled and dreamt of a secular state, whereas others offered a more irenic religious solution wherein Protestantism and Catholicism would be reintegrated into a Christian whole.[119] Yet even those Protestants who embraced a dream of homogeneity in an increasingly heterogeneous nation-state were forced by events to alter their strategies. This was in large part because of their debates with Catholic Americans, who were more likely to hew to a solution that stressed the heterogeneity in the United States. But as we shall see in the next chapter, Roman Catholics in America had their own challenges to confront and this more capacious solution engendered a conundrum of its own.

---

[119] For example, the Mercerburg school, led by Philip Schaff and John Williamson Nevin, envisioned a theological path that resulted in some sort of amalgamation within Christianity.

2

The Catholic Conundrum

> The question now pressing itself upon the American people is, to determine their Religion, as our fathers did the character of their political institutions. ... With the free exertion of Reason, with the natural impulses of our instincts, and with the silent influences of our noble institutions, the American people will rise in the strength of its manhood and proclaim itself Catholic.
>
> Isaac Hecker, 1857[1]

In 1836, John Hughes, who would later become archbishop of New York City, and John Breckinridge, secretary and general agent of the Board of Education of the Presbyterian Church, engaged in a series of debates in Philadelphia considering whether either Roman Catholicism or Presbyterianism was inimical to civil or religious liberty in the United States (see Fig. 3).[2] The debate was long in coming. As early as 1832, Breckinridge tendered a challenge in the periodical *Christian Advocate* to anyone who wished to debate whether the "Protestant Religion" was the "Religion of Christ." Hughes, who had been ordained to the priesthood only six years before and who would become a towering figure in American Catholicism, took up the challenge. Once they agreed on the ground rules of the debate, each developed his arguments, which were published in sectarian journals beginning in 1833. Three years later, Breckinridge and Hughes met in another series of debates, the content of which was also published.[3]

---

[1] I[saac] T. Hecker, *Aspirations of Nature*, 4th ed. (New York: J. B. Kirker, 1857; New York: Catholic Publication House, 1869), 360.

[2] On the debate, see Billington, *The Protestant Crusade, 1800–1860* (New York: Macmillan, 1938), 62–65; "Religious Discussions," *Catholic Encyclopedia*, 1912, http://www.newadvent.org/cathen/05034a.htm. The question was "Discussion of the Question, Is the Roman Catholic Religion, in any or in all its Principles or Doctrines, Inimical to Civil and Religious Liberty? and of the Question, Is the Presbyterian Religion, in any or in all its Principles or Doctrines, Inimical to Civil and Religious Liberty?"

[3] Billington, *Protestant Crusade*, 62–65; Mary Ann Meyers, "The Children's Crusade: Philadelphia Catholics and the Public Schools, 1840–1844," *Records of the American Catholic Historical Society of Philadelphia* 75 (1964): 104–5. The *Catholic-Herald*, which would become a significant newspaper among Philadelphia Catholics, was established to publish Hughes's arguments. We have access to the content of the debates because of their publication. See *Controversy between the Rev.*

FIGURE 3. John Hughes, archbishop of the Archdiocese of New York, engaged in a series of famous debates over the question of whether Catholicism or Protestantism best promoted civil liberty in America. (Brady-Handy Photograph Collection, Prints and Photographs Division, Library of Congress, LC-DIG-cwpbh-02511)

These debates nicely framed a number of issues of state, religion, and civil society that drew the attention of many Americans. First, the debate itself was emblematic of recurring intellectual controversies that electrified people in the antebellum era. A relatively common event particularly in the 1830s, the religious debate was a public display of rhetorical skills that pitted clergymen against one another and drew interested listeners into crowds that cheered wildly the theological contentions of their favored speaker and disparaged the voice of the opponent. These public discussions had not, in fact, originated as debates as such, but as meetings where religious beliefs were affirmed. In 1832, the newly founded New York Protestant Association organized meetings focused on the evils of Catholicism that attracted fifteen hundred auditors. Soon, however, Catholics as well as Protestants attended the meetings, and the volatile mix of those of confessional difference could erupt in violence. A bloody riot, for example, in 1835 marred a debate over whether popery was compatible with civil liberty; the doors of the Broadway Hall were broken down during the debate, the speakers escaped out the back doors, and the intruders destroyed the hall's interior.[4] The religious debates soon spread beyond New York. Not only would there be the Hughes-Breckinridge debate set in Philadelphia, but Bishop John F. Purcell and Alexander Campbell, the founder of the restorationist Disciples of Christ, would debate "on the Roman Catholic religion" in Cincinnati in 1837. And, as late as 1854, the Catholic convert Orestes Brownson declined an invitation to engage in debate with Protestants in St. Louis.[5]

Second and more significantly for our purposes, these debates were only one medium of a continuous dialogue that considered the correctness of religious belief and the implications of varying religious forms for the social, political, and economic development of the United States. They not only mobilized religious groups, but at heart they pondered the contributions and shortcomings of the variety of confessions that were vying for influence in the young American republic. A flood of printed literature complemented the oral arguments and provided the foundation for an uninterrupted debate about confession and state in the antebellum era. As we saw in the previous chapter, Americans, as they

John Hughes, of the Roman Catholic Church and the Rev. John Breckinridge, of the Presbyterian Church, Relative to the Existing Differences in the Roman Catholic and Protestant Religions (Philadelphia: Joseph Whetham, 1833); and *A Discussion of the Question, Is the Roman Catholic Religion, in any or in all its Principles or Doctrines inimical to Civil and Religious Liberty? and of the Question, Is the Presbyterian Religion, in any or in all its Principles or Doctrines, inimical to Civil and Religious Liberty?* (Philadelphia: Carey, Lea and Blanchard, 1836).

4 Billington, *Protestant Crusade*, 60.

5 For Alexander Campbell's assessment of the Breckinridge-Hughes debate, see "Catholic Controversy," *Millennial Harbinger* 4 (1833): 537–41. Campbell argues that the Protestant side was "triumphant," even if Hughes "often brought Mr. Breckinridge to his knees." For a critical Unitarian view of both the Breckinridge-Hughes and Campbell-Purcell debates, see "Debates on the Roman Catholic Religion," *Christian Examiner* 23 (1838): 53–64. If Campbell saw Breckinridge's weakness in the debate, the *Christian Examiner* suggested that Purcell won the debate with Campbell (60). On Brownson's offer to debate in the 1850s, see Thomas R. Ryan, "Orestes A. Brownson's Lectures in St Louis, Missouri, 1852 and 1854," *Records of the American Catholic Historical Society of Philadelphia* 89 (1978): 57.

pondered their nation's future, often wedded myths of nation to religious belonging, and implicitly – and sometimes explicitly – to the unsuitability of other confessions to the national project. This, in fact, was the underlying question in the crowded auditorium where Hughes pitted his forensic skills against those of Breckinridge. And it was Hughes's challenge to present a Catholic counternarrative to that which was becoming the Protestant story of national development and which, not coincidentally, was presented by Breckinridge in the debate.

Throughout the debates, both Hughes and Breckinridge deployed commonly avowed prejudices to galvanize their supporters and build their respective cases. Breckinridge cited many of the arguments introduced in the previous chapter. He trotted out complaints that were commonly expressed by his countrymen: Roman Catholicism was an institution of unfreedom, authoritarianism, and changelessness. The Church, he argued, created a "voluntary slavery," the most ignoble of all forms of slavery because it was not coerced. "The papacy, by *restraining liberty of conscience*," Breckinridge reasoned, "is a system of oppression. *Its doctrines* are *forced* on *man* ... on every subject; and they who reject them are punished *civilly*, and *temporally*, and once more *mortally*; for heresy was *death* by the *law*." Because "all *good Catholics choose* to submit" and "*abandon their rights of conscience* rather than expose themselves to her wrath and damnation," it followed that they were voluntary slaves.[6] This slavery, foreign to an independent republican citizenry, was fostered by the authority of the Church. Whereas the "American system" was one of protection and toleration of religious faith, Roman Catholicism was despotic.

Hughes told a different story. He not only affirmed his allegiance to the United States but also attempted to illustrate the many ways in which Catholicism conformed to American values, and the many ways in which Protestantism did not. He was able to put his remarkable autobiography to good use. Born in County Tyrone in 1797, Hughes would recount throughout his life the depredations of English colonialism in Catholic Ireland. Arriving in America with his family in 1817, Hughes set about to become a priest, an ambition he realized at age twenty-nine, six years before the debate with Breckinridge.[7] In the debate, Hughes set his story into a larger context of immigrant loyalty and an appreciation of economic mobility and political and religious freedom. "I am," he stressed, "an American citizen – not by *chance* – but by *choice*." Utilizing a commonly expressed belief that immigrants were in fact the best sort of Americans because they chose to join the republic, Hughes contended that American tolerance was central in his family's decision to leave Europe. "I was born under the scourge of

---

[6] *Discussion of the Question*, 36, 62 (italics in original).

[7] See, for example, Richard Shaw, *Dagger John: The Unquiet Life and Times of Archbishop John Hughes of New York* (New York: Paulist Press, 1977); Henry A. Brann, *Most Reverend John Hughes, First Archbishop of New York* (New York: Dodd, Mead, 1892); John R. G. Hassard, *Life of the Most Reverend John Hughes, D.D., First Archbishop of New York* (New York: Appleton, 1866); and William J. Stern, "How Dagger John Saved New York's Irish," *Urbanities* 7 (1997), http://www.city-journal.org/html/7_2_a2.html.

Protestant persecution, of which my fathers in common with our Catholic coun-trymen have been victim for ages." As a result, he continued, "I know the value of that civil and religious liberty, which our happy government secures for all." And if any sect was attempting to put an end to this liberty, it was the Presbyterians, who were trying "to destroy the civil and religious liberty of Catholics." If any denomination should be expelled for persecution, Hughes concluded, setting Breckinridge's argument on its head and belittling his point about Protestant malleability, it should be the Presbyterians.[8]

In fact, Hughes argued, Protestant intolerance placed in question the entire myth about immigrants, freedom, and America that was taking hold among many in the antebellum period. "Poor foreigners," Hughes observed, were "escaping from the oppressions of their various countries, seek asylum on these shores." These immigrants were coming to America "to better [their] condition"; they were "foreign," but their children would be American and their grandchildren "will wear gold spectacles." Perhaps they were poor, perhaps they were ignorant, but the "great body" of them were "industrious, hard-working people, who live, not by *knavery*, but by their daily toil." And who greeted these immigrants? It was "ministers of the gospel," who "are guarding the coast against the landing of the emigrant who comes to better his condition, and to breathe ... the air of religious freedom and civil freedom." Because he was a Catholic who worships God according to the dictates of his conscience, he was denounced. Who, Hughes implied, was not the American here?[9]

If Hughes consistently took notice of the rich contributions that the Church and its adherents would make to American life, he scorned those of Presbyterians. Reflecting a narrative that I will discuss shortly that glorified the contributions of Roman Catholics to the American republic,[10] Hughes reminded his audience of past Protestant depredations and enumerated Protestant faults at present. For one thing, the doctrine of predestination, the belief that God has foreordained all that will come to pass, in fact removed all forms of liberty, turned individuals into machines, and made a mockery of the human conscience. Presbyterianism, Hughes contended, was equally dangerous in civil society. Although some Presbyterians were almost "*idolaters*" of the American Constitution, Hughes noted with tongue in cheek, others denounced it as "a GODLESS INSTRUMENT"

---

[8] *Discussion of the Question*, 20.

[9] Ibid., 312.

[10] See, for example, M. J. Spalding, *D'Aubigne's "History of the Great Reformation in Germany and Switzerland," reviewed; or, The reformation in Germany examined in its instruments, causes, and manner, and in its influence on religion, government, literature and general civilization* (Baltimore: John Murphy, 1844); and *Miscellanea*, which was later published as *The Church, Culture and Liberty* (New York: Joseph F. Wagner, 1923). These American works by Catholic apologists were buttressed by European scholars. For example, Rev. Jaime Balmes's comparisons of Protestantism and Catholicism were translated and published in the United States as *European Civilization. Protestantism and Catholicity Compared in Their Effects on the Civilization of Europe* (Baltimore: John Murphy, 1850).

because it does not explicitly acknowledge God.[11] It was the Presbyterians who were opposed to civil and religious liberty, and it was they who were conspirators against the American republic. In attempting to make Presbyterianism the dominant religion in the country, they had used a variety of tactics. Once their attempt to stop the Sunday mail failed, they moved to a "more popular, more cunning, and therefore, a more dangerous expedient for the accomplishment of its unhallowed purpose." This plot, Hughes contended, aimed first to combine Protestant sects against the most unpopular religious elements and then move forward until all denominations had been overpowered and Presbyterianism was predominant.[12]

Although few Protestants would admit it at the time, Hughes probably won the argument. Protestant journals rehashed the debate in a nineteenth-century version of spin and pointed to lines of reasoning that Breckinridge missed on the first pass. In due course, Protestants, who initiated the public discussions of Catholicism, lost interest in the spectacle, another mute testimony to Hughes's forensic success.[13] Ultimately, urban Americans moved on to other public amusements, many of which also placed confessional difference at their center.[14]

If Hughes was able to display his forensic skill in the debate, however, his argument also clearly illustrated the manifold challenges faced by Catholics in antebellum America. In the first place, Catholics had to make a case for their belonging in the United States. The first section of this chapter illustrates how Catholics in fact wrote a counternarrative to the Protestant story and thereby asserted their membership in the nation. Their narrative utilized history to illustrate both the consequences of American opportunity for Roman Catholics and the contributions of Catholicism and Catholics to the unfolding American drama. As we shall see, Catholics brought civil liberty to American shores; they fought in the Revolution; some among them signed the Declaration of Independence; and they continued to contribute brains and brawn in advancing the antebellum American republic. Catholics next had to rebut the argument that their faith in the United States and elsewhere was regressive. Again drawing on historical examples, they argued that Catholicism was a positive force in the history of the world because it constructively fused progressive and conservative impulses. Although Catholicism was at the forefront in historical developments such as the end of slavery and the liberation of women, it simultaneously provided a solid brace that would sustain society and impede the development of unsalutary

---

[11] *Discussion of the Question*, 391. Hughes consistently hammered the theme that Presbyterian predestination did not fit the modern world. "Any religion that holds, as a 'tenet of faith revealed by Almighty God,' that 'whatsoever comes to pass' was 'unchangeably foreordained,' is opposed and dangerous to civil and religious liberty, by reducing *its votaries* from the position of moral, free, responsible agents, to that of the mere instruments of God's eternal decree, for the execution of 'whatsoever comes to pass'" (286).

[12] Ibid., 281–82.

[13] This is Billington's argument. See *Protestant Crusade*, 66.

[14] See R. Laurence Moore, *Selling God: American Religion in the Marketplace of Culture* (New York: Oxford University Press, 1994), for a compelling view of the ways in which religion was influenced by various forms of commercial entertainment.

impulses in society. In the end, republican America needed Catholicism as much as members of the Church benefited from membership in American society.

The more daunting challenge, addressed in the second section of this chapter, was the complicated relationship between the Catholic Church and the American state. Catholic leaders in America, illustrated by Hughes and others, celebrated the separation of church and state because it provided freedom of religion, but, because of the particularistic orientation of their church, they were less inclined to accept a denominationalism as it was developing in the United States. As they maintained the primacy of the spiritual over the temporal and the supremacy of the Church over spiritual matters, they continued to encounter misgivings among a suspicious Protestant majority.[15] The conundrum that they faced, simply stated, was how they could be pluralist and liberal, on the one hand, and particularistic, on the other.

The Catholic Counternarrative

The boasted Reformation trampled in the dust every important object of free government: security to life, to character, to property, to the pursuit of happiness, to personal liberty. And still we are to be told, that to it we are indebted for all the liberties we possess! Martin J. Spalding, 1860[16]

Catholic Americans did not passively witness a process of mythmaking and nation building that wrote them out of the story. Indeed, they created their own myths that justified their place in the United States and their contribution to it.[17] In many ways, the Catholic narrative in the United States paralleled the themes articulated by prominent Protestants. Reflecting on the American past, Catholics – like Protestants – argued that their faith was instrumental in creating

---

[15] To be sure, many particularistic church bodies in the United States encountered these challenges. Protestant confessional sects, for example, also faced difficulties folding their beliefs into a national identity. But these obstacles were particularly acute for Catholics in large part because of the Protestant majority's enduring suspicion of the Church. See Walter H. Conser, Jr., *Church and Confession: Conservative Theologians in Germany, England, and America, 1815–1866* (Macon, GA: Mercer University Press, 1984).

[16] Martin J. Spalding, *A History of the Protestant Reformation in Germany and Switzerland, and in England, Ireland, Scotland, the Netherlands, France and Northern Europe. In a Series of Essays Reviewing d'Aubigné, Menzel, Hallam, Bishop Short, Prescott, Ranke, Fryxell, and others* (Louisville, KY: Webb and Levering, 1860), 366.

[17] Mythmaking by minority groups in the United States that aimed at both enabling membership in the American nation and fostering ethnic identity has been widely treated by historians. See, for example, Orm Øverland, *Immigrant Minds, American Identities: Making the United States Home, 1870–1930* (Urbana: University of Illinois Press, 2000); and Russell A. Kazal, *Becoming Old Stock: The Paradox of German-American Identity* (Princeton, NJ: Princeton University Press, 2004). The Catholic counternarrative, by fostering an appreciation of Catholic contributions to the United States, also attempted to illustrate the benefits of Catholicism for the United States and those of the United States for Catholics. On the Catholic contribution to conceptions of national identity, see R. Laurence Moore, *Religious Outsiders and the Making of Americans* (New York: Oxford University Press, 1986), 48–71.

and fashioning the American nation. From the colonial period onward, they would cite instances of their contributions to the accretion of rights and liberties that characterized American society in the nineteenth century. As a religious minority, Catholics celebrated a state that guaranteed freedoms of belief, a guarantee that was lacking in many other areas in the world. Catholics also agreed that Christianity ought to be a foundation of the American state and that it was the moral basis for the favorable advance of the United States. As we shall see, some Catholics even recognized an American mission that resembled in many ways the Protestants' providential vision. Their narrative, in short, was remarkable in the ways that it mirrored the dominant Protestant myth.

The Catholic counternarrative took account of the perceived opportunities that the United States offered its residents, native born and immigrant alike. Like Hughes, many immigrants left Europe *because* of circumstances at home and the perceived prospects in America. "The Irishman as he loses sight of his native shores," wrote the Irish Catholic *Boston Pilot* in 1844, "feels by anticipation that chains, and persecution, and beggary are no more to be his portion" and he feels "a heart rendered ductile by gratitude" as he approaches the American shore.[18] He was at heart a republican, the *Boston Pilot* observed elsewhere, because "the desire of escaping the overlaying pressure of a proud aristocracy, a truculent oligarchy, and a heartless Monarchy" causes the emigrant to "forsake all that is near and dear to them on this side of the grave, and come to America to enjoy the blessing of her Republican Institutions." Could anything be more palpable, the *Boston Pilot* concluded, than that every act of emigration from Ireland was a renunciation of monarchy and despotism and "an actual adhesion to the principles of freedom and the institutions of Democracy"?[19] Given this premise, it was folly to accuse Catholic immigrants of hostility to American ideals. Of all the charges made against Irish Catholics, the *Boston Pilot* maintained, none was more "unfounded, slanderous and calumnious" than that they brought antirepublican prejudices to the United States. Indeed, given his predispositions, it was "impossible that [the Irish immigrant] should not become a good citizen."[20]

These expressions of allegiance to American principles, as I have argued elsewhere, were often nested in a complementary devotion to ethnic group.[21] Members of many national and religious backgrounds in the nineteenth century commonly expressed the "complementary identity," which simultaneously fostered an enhanced allegiance to nation and to ethnic subgroup. The Irish Catholic predisposition to maintain a complementary identity was no exception, a fact visibly demonstrated by the masthead of the *Boston Pilot* itself. Erin, clad in a green dress and emblematic of Ireland, is embraced by Columbia, who comforts her sister and welcomes her to America. Behind them stands Liberty, who wields a sword, wears

[18] "New York City Election," *Boston Pilot*, 20 April 1844.
[19] "Common Schools and Catholic Children," *Boston Pilot*, 13 June 1840.
[20] Ibid.; "New York City Election," *Boston Pilot*, 20 April 1844.
[21] Jon Gjerde, *The Minds of the West: Ethnocultural Evolution in the Rural Middle West, 1830–1917* (Chapel Hill: University of North Carolina Press, 1997), 59–66.

the cap of freedom, and extends a blessing and promise to beleaguered Erin as she confirms the words of solace from Columbia.[22]

If America enhanced the condition of Irish Catholic immigrants, proponents of the Catholic counternarrative focused simultaneously on the benefits of Catholicism for America. When Catholics wrote their specific myth, their story was a three-part history that illustrated the beneficial attributes of Catholicism, the injuries to society stemming from the rise of Protestantism, and the inevitable triumph of the Church in the United States. The first chapter of the story was set in Europe and rebutted the allegation that Catholic Europe was a seat of regression, arguing instead that it was the Reformation that ushered in an era of degeneration. In the second segment of the myth, the setting moved to the Americas but the moral remained the same: Catholic colonization was more salutary than its Protestant counterpart and the American Revolution was as much a Catholic triumph as a Protestant one. The concluding episode in the narrative was situated in the present. Not only had the unsavory character of Protestantism endured, but the American republic needed the helpful influences of Catholicism now more than ever. Simply put, the American nation was dependent on a flourishing Catholicism for its very survival.

The American authors of this story borrowed heavily from Catholic scholars such as the Spaniard Jaime Balmes, the Frenchman Joseph de Maistre, and the German Johann Joseph Ignaz Döllinger, each of whom provided a framework for understanding the resilience of Catholicism and the unfavorable outcomes of the Reformation from a European perspective.[23] Yet they also made use of American writers, including historians (especially William H. Prescott and Hubert Howe Bancroft), literati (including James Fenimore Cooper and Herman Melville), and politicians to write their myth. The foremost example of this project was the work of Bishop Martin J. Spalding. Born in Kentucky in 1810, Spalding was named bishop of Louisville in 1848 and archbishop of Baltimore in 1864. He was also a prolific author of a variety of texts ranging from a lengthy rebuttal of D'Aubigné's history of the Protestant Reformation to an eight-hundred-page tome

---

[22] "To Our Readers," *Boston Pilot*, 1 January 1848, describes the masthead. Erin is unhappy, explains the *Boston Pilot*, because her spiteful half-sister Britannia torments Ireland. Britannia, the paper continues, once ruled America, but Liberty and George Washington drove her back to her "own miserable Island" and now "America is the happiest country in the world." But Britannia continues to torment Ireland, and O'Connell, the one man who had a soul like Washington, is dead and Erin is very sad.

[23] In English translation, see Balmes, *European Civilization*; Joseph de Maistre, *The Works of Joseph de Maistre*, trans. Jack Lively (New York: Macmillan, 1965); and Johann Joseph Ignaz Döllinger, *A History of the Church*, trans. Edward Cox, 4 vols. (London: C. Dolman, T. Jones, 1840–42). Catholic critics also used Jacques Bénigne Bossuet, *The History of the Variations of the Protestant Christianity* (New York: D. and J. Sadlier, 1845). See Hartmut Lehmann, *Martin Luther in the American Imagination* (München: Wilhelm Fink Verlag, 1988), 164–76, for a useful overview of Catholics' critique of Luther and their arguments on the indispensability of Catholicism in the United States in the nineteenth century.

on Catholicism and Protestantism in world historical development.[24] Spalding's work was complemented by that of the convert Orestes Brownson, the Irish nationalist Thomas D'Arcy McGee, and Hughes, among others, and by Catholic periodicals such as the *Boston Pilot* and the *United States Catholic Magazine*. Together, these commentators – clerics and laity, immigrants and native born – created a remarkably consistent narrative that told a story almost diametrically opposed to the views of Protestants with regard to their religion and state.

The Catholic counternarrative began in Europe when the birth of civil liberty occurred in a pre-Reformation Catholic era. Although Christianity's primary objective was not of this world, Spalding argued that it had a direct influence on civil governments "by elevating and ennobling man's nature, – by dissipating the errors of his mind, by expanding the affections of his heart, it has necessarily promoted even his earthly happiness, and improved his social condition."[25] This was a stage in human development that ushered in the end of slavery and prepared humankind for an era of "full and perfect liberty." Specifically, the Catholic era was marked by advances embodied in the "Magna Charta, trial by jury, no taxation without representation, habeas corpus, stationary courts, and wise municipal laws and polity."[26] It was the Church that "rescued Europe from barbarism and re-established social order and well administered law."[27] As Balmes argued, "before Protestantism, European civilization had reached all the development that was possible for it."[28]

If the Catholic era enabled civil liberty, the Protestant ascendancy in Europe was an epoch when the "democratic principle" was weakened and the arm of monarchy fortified. The Reformation, in short, was a regression in civil liberty, and in those countries where it was most successful "an absolute despotism was established on the ruins of whatever institutions of human liberty had sprung up in the 'dark ages.'"[29] As Balmes contended, "Protestantism perverted the course of civilization, and produced immense evils in modern society; the progress which has been made since Protestantism, has been made not by it, but in spite of it."[30] Spalding placed the puzzle in an American context. How odd it was that Catholicity was accused of being the sworn enemy of republicanism in the United States when it nurtured European freedom and civil liberty.[31]

[24] Spalding, *D'Aubigné's "History of the Great Reformation in Germany and Switzerland,"* reviewed.

[25] M. J. Spalding, "Influence of Catholicity on Civil Liberty," in M. J. Spalding *Miscellanea: Comprising Reviews, Lectures, and Essays on Historical, Theological, and Miscellaneous Subjects*, 4th ed. (Baltimore: John Murphy, 1866), 132.

[26] Spalding, "Influence of Catholicity on Civil Liberty," "Our New 'American' Literature," in *Miscellanea*, 132, 768–69.

[27] Spalding, "Influence of Catholicity on Civil Liberty," "Our New 'American' Literature," in *Miscellanea*, 132, 769.

[28] Balmes, *European Civilization*, 419.

[29] Spalding, "Webster's Bunker Hill Speech. Relative Treatment of the American Aborigines by the English and Spanish Colonists," in *Miscellanea*, 337.

[30] Balmes, *European Civilization*, 419.

[31] Spalding, "Influence of Catholicity on Civil Liberty," in *Miscellanea*, 148.

Yet another prong in the Catholic narrative was a rebuttal of the common misperception that the Protestant lands of nineteenth-century Europe were "more free, more enlightened, more industrious, more enterprising, more prosperous, more moral and more happy" than their Catholic counterparts. In this discussion, Catholic apologists shifted their attention from civil liberty to economic justice. It was true that England reigned supreme in Europe, but Spalding pondered whether that nation's "grasping ambition, and her quenchless desire to accumulate wealth and to extend her power by all means, whether lawful or not," was deserving of any "higher reward." Perhaps, he suggested acidly, the secret to England's commercial greatness was that England was "emancipated by the reformation from the harassing thralldom of a conscience."[32] Perhaps the Reformation allowed this Protestant land to overlook a growing social inequality. Spalding's portrayal of England was of a dystopia: "a land of the boldest social contrasts, overgrown fortunes in the few and squalid misery in the many," a world of

splendid palaces, and miserable hovels; men and women rolling in brilliant equipages, and haggard multitudes crying aloud for bread to prevent starvation, at their very carriage windows; speculators amassing enormous wealth in the manufacturing districts, and a mass of wretched operatives worked almost to death, and nearly starving in the midst of their hard labor to sustain life; immense profits realized by avaricious capitalists, while the price of labor is cut down to the very starving point.[33]

England's empire of "colossal power and grandeur," moreover, also embraced "millions of crouching slaves who tremble under her iron scepter abroad." Like the Roman Empire, England had extended its power over the world; but again like Rome, she had not improved the condition of those under her thrall.[34]

Empire and poverty in fact stemmed from the same root. "The Protestant principle of private judgment," Spalding argued, "tends to isolate from the rest of society those who profess it, and to foster in them a spirit of individualism, of pride, and of avarice."[35] This principle might make Protestants more wealthy, but at what cost? By cultivating individualism, it isolated humans from one another and promoted a sterile and uncharitable society. Popular amusements in Protestant Europe – theaters, boxing matches, cock fights – were no longer innocent like Catholic holy days. Protestant Europe was swept away by "the gloomy tendency of a *new* religion, and by the breadth of mammonism, the cardinal maxim of which is – *time is money*."[36] All of this led to a less amicable, less compassionate society where Christian charity had vanished, where the poor had been crushed and banished, and where "gripping, hard-hearted avarice" had been ingrained in the people.[37]

---

[32] Spalding, "Catholic and Protestant Countries," in *Miscellanea*, 460.
[33] Ibid., 461.
[34] Ibid., 492–93.
[35] Ibid., 473.
[36] Ibid., 481.
[37] Ibid., 504.

Writers of the Catholic story stressed that the contrasts so apparent between Catholicism and Protestantism in Europe were transplanted to American soil. And they warned, as we will see in Chapters 4 and 6, of the deleterious effects of Protestant attitudes in contemporary America. Spalding cautioned that Americans were "imitating England in the very worst features of her social condition" and thereby nurturing "the fatal seeds of decay and ruin." He urged that the proper remedy be applied – "a substitution of the spirit of Catholic, social charity for that of Protestant individuality and avarice" – before the evil became incurable.[38] Yet Catholic apologists, to show the development of the Americas over the *longue duree*, also underscored the deep roots of these differences in the American past. Thomas D'Arcy McGee often skirmished with the Catholic clergy over his nationalist designs, but he did write a story about the Catholic contribution. To begin, Catholic Europe was responsible for the discovery of America. Thereafter, Catholic missionaries began the conversion of the aboriginal population. "They first planted the cross in the wilderness," McGee observed, "and shed their blood cheerfully at its base."[39]

Others made more detailed and pointed comparisons of the fate of Indians in Puritan New England and Catholic New Spain. In order to challenge the allegations that New Spain lacked liberty, Spalding, for example, deprecated the brutality and intolerance in New England. Equally important, Spalding wed the Spanish encounter with conversion rather than with genocide. In his response to Daniel Webster's nationalist speech commemorating the completion of the monument on Bunker Hill in 1843, Spalding rejected Webster's paean to American religious liberty by focusing on the fate of the American Indian. The native populations of New England, Spalding contended, "disappeared from the face of the earth, thanks to the cold-blooded policy and heartless cruelty of the Puritans!" American policy was ruthless; the Indians were exploited in trade, hemmed into restricted territories, goaded into war, and then "exterminated by fire and sword." In contrast, Spanish America assimilated and Christianized the aborigines. The Spaniards, he continued, "intermarried with them and become one people with them." The failure of Spanish America to exterminate its Indians, rather than the absence of religious liberty in Spain, was the reason that the Latin American states were less prone to civil liberties that Americans celebrated. Tragically and ironically, an Indian holocaust engineered by the United States enabled Webster to boast of his nation's "superior refinement and greater purity of blood" and "taunt the Spaniards with their humanity." Yet again, colonized peoples of the world enjoyed greater security under the aegis of Catholic rule.[40]

---

[38] Ibid., 505.

[39] Thomas D'Arcy McGee, *The Catholic History of North America. Five Discourses to Which Are Added Two Discourses on the Relations of Ireland and America* (Boston: Patrick Donahoe, 1855), 66. On the importance of the "discovery" of America as a component in the myth of many subgroups in the United States, see Øverland, *Immigrant Minds*, 54–86.

[40] Spalding, "Webster's Bunker Hill Speech. Relative Treatment of the American Aborigines by the English and Spanish Colonists," in *Miscellanea*, 348, 334–36. Spalding's reply to Webster's

And "Protestantism may boast its missionary zeal," Spalding concluded his essay on Catholic missions in the American Northwest, "but it is only Catholicity which can reclaim the savage, tame his ferocity, and effectually teach him the arts of civilization."[41]

If the history of Puritan New England was a shameful one in relation to the Indians, it was not much better with regard to religious liberty. In his exploration of the "blue laws" of New England, Spalding uncovered a "cardinal principle" that reestablished "a complete theocracy" in the region. If the "Pilgrim fathers" themselves had been victims in the Old World, they took most special care to establish crimes against religion that were "always rigid, sometimes wantonly cruel."[42] The *Boston Pilot* in 1841 agreed by citing the legal impediments that Catholics encountered in many British American colonies, such as the New York law that condemned Catholic priests to perpetual imprisonment and death should they escape.[43] Spalding paid special attention to the travails of his co-religionists, but he was also careful to recount the intolerance aimed at the Quakers and the witchcraft frenzy.[44] If Protestants dwelt on the Spanish Inquisition, Catholic critics were ever ready to consider another example of religious intolerance that was closer at hand both in time and space.

This long historical record of intolerance permitted Catholic commentators to draw comparisons with contemporary events. Following the 1834 burning of the Ursuline convent, for example, some observers wondered if this was merely the latest manifestation of Puritan intolerance, an intolerance that was shielded by the heady rhetoric of the Protestant roots of religious liberty.[45] The "systematic attempt . . . to fasten all the odium of narrow-mindedness and persecution on the Catholic Church," Spalding argued, had deep roots as did the contemporary battle cry of those who sought "in this free country, to render Catholics hateful

speech is an apt example of the Protestant-Catholic conversation in antebellum America. If Webster's speech is replete with flourishes of the Protestant role in the thriving American republic, Spalding focuses on Webster's hubris; his misstatements of history; and the blemishes of American behavior, varying from America's treatment of Indians to the riots aimed at Catholic citizens of the United States. Spalding was particularly attentive to the Catholic interaction with Indians, and he wrote numerous essays reviewing the histories of Bancroft and Prescott. See "The Spanish Inquisition: Prescott's View," 213–34; "Prescott's Conquest of Mexico: Character of the Conquerors," 250–74; "Prescott's Conquest of Mexico: The Religious Point of View of the Conquest," 275–97; and "Early Catholic Missions in the North West: Bancroft's Account," 311–21, all in *Miscellanea*.

41 Spalding, "Early Catholic Missions in the North West," in *Miscellanea*, 311. See also E. Rameur, "The Progress of the Church in the United States," *Catholic World* 1 (1865): 1–19, which provides a historical overview of Roman Catholic contributions to the American past.
42 Spalding, "Our Colonial Blue Laws," in *Miscellanea*, 359.
43 "The Irish in America," *Boston Pilot*, 16 January 1841.
44 Spalding penned two extensive articles on colonial blue laws: "Our Colonial Blue Laws: Union of Church and State," 353–68; and "Our Colonial Blue Laws: Heretics, Quakers, and Witches," 369–82, both of which appeared in *Miscellanea*.
45 See, for example, the editorial in the *Cincinnati Telegraph*, 10 April 1835, cited in Committee of Publication, *Supplement to "Six Months in a Convent," Confirming the Narrative of Rebecca Theresa Reed, by the Testimony of More than One Hundred Witnesses, Whose Statements Have Been Given to the Committee* (Boston: Russell, Odiorne, 1835).

to their fellow-citizens, and to deprive them even of their undoubted civil rights."
In his day, "this undisguised effort to crush Catholic liberty and rights" was made
"with strange inconsistency . . . in the name of liberty itself!"[46] "Much as we regret
to write it," Spalding concluded, "the narrow-minded persecuting spirit of the
Puritans still survives in their descendents."[47]

If examples of religious tolerance were to be found in British North America,
they were based in Catholic, and certainly non-Puritan, colonies. Catholic
chroniclers paid special attention to instances of religious freedom that were
associated with Catholic influence. The colony of Maryland was a major topic of
conversation. The passage of the Toleration Act of 1649, McGee observed, was
the "first ordinance of its kind known in America."[48] Likewise, Spalding argued
that "it was the Catholic Lord Baltimore, and the Catholic colonists of Maryland
who in 1648 proclaimed on these shores the great principle of universal toleration,
while the Puritans were persecuting in New England, and the Episcopalians in
Virginia."[49] "While the Puritans were persecuting their Protestant brethren in
New England," the *Boston Pilot* observed, "the Catholics, against whom the
others were combined, formed in Maryland a sanctuary, where all might worship
and none might oppress."[50] The lesson was clear to Spalding: Maryland "did at
least as much for civil liberty as the pilgrims, and much more than they for religious
liberty."[51]

When Americans declared their independence, the Catholic Church was there.
Despite the persecution that Catholics faced in the eighteenth century in the British
American colonies, McGee claimed, they "thought only of the common cause" of
the Revolution; "a large share of Catholic blood, talent, and treasure," in sum,
"contributed to your independence."[52] Using a possessive pronoun to emphasize
the Catholic contribution, Spalding figured that "half of the generals and officers
in our revolution" were Catholic. In an unspoken reference to Benedict Arnold,
moreover, Spalding noted that there was "no Catholic traitor during our revolution."[53] Some suggested that the Revolution itself was divinely inspired to create a
new order of the ages. As the *Boston Pilot* phrased it, "God fought at the back of
Washington, and he willed that an Asylum for the oppressed of the old world
should be opened here, that the unfettered developments of the human mind,

---

[46] Spalding, "Our Colonial Blue Laws," in *Miscellanea*, 353.
[47] Ibid., 354.
[48] McGee, *Catholic History of North America*, 70.
[49] Spalding, *D'Aubigné's "History of the Great Reformation in Germany and Switzerland,"*
    reviewed, 273–74.
[50] "The Irish in America," *Boston Pilot*, 16 January 1841.
[51] Spalding, "Webster's Bunker Hill Speech. Relative Treatment of the American Aborigines by the
    English and Spanish Colonists," in *Miscellanea*, 334. Plymouth Rock, Spalding concluded, was
    the Blarney Stone of New England.
[52] McGee, *Catholic History of North America*, 84.
[53] Spalding, "Influence of Catholicity on Civil Liberty," in *Miscellanea*, 150. The Catholic military
    leaders listed by Spalding were Lafayette, Pulaski, Count de Grasse, Rochambeau, DeKalb, and
    Kosciusko. See also "Foreigners and the Right of Suffrage," *Boston Pilot*, 28 August 1841, which
    makes a similar argument.

should form this meridian mark, and direct the effeminate and declining races of Europe."[54] Archbishop Hughes agreed. The Revolutionary era resulted in "a land of religious freedom and equality" that was neither a Catholic nor a Protestant country.[55] Seen in this light, the American Revolution against Protestant England and abetted by Catholic France was a story that was not so much the triumph of a Protestant new world order as the birth of a multiconfessional society with basic freedoms of conscience, freedoms that originated in Catholic Europe.

Following the Revolution, Catholics continued to participate, both intellectually and materially, in the building of the United States. The material contribution was readily apparent. The mass of immigrants, who brought with them "athletic frames, robust, inured to labor and industry," the *Boston Pilot* argued, "are the secret of this great country's giant progress."[56] McGee made a similar observation when he remarked that "a steady supply of cheap labor, a force which could be freely moved from point to point of national development, which could content itself to camp in shanties, and to turn its hand to any thing ... was the great want of this republic in the last half century." And "that want," he concluded, "Catholic Ireland supplied."[57] Others in addition to McGee stressed the correlation between immigrant labor and economic growth. The economist Louis Schade, who conducted a comprehensive statistical study of immigration, concluded that "but for the influence of immigration, the wonderful works of improvement, which have added so much to our national wealth and prosperity, could not have been accomplished." Immigrants were in large part responsible for the construction of canals and railroads and the growth in arable land and the labor that facilitated industrial pursuits. The immigrant contribution, Schade concluded, enabled the United States to be "the most happy, and prosperous, and powerful nation on the earth" and provide "our republican example to shake the hoary thrones of monarchs in the Old World"; without them, "we should be a fourth rate national power, subject to constant dangers of foreign invasion."[58] In an essay written in a moment of white-hot nativism in the 1850s, Spalding reminded Americans what "foreigners" had done for the nation.

They have filled our army and navy; they have fought our battles; they have leveled our forests, peopled our vast unoccupied territory, and filled our cities with operatives and mechanics; they have dug our canals, built our turnpikes and railroads, and have thus promoted, more perhaps than any other class, the improvement of the country and the development of its vast resources.

[54] "The Mission of America," *Boston Pilot*, 18 March 1848.
[55] John Hughes, "The Catholic Chapter in the History of the United States," 8 March 1852, in *The Complete Works of the Most Rev. John Hughes, D.D., Archbishop of New York*, ed. Lawrence Kehoe (New York: American News, 1865), 2:104.
[56] "Foreigners and the Right of Suffrage," *Boston Pilot*, 28 August 1841.
[57] McGee, *Catholic History of North America*, 102.
[58] Louis Schade, *The Immigration into the United States of America, from a Statistical and National-Economical Point of View* (Washington, DC: Union Office, 1856), 12–13. See also "Boston Emigrant Society," *Boston Pilot*, 23 January 1844, which also stresses the economic benefits of immigration.

"In a word," Spalding concluded, "[foreigners] have, in every way, largely contributed towards enhancing the wealth and increasing the prosperity of the republic."[59]

In so doing, immigrants contributed to nation and faith. "America has no better citizens," the *Boston Pilot* concluded, "none who would soon breast the steel of her enemies, or pour out their bloods more freely in defense of her soil and liberties than those, who ... have severed the ties of relationship and country, and sought on her shores a *New Home*."[60] Yet as they made a new home, Catholic immigrants built up their church. When the Yankee factory owner paid their hard-earned wages to his Irish operatives, McGee observed, "little he dreamed that on the morrow a part of that Puritan capital would go to build a Popish church, or pay a priest, or to erect a Catholic school." Although the Puritan became rich, McGee concluded, "the Catholic in his poverty was to come after him, to win wages from him by industry, and to erect in the land of the Puritans, with the money of the Puritan himself, the cross the Puritan had so long rejected."[61]

Despite their manifest contributions to the growth of the United States, Catholics noted that the struggle between Protestantism and Catholicism endured into the nineteenth century. The intolerance that characterized Puritan New England, Catholic apologists contended, found new expression in anti-Catholicism and the Know Nothing movement, a rearguard action by Protestants, who would face inevitable defeat. Anti-Catholics could rile up the American people for only so long with calls against the priesthood and for the use of the King James Bible. But eventually Protestantism would destroy itself with its strange mixture of latitudinarianism and fanaticism. This result would be beneficial for the American people as well as for their state and society for a variety of reasons. Because Catholicism promised true freedom, Americans would benefit; because it fostered justice, the divisions in society would be ameliorated. In the end, the struggle in the United States would be between Catholicism and infidelity. Because the nation-state had to be bolstered by religious faith, it would have to rely on the Church for support against the havoc wrought by the forces of infidelity.

If Catholics respected their contributions to American economic growth, then, the intellectual and spiritual contributions to the development of the United States were more complex and ultimately more important. Writers of the Catholic counternarrative built their thesis on the weaknesses of Protestantism, evident in the past and the present, and the assets of Catholicity in providing its believers a freedom absent in the Protestant faith and in furnishing state and society a bulwark against the precarious circumstances inherent in a republic undergoing massive economic and social change. Catholicity, in short, was the great hope for America owing to the very nature of Catholicism itself.

[59] Spalding, "Introductory Address, To the Impartial Public; on the Intolerant Spirit of the Times," 1855, in *Miscellanea*, lv.
[60] "The Emigrant," *Boston Pilot*, 30 May 1840.
[61] McGee, *Catholic History of North America*, 104–5.

The weaknesses of Protestantism were obvious to Catholic writers. The narrative of Protestant defects began in Europe, which resembled a mirror image of the Protestant map of European morality. The core of the problem, in Spalding's mind, was the shattering of the unity of Christianity – apparent in the Church – which segmented church and state. Before Luther, Hughes agreed, all had been unified and therefore all subsisted in the harmony of one belief. "There was," Hughes continued, "one ideally perfect, central rallying point, on which men's minds were united – the beauty, simplicity, and *Unity* of the faith of the Catholic Church, which God had established for the salvation of men."[62] Catholic Europe remained a site of economic justice in contrast to the rapacious Protestant nations best exemplified by a growing English empire. Spalding remarked that the Protestant shortcomings were apparent in the United States as well. Here was a society without unity as exemplified by a flourishing denominationalism and stamped by excess illustrated by the nativist violence that increasingly terrorized his co-religionists at midcentury. Americans, as a result, were victim to a variety of intellectual and spiritual impulses. Latitudinarianism, fanaticism, and infidelity characterized the Protestant world in the early American republic.

The first deficiency of American Protestantism was what Spalding called its "religious liberality," or what might more properly be called latitudinarianism. These excessive freedoms of belief could in turn lead to tolerance for heresies such as Pelagianism (which denied original sin, proclaimed free will, and perceived Jesus as merely a moral teacher) and Socinianism (which saw Jesus as a human moralist). Such a "fashionable theory" held that as long as a person was "a moral man and a good citizen," he or she had no concerns about the teachings of Jesus or the doctrines of Christianity. Catholics argued that this posture, increasingly maintained by Protestant America, subverted Christianity because it discounted Christian doctrine and fostered a vague moral attitude in its place.[63] The tendency was to depose "the noble and sublime truth of religion" and replace it with a "low level of merely earthly knowledge," a tendency that not only was wrong but also debased and degraded what Spalding called "this heavenly science." Hughes agreed. Whereas New England originally was a land of stern Puritans, he contended, it had now devolved into "a land of Socinians – a land of infidelity."[64]

With the age-old principle of religious authority superseded, discipline was replaced by the mischief of religious individualism and denominationalism in American society. Believers were encouraged to decide for themselves which Protestant sects were temporally the most appealing. A system of logic was thus put in place that flattered human pride and pandered to human passion. The "distracting and disorganizing" principle of individuality, Spalding stressed,

---

[62] John Hughes, "The Decline of Protestantism, and Its Cause," 10 November 1850, in Kehoe, *Complete Works of the Most Rev. John Hughes*, 2:88.

[63] Spalding, "Introductory Address, To the Impartial Public; on the Intolerant Spirit of the Times," xxvii.

[64] Hughes, "Decline of Protestantism, and Its Cause," 98.

opposed "the great conservative principle of an authority ... secured from error by Divine promise." The outcome was "the prolific brood of jarring sects which overspread the land," which grew forth proclaiming their own versions of the truth.[65] If scripture observed "there is nothing new under the sun," it was belied, Spalding sarcastically observed, by the "prophetic vision of our enlightened age."[66] The celebration of freedom for its own sake, in sum, was undermining the authority of the clergy as sect after sect, each one more ridiculous than the one before, was formed. "The very pulpits, built for the purpose of preaching the doctrines of the Trinity," Hughes argued, "have been turned into places for preaching against the divinity of the Son of God!" Elsewhere, he continued, "you have your Father Millers also, who turned votaries of private interpretation, crazy with the idea that the last day has come, or was to have come four years ago. And who can stop him? Who among Protestants has the authority to say to him, 'Unhappy man, you are not a Protestant if you say so, and you must cease?'" The Protestant clergy might preach obedience from their pulpits, Hughes concluded, "but what authority are they? None at all."

The proliferation of sects fostered by the primacy of individual religious belief, Catholic critics continued, not only destroyed religious unity and ecclesiastical authority, but it also spawned a curious mixture of religious excitement that smacked of fanaticism and indifferentism. On the one hand, Spalding observed, "we hear an endless cant about the Sabbath and the Bible, about revivals and 'getting religion,' about tract societies and missionary societies, about money to support the missionaries, and their wives and children." Yet curiously, this fervor, on the other hand, was juxtaposed with a lackadaisical "indifferentism," a belief that variations in religious doctrine and practice were unimportant. If fanaticism garnered the greatest attention, indifferentism, resembling "an ominous silence, as of the grave," gained the most proselytes.[67]

The combination of sectarian division, indifference, and fanaticism boded ill for Protestantism. The individualism inherent in American Protestantism foretold sectarian divisions. "Torn and distracted within, split up into a hundred warring sects already, and yearly witnessing new divisions," Spalding predicted, Protestantism sooner or later would "become victim of those warring elements of dissolution which are festering in its very bosom."[68] Fanaticism was a reflection of desperation. "The undeniable fact," Brownson claimed, was "that Protestantism as a religion is in this country on its last legs" and that its ministers were attempting to recover their standing and influence by orchestrating an aggressive persecution against the Catholic Church. But as anti-Catholicism and other reform movements ran their course, the victory of indifferentism among

[65] Spalding, "Spirit of the Age," in *Miscellanea*, 392–93.
[66] Ibid., 383, 386.
[67] Ibid., 393.
[68] Ibid., 390–91.

Protestant sectarians was at hand.[69] "The present desperate effort of Protestantism to put down Catholicity in this *free* republic," Spalding mocked, was "spasmodic and can not last long." Fierce and animated, anti-Catholicism was only the first chapter in the great coming struggle between Catholicism and unbelief.[70] Boston exemplified this progression. It was a "paradise of infidels, and of sects bordering on the very verge of infidelity" and "a center of Universalism, Unitarianism, Fourierism, Parkerism, Transcendentalism." "How sadly," Spalding asked rhetorically, "have the children of the Puritans degenerated from the rigid orthodoxy of their sires" into a stronghold of "downright infidelity?"[71] As Brownson put it, "the half-and-half religion of Protestantism no longer satisfies their hearts" and "blinds or confuses their intellectual vision."[72]

The conclusion drawn by a variety of Catholic writers was unmistakable. Given the movement of history and the obvious defects of American Protestantism, the "great coming struggle in our age and country," Spalding concluded, would not be between Catholicism and Protestantism, but "between Catholicity and indifferentism and infidelity."[73] The struggle grew more troublesome around 1850 because of the immigration not of Catholics, but of radicals fleeing the chaos of revolution. The greatest danger to the institutions of the American republic, Spalding argued in 1855, were "infidels in religion, and red republicans, or destructionists of all social order" who were thrown against American shores following the convulsive European revolutions in 1848.[74] Brownson defined this "most dangerous class of immigrants" as those "imbued with the infidel and anarchical principles of the mad European revolutionists," who carried on "their machinations against legitimate authority and social order in a language which very few of our countrymen are able to understand." With no religion to supply their lack of respect for civil authority, this non-Catholic mass of immigrants was a dangerous class.[75] Because many American-born individuals would soon join these European infidels as Protestantism lost credibility, the importance of Catholicism only increased in what promised to be a titanic battle between religion and infidelity.

The future, in short, portended the growing importance of the Catholic faith and its pivotal role in the development of American society. Given the imminent demise of Protestantism, one benefit that Catholicism would confer on the

---

[69] Orestes Brownson, "The Papal Conspiracy Exposed," *Brownson's Quarterly Review* 3 (April 1855): 252–53; Spalding, "The Spirit of the Age," in *Miscellanea*, 390–91.

[70] Spalding, "Spirit of the Age," in *Miscellanea*, 393.

[71] Ibid., 391.

[72] Brownson, "Papal Conspiracy Exposed," 254.

[73] Spalding, "Spirit of the Age," in *Miscellanea*, 393. Brownson also used nearly the same wording as Spalding: "The day is near at hand when [the American people] must make their election between Catholicity and no religion." Brownson, "Papal Conspiracy Exposed," 254.

[74] Spalding, "Introductory Address, To the Impartial Public; on the Intolerant Spirit of the Times," lvii.

[75] Orestes Brownson, "Native Americanism: A Few Words on Native Americanism," *Brownson's Quarterly Review* 3 (July 1854): 343.

United States was its role as a spiritual bulwark for American state and society. Although "America [was] the country of the Future," argued Isaac Hecker, it was also in a moment of crisis at midcentury because no people could become great without religion and the destiny of the United States was to be decided in the present through an acceptance of Catholicism.[76] After all, even many Protestants would agree that religion was a necessary element for political stability and if the battle pitted Catholicity against infidelity, it was clear on which side they would fall. The Catholic population, moreover, would continue to shore up the nation. Brownson, who was certainly no unconditional advocate of European Catholics, nonetheless perceived that "the really Catholic portion of our foreign population ... are at present the most conservative body in the country." Catholic immigrants possessed principle and conscience that boded well for their republican education; they were a group that neutralized the unsavory influence of the radical immigrants that swarmed onto American shores after 1848.[77] The stabilizing influences of Catholics would only continue with the decline of Protestantism.

Another contribution of Catholicism to American society was the deliverance that it would provide those who converted to the faith. One facet of this liberation, which I will discuss in greater length in the chapters that follow, was the role that Catholicism would play in contesting the materialism and individualism that plagued American society and in providing a salve to the poor and vulnerable. When Spalding disparaged the quality of life in England, he was casting his gaze at unsalutary developments in the United States as well. Still another component of the Catholic deliverance, an unmistakable truth that Protestant Americans willfully ignored, was that Catholic belief set people free. Although Protestants believed that Catholics were "deprived of all freedom, and are mere slaves to our priests," Brownson argued, nothing was further from the truth. As a convert to Catholicism, Brownson could observe that the most remarkable aspect of conversion was that everything was "free, natural, spontaneous." The Catholic "feels that he has suddenly burst from darkness into light, from the most galling slavery into the glorious liberty of the children of God."[78] But because of the authority of the Church, this freedom was not unrestrained license. If nineteenth-century liberals felt that true liberty was a freedom from right as well as wrong, wrote a Catholic, "we assert that it is freedom only from wrong."[79]

Catholic spokesmen, who gathered historical, theological, and contemporary evidence, drew what they considered an inevitable conclusion: Catholicism by its very nature was destined to play a pivotal role in the American story, a role that

---

[76] Hecker, *Aspirations of Nature*, 45–48.
[77] Brownson, "A Few Words on Native Americanism," 348.
[78] Brownson, "Papal Conspiracy Exposed," 266, 261.
[79] "Hungary," *New York Freeman's Journal*, 1 September 1849, 1, cited in John T. McGreevy, *Catholicism and American Freedom: A History* (New York: W. W. Norton, 2003), 36–37. Some years later, Pope Leo XIII, in an 1888 encyclical, put it well: "The true liberty of human society," he wrote "does not consist in every man doing what he pleases," but rather "supposes the necessity of obedience to some supreme and eternal law." Also cited in McGreevy, 37.

would benefit the American people and their state and society. The convert Isaac Hecker would proclaim the truth that Christianity was the only religion that could "claim the attention of all mankind" but that its Protestant form contradicted reason, shocked the convictions of conscience, and was subversive of all human dignity. In the end, "with the free exertion of Reason, with the natural impulses of our instincts, and with the silent influences of our noble institutions," Hecker assured his readers, "the American people will rise in the strength of its manhood and proclaim itself Catholic."[80]

Perhaps Orestes Brownson, in his 1856 essay entitled "The Mission of America," best synthesized notions of American progress and the indispensability of Catholicism. In it, Brownson contended that Catholicism was not merely an ingredient, but was a crucial requirement for American democracy. Brownson tapped into the coinage of American exceptionalism. "We look upon ourselves as a providential people," he wrote, who possess "a destiny glorious to ourselves and beneficent to the world."[81] Americans were "the people of the future." The manifest destiny of the United States, he continued, was "something far higher, nobler, and more spiritual" than territorial expansion. It was "the realization . . . of the Christian ideal society for both the Old World and the New."[82]

Brownson concluded that Catholicism sustained the United States, just as America was the future of the Catholic Church. "It is but simply truth to assert," he continued, "that ours, at present, is the country towards which Catholics throughout the world should turn their hopes." America was "the future of the world," and those who wished to be part of the new order of civilization should look to the United States. Yet this future, this destiny, this new order of the ages was only possible through Catholicity. "The Catholic Church . . . comes not to destroy the natural," Brownson argued, "but to fulfill – to purify, elevate, direct, and invigorate it. . . . As our country is the future hope of the world, so is Catholicity the future hope of our country."[83] In contrast, the Protestant story was "a chronicle of decline" because "Protestantism has not been able to retain life and vigor enough to suppress our American civilization," and therefore "has

---

[80] Hecker, *Aspirations of Nature*, 358–59.

[81] "The Mission of America," *Brownson's Quarterly Review* 1 (July 1856): 409–44. Also in Orestes A. Brownson, *The Works of Orestes A. Brownson*, comp. Henry F. Brownson, vol. 11 (Detroit: T. Nourse, 1882–1887), 551–84 (quotation from 567). Brownson also lectured on the American mission, rejecting the idea that the destiny of the United States was related to pure democracy. "The mission of the American people was to subdue this new world, to cover it with a new civilization, and with new institutions, with as much freedom for the individual and communities as is compatible with the frailty of our nature. . . . But instead of this, we have conceived it to be our mission to propagate to other States, Democracy as a creed. . . . The hope of America is not in the intelligence, or even in the virtue of the people, but in the Church of God. To the conservative influence of Catholicity, are we to look for a check on the rampant spirit of democracy, the tendency to the absolute will of the people." See Thomas R. Ryan, "Orestes A. Brownson's Lectures in St Louis, Missouri, 1852 and 1854," *Records of the American Catholic Historical Society of Philadelphia* 89 (1978): 54–55.

[82] Brownson, *Works*, 567.

[83] Ibid., 571–72.

been forced to give way before it."[84] Brownson's point was clear: the United States was a nation of providential importance, but it could fulfill its destiny *only* through the conversion of the nation to Catholicism. And the implication was equally clear: the progress of the United States was not one of religious pluralism, but rather was achieved through a symbiosis of Americanism and what Brownson called "Catholicity." The Catholic Church not only was the medium of human salvation, but it was "only through Catholicity that the country can fulfill its mission [for the world]."[85] In sum, Brownson perceived both the Constitution and the American state to be Catholic in origin and able to operate properly and fulfill their destinies only with Catholic principles.

Despite the optimism inherent in this prediction of Catholic success, the dream of a Catholic America faced a harsh reality in the antebellum era. Perhaps the Catholic contribution to American greatness had been palpable. Perhaps the nativist violence aimed at Catholic churches, clerics, and laity portended the beginning of the end of Protestant hegemony in the United States. Perhaps Catholicism would provide the foundation of freedom and justice amid the roiling changes in American society. Perhaps the Catholic faith would eventually be intertwined with the American mission. But a stark certainty nonetheless remained: Protestant America endured as a powerful force in the nation, and the demise of Protestantism, should it occur, would be a process that would take considerable time. In the meantime, the Church had to find its place in a multiconfessional society that had come to be established on a denomination-alist system. Many of its spokesmen would argue that Catholics, more than other Americans, understood that their nation was a place of religious freedom that contained a variety of faiths. Yet as they acquiesced to a multiconfessional society while awaiting a Catholic America, they also had to grapple with their own conundrum of faith.

The Catholic Conundrum

God is the author of religion, and through religion the author of civil government. . . . To protect society, the human law must repose on the eternal basis of spiritual law, whose witness is the eye of One who penetrates into the deepest recesses of the soul. Were it not for this influence, human law would be weak and inefficient. John Hughes, 1856[86]

If Catholic thinkers developed myths about Catholicism's place in the United States and its role in American destiny, an even more complicated challenge that they faced was to integrate their views of church, state, and society in the context

---

[84] Ibid., 568.

[85] Ibid., 576. On Brownson's belief in the primacy of religion as the mission of society, see Francis E. McMahon, "Orestes Brownson on Church and State," *Theological Studies* 15 (1954): 189.

[86] John Hughes, "The Relation Between the Civil and Religious Duties of the Catholic Citizen," 27 June 1856, in Kehoe, *Complete Works of the Most Rev. John Hughes*, 2:145.

of American society.[87] Roman Catholics did not speak with one voice on this matter, and their views shifted in the face of contemporary events. Yet they nonetheless were in broad agreement with Protestants that Christianity, however defined, was a necessary force to undergird the state. As Brownson, shortly before his conversion to Catholicism, wrote in the *United States Magazine and Democratic Review* in 1843, "I frankly confess that I am unable in my own mind to settle down on a political theory that shall be equally acceptable to the Christian and the Infidel." He simply could "accept no theory of government," he confided to his readers, "that does not imply as its basis the truth of Christianity ... as a gracious scheme, devised by Infinite Love and Mercy for the practical redemption and sanctification of mankind."[88]

If Catholics agreed with the Protestant clergy on Christianity's essential role in government and society, however, their stress on the ecclesiastical role and the institutional interdependence of their church and the state divided them from American Protestants. Put simply, in the face of calls for an explicit separation of church and state, could the spiritual authority of the papacy and prelacy be separated from temporal political power?

Early Catholic leaders, such as Bishop John Carroll, cautiously contended that ecclesiastical intervention in civil affairs was unacceptable in the new United States. Wary of any affiliation with the "foreign," Carroll argued that political authority was national and no Catholic should expect extranational intervention. Conversely, membership in a church whose principal authority resided outside the United States was nonetheless protected by proclamations of religious liberty.[89] Bishop John Ireland, who clarified and elaborated on Carroll's views, clearly distinguished between church and state. As a strict constructionist of the Constitution, Ireland contended that legislators were to enact laws only for the "temporal welfare of the state." The people were the source of temporal power, which was "entirely distinct from the source of the pope's spiritual authority." Indeed, any pronouncement by a Catholic authority had no binding force because it was forbidden by natural law. Given this strict separation, no American could reasonably object to the spiritual authority of the pope.

This optimism of a liberal Roman Catholicism in the early national period was not without cause. The Catholic world in the United States in fact did differ in many ways from the Church in Europe, not least because of the absence of a state church. Clerics expressed admiration for religious organizations nurtured in a free church environment.[90] And the laity commonly expected that the

---

[87] See McGreevy, *Catholicism and American Freedom*, on the question of freedom in the American Catholic past.

[88] Orestes Brownson, "On the Origin and Ground of Government," *United States Magazine and Democratic Review* 13 (September 1843): 257.

[89] I rely here on Elwyn A. Smith, "The Fundamental Church-State Tradition of the Catholic Church in the United States," *Church History* 38 (1969): 486–505.

[90] See, for example, Jay P. Dolan, *In Search of an American Catholicism: A History of Religion and Culture in Tension* (New York: Oxford University Press, 2002); and McGreevy, *Catholicism and American Freedom*. For specific community studies of Catholicism in the early national era, see

Church would adapt to a new republican environment replete with a voluntary church and less state intervention in religion, an expectation reflected in the confidence of a lay trustee system that placed the laity, rather than the prelacy, in possession of church property.[91]

As the century progressed, however, these rather secular and pluralist notions gave way to views that more closely linked religion and the state, views that were reflected in Hughes's interventions in his debate with Breckinridge. The thought of Hughes and Brownson frame the Catholic perspective. Brownson's views, because he was such an intellectual gadfly, are difficult to encapsulate.[92] Born in Vermont in 1803 to a Presbyterian family, Brownson flirted with Unitarianism and transcendentalism before his conversion to Catholicism in 1844. Despite his religious journey, Brownson remained remarkably consistent in many of his beliefs. First, as already mentioned, Brownson throughout his life marveled at the American constitution, which created a unique governmental form that was both the only viable form of government for America and the precursor of an advancement of governance in general. The constitution of society, which existed prior to the written documents on which it ultimately was based, provided safeguards that protected the right of conscience. Second, Brownson insisted that a close connection existed between religion and politics that was essential not only for the governed but also for the well being of the state. This is not to say that the temporal and spiritual were equal; indeed, the former was consistently dependent on a higher moral law based on divine sovereignty that ordered all life. Nor is it to say that the state was not independent in its own realm. A secular state could not suffice in and of itself without a moral foundation because it had no spiritual jurisdiction. A democracy based solely on majority rule, moreover, was only one more form of tyranny. True democracy could exist only through the "absolute sovereignty of *Justice*," a justice that could only be identified with God.[93] The third point followed from the second: the vitality of the American republic depended on its religious character. If citizens were thrown back on their human nature alone, they would be tempted by vice and corruption. The spiritual was not a supplement, but rather a vital necessity to the virtue of an American democracy.[94]

David A. Gerber, *The Making of an American Pluralism: Buffalo, New York, 1825–1860* (Urbana: University of Illinois Press, 1989); and Dale B. Light, *Rome and the New Republic: Conflict and Community in Philadelphia Catholicism between the Revolution and the Civil War* (Notre Dame, IN: University of Notre Dame Press, 1996).

[91] See Patrick W. Carey, *People, Priests, and Prelates: Ecclesiastical Democracy and the Tensions of Trusteeism* (Notre Dame, IN: Notre Dame University Press, 1987), 155ff.

[92] Much has been written about Brownson, but see Patrick W. Carey, *Orestes A. Brownson: American Religious Weathervane* (Grand Rapids, MI: Wm. B. Eerdmans, 2004), for the best recent biography of him.

[93] On these points, see Richard M. Leliaert, "The Religious Significance of Democracy in the Thought of Orestes A. Brownson," *Review of Politics* 38 (1976): 3–26, esp. 10; and McMahon, "Orestes Brownson on Church and State," 175–228.

[94] Leliaert, "Religious Significance of Democracy in the Thought of Orestes A. Brownson," 17; McMahon, "Orestes Brownson on Church and State," 189–96.

In many significant ways, Brownson shared beliefs with his Protestant counterparts that the secular was integrally connected with the spiritual and that society needed religious belief to operate properly. Yet for Brownson, the most significant outcome of these beliefs was his view of the role that Catholicism played in American development. Brownson admitted that non-Catholic religious bodies had religious freedom; indeed, he celebrated the fact that the state did not enter into entangling alliances with any church. Yet he also stressed in 1848 that the state had "no spiritual competency." A year later he wrote that "our absolute and unconditional subjection to [God] excludes all other subjection." Because there existed "no liberty before God," liberty itself was "rightly defined [as] full and entire freedom from all authority but the authority of God."[95] Brownson's answer to questions of where this authority was found, moreover, was simple. It rested with God and, on earth, with the Church. Separation of church and state did not mean that the unifying fabric of the spiritual and temporal was rent. Rather, there remained an institutional independence of church and state. The church, however, affected humankind through its reason and conscience. It was, writes Elwyn A. Smith, "the soul of the society, not its governor; its influence is pervasive, profound, and inward, even though legally restricted."[96]

The thought of Archbishop Hughes, the leading prelate in the antebellum United States, mirrored Brownson's pronouncements in many ways.[97] Already in 1835, in his debate with Breckinridge that introduced this chapter, Hughes had developed an outlook that he would hold for decades. On the face of it, Hughes constructed a remarkably pluralist, liberal argument about American religious liberty and the place of Catholicism in the United States. Protestant sects, it seemed, implied that the United States was a Protestant country. Yet any religion that taught that civil magistrates were bound to protect Protestantism to the exclusion of other faiths was dangerous to civil liberty. Indeed, Hughes continued, it was the Protestant clergy who were not liberal or pluralist. On the one hand, they distorted, through "the exhibition of caricatures, and the concoction of old slanders with modern seasoning," the Roman Catholic Church and its adherents. More treacherous, on the other hand, was their concerted attempt to erode a wall of separation between church and state. In a succinct passage that encapsulates Sabbatarianism, the Bible controversy in the schools, appeals for a Protestant political party, and anti-Catholicism, Hughes condemned Presbyterianism's

recent efforts to disturb petitions to Congress to have the Sabbath sanctified by legislative enactments; their attempt to drive out of circulation every elementary book, of education not favourable to their doctrine of arrogance, as well as despotism; their attempt . . . to

---

[95] Allen Guttman, "From Brownson to Eliot: The Conservative Theory of Church and State," *American Quarterly* 17 (1965): 487.

[96] Smith, "Fundamental Church-State Tradition of the Catholic Church," 492.

[97] In one of his clearest statements on the matter, see Hughes, "Relation Between the Civil and Religious Duties of the Catholic Citizen," 2:144–48. See also Smith, "Fundamental Church-State Tradition of the Catholic Church."

"form a Christian party in politics;" these were the beginnings of that intolerant policy which in the name of *God Almighty* calls upon all Presbyterians to labour "according to each one's place and calling," to "*remove* all false worship, and all the monuments of idolatry."

Clearly, Hughes argued, Presbyterians either were traitors to the Constitution, which "protects those 'false worships,'" or they were faithless to a God who, "according to their narrow and intolerant creed ... commanded them to '*remove*'" such false beliefs.[98]

All of this was meant in part to sustain the Catholic counternarrative that asserted that Catholics were trustworthy citizens and that the Church was not a danger to the American state. Hughes repeatedly celebrated the possibilities of the United States, a state not only favored with "broad land, free institutions, and a Constitution on which the happiness of the people is based," but one that "leaves spiritual order intact." Given these freedoms, why would Catholics not love their country? Rehearsing a commonly voiced argument, Catholics "have shed their blood as freely ... as any other denomination." They obey their clergy, whose mission to make them good Christians inevitably causes them to be good citizens.[99]

Yet even more than Brownson, Hughes maintained particular views on the relationship between the state and church and the duties performed by Catholic citizens, which underscored the special place of the Church and its hierarchy in American society. Humans, Hughes argued, were indeed subject to two unified orders, the sacred and the temporal. Whereas the latter regulated humankind's duties to their fellow citizens, the former regulated duties to God and the Church. The two orders were perfectly compatible; because God was the author of both, any conflict was the result of an encroachment of one on the legitimate rights of the other. If they were complementary, however, the spiritual and temporal were not equal. In fact, the error in many nations was to see the state as "the fountain of all good," an idea that was extraordinarily dangerous. The correct disposition, a view that obtained in the United States, was to privilege the sacred. The state, Hughes argued, relies on the "religious principle." To protect society, "the human law must repose on the eternal basis of spiritual law, whose witness is the eye of One who penetrates into the deepest recesses of the soul." Without this witness, human law would be weak and unable to restrain crime. Society was kept together by the "unspoken but efficient voice" of the spiritual world, "even when it is not audible." More to the point, Hughes believed not only that "the spiritual is far more important than the temporal" but also that "the temporal can be sanctified as the auxiliary of the spiritual." Simply put, "the man that is truest to God, is truest to the State."[100] Yet all of this begs the role of the Church and Protestant sects in the "spiritual." If Hughes did not imply that the Protestants were *not* good citizens, he hinted that their sects did not

---

[98] *Discussion of the Question*, 319 (see n. 3 above).
[99] Hughes, "Relation Between the Civil and Religious Duties of the Catholic Citizen," 2:147–48.
[100] Ibid., 2:144–47.

have a special role in spiritual matters of religion or the state. This, for many Protestants, was the rub.

Historians often focus on the intellectual conflict between Hughes and Brownson. They differentiate Brownson's Americanist vision from Hughes's role as an immigrant tending to a growing flock of immigrant Catholics, which resulted in policy disagreements over issues such as the parochial school. Or they ponder their subsequent differences during the Civil War over the question of slavery.[101] These contrasts were very real, but it bears emphasizing that Brownson and Hughes were in fundamental agreement on many points regarding Catholic doctrine with respect to the relationship between church and state. They both treasured the relationship between church and state; they both marveled at the special characteristics of the United States and shared with many Protestants a vision of American providence; and they both privileged the spiritual authority of their church and its earthly representatives. Insofar as they had differences, Hughes's view – because he *was* a clergyman – carried the day at midcentury. The general conclusions of the Second Plenary Council in 1866, for example, resolved that there did exist a difference between the Church and Protestant sects. "The State," it wrote, "is bound to recognize [the authority of the Roman Catholic Church] as supreme in its sphere – of moral, no less than dogmatic teaching," an unnecessary requirement for Protestant sects because they lacked divine sanction.[102]

It should come as no surprise that many Protestant critics believed that an inherent contradiction existed between the Catholic leaders' pronouncements of religious pluralism and the particularist teachings of the Church. The frequently voiced paean to a liberal society with full civic liberty, they argued, was disingenuous. One need only look to the past to see that Roman Catholicism had been anything but blameless. It was a source of intolerance and fanaticism, the instigator of the Inquisition. Its record in contemporary Europe and the Americas was hardly better. Whereas a freethinker in an 1850s novel voiced the view that Protestant Christianity tended to "improve our race," to cite one example among many, he pronounced popery as evil, "everywhere and always working mischief; at war with light and opposing liberty!"[103] Notwithstanding the Catholic counternarrative, then, many Americans believed that the freedoms that they treasured not only were denied in Catholic lands but were at risk in America as well.

---

[101] See, for example, Moore, *Religious Outsiders*, 52–57; and McGreevy, *Catholicism and American Freedom*, 80–81.

[102] Peter Guilday, *The National Pastorals of the American Hierarchy, 1792–1919* (Washington, DC: National Catholic Welfare Council, 1923), 206. See also Smith, "Fundamental Church-State Tradition of the Catholic Church," 494; and Elwyn A. Smith, *Religious Liberty in the United States: The Development of Church-State Thought Since the Revolutionary Era* (Philadelphia: Fortress Press, 1973), 185–99.

[103] Isaac Kelso, *Danger in the Dark: A Tale of Intrigue and Priestcraft* (Cincinnati: Moore, Anderson, Wilstach, and Keys, 1854), 37.

Yet what about the fact of Protestantism's failings in the past? When confronted with the misdeeds of their forebears, Protestants referred to what they considered an important distinction between Catholicism and their faith. Protestantism was adaptive, whereas the Catholic faith boasted that it was both unchangeable and infallible. *Because* it was changeless, it could be held accountable for its past misdeeds. If Protestant American churches had renounced the alliance of church and state and therefore "have adopted American principles," Breckinridge argued, "*American Papists change not*" because they cannot change.[104] The Catholic pride of unity and infallibility thus was dangerous because there could be no reform or improvement.[105] This changelessness was perilous for the American republic because any evidence that the Church was modifying and assimilating to the American system was a deceitful ruse.

Perhaps even more damning was the apparent contradiction between a realization of a religious pluralism in the United States and the Catholics' construction of rights, a tension already apparent in Hughes's views in the mid-1830s. While the terms of the dispute seem somewhat arcane to us today, they clearly illustrate the Protestants' concern that Catholics advocated what at heart was an impossibility: a pluralist society *and* the supremacy of their faith. For Hughes, rights were privileges of two types. The first category was rights that derived from an extrinsic source, which in turn were separated into three sorts, the divine, the political, and the religious. Extrinsic rights drew from various sources of power: divine rights were derived from neither nature nor civil authority, but stemmed from an authority vested in certain religious leaders; political rights were residual of natural liberty, which was not required by law to be sacrificed to "public convenience"; and ecclesiastical rights were privileges given to individuals because of their stations in religious life.[106] Not surprisingly, Protestants took issue with divine and ecclesiastical rights, which seemingly were vested entirely in the Catholic Church itself and which were used to found a hierarchy that claimed exclusive authority. If rights were so configured, those that were divine and ecclesiastic would certainly enter into conflict with natural rights, and one would have to give way to the other.[107]

In a philosophical world so constructed, a liberal notion of rights was chimera. As a Presbyterian put it, Hughes's system nullified natural liberty because

---

[104] *Discussion of the Question*, 50–52.
[105] Kelso, *Danger in the Dark*, 43–44. H. A. Boardman agreed that Catholicism would never be changed, "but will continue a corrupt system until it is finally *destroyed*." See Boardman, *A Lecture Delivered in the Walnut Street Presbyterian Church, Philadelphia, on Sunday Evening, December 28th, 1840* (Philadelphia: Hooker and Agnew, 1841).
[106] *Discussion of the Question*, 50–52.
[107] A useful discussion of the debates is found in "A Discussion of the Question, Is the Roman Catholic Religion, in any or in all its Principles or Doctrines inimical to Civil and Religious Liberty? and of the Question, Is the Presbyterian Religion, in any or in all its Principles or Doctrines, inimical to Civil and Religious Liberty? By Rev. John Hughes and Rev. John Breckinridge," *Princeton Review* 9 (1837): 238–66, 326–49, 487–509. This three-article review takes up points that Breckinridge missed in the first debate.

it was absorbed into civil and political power; the state did not protect the people's inalienable rights in society, but subsumed them. Ultimately, Hughes's arrangement of rights, the complainants continued, derived from a "European system of political science," whose origin was the throne and whose mission was "the art of governing subjects." In contrast, the source in the United States was the natural rights of man and "the art of preserving the order and peace of society with the least possible government."[108] In the end, the Catholic system privileged the rights of the hierarchy that would enable it to etch out a status independent of natural rights and civil liberty and allow it to maintain a position of power that differed fundamentally from those afforded its confessional competitors. This system, in which divine rights possessed by a particularistic faith compromised natural ones, was anything but liberal.

And what about the religious liberty for individual believers? Brownson argued that whereas religious liberty was the natural and inherent right of every person, "the liberty of heresy and unbelief is not a *natural* right, for by the law of nature, as well as the divine law, every man is bound to be of the true religion, and has no right to be of any other." Because sects have no rights under the law of nature or the law of God, their believers were neither wronged nor deprived of liberty if the state refused to grant them any rights at all. Brownson conceded that the American state placed all forms of religion on a footing of perfect equality before the law. But his distinction between the freedoms of religion and those of heresy certainly could not be comforting to Protestants, who were clearly placed by Brownson in the latter category.[109] If it followed that Protestantism was heresy, individual Protestant belief was not a natural right. Any argument that denied individual belief and human conscience, which was, as I argued in Chapter 1, a mainstay in the Protestant ethos, was anathema to American Protestants.

Catholic leaders therefore grappled with their own conundrum of faith. As a minority faith, they celebrated the separation of church and state and the freedom of religion that characterized the United States. Nineteenth-century America was neither a Catholic country nor a Protestant country, Hughes contended in 1852, but rather "a land of religious freedom and equality."[110] Like many religious leaders in America, Catholic leaders stressed the benefits that accrued both to the

---

[108] Ibid., 333.

[109] Orestes Brownson, "A Review of George Bancroft's *History of the United States, from the Discovery of the American Continent*," *Brownson's Quarterly Review* 6 (October 1852): 156. Elsewhere, Brownson condemned Protestant belief: "The men who adhere to Protestantism," he wrote, "know perfectly well that they adhere to it only because it emancipates them from all religion, by subjecting religion now to the state and now to the individual judgment or caprice." Brownson, never one to mince words, continued by describing the Reformation as "simply a rebellion against God, prompted by the flesh, incited by the Devil. ... We must oppose Protestantism," he concluded, "not as a false theology, but as a revolt of the flesh against God." "Protestantism not a Religion," *Brownson's Quarterly Review* 1 (January 1853): 110. See Stephen Colwell, *The Position of Christianity in the United States, in its Relations with our Political Institutions, and Specially with Reference to Religious Instruction in the Public Schools* (Philadelphia: Lippincott, Grambo, 1854), 144, 156.

[110] Hughes, "The Catholic Chapter in the History of the United States," 2:104.

polity and to the churches as a result of this separation. Religious freedom enabled believers both a purity of belief and the steadfastness of the society in which they lived.[111] They concurred with their Protestant adversaries that the spiritual was a central building block for a state and society that was both moral and prosperous.

Despite what appeared to be pluralist and irenic pronouncements, however, the Catholic leadership envisaged a particularistic role for their church not only spiritually but also in its relationship with the state. Occasionally, their unambiguous language was jarring to Protestant critics. Hughes, for example, observed that "everybody should know that we have for our mission to convert the world – including the inhabitants of the United States – the people of the cities, and the people of the country, the officers of the navy and the marines, commanders of the army, the Legislatures, the Senate, the Cabinet, the President, and all!"[112] Brownson concurred when he reportedly declared that "we Catholics are a *missionary* people" who "are here to *Catholicize* the country." He concluded that as "God's chosen instruments for that purpose," it remained for "Catholics to make [the United States] morally, intellectually, spiritually great."[113]

The Catholic conundrum, moreover, became ever more problematic in an era of nativist hostility at midcentury. Catholicism of course had faced a barrage of criticism even before the United States was a nation-state. As the nation-building project went forward in the nineteenth century, this criticism was amplified (and it would become even more shrill when untold thousands of Catholic immigrants arrived on American shores beginning in the mid-1840s). The criticism's focus on the dangers of Catholicism to a fledgling American republic, on its characteristics of unfreedom and on its indebtedness to conservative forces in Europe, was only exacerbated by pronouncements by Catholic leaders. Despite assurances that the Church was in accord with the American mission, Protestants increasingly saw Catholicism to be part of a complex conspiracy amassing resources – in capital, leadership, and individual members – aimed at systemically invading and subverting the American republic, an experiment that many Americans claimed was the last best hope for humankind.

Outcomes

A modern observer might argue that the dissimilar views between Protestant and Catholic leaders were simply the narcissism of small differences. Both leaderships tended to agree that Christianity was central to state and society, at the same time that they claimed that the church benefited from some separation

---

[111] On the widely held belief that religious freedom made churches more pure, see Jon Gjerde and Peter Franson, "'Still the Inwardly Beautiful Bride of Christ': The Development of Lutheranism in the United States," in *Luther zwischen den Kulturen*, ed. Hans Medick and Peer Schmidt (Göttingen: Vandenhoeck and Ruprecht, 2004), 190–211.

[112] Hughes, "Decline of Protestantism, and Its Cause," 2:100–101.

[113] Brownson, cited in Anna Ella Carroll, *The Star of the West; or, National Men and National Measures* (New York: Miller, Orton, 1857), 461.

from it. They ostensibly celebrated the freedom of religion that characterized their nation and shared a belief that the United States had a special destiny that would forever change society and that the nation's mission was somehow sustained by Christianity. In fact, however, the disagreements were profound, and they created quandaries that would trouble Protestants and Catholics for years.

The Protestant puzzle was to integrate an increasingly large mass of American citizens who not only rejected Protestantism but also were seemingly hostile to its advancement. For those who believed that the genius of the United States had a Protestant foundation and that the individual conscience was a linchpin in fostering religious as well as social and economic progress, Catholic claims that their church was pivotal in the American future and faultless in the American present were jarring. The Catholic conundrum, in contrast, was how the Church could be pluralistic and liberal, on the one hand, and particularistic on the other. If the Catholic leadership affirmed both that a spiritual dimension was central to the arrangements of the temporal and that these rights were vested in ecclesiastical authority, Protestants perceived an inherent contradiction that only offered greater evidence of the gravity of their own puzzle. As Catholics explained the ways in which their church could be integrated into a republic based on representative rule, they, as a minority faith, were forced to grapple with the contentions of the Protestants. Even with – or, perhaps, because of – an overzealous nativism, the Catholic conundrum became even more acute from the 1830s onward. As Catholic immigration swelled in the 1840s and 1850s, many Protestants viewed what they deemed to be an increasingly large and arrogant Catholic church as disadvantageous for the future of the American state and society. And as the Church faced challenges in Europe at midcentury and lurched rightward, the repercussions created even greater discord.

The divisions between Protestants and Catholics, then, became, if anything, more knotty in the years after Breckinridge and Hughes debated. The conversation and contention between Roman Catholics and Protestants that resulted touched on virtually every aspect of life, from the family to state and politics. In the chapters that follow, we will consider a series of events during which Americans grappled with the question of how the differences between a Catholic world and a Protestant world might be bridged. As such, we will grapple with two overarching themes.

The first rubric for discussion is the fundamental differences between the Catholic and Protestant disputants on the nature of society. Their reliance on structures of authority led Catholic leaders to embrace an organic theory of state and society. In this view, which we have seen expressed repeatedly in this chapter, individuals in the state lived only through their relationships with the corporate whole. Brownson was particularly influenced by the humanitarian socialist Pierre Leroux's concept of communion, which argued that one law circulated among humans that in turn rendered society analogous to a living organism. The state, then, was more than the sum of its individual members; it was, rather, an organic whole. Complementary to these ideas of a relational and organic state and society were the nature of liberty and, more particularly, the role of the Church in reform.

Americans had the liberty to act, but as Brownson would stress, Christian liberty was freedom only to disobey the guidelines of an illegitimate ruler.[114] In sum, Brownson, who was also influenced by the Catholic apologist Joseph de Maistre, came to believe that liberty was possible only through order. Brownson also argued that progress was based on some power extrinsic to humanity; it was only through some supernatural force that it could proceed. As he wrote to his fellow convert Isaac Hecker late in 1843, "Man can Institute nothing greater than himself; therefore, man can never, of himself, as mere man, found anything which will raise the age above what he himself really is." "No *man*," Brownson concluded, "can be a reformer."[115] The reforming force, of course, was the Church, which enabled the orderly advancement of humankind. Those without a higher reformer – socialists, abolitionists, most Protestants – had no external rudder to direct them; their beliefs inevitably led to relativism. In contrast, the Church provided individuals with the ability to change, the possibility of reform, and the hope of progress.[116]

Protestants tended to conceive of the world differently and increasingly put a premium on the correct behavior of the individual. In a construction that placed more and more salience on a liberal world informed by the sum total of decisions made by its members, they rejected an organic view of society. Theirs was a worldview that Catholics could only describe as dangerous relativism. The articulation of these deep structures, as we shall see, were not merely the pronouncements of the theological elite. They were reflected as well in a series of debates that pondered the market, the family, slavery, and westward expansion in the antebellum era.

The second theme is an exploration of the twists and turns in the engagement with the varieties of religious belief in private and public life. As we will observe in the next chapter, one solution to the dilemmas confronting Catholics and Protestants was simply the hope of conversion. If Catholics, and especially Catholic immigrants who breathed in American freedom, were shown the light and treated kindly, Protestants reasoned, Catholicism might wither on the vine. Yet it soon became clear to many Protestants that conversion was not necessarily a one-way street, and Protestants warily viewed both the conversion of influential Europeans and the prospects of Catholic converts in America. From both perspectives, conversion was a potential solution to the quandaries faced by

---

[114] Leliaert, "Religious Significance of Democracy in the Thought of Orestes A. Brownson," 13–15. Put differently, Leroux argued that human life was the result of the intercommunication of subject and object, which meant that humankind – the subject – could not in and of itself create progress. See James E. Barcus, "Structuring the Rage Within: The Spiritual Autobiographies of Newman and Orestes Brownson," *Cithara* 15 (1975): 55.

[115] Brownson to Hecker, 8 November 1843, in *The Brownson-Hecker Correspondence*, ed. Joseph F. Gower and Richard M. Leliaert (Notre Dame, IN: University of Notre Dame Press, 1979), 76.

[116] On this, see Barcus, "Structuring the Rage Within," 55; Mark S. Burrows, "Catholic Revision of an American Myth," *Catholic Historical Review* 76 (1990): 32–37; and Patrick W. Carey, "Christian Socialism in the Early Brownson," *Records of the American Catholic Historical Society of Philadelphia* 99 (1988): 30–33.

Catholics and Protestants. If the American world could be transformed into a Protestant or Catholic nation, the problem of a pluralist religious world might be solved. Yet despite their greatest hopes, the United States retained its religious heterogeneity as a denominationalism came to characterize American society. Rather than realize a millennial dream of Protestant homogeneity, the denominationalism that took hold was part of a religious structure that divided a relatively united Protestantism from their Catholic adversaries.

If conversion would not transform the American, state institutions such as the schools became an environment where children might be edified; this posture ushered in a titanic battle explored in Chapter 4. It is well known that many Americans in the antebellum era came to see the school as a pivotal institution in instilling virtue and learning in the minds of American youth. It is also often noted that this virtue generally meant the benefits that Protestantism provided in undergirding American society. Not surprisingly, these conventions were resisted by Catholic America, which agreed that children should be edified but believed that they should be enlightened in a Catholic system of belief as well as in the duties of citizenship. The outcome was a pivotal battle fought most notably in New York City in the 1840s. The Protestants won the battle but lost the war, as they resisted Catholic intrusions into the instruction of youth in the public schools but found that Protestant teaching was now also mistrusted. If the public schools became increasingly secularized, Catholics responded by withdrawing from them and forging a parochial school system that would be a focal point of their institutional structure for years to come. They stressed the fact that schools were just one arena in a complex institutional structure that included the church and the home. These institutions fostered the teaching of Catholic virtue and, in so doing, advanced a growing belief that Catholics should be wary of interaction with other Americans. In the end, the school controversy neither nurtured a Protestant school system that would edify America's youth nor integrated Catholics into an American whole.

If the school became a site of controversy rather than a resolution to the problem, the family was another arena of contention between Protestants and Catholics, as seen in Chapter 5. Some Protestants came to believe that the home buffered religious belief from the hurly-burly world of the religious revival. It supplied the nurture necessary for a Christian republic. Yet again, however, Catholicism intruded into this idyll. As they invaded the domestic world, the institutions of the Church threatened arrangements between parent and child and husband and wife. In contrast, Catholics viewed the Protestant American family to be emblematic of the shortcomings of American society generally.

Amid the vast economic changes in antebellum America, the issue of economic justice was a topic of great moment to Protestant and Catholic moralists, a topic explored in Chapter 6. As we have observed in this chapter, many Catholic leaders rued the growth of an economy in industrializing – and, not coincidentally, Protestant – Europe and America that endangered the condition of labor. They again tried to foster what we might consider an antimodern worldview of corporatism that stood in stark contrast to what would become the dominant liberal outlook of Protestant America. How labor was to be integrated fairly into an economy increasingly based on industrial work not only affected workers in the city but also became the basis of a great debate surrounding slavery that divided Americans and animated Protestant and Catholic clergy alike. In short, competing conceptions of economic justice, particularly as they related to the changing nature of the marketplace, informed the slavery debate.

The slavery question and the issue of the role of Catholicism in the United States, which had become increasingly rancorous at midcentury, found expression in American political discussion. Anti-Catholicism, after all, became the basis for the rise of the American Party. A political movement that epitomizes great success and dismal failure, the American Party rose to spectacular heights in the 1850s only to decline in a matter of months. For our purposes, the party, despite its ruthless nativism, was a political movement where the theological aspects of the debate were muted. After the demise of the American Party, the sectional crisis and the Civil War profoundly changed most aspects of American life. Yet disputes about the role and the place of Roman Catholicism endured into the 1870s.

As I shall stress in the chapters that follow, the trajectory of the debate became increasingly public in the middle decades of the nineteenth century. If Protestant leaders placed great hope on the private decisions, such as conversion, that would diminish the influence of Catholicism or on edification within the family in the earlier eras, they altered their strategies toward state institutions like the school and, ultimately, toward electoral politics at midcentury.

As this debate played out in a variety of settings, moreover, we shall see how the outcomes were not always as the combatants envisioned they would be. When the dream of Catholic conversion to Protestantism failed, for example, the outcome was not the unity of Christian belief, but rather a denominationalist religious structure that institutionalized theological difference. More significantly for our purposes, denominationalism became a powerful force that permitted Protestants to accept theological variation as they differentiated themselves as a group from Catholicism. A hope for national conversion, in short, resulted in a segmented religious landscape. To cite another example discussed in Chapter 4, Protestants attempted to sustain the social and political significance of their faith through the nation's public schools. But this effort failed to incorporate Catholics into a state-run institution that instructed its children to revere the nation and a developing conception of civil religion. Rather, it resulted in a growing secularization of the common school, on the one hand, and a widespread retreat of Catholic children into parochial schools, on the other.

Likewise, the outcome for Catholics was perhaps not what was expected by the Church's leadership. Although Catholic leaders continued to voice a belief in a complementary identity that posited a role for Catholicism in the American nation and even as they remained involved in American institutions, for example, they also retreated into an increasingly separate world. Indeed, as dreams of Catholic conversion in the United States faded, the Catholic strategy was one of pillorization, which shielded its believers from the unwashed at the same time that it conceded the fact that the United States would remain a society based on denominationalism and, ultimately, of Protestant dominance. As a result, the Catholic critique of American society, varying from critical assessments of family life and economic justice, would become marginalized as well. For both Protestants and Catholics, their conversation with each other was ultimately a story with many strands of unintended consequences and of missed opportunity for its participants and the people of the United States as a whole.

3

Conversion and the West

No human means can so certainly meet and repel this invasion of Catholic Europe as a competent evangelical ministry and revivals of religion. These speedily will throw all mischief into the distance, and render our salvation like the waves of the sea, and our glory like the unsetting sun. ... May God, my brother, guide your understanding and fire your heart to act immediately and efficaciously in behalf of the West; to blow the trumpet around you, and rally the sacramental host for the onset that is coming on here; for if we fail to hold our own in our own land, how shall we lead in the aggressive movement for the conversion of the world? I am on the field. The battle is begun.

Lyman Beecher, 1842[1]

Lyman Beecher bore a heavy burden in 1835 (see Fig. 4). Three years before, the noted Presbyterian clergyman had moved his family to Cincinnati, where he was to become the president of Lane Seminary. The population of Cincinnati – a hodgepodge of blacks and whites, Northerners and Southerners, Europeans and Americans – reflected its role as a western outpost that linked north and south. As such, it became a site embroiled over the battle to extend or restrict slavery and, importantly for our purposes, a staging ground for northern evangelical Protestants to convert the West. It was in this context that Lane Seminary was founded in 1829 to bring evangelical Christianity to the West and, not incidentally, to battle the vices of barbarism, on the one hand, and Romanism, on the other. The move, however, was star-crossed from the start. As they approached the city, the family had to tarry at Cincinnati's boundaries because of a cholera epidemic raging within. Matters did not improve on their arrival. Within a year, the majority of the students at Lane Seminary had rebelled because of Beecher's lukewarm attitude toward abolition and had gone to study with Beecher's long-time rival Charles Finney. Moreover, Beecher's second wife, unable to withstand the rigors of life on the frontier, had died. Also, although eventually exonerated,

---

[1] Lyman Beecher to Albert Barnes, 11 July 1842, cited in Lyman Beecher, *Autobiography, Correspondence, Etc., of Lyman Beecher, D.D.*, ed. Charles Beecher (New York: Harper and Brothers, 1865), 2:453–54.

FIGURE 4. Presbyterian clergyman Lyman Beecher anticipated the coming of the millennium through the conversion of the American West. (Brady-Handy Photograph Collection, Prints and Photographs Division, Library of Congress, LC-DIG-cwpbh-02529)

Beecher had been accused of heresy. Identified as a coward by abolitionists and a heretic by Presbyterian conservatives, Beecher might well have despaired.

Amid these tribulations, however, Beecher's perspective on the world was surprisingly optimistic. Indeed, he saw his labors in the West as part of a momentous time in history. When he published *A Plea for the West* in 1835, he foresaw the coming of the millennium resulting from the Christianization of the West under the favorable auspices of the American nation.[2] A colleague who wrote to Beecher as the clergyman was pondering whether to move west expressed Beecher's overarching sentiment: "arm the spirit which now reigns in the evangelical churches with just views of moral government and agency, and you bring the Millennium to the very doors." And move west, Beecher's colleague continued, because nowhere "in all the world can you do half as much to impart and disseminate such views as in the great Western Valley – the Valley of Decision."[3] Amid its ethnic and religious diversity, Cincinnati became a starting point for Beecher to stage efforts to Christianize the West by bringing it the light of evangelical Protestantism.

As it did for many evangelical Protestants, the menace of Roman Catholicism weighed heavily on Beecher's mind. And like many Protestants, he believed that one way to address the heterogeneity that increasingly characterized American society was to transform and ultimately homogenize its diverse elements. If immigrants would become American, a heterogeneous mass could speak in a more unified voice. And if Catholics could be converted, the religious conundrum faced by Protestant Americans could be averted and the future of a Protestant republic might be assured. Nowhere was this hope expressed more fervently by American Protestants than with regard to the West, the rapidly evolving areas in the Mississippi region whose future by all accounts would be critical for the nation. Nowhere was the question more troubling than in the West, a region that was both so unsettled and so unformed. This proving ground for Protestant conversion, as a result, was complicated not least because of its diverse population and its embryonic society.

Amid this hope, there existed a counternarrative that was less optimistic for evangelical Protestants. As prominent Catholics noted, America could become a recruiting field for Catholicism. Indeed, as the first section of this chapter argues, many observers, Catholic and Protestant alike, saw in the existence of a free church environment the possibility of a Roman Catholic conquest of the American nation. Ironically, freedom of religion – one of the pedestals of future American greatness – might be a contributing factor to the victory of the Roman Catholic Church in the United States.

Yet, as we shall see in the second section of this chapter, Protestant expectations, based on a developing national narrative, buoyed the hopes of evangelical Protestants. Anticipation of the millennium, expressed by Beecher among

---

[2] Lyman Beecher, *Plea for the West* (Cincinnati: Truman and Smith, 1835). On Beecher, see Vincent Harding, *A Certain Magnificence: Lyman Beecher and the Transformation of American Protestantism, 1775–1863* (New York: Carlson, 1991); James W. Fraser, *Pedagogue for God's Kingdom: Lyman Beecher and the Second Great Awakening* (Landham, MD: University Press of America, 1985); and Constance Mayfield Rourke, *Trumpets of Jubilee* (New York: Harcourt, Brace and Co., 1927). See also Robert Dunne, "A Plea for a Protestant American Dream: Lyman Beecher's *A Plea for the West*," *Old Northwest* 16 (1992): 189–97.

[3] Dr. Skinner to Lyman Beecher, 16 February 1832, cited in Fraser, *Pedagogue for God's Kingdom*, 113.

others, centered on a mission field in the American West that foresaw the fulfill-ment of Christian hopes. The West was considered a region that harbored the American destiny; it was seen as the future seat of the American empire. Economically, it was the site of fertile land that would enrich the nation. For Northerners, it was a place of freedom that stood in stark contrast to the growing threat of slavery in its westward push. Roman Catholicism was a central subject in all of these developments.

These millennial hopes had wide-ranging implications. They were part of a belief that the destiny of America was tied to a larger Christian advance. As such, they were a motivating force in the United States toward reform and they placed a huge burden on the American republic to fulfill its destiny. Because the place of the Catholic Church was critical to the millennial narrative in the United States, the conversion of Roman Catholics was of great concern. Evangelical Protestants coalesced to form societies to bridge sectarian differences (in an era of disestablishment), to foster the coming of the millennium, and to address general concerns regarding religion. A variety of organizations formed begin-ning in the 1820s that worked to bring the Word to Americans, to evangelize, and to bring about social reform.

In the end, the millennium did not arrive as expected. Neither was there a widespread conversion of Roman Catholics to the Protestant faith. Instead, a denominationalist structure developed that pitted an occasionally fractious group of Protestant denominations against the unity of Catholicism. These disappointing outcomes had broad implications for religion and society in the United States. On the one hand, they resulted in a religious arrangement that reified and reinforced the divisions between Protestant and Catholic. On the other hand, they suggested to Protestants that more coercive measures would have to be undertaken to assimilate Catholics into the American nation.

American Religious Freedom and Catholic Conversion

Religious freedom was one component of a group of privileges that many "white" Americans – Protestant and Catholic alike – celebrated and that culti-vated among them an optimism about the future of the American nation. This constellation of entitlements included a relatively generous naturalization and citizenship law that permitted immigrants to become members in good standing of the nation. It offered political rights that gave male voters the power to influence government representation. It guaranteed at least a perception of social mobility and improved well-being in the American economy. And, of course, it offered a freedom of religion that rejected an established church and enabled people to worship as they pleased. The combined opportunity to be members of a body politic and of a church was often received, for a number of reasons, with optimism among clergy and laity alike in the nineteenth century. On the one hand, it conceivably could reduce religious conflict and thereby enhance state and society. The Swiss-born Philip Schaff optimistically portrayed the state of religious difference in 1855. "In the United States," he contended, "all nations, all churches and sects, all the good and evil powers of the old world, meet without blows or bloodshed; and while Europe began with paganism and barbarism, America begins with the results of Europe's two thousand years' course of civilization, and has vigor, energy, enterprise, and ambition enough to put out this enormous capital at the most profitable interest for the general good of mankind."[4] European-born church leaders, on the other hand, praised religious freedom because it strengthened the church. Schaff, who immigrated to the United States in 1843, quoted Luther's observation that "faith is a free thing, which can be forced on no one" and argued that "the civil equality of all churches and sects in America, and the voluntary system inseparable from it, have aroused and are sustaining a great mass of individual activity." Schaff argued that the United States was the most religious and most Christian country in the world "because religion there is most free."[5] John Henry Hobart, the Episcopal bishop of New York, agreed. "It is the *religious freedom* of my country," he wrote in 1825, "that constitutes, in my view, one of her proudest boasts."

Protected as religion is by the state, which finds in her precepts and spirit and sanctions the best security for social happiness and order, she is left free to exert her legitimate powers, uninfluenced and unrestrained by any worldly authority whatsoever.[6]

For both Schaff and Hobart, American freedoms enabled religious belief.

Lutherans in the United States made similar observations. Two Lutheran leaders – one German, one Norwegian – compared the conditions of Lutheranism in the United States and in Europe. C. F. W. Walther, a leader among German American Lutherans, contended that "we live here in a State in which the church enjoys a freedom unsurpassed since its origin, and at present to be found scarcely anywhere else in the world. ... We have here full liberty to regulate everything according to God's Word and the model of the church in its best days and to give our church a truly Christian and apostolic form." Walther, who left Europe in 1838 because of his dissatisfaction with the state of Lutheranism there, concluded, "if we take a glance at our old German Fatherland, how entirely different do we find it! There the church is bound in chains."[7] These beliefs endured. When the Norwegian Georg Sverdrup spoke in Minneapolis in 1875, he used strikingly similar imagery. He noted that the United States was a place where there existed "a free people, in a free

---

[4] Philip Schaff, *America. A sketch of the political, social, and religious character of the United States of North America, in two lectures, delivered at Berlin, with a report read before the German church diet at Frankfort-on-the-Maine, Sept., 1854* (New York, 1855), xviii.

[5] Ibid., xii.

[6] John Henry Hobart, "Bishop Hobart's Estimate of the Church of England: A Review of *The United States of America Compared with Some European Countries, Particularly England*" (New York, 1825), cited in Robert T. Handy, *A Christian America: Protestant Hopes and Historical Realities* (New York: Oxford University Press, 1971), 54.

[7] Walther is quoted in Henry Eyster Jacobs, *A History of the Evangelical Lutheran Church in the United States* (New York: Christian Literature, 1893), 404.

congregation, with Christ among us." To stress his point, he repeated that "Christ was not gone, even if the people were set free." In contrast, Sverdrup argued that there "lies a distant land, Norway," where there was a struggle and that "there too it is all about freedom or bondage for the Church of Christ."[8] The differences between the freedoms of America and the rebellion and reaction of Europe were, in Sverdrup's mind, palpable.[9]

Catholics, despite episodes of religious intolerance, also celebrated the freedom of religion in the United States. Orestes Brownson, as he complained about the abuses of the nativist Know Nothing movement in the 1850s, nonetheless argued that "there is no country where the church is freer than she is here." It was true, he continued, that "annoyances, vexation, and petty persecutions we have always suffered," but the United States nonetheless was "probably the only country where the Catholic press is absolutely free."[10]

The constellation of rights, of course, signaled perils as well as prospects for the American future. Some Americans rued the uncomplicated route to citizenship for immigrants, whereas others feared the outcome of too much democracy conveyed by the voting rights of poor and immigrant men. And if religious freedom was one of the treasures of an American inheritance, it created a variety of challenges for the churches that dwelt under its aegis. These challenges only grew when churches were disestablished by state governments, culminating in 1833 when Massachusetts ended its relationship with Congregationalism. Indeed, Lyman Beecher, before he became convinced of its benefits, contended in 1812 that with disestablishment "we shall become slaves, and slaves to the worst of masters."[11] Europeans frequently shared the concern of their American-born brethren about disestablishment. Protestants often observed that the challenges were most dangerous for the future of their faiths, not only because of the Catholic threat but also because the Protestants did not possess the authority to enforce deference. The possibility of freedom, in short, offered perils as well as promise.

For American Protestants, the most ominous and ironic outcome of religious freedom was the potential for conversion to Catholicism. Catholic spokesmen often confidently – and sometimes arrogantly – affirmed that their faith would

---

[8] Georg Sverdrup, *Samlede Skrifte i Utvalg* (Minneapolis, 1909), 3:93, cited in Vidar L. Haanes, "Pastors for the Congregations: Transatlantic Impulses," in *Crossings: Norwegian-American Lutheranism as a Transatlantic Tradition*, ed. Todd W. Nichol (Northfield, MN: Norwegian-American Historical Association, 2003), 12–13.

[9] For a fuller discussion of this issue, with a consideration of the "perils" as well as the prospects of religious freedom for European churches, see Jon Gjerde and Peter Franson, "'Still the Inwardly Beautiful Bride of Christ': The Development of Lutheranism in the United States," in *Luther Zwitschen den Kulturen*, ed. Hans Mednick and Peer Schmidt (Gottingen: Vandenhoeck and Ruprecht, 2004), 190–211; and Jon Gjerde, "The Perils of 'Freedom' in the American Immigrant Church," in Nichols, *Crossings*, 3–29.

[10] Orestes Brownson, *Brownson's Quarterly Review* (July 1855): 408, cited in Schaff, *America*, 233.

[11] Lyman Beecher, *Autobiography of Lyman Beecher*, ed. Barbara M. Cross (Cambridge, MA: Harvard University Press, 1961), 1:192.

emerge victorious in the battle for America's hearts and minds. In 1848, the *Freeman's Journal*, a Roman Catholic newspaper, awkwardly proclaimed that it would show Protestantism for what it was – "effete, powerless, dying out ... and conscious that its last moment" would be its encounter with "Catholic truth."[12] Two years later Archbishop John Hughes was more specific. The conversion of the world to Catholicism, he announced in a homily entitled "The Decline of Protestantism and Its Causes," was manifest. "There is no secret about this," he continued. "The object we hope to accomplish in time is to convert all pagan nations and all Protestant nations – even England, with her proud parliament and imperial sovereign." "Protestantism pretends to have discovered great secrets," he went on, but it was really no secret at all. "Everybody should know," he affirmed, "that we have for our mission to convert the world."[13] Orestes Brownson concurred. "No matter who writes, who declaims, who intrigues, who is alarmed," he wrote, "this is to be Catholic country; from Maine to Georgia, from the broad Atlantic to the broader Pacific."[14]

Hughes, in affirming the doomsday scenarios that Protestants had been trumpeting for decades, was perhaps impolitic.[15] But he was only one among a group of observers – Protestant and Catholic alike – who marveled at the possibilities of the growth of Catholicism in the United States. The most famous observer to remark on the compatibility of Catholicism and American society was Tocqueville. He noted not only that Catholics made excellent citizens in the American republic but also that Roman Catholicism was gaining converts in the United States. Tocqueville argued that humans regulated their temporal and spiritual institutions similarly or, as he put it, endeavored "to *harmonize* earth with heaven." British Protestants in America, he noted, styled "a democratic and republican religion" that was central in the establishment of a democratic civil society. The Irish Catholics who followed, in contrast to how they were commonly portrayed, in fact constituted "the most republican and most democratic class in the United States." This democracy stemmed from both the status of the laity and the role of the priest. Because Catholic doctrine placed all of its followers on a common plane, Tocqueville considered it to be "one of the most favorable to equality of condition among men." Protestantism, in contrast, made humans more independent rather than more equal, which presumably created an inequality of condition and an inequality of outcomes among individuals. Tocqueville also believed that the clergy, when they entered politics, were "naturally disposed" to "transfer the doctrine of the equality of condition into the political world." Although the priesthood maintained doctrines of

---

[12] *Freeman's Journal*, 4 March 1848, cited in Ray Allen Billington, *The Protestant Crusade, 1800–1860* (New York: Macmillan, 1938), 290.

[13] John Hughes, "The Decline of Protestantism, and Its Cause," 10 November 1850, in *The Complete Works of the Most Rev. John Hughes, D.D., Archbishop of New York*, ed. Lawrence Kehoe (New York: American News, 1865), 2:26.

[14] Edward Beecher, *The Papal Conspiracy Exposed, and Protestantism Defended, in the Light of Reason, History, and Scripture* (Boston: Stearns, 1855), 17 (citing Orestes A. Brownson).

[15] Billington, *Protestant Crusade*, 290–94.

a revealed religion that were not subject to debate, the other part of their intellectual world was politics, "which they believe the Deity has left open to free inquiry." As "the most submissive believers and the most independent citizens," Tocqueville assured his reader, Catholics would continue to play a salutary role in the unfolding of American democracy.[16]

Undoubtedly more troubling to Protestant observers than the Catholic's constructive role in the polity was Tocqueville's belief that the Catholic Church was gaining in power in the United States. It was true, Tocqueville observed, that some Catholics were lapsing into infidelity. Yet these departures from Catholicism were more than offset by the conversions of Protestants to Catholicism. The reason for this turn to Rome was simple. Although the modern world tended to be agnostic, any religious inclination evoked "a secret admiration for [Catholicism's] discipline" with its great unity and therefore "a latent instinct that urges them unconsciously towards Catholicism." Tocqueville's conclusion – "that our posterity will tend more and more to a division into only two parts, some relinquishing Christianity entirely and others returning to the Church of Rome" – was of little comfort to American Protestants.[17] A society based on either irreligion or Catholicism, an outcome that many Catholic leaders in fact predicted, was anathema to a Protestant elite.

Thomas F. Knox, a Catholic, writing from Boston to his friend John Henry Newman in England in 1846, agreed with Tocqueville. The religious environment in the United States, he contended, fostered the growth of Roman Catholicism and "no-churchism," with the implication that Protestantism would eventually die away. Boston, "a city of isms," harbored religions and creeds of every sort and description that forced its residents to confront the teachings of Roman Catholicism. "The question of Church & no Church," he wrote, was agitating minds in the city both negatively and positively. "By negatively," he continued, "I mean people are trying to get along with the Church, without the notion of a Church being adopted." His positive view of the question was that "a church and The Church are growing to be synonymous."[18] Try as they might, Bostonians could not ignore the Roman Catholic Church.

Tocqueville and Knox were not the only Europeans – or Americans – who marveled at the seeming tendency of Americans to drift toward Rome. They were joined by Frederick Marryat, Charles Augustus Murray, Harriet Martineau, and Fanny Trollope, among others, all of whom perceived a growing conversion to Roman Catholicism that stemmed from a variety of causes. Some asserted, following Tocqueville, that Catholicism would win the war of prose-lytization *because* of its unequivocal structure of authority. The British traveler

---

[16] Alexis de Tocqueville, *Democracy in America*, ed. Philips Bradley (New York: Vintage Books, 1990), 1:300–3.

[17] Tocqueville, *Democracy in America*, 2:30–31.

[18] John Tracy Ellis, "An English Visitor's Comments on the American Religious Scene, 1846," *Church History* 36 (1967): 36–44 (quotations from 38, 41).

Captain Frederick Marryat, for example, after one of his visits to the United
States in the 1830s, criticized what he called the "voluntary system" of religion
in the American republic. Whereas the "established church" tended to "cement
the mass, cement society and communities, and increase the force of those
natural ties by which families and relations are bound together," the voluntary
system produced the opposite because "it has broken one of the strongest links
between man and man." In the United States, "any one is allowed to have his
own peculiar way of thinking [without any] right to watch over each other; there
is no mutual communication," he concluded, "no encouragement, no parental
control."[19] Moreover, because of a democratic impulse in the American republic, the ministers of religion, as exemplars of authority, were treated with
"tyranny and contumely." The ministry, Marryat argued, is "deprived of its
primitive and legitimate influence, and the ministers are tyrannized over by the
laity, in the most absurd and most unjustifiable manner." Although they were
sent to instruct the people, ministers had to give voice to their congregations or
surrender their trust. Because of a contempt for authority and a free church
environment in which their salaries were paid by the laity, the ministers lost "all
their dignity and become slaves of the congregation."[20]

The end result of these developments, according to Marryat, was a combination of confusion and lack of conviction among the population, a diagnosis that
resembled the division predicted by Tocqueville and the "indifferentism"
observed by Catholics in the last chapter. The confusion was exacerbated by
American materialism that muted the firmness of spiritual belief. "No one can
serve God and Mammon," Marryat asserted confidently. The Protestant faith,
as a result, was "growing weaker every day with disunion and indifference,"
while the Catholic Church was "advancing," especially in the West, where
immigration and conversion increased the numbers of those of a "Catholic
persuasion." Slowly but surely, Catholic power was increasing, so that observers
could faithfully assert that "all America west of the Alleghenies will eventually
be a Catholic country." Indeed, they would soon affirm "that *all* America will be
a Catholic country."[21]

For Marryat, this development portended a monumental shift in the political
direction of the United States. With Protestantism in America rife with division –
"a house divided against itself cannot long stand," Marryat, citing scripture,
predicted – the Catholic Church will increase in power. In opposition to
Tocqueville, who did not see the Catholic Church as "the natural enemy of

[19] Frederick Marryat, *Diary in America with Remarks on its Institution* (London: Longman, Orme,
Brown, Green and Longmans, 1839), 3:96–97.
[20] Ibid., 3:134, 104–5. Marryat was amazed at a conversation he had with an American who
implicitly compared business with scripture. The American, Marryat wrote, "pronounced that
the laity were quite right, and that it was the duty of the minister to preach as his congregation
wished. His argument was ... I expect it to be made exactly after the pattern given; if not, I will not
take it: so it is with the minister: he must find goods exactly suited to his customers, or expect them
to be left on his hands!" *Diary in America*, 3:105.
[21] Ibid., 3:143–44, 157–58, 163, 166.

democracy," Marryat suggested that a "hierarchy may ... be raised, which, so far from *advocating the principles of equality*, may serve as a *check* to the spirit of democracy become more powerful than the Government, curbing public opinion, and reducing to better order the present chaotic state of society."[22] If Marryat perceived some constructive results from the ascent of Catholic power, then, on balance he feared the consequences.

Charles Augustus Murray, an Englishman who journeyed through North America in the late 1830s, also rued the effects of religious freedom. Although the United States possessed favorable circumstances for Christianity to flourish, such as a toleration of religion and a relatively educated laboring class, Murray believed that its prospects were "neutralized by the pernicious influence of the 'voluntary' system." The circumstances were curious. Although Americans believed that religion was the basis for a sound morality, Murray argued, they left it to the popular whim of the day. The evils that ensued were many. First, a clergyman was so dependent on the "caprices" of his congregation that he had either to "sacrifice his daily bread, or refrain from conscientiously preaching to them unpalatable truths." Second, the ministry's low status was complemented by small salaries that lessened the quality of the clergy itself. Third, the voluntary system fostered a variety of sects, "some of them most absurd, others the most extravagant, that have hitherto appeared in the civilised world." In this context, Catholics were increasing rapidly for two reasons. One was that the Church possessed "the plastic readiness" to adapt itself to circumstances in the United States. The second cause was the "zeal and enterprise" of the priesthood, which labored amid Indians and African Americans, among others.[23]

The British writer Harriet Martineau, who also perceived the gains made by Roman Catholicism in America, focused more on theological than on sociological causes. Martineau, who repeatedly expressed hostility to the practice of Christianity in the United States, was quick to allude to the hypocrisy of American churchgoers, whether they were Southern slaveholders or "the Presbyterian clergyman who preached three long denunciations against the Catholics in Boston, the Sunday before the burning of the Charlestown convent." Her discussion of the theories of the Catholic presence in America, therefore, concentrated less on the reputed plot of the pope to "explode the Union" than on the real gains in Catholic membership that resulted from conversion, a conversion that stemmed from varying theological predilections. "While the Presbyterians preach a harsh, ascetic, persecuting religion," she argued, "the Catholics dispense a mild and indulgent one; and the prodigious increase of their numbers is a necessary consequence." Unlike American Protestant critics, Martineau found Catholicism in America to be salutary. "The Catholic body is democratic in its politics," she continued, "and made

---

[22] Ibid., 3:159.
[23] Charles Augustus Murray, *Travels in North America, Including A Summer Residence with the Pawnee Tribe of Indians, in the Remote Prairies of the Missouri, and a Visit to Cuba and the Azore Islands*, 3rd ed. (London: Richard Bentley, 1854), 2:286–89.

up from the more independent kind of occupations." If it were "modified by the spirit of the time in America ... let alone, and treated on genuine republican principles," Martineau concluded, "they may show us how the true, in any old form of religion, may be separated from the false."[24]

Whether one feared or celebrated this advance of Catholicism, the common focus was on the status of the church in the United States. And the ultimate irony, for Americans who dreaded the growth of Catholicism, was that the jewel in the crown – a religious freedom in conjunction with a disestablished church – might become the ingredient that assured the triumph of Catholicism. Some critics argued that it would be well should it be so. Fanny Trollope, a prolific English essayist whose acerbic pen often cast the United States in a highly negative light, reviled the "almost endless variety of religious factions." Following her extended stay in Cincinnati, she contended that each sect created its own church government, invariably with "the most intriguing and factious individual" as its head and "some queer variety of external observance that has the melancholy effect of exposing *all* religious ceremonies to contempt." In such an environment, she saw the clear advantages of an established church, as well as the dignity of Catholicism. Unlike the bewildering array of American sects, the influence of the pope apparently prevented "the outrageous display of individual whim which every other sect is permitted."[25]

The Catholic threat in the "free" United States was an even more ominous prospect when coupled with the successes of the Church in Europe. Amid years of revolution, the Church was able to endure and from some viewpoints was strengthened. A Catholic revival in England, Germany, and elsewhere, fostered by a Marian revival, increasingly inspired and reincorporated the common Catholic believership.[26] Significantly, this revival was fostered by influential converts who were infusing an increasing intellectual vigor into the faith at the same time that their conversion gave Catholicism greater legitimacy. The Oxford Movement, for example, was evidence of the actual growth of Catholicism in England, of all nations. The Catholic revival affected common people as well as intellectuals. A growing institutional structure in the form of schools and fraternal organizations, in combination with a ritual revival, gave

---

[24] Harriet Martineau, *Society in America* (London: Saunders and Otley, 1837), 3, pt. 4:236–37.

[25] Fanny Trollope, *Domestic Manners of the Americans*, ed. Pamela Neville-Sington (London: Whittaker, Treacher, 1832; London: Penguin Books, 1997), 84. (Citations are to the Penguin edition.) Trollope's shift to a conservative worldview is reflected in her belief that religious observance is better when it "is confided to the wisdom and experience of the most venerated among the people, than when it is placed in the hands of every tinker and tailor who chooses to claim a share of it" (85).

[26] See, for example, Jonathan Sperber, *Popular Catholicism in Nineteenth-Century Germany* (Princeton, NJ: Princeton University Press, 1984); Margaret Lavinia Anderson, "The Divisions of the Pope: The Catholic Revival and Europe's Transition to Democracy," in *The Politics of Religion in an Age of Revival: Studies in Nineteenth-Century Europe and Latin America*, ed. Austen Invereigh (London: Institute of Latin American Studies, 1999), 22–42; and Patrick Allitt, *Catholic Converts: British and American Intellectuals Turn to Rome* (Ithaca, NY: Cornell University Press, 1997).

Catholicism greater relevance to its parishioners. And the Church remained active in converting unbelievers and retaining its laity in the faith.

To exacerbate matters, European Protestants feared that their churches were weakening as Roman Catholicism gained in strength. Observers already in the 1840s were noting the contemporary varieties of Christianity. Samuel Laing, a Scottish agricultural reformer and translator of Norse sagas, argued in 1844 that Christianity was separating itself into two great divisions: "a Christianity pure, spiritual, scriptural and altogether purged from ceremonial forms of worship" and "a Christianity altogether ceremonial ... a religion of show, relics, ... saint worship [and] pilgrimages."[27] If the latter obviously was the Church of Rome, pure Christianity was exemplified – not surprisingly – by Laing's church in Scotland. Yet there also existed the "halfway houses" of Lutheranism and the Church of England that repudiated Rome but nonetheless retained the super-stitious ceremonies and usages of the Church. These halfway houses would eventually have to take shelter in one of the two extremes, Laing argued, and he remained hopeful that they would move to the purer form of Christianity.

Three years earlier, however, Henry Augustus Boardman had been less sanguine. Boardman, who would maintain a forty-year tenure as a Presbyterian minister in Philadelphia, offered a thoughtful appraisal that expressed fear of the advantages of the ceremonial over the spiritual, of the inane over the pure. He renounced any persecution of Roman Catholics because "liberty of conscience is a fundamental principle of Protestant Christianity." Yet he stressed, nonetheless, that the Church was a threat in America for a number of reasons. Some bases for fear of Catholicism were familiar. For one, the Church had vast resources at hand that it could use to spread across the globe. "The condition of things in the valley of Mississippi," he observed, "is probably much better known at the College of the Propaganda at Rome, than it is among the Christians [in Philadelphia]."[28] For another, Americans generally misappre-hended the true character of Romanism, which was not merely a religious institution, but rather "essentially a *politico*-ecclesiastical Institution" replete with a temporal sovereign who claims both spiritual and temporal jurisdiction over the whole world.[29] Americans' celebration of their nation as an asylum taught them to open their arms to all. Yet this was a faulty perspective. Using deceitful trickery and boundless resources, Roman Catholicism was making inroads into the political and cultural fabric of the United States as Protestants naively made empty pronouncements of their nation as a haven of freedom.

If these were routinely voiced concerns, Boardman's other cautions are per-haps more noteworthy. First, he argued that Catholicism was an undemanding

---

[27] Samuel Laing, *Notes on the Rise, Progress, and Prospects of the Schism from the Church of Rome, called the German-Catholic Church* (1844), cited in E. E. T., "The American Catholic Church," *New Englander and Yale Review* 5 (January 1845): 136–39.

[28] H. A. Boardman, *A Lecture Delivered in the Walnut Street Presbyterian Church, Philadelphia, on Sunday Evening, December 28th, 1840* (Philadelphia: Hooker and Agnew, 1841), 14–17.

[29] Ibid., 21.

faith that "appealed to the sympathies of the human heart." Because the pure doctrine of the Bible – the depravity of human beings, for example – was daunting, the Catholic rules of absolution appealed to human nature. Here was a religion that made salvation "easy and cheap," Boardman warned his listeners, so that "men will be found predisposed even to believe impossibilities and to practice the most senseless mummeries, if they are taught that they can thereby get to heaven without sacrificing their lusts or renouncing their self-righteousness." The second concern followed from the first: the "alarming progress" made by Romanism throughout the world. Although the ratio of Protestants to Catholics in the United States was fifteen to one, Boardman calculated that the rate of Catholic increase in 1840 was three to four times that of Protestants. And as Catholicism grew, Protestants were becoming both less vigilant and less resolute. Because Protestantism had been undergoing a "gradual deterioration," Boardman stressed that this was not the time for a false complacency. Even at a time when knowledge was diffusing, Americans ought not feel confident that "the progress of knowledge will necessarily be fatal to a system which has, to say the least, stood its ground in spite of the immense progress which knowledge has made."[30]

A decade after Boardman's sermon, American theologians continued to puzzle over the seemingly inherent advantages of Catholicism in the modern world. The *New Englander and Yale Review*, for example, in its account of the Irish economist and logician Richard Whately's work on the "errors of Romanism," argued that humans were "willing dupes and slaves of a priest-hood," if they could escape personal responsibility. And this was no less true in the United States than in other, less free environments. "Man," the journal argued, "is a Roman Catholic by nature." Humans tended to possess "a disposition to serve God by proxy" and "to rely on some system of priestly rites and ceremonies." They will accept "any system which will give ease to conscience and a comfortable hope, which it frees from personal and direct responsibility to God." Anyone who blithely believed that there was no danger from Roman Catholicism in this "free country" needed to understand that the peril existed "everywhere where there is human nature."[31]

The situation was fraught with irony. The Irish-born Protestant convert Nicholas Murray contended that popery was "the religion of children, of low civilization," whereas "Christianity is the religion of men, and of high civilization, where the virtues and graces most flourish."[32] The Church, he wrote elsewhere, was "the merest caricature of Christianity, with "its ritual ... addressed to the eye, and its whole worship ... a ludicrous pantomime, in which the priests are the actors, and the altar the stage, and the ignorant

---

[30] Ibid., 10–13, 18, 40, 45.

[31] "Vicarious Religion," *New Englander and Yale Review* 10 (1852): 516, 520.

[32] Kirwan [pseudonym of Nicholas Murray], *Letters to the Right Rev. John Hughes, Roman Catholic Bishop of New York* (New York: Harper and Brothers, 1855), 329.

attendant, not knowing what they worship, the spectators."[33] Yet it was in the United States where the Catholic challenge lay. Although Murray ultimately expressed confidence about the decline of Catholicism, the question nonetheless remained whether immigrants from Ireland would be able to become independent individuals or whether they would be "content to be slaves in a country of freedom" where they had the potential to be both spiritually and civilly free.[34]

Here, in short, was another version of the Protestant conundrum posed by Roman Catholicism. Freedom of religion had become an American birthright in large part because of the Protestant underpinnings of the American nation. Yet this very freedom engendered societal challenges from all directions. From one side, Protestants warned against the infidelity and barbarism that might evolve if Americans lost their faith. From another side, freedom of religion fractured Protestant unity in the face of a unified Catholic Church. More ominously, that same freedom created a marketplace of creeds in which Catholicism had no small advantage, *because* it was "easy and cheap." Another conundrum, in sum, plagued American Protestants who celebrated a religious liberty that might inexorably lead the nation either to infidelity or Roman Catholicism, a progression that in either case would inevitably destroy the fabric of the American nation.

It did not help matters that thousands of Americans were indeed converting to Catholicism. According to one estimate, some 57,400 American converts took the path to Rome between 1831 and 1860.[35] An equally striking fact was that prominent Americans such as Sophia Ripley, Orestes Brownson, and Isaac Hecker converted to Roman Catholicism.[36] By many accounts, their conversion was not the result of an astonishing epiphany, but rather occurred after considerable contemplation. Reason was central to the process.[37] Yet reason was complemented by an awesome sense of relief and release. For such converts, Catholicism was anything but "easy and cheap."

Catholic converts defended their change of heart by providing very different rationales than those described by their Protestant detractors. The combination of the converts' theological reasons with their status as social outsiders, moreover, fostered an acute ability to criticize dominant Protestant culture. Hecker, for example, succinctly inverted Ralph Waldo Emerson's prescriptions for

---

[33] N[icholas] Murray, *The Decline of Popery and Its Causes: An Address Delivered in the Broadway Tabernacle, on Wednesday Evening, January 15, 1851* (New York, 1851), 337.

[34] Kirwan, *Letters to the Right Rev. John Hughes*, 325–26.

[35] Christine M. Bochen, "Personal Narratives by Nineteenth-Century American Catholics: A Study in Conversion Literature" (Ph.D. diss., Catholic University of America, 1980), 57ff., cited in Jenny Franchot, *Roads to Rome: The Antebellum Protestant Encounter with Catholicism* (Berkeley: University of California Press, 1994), 280.

[36] On antebellum Catholic converts, see Franchot, *Roads to Rome*, 197–349; and Allitt, *Catholic Converts*, 43–106.

[37] Both Franchot and Allitt make this point. Franchot, *Roads to Rome*, 282–83; Allitt, *Catholic Converts*, 3–4.

independence in the antebellum world. "Substitute humility to obey, for 'self-reliance,'" Hecker argued, "courage to believe, for 'trust thyself'; – deny thyself, for 'act out thyself'; – master thy instincts, for 'obey thy instincts'; – self-sacrifice, for 'self-culture'; – surrender thyself to God, for 'be thyself.'"[38] As Jenny Franchot argues, these converts sought to escape Protestant hegemony, para-doxically, by allying themselves with "the proverbial captivity to Old World orthodoxy."[39]

American converts also occasionally suspected the wisdom of a society that celebrated the liberty to choose one's religion. Hecker, for example, agreed with William Ellery Channing that "'sects are essential to freedom and progress,'" but only "where error and not truth lies at the foundation." "Error disunites, isolates, and produces harsh discord," he continued, "while truth brings men together in bonds of common brotherhood, producing love and perfect unity."

It is a proof of a secret and painful tyranny exercised over the mind, and a mark of a radically false religion, where freedom and progress can only be preserved by hostile sects, and by causing violent divisions among men. This thraldom accounts in a great measure for the constantly increasing sects in Protestant communities; and explains why the great body of intelligent men stand aloof, and look with indifference, if not contempt, at the countless sects of the Protestant Religion.[40]

Apparently content that he had the freedom to convert to Catholicism, Hecker nonetheless rued the outcomes of religious freedom if they resulted in chaotic religious heterogeneity. Brownson too saw the centrality of the Church in relation to the proliferation of the many Protestant sects. "The dispositions of the American people are much less unfavorable," he wrote to Hecker in 1857, "to the Church than is generally supposed." Here Brownson echoed the obser-vations about sectarianism made by others. "Owing to the breaking up of Protestantism, and the wild, fanatical, & offensive course of its ministers on a great variety of subjects," he continued, "[America's] attention is turned to the study of Catholicity as it never has been before." If these people were approached in a proper manner, Brownson concluded, "I cannot [but] believe that a rich harvest of souls will be reaped."[41]

Some Protestant Americans claimed not to be threatened by these spiritual transformations. In writing about Brownson's conversion, one transcendentalist contended that "the conversions to Romanism are mere eddies in the stream, – dimples of water turning backward, and showing thereby the power with which the main current is setting forward."[42] The converts obviously had a profoundly

---

[38] Isaac Hecker, *Questions of the Soul*, 6th ed. (New York: Catholic Publication House, 1855), 282, cited in Franchot, *Roads to Rome*, 302.

[39] Franchot, *Roads to Rome*, 280.

[40] Hecker, *Aspirations of Nature*, 4th ed. (New York: J. B. Kirker, 1857; New York: Catholic Publication House, 1869), 167–68.

[41] Letter from Orestes Brownson to Isaac Hecker, 5 August 1857, in *The Brownson-Hecker Correspondence*, ed. Joseph F. Gower and Richard M. Leliaert (Notre Dame, IN: University of Notre Dame Press, 1979), 194–95.

different view. Hecker wrote Brownson that "Divine Providence has by singular events prepared the American people for conversion to the Catholic faith." A series of movements, he believed, including the "transcendental movement, the Beecher movement, the memorial papers [referring to the Muhlenburg Memorial], the Know-Nothing movement, and that of Abolishonism [*sic*], & by the character of American institutions, that all these things are by the Providence of God so many ways of leading our people to the Catholic truth."[43] By making their way to the one true church, they contended that they were merely the first among many who would convert to Roman Catholicism. Indeed, as we saw in the previous chapter, they argued that wide-spread conversion to Catholicism was a precondition for the march toward American greatness.

These beliefs, as well as this Catholic confidence, would endure. By 1860, E. Rameur, yet another European visitor writing about his sojourn in the United States, summed up the state of conversion and the progress of the United States from an explicitly Catholic perspective. The most notable fact, he observed, was simply the growth of Roman Catholicism in the United States. Whereas only one American out of sixty-five was Catholic in 1808, the 4.4 million Catholics in the United States in 1860 accounted for one-seventh of the population. Although immigration clearly was responsible for much of the increase, conversion was also significant in augmenting the size of the Church. Missionaries, "simple and dignified, ... austere without fanaticism," made inroads in the Protestant population. The Protestant clergy, whose ministry and teaching "cannot fully satisfy the soul," witnessed their parishioners studying Catholic doctrine. When this occurred, three-quarters of those who "honestly study the faith" converted to Catholicism. Because Americans were "a people of a strong religious bent," the turn to Rome is especially pronounced among Protestants in the United States.[44] As always, these conversions were common in the West. A great wilderness only a few years before, the West had been transformed into a region of immense consequence. Catholicism grew there as well, with Catholics comprising nearly one-fifth of the population of Missouri, Illinois, Michigan, Wisconsin, and Minnesota, and it was destined to become the dominant religious organization in the region. The West was, in short, a "glorious mission field," whose future gave as much promise as had its past.[45]

As in many European narratives, Rameur grappled with the influence of American liberty on religious change and of Catholicism on the "American race." It was true, he contended, that religious toleration – even before the Bill of Rights – had enabled Catholic missionaries to proselytize among Protestant

[42] James Freeman Clarke, "Orestes A. Brownson's Argument for the Roman Catholic Church," *Christian Examiner* 47 (1849): 247, cited in Franchot, *Roads to Rome*, 337.

[43] Letter from Isaac Hecker to Orestes Brownson, 24 October 1857, in Gower and Leliaert, *Brownson-Hecker Correspondence*, 207.

[44] E. Rameur, "The Progress of the Church in the United States," *Catholic World* 1 (1865): 14–15.

[45] Ibid., 11–12.

Americans, especially when compared with the fate of orders such as the Jesuits, who were excluded from some European states. Such an opportunity was providential because Americans, despite their good qualities, also exhibited a variety of faults, such as "the decay of thoughtful, systematic, methodical intelligence" and "narrowness of mind." The role of the Catholic Church was to combat these failings, which were leading to a "serious and rapid degeneracy of the Anglo-American race," and it would thereby "render a signal service to the United States in return for the liberty which they have granted it."[46] If American freedom enabled the growth of Catholicism in the past, the Catholic Church would be a necessary support in the American future.

Again, one detects a parallel narrative between this Catholic view of conversion and its evangelical counterpart. The United States played a special role in the providential unfolding of history. Religion – in this case, Catholicism – was crucial in the evolution of the narrative. Americans focused on their liberties, but liberty existed in good and evil forms. Catholicism not only tempered the latter and enabled Americans to foster "well-regulated liberty," but the liberty enabled the Church to advance in the world. For the United States was, in fact, a cradle for nurturing Catholicism in an era of freedom. And successes in America would roll back to Europe and defeat the "intolerant fanaticism" that now characterized parts of the Old World. The United States could not advance without the Church; the Church in turn profited from its relationship with the American nation.[47]

The Protestant Conversion

Such were the challenges that evangelical Protestants faced in a brave new world of religious freedom. Although events seemed to indicate a move toward freedom, a move that was enabled by American progress, they were twinned with troubling instances of regression and conflict embodied in the Church. Perhaps the ritualistic mystery of Catholicism was fascinating and its religious temples were impressive, but it was a force of the Old World and its power, so the argument went, was destined to wane. Yet curiously the Church remained a potent cultural force – because of religious freedom, because of its undemanding obligations – and its presence paradoxically placed a stamp of regression on the peoples over whom it held sway. This was all very troubling for American Protestants because it challenged many of their premises about world development. In geographical terms, Protestantism was marching westward and it would inevitably come into conflict with Catholic lands to the north and south. The example of America would reverberate back to Europe and bring with it the prospect of liberty, but the Catholic Church seemed to be making inroads among both the uneducated laity and the intellectual leaders not only on the Continent but in England as well. Yet the most knotty challenge of all for

---

[46] Ibid., 3, 16.
[47] Ibid., 16–17.

American Protestant evangelicals remained the state of religion in the United States.

These concerns, however, were curiously accompanied by expressions of an almost improbable confidence in religious progress that would have a transformative influence on the American state and perhaps on world history. If Americans could convert to Catholicism, so the logic went, Catholics in turn could become Protestant and, by implication, American. On a secular level, then, Protestant conversion would be a balm to the state by solving many of its problems. A homogenous society, freed of the trappings of Catholic authority, would consist of citizens who were free to act in the best interests of the state. A heterogeneous mass today would become a homogeneous whole in the future. Most marvelous of all, these developments might be part of a process that would end in an event that many nineteenth-century Americans believed was nigh: the coming of the millennium.

These concerns and hopes found particular expression in the unformed "West," the region west of the Appalachian Mountains and a site of rapid growth and change in the early decades of the nineteenth century. Not only was it a region characterized by enormous religious and ethnic diversity and therefore a place where religious conflict might result, but the West was also a location that seemed to hold immense future meaning for the American republic. Its importance grew both demographically and symbolically, a fact well understood by Protestants and Catholics alike.[48] As both American-born *and* European-born whites pushed westward, a balance of power inexorably seemed to tilt toward the western regions. Many observers, European and American alike, celebrated its possibilities.

For many evangelical Protestants, the West became a focal point in the battle for America's hearts and minds. Not only was it the future site of empire, but a Protestant West would drive a wedge between Catholic hinterlands, both to the north and to the south. To the north, Canada symbolized a nation in which Catholicism festered and it would continue to pose the possibility of conflict between Catholics and Protestants. To the south, the Latin American states, principally Mexico, remained touchstones of a regressive Catholicism. Following the Mexican-American War, moreover, large tracts of Mexico with their Catholic populations were absorbed by the United States. From one perspective, Americans were confident of the conquest of these Catholic lands and the destiny of their Protestant nation. Viewed differently, however, the Catholic hinterlands, if they remained wedded to the Church, resembled a vise that

---

[48] The *Boston Pilot* published a series of articles guiding the Catholic migrant westward. See, for example, "Emigration," 22 January 1848, 5 February 1848, and 4 March 1848; "The West's Awake," 19 February 1848; and "Emigrant's Guide," 25 August 1849. Catholic leaders also saw the West as a refuge from the nativism and intolerance in the East. See Jon Gjerde, *The Minds of the West: Ethnocultural Evolution of the Rural Middle West, 1830–1917* (Chapel Hill: University of North Carolina Press, 1997), 52–53.

confined the advancement of American Protestantism, especially if Catholicism pervaded the American West.

To be sure, some Protestant observers continued to express concerns about the inherent weaknesses of Protestantism in a free church environment and predicted devastating results. Marryat, for example, concluded that the West would eventually become a Catholic country. Catholics were already in the majority in areas west of the Alleghenies, he reported, and there was nothing to prevent them from establishing their faith as the religion of particular states.[49] Catholicism was gaining in numbers in the West relative to Protestantism, agreed the Canadian Thomas Chandler Halliburton, through immigration, natural increase, *and* conversion. When Catholics became the national majority, Halliburton predicted, the United States would become a Catholic country, a prospect that for Marryat was "one of the dark clouds which hang over the destiny of the western hemisphere."[50]

Yet many other Protestant leaders, when they focused their gaze on the West, saw reason for confidence. Like Halliburton and as in the narratives that foretold Catholic victory in America, the categories of Protestantism, Catholicism, and indifferentism (or "barbarism" or unbelief) were utilized. They were used, however, to tell the story of the triumph of Protestantism. Rather than envisioning the disappearance of Protestantism and the conquest of a combination of Catholicism and unbelief, these observers foresaw a battle of monumental importance that would ultimately be won by Protestants and would enable the erasure of both unbelief and Romanism.

And so we return to Lyman Beecher, who published his *A Plea for the West* in 1835, a few years after his arrival at Lane Seminary in Cincinnati. The "plea" was based on a series of sermons that Beecher had delivered in previous years. In it, he marveled, as did many Americans, at the possibilities of the West, just as he saw the dangers of barbarism and Catholicism taking root in the region. The challenge, as Beecher foresaw it, was the unformed character of the West, which made it vulnerable to forces that would guide it in directions unfortunate for the nation and the world. One path might lead the region to barbarism; another route could end in a dearth of religious belief. Beecher was not alone in voicing these fears. Americans in the east, for decades, had feared the growing influence and seeming boorishness of the settlers in the West. Timothy Dwight, a theologian and the president of Yale College, who often criticized those moving westward, in 1822 called the western pioneers "too idle; too talkative; too passionate; too prodigal; and shiftless; to acquire either property or character."[51] In 1847, twelve years

---

[49] Marryat, *Diary in America*, 3:163.

[50] Thomas Chandler Haliburton, *Judge Haliburton's Yankee Stories* (Philadelphia: Lindsay and Blakiston, 1846) 124; Marryat, *Diary in America*, 3:164. Haliburton was a Canadian jurist and author whose writings included satirical sketches of American life and practices. The first of his popular *Clockmaker* series was published in 1836.

[51] Timothy Dwight, *Travels; in New-England and New-York* (New Haven, CT, 1821), 2:459. See also Ruth H. Bloch, "Battling Infidelity, Heathenism, and Licentiousness: New England Missions in the Post-Revolutionary Frontier, 1792–1805," in *The Northwest Ordinance: Essays in Its*

after the publication of *A Plea for the West*, Horace Bushnell, a clergyman and theologian, argued that barbarism was the first danger of the West and that the region's future was grim if it were not addressed.[52] Here might dwell "a wild race of nomads roaming over the vast western territories of our land – a race without education, law, manners or religion." Bushnell's argument was historical and sociological: all migrating societies – even the early New Englanders – endure social decline, in part because they lacked the institutional framework of their former communities, in part because all restraint was loosened in the new home. Yet Roman Catholicism was for Bushnell the second danger, because it could succeed in converting the masses only through "the gate of superstition," which was enabled by barbarism. Superstition, moreover, already had "a wide and terrible sway over the western mind," as evidenced by the growth of Mormonism. "If we persist in training a barbarous people," Bushnell concluded, "let us indulge no regrets that Romanism gives them a religion as they are capable of receiving." Both Bushnell and Beecher, then, perceived the power and the threat of the Roman Catholic Church to American development.[53]

Perhaps the most notable aspect of Beecher's plea, however, is its hopefulness, grounded in a historical and geographic movement that associated the West with the improvement of humankind through the introduction of religious truth. Even more remarkably, he predicted that these developments might result in the end of time. Beecher, in short, presented an overarching argument that knit together the fate of America, the significance of the West, and the coming of the millennium. It was true, he noted at the outset, that people have ridiculed "efforts of the church to evangelize the world and predicted their failure." These pessimists claimed that the world could never be converted to Christianity by the power of humans. Yet it was God, Beecher continued, who had promised this conversion and signs of this prospect were afoot in the world. "The rapid and universal extension of civil and religious liberty," he stressed, was "introductory to the triumphs of universal Christianity." This global extension of liberties was based in the United States, which would be the site of the millennium. And the West – "a young empire of mind, and power, and wealth" – was the location where religious and political destinies were to be decided. Americans needed to be "harnessed for the work" of leading the way toward a moral and political emancipation of the world, and the destiny of the West was central in this progression.[54] Significantly, this vision fostered what Nathan

Formulation, Provisions, and Legacy, ed. Frederick D. Williams (East Lansing: Michigan State University Press, 1989), 39–60.

[52] Horace Bushnell, *Barbarism the First Danger. A Discourse for Home Missions* (New York: William Osborn, 1847), 24–25.

[53] Ibid. Beecher's tract was not the only expression of fear published in 1835. Samuel F. B. Morse also anonymously published a pamphlet that argued that Catholicism was used simply as a means to political ends. Forces of European tyranny controlled the Church, Morse contended, and their aim was to destroy American republicanism and replace it with despotism. See *Foreign Conspiracy against the Liberties of the United States: The Numbers of Brutus, originally published in the New York Observer* (New York, 1835).

[54] Beecher, *Plea for the West*, 7–11.

Hatch terms "republican millennialism," which politicized the sacred and invested the state and civil rights with spiritual meaning.[55] As the deeply anti-Catholic German and Dutch Reformed clergyman Joseph Berg argued, if infidelity was the source of anarchy and confusion and if popery embodied despotism, Protestantism *was* liberty resting on law. Protestantism was a middle way that provided freedom of conscience and the rule of faith and hence a force that fostered American exceptionality.[56]

Despite this optimism, Beecher's plea recognized the dilemma that Protestants faced in their struggles with the Church. Indeed, it was in large part a petition against Catholicism. The Catholic hierarchy, armed and abetted by the papacy and the monarchies of Europe, controlled its minions by stressing its spiritual singularity. As it amassed its strength, Romanism was poised to arrest the extension of religious and civil liberty and thereby impede the coming of the millennium. From this perspective, the Catholic Church was not simply one Christian denomination among many. Rather, by portraying itself as the one true church, it fostered a sectarian notion that it was a singular religion with a special dispensation that enabled it to keep its adherents in check. In this unbalanced condition, Beecher had to weigh his millennial dreams in relation to his respect for civil and religious liberty. Unwilling to restrict a Catholic's right of religious belief, he stressed the power of Protestantism to bring light to the benighted Catholics. Beecher's prescriptions focused on the aid that evangelical Protestants might offer the West. The cultivation of schools, churches, colleges, and seminaries, supplied by those from the civilized East, would provide westerners with an institutional framework to nurture civil and religious liberty. Beecher saw the conversion of the Catholic immigrant as a way out of both the western dilemma and what I termed the Protestant conundrum in Chapter 1. Catholic believers, Beecher wrote, "are not to be regarded as conspirators against our liberties," but rather as people manipulated by their leadership and "unconscious of their tendency."[57] If the "evangelical light" could be extended to the Catholic population of the United States, Beecher concluded, they might be able to think for themselves and thereby free themselves from the grip of Catholicism. They might become a positive force for, rather than an ominous threat to, religious progress.

A Plea for the West, by emphasizing both the importance and challenges of the West, therefore limns the hopes and concerns that evangelical Protestants would express for the next quarter of a century. It illustrates the oft-expressed

---

[55] See Nathan O. Hatch, *The Sacred Cause of Liberty: Republican Thought and the Millennium in Revolutionary New England* (New Haven, CT: Yale University Press, 1977), 170–74; H. Richard Niebuhr, *The Kingdom of God in America* (New York: Harper and Brothers, 1937); Ernest Lee Tuveson, *Redeemer Nation: The Idea of America's Millennial Role* (Chicago: University of Chicago Press, 1968); and J. F. Maclear, "The Republic and the Millennium," in *The Religion of the Republic*, ed. Elwyn A. Smith (Philadelphia: Fortress Press, 1971), 183–216.

[56] Joseph F. Berg, *Trapezium; or, Law and Liberty versus Despotism and Anarchy. A Vindication of Protestantism from Papal Assailants, and Infidel Advocates* (Philadelphia: E. S. Jones, 1851), 5–6.

[57] Beecher, *Plea for the West*, 170–71.

anticipation of America's role in the coming of the millennium, an expectation that bears deeply on the question of Roman Catholicism in the United States. The future augured not only the march of progress of the American nation but also the integration of its motley elements through a conversion to Protestant Christian (and, not coincidentally, to American) belief.

To the modern ear, these millennial expectations are jarring. But they have deep roots in American theology and are fraught with concern about the place of Catholicism in the New World. Jonathan Edwards, for example, identified the "abundant outpouring of the Spirit of God" that portended that a time would come "when all nations, through the whole habitable world, should embrace the true religion, and be brought into the church of God." For his part, Edwards also identified the papacy with the Antichrist and, following the words in the Book of Daniel, saw the fall of the Antichrist as historically significant.[58] Millennial optimism, if anything, would wax in the nineteenth century as Americans wed scriptural dogma to the perceived trajectory of the American nation and "republican millennialism."[59] To be sure, not all theologians were sympathetic to the reading of contemporary events into the coming of the millennium. Such respected biblical scholars as Moses Stuart, for example, warned against overzealous predictions of an imminent millennium.[60] The disappointments of the followers of William Miller, moreover, who studied the Books of Daniel and Revelations and foresaw the millennium occurring in 1843 (then in 1844), only increased doubts.[61]

Yet many respected and respectable evangelical Christians were in the forefront of millennial expectations that joined the American narrative to the

[58] Jonathan Edwards, "An Humble Attempt to Promote Explicit Agreement and Visible Union of God's People in Extraordinary Power," in *Apocalyptic Writings*, ed. Stephen J. Stein, vol. 5 of *The Works of Jonathan Edwards*, ed. John E. Smith (New Haven, CT: Yale University Press, 1977), 23, 329. Edwards's eschatological views are treated by Stein in his introduction to *Apocalyptic Writings* (1–93).

[59] Hatch, *Sacred Cause of Liberty*, 139–75. See also Maclear, "Republic and the Millennium," 183–216; Richard G. Kyle, *The Last Days Are Here Again: A History of the End Times* (Grand Rapids, MI: Baker Books, 1998); Ronald G. Walters, *American Reformers, 1815–1860* (New York: Hill and Wang, 1978); Nathan O. Hatch, *The Democratization of American Christianity* (New Haven, CT: Yale University Press, 1989); and Paul E. Johnson, *A Shopkeeper's Millennium: Society and Revivals in Rochester, New York, 1815–1837* (New York: Hill and Wang, 1978).

[60] Moses Stuart, *Hints on the Interpretation of Prophecy* (Andover, MA: Allen, Morrill and Wardwell, 1842); and Moses Stuart, *Commentary on the Apocalypse* (Andover, MA: Allen, Morrill and Wardwell, 1845). See also "Review of *The Apocalypse of St. John; or, Prophesy of the Church of Rome, the Inquisition, the Great Revolution, the Universal War, and the Final Triumph of Christianity; being a new Interpretation*," *Christian Examiner and General Review* 8 (1830): 146–59; "Review of *Christ's Second Coming*," *Biblical Repository and Princeton Review*, 59 (1847): 564–79; and "Review of *The Second Advent; or, What do the Scriptures teach respecting the second coming of Christ, the end of the World, the Resurrection of the dead, and the General Judgment*," *Church Review and Ecclesiastical Register* 3 (1850): 61–78.

[61] William Miller, *Evidence from Scripture and History of the Second Coming of Christ about the Year 1843, Exhibited in a Course of Lectures* (Boston: B. B. Murray, 1840).

Christian creed. Three examples might suffice. Well before publication of *A Plea for the West*, Beecher had founded a journal, the *Spirit of the Pilgrims*, that laid out the importance of the United States for global development. Whereas Europe contained within "her bosom the elements of one mighty moral earthquake," the United States, with its civil and religious freedom, stood as "a luminous example to the world." Beecher detected "special indications of the high designs of God" in the ever-increasing religious revivals whose spirit was one of Christian enterprise. It was clear to Beecher that America was "destined, in the providence of God, to take a prominent and leading part in the moral regeneration of the world."[62] Charles Finney's journal, the *Oberlin Evangelist*, agreed. "The golden age of our race is yet to come," it observed in 1841, "and numerous indications of Providence seem to show that it may not be very distant." In preparation for the coming of the millennium, Christians were urged to preach the Gospel, "fight the fight of faith, and hasten forward the promised reign of Jesus." Because the day drew nigh, readers were asked whether they wished to meet "the Man of Calvary" as a friend or a foe.[63] For his part, in 1830 the prominent religious reformer and educator Alexander Campbell saw the American Revolution as a precursor to a revolution "of infinitely more importance to mankind." For "a more glorious work" was reserved for Americans in the present day: "the emancipation of the human mind from the shackles of superstition, and the introduction of human beings into the full fruition of the reign of heaven."[64]

These theologians, who certainly were not of one mind on many matters religious, nonetheless agreed that a realization of the millennium was linked to political and religious advances in the United States and to a dissociation from Europe and especially from Roman Catholicism.[65] "Tired and jaded with the conflicts of Papal Rome," Campbell argued, Americans sought a city of refuge where they devised a government without religion that secured the greatest amount of political and temporal happiness enjoyed by any people and that will continue to do so "till Christianity conquers the world."[66] Beecher's vision was even more apocalyptic. Europe's problem was its intimate connection to the papacy, "that scourge of the earth, and abominable thing in the eyes of heaven." A time will soon come, Beecher assured his readers, when this "great Babylon, this mother of harlots and abominations of the earth" will be blotted out and when "the tumult of the nations will create one mighty vortex, whose centre

---

[62] "Hints on the Relative Importance of the United States to the Rest of the World, In a Moral and Religious View," *Spirit of the Pilgrims* 1 (1828): 281–84. It is not surprising that the journal also applauded the role of New England in these developments (337–43).

[63] H. C., "The Millennium, No. 23," *Oberlin Evangelist* 3 (1841): 204.

[64] Alexander Campbell, "An Oration in Honor of the Fourth of July, 1830," in *Popular Lectures and Addresses* (Philadelphia: James Challen and Son, 1863), 374–75.

[65] On the connections between millennialism and anti-Catholicism, see Whitney R. Cross, *The Burned-Over District: The Social and Intellectual History of Enthusiastic Religion in Western New York, 1800–1850* (Ithaca, NY: Cornell University Press, 1950), 231–33.

[66] Campbell, "Oration in Honor of the Fourth of July, 1830," 372.

shall be at the heart of Europe, drawing into its whirlpool everything in the civilized world, which now throws its iron hand over human intellect and the holier aspirations of the human heart."[67] Finney's journal utilized scripture to predict both that the millennium was imminent and that the destruction of Rome was at hand. This might create an "awful impression" of the damnation of hundreds of millions of Romanists, it continued, and "we gladly hope that not all of this vast number will be the victims of strong delusion and swift damnation." Although "the Romish church resists conversion to simple gospel" with greater vigor than any class of people on earth, the Finneyite hope was simple: "May God spare and save as many as can wisely be."[68]

Thought about the millenium in relation to the place of Roman Catholicism and Roman Catholics within it thus was fraught with ambivalence. On the one hand, many – like Beecher, Finney, and Campbell – continued to see the Church as the Beast of the Apocalypse as described in the Book of Revelation. On the other hand, they actively proselytized to bring the Word to the unwashed and, as in the case of Finney, feared the horrific outcome of the Apocalypse for the unredeemed. Consequently, they hoped to bring as many Roman Catholics as possible into the (Protestant) Christian fold, a conversion that would save the degenerate and illustrate the progression toward an end of times.

These cosmic expectations begat prosaic enterprises. Evangelical Protestants, in this an era of revival, proselytization, and conversion, established a cluster of organizations that tended to the cultural and religious well-being of the nation. The American Bible Society, founded in 1816, was followed by the Philadelphia Sunday and Adult School Union (founded in 1817 and later called the American Sunday School Union) and the American Tract Society (1825). These organizations were complemented by the American Society for the Promotion of Temperance (1826), the American Peace Society (1828), and the American Anti-Slavery Society (1833).[69] Perhaps the most notable organization was the American Home Missionary Society (AHMS), founded in 1826.[70] As part of a larger strategy to address perceived social ills, the AHMS aimed at bringing the Gospel to benighted realms, including the West. As such, the efforts of the AHMS and its partner societies illustrate the aspiration to use conversion as a means of grappling with an increasingly pluralist society. Yet the groups' focus on the West also reflected Beecher's conviction that the region was of singular

---

[67] "Hints on the Relative Importance of the United States to the Rest of the World," 283.

[68] H. C., "The Millennium, No. 10," *Oberlin Evangelist* 3 (1841): 101.

[69] See David Paul Nord, "Benevolent Capital: Financing Evangelical Book Publishing in Early Nineteenth-Century America," in *God and Mammon: Protestants, Money and the Market, 1790–1860*, ed. Mark A. Noll (New York: Oxford University Press, 2001), 147–70; and John T. McFarland, Benjamin S. Winchester, Robert Douglas Fraser, James Williams Butcher, eds., *The Encyclopedia of Sunday Schools and Religious Education* (New York: Thomas Nelson and Sons, 1915), 1:341.

[70] See Colin Brummitt Goodykoontz, *Home Missions on the American Frontier With Particular Reference to the American Home Missionary Society* (New York: Octagon Books, 1971), for a detailed treatment of the AHMS.

importance to the world, as well as to the nation. Some exuded a confidence that reflected their belief in a millenarian future. As late as 1855, the *New Englander and Yale Review* contended that "there can be no question, that the American Republic was designed by Providence to accomplish a work in history surpassed by no nation under Heaven." The United States was "just far enough remote from the old [world] to escape the evil influence of European corruption and vices, and just near enough to feel the good influence of what was best in European civilization."[71]

Missionaries, who fanned out across the West, frequently extolled the character of the region's residents. Stephen Peet, for example, worked in the Wisconsin Territory beginning in the late 1830s. He observed that many in the territory were "the best class of emigrants from the eastern states – intelligent, enterprising, and decidedly in favor of education and religious institutions." As a representative of the AHMS, Peet was pleased to observe that "there is a large amount of educated mind in Wisconsin," including "a great number of females of refined and finished education, qualified to fill any station." All of this, Peet concluded, "augurs well for the future character of our population."[72] Three years later, he reported a growing number of Sunday schools, an abstinence society, interest on "behalf of the downtrodden," and the good works of women, who led a revival. Again he waxed confidently that we "hope soon to see this wilderness everywhere ... becoming as the garden of the Lord."[73] If Peet commented on the intelligent and educated class from the eastern states, however, he also observed the illiterate "Roman Catholics who are generally kept in ignorance according to the genius of their religion and the designs of their priests."[74] Here, then, was the realm that, according to the New School Presbyterian Albert Barnes, "may now be regarded as the great battle-field of the world – the place where probably, more than any where else, the destinies of the world are to be decided."[75]

The future of the West, as a result, was as uncertain as it was important. From one perspective, it was a milieu where, if adequate missionary work was performed, Protestants could convert and church the unwashed and undergird the American republic. The Roman Catholic Church, in a weakened state, could not care for its adherents in this unsettled region. Catholic immigrants, freed of the garish trappings of the Church, would find their way to a Protestant and republican liberty. From another perspective, however, the fluid and unformed character of western society might result in a populace that would not be churched at all, or worse yet, would join the wrong church. Presbyterian and

[71] "The Moral of Statistics," *New Englander and Yale Review* 13 (1855): 184.
[72] Stephen Peet, letter to the Secretaries of the American Home Missionary Society, 20 July 1839, Records of the American Home Missionary Society, Wisconsin State Historical Society Archives.
[73] Stephen Peet, narrative of the state of religion, to the American Home Missionary Society, 1842, Records of the American Home Missionary Society, Wisconsin State Historical Society Archives.
[74] Stephen Peet, letter to the Secretaries of the American Home Missionary Society, 20 July 1839, Records of the American Home Missionary Society, Wisconsin State Historical Society Archives.
[75] Albert Barnes, *Home Missions* (New York: William Osborn, 1849), 19.

Congregational missionaries fretted not only about Roman Catholicism but also about other religious movements, such as Mormonism. The solution was a proper institutional structure that would chart a middle way between a dearth of religious discipline, as represented by ecstatic revivals, and excessive authority, as embodied in the Church. The "American Church," wrote a Presbyterian journal in 1832 referring to the Protestant church, "shall do its duty," or otherwise it would "see the Valley of the Mississippi the strong hold of Popery; a prey to every fanatical teacher; wasted by infidelity; and DESERTED OF THE LORD!"[76] To make matters worse, a disestablished church in the United States promised widespread instability and uncertainty. Church organizations might change; they might merge; they might disappear. More important, the West was the future seat of the American empire. The outcome of this battle – and it was perceived to be a warlike battle – was of monumental importance to American observers in the East.

As the battle was joined in the present, many argued that the influence of the West would only increase in the future. "No one can cast his eye over the map of this continent," wrote the *Princeton Review* in 1832, "without being struck with the almost unexampled advantage in many respects possessed by the great Valley of the Mississippi." Amid this growing influence, Protestant missionaries perceived their duty to be to fill the region with Christian belief that, in turn, would enhance the integrity of state and society. "If the West is filled with the Gospel, if every town and neighborhood is pervaded by the doctrine which came down from heaven, and whose effect is to strengthen the authority of law, to teach men industry, temperance and justice, and to lead quiet and peaceable lives in godliness and honesty," wrote the *Home Missionary* in 1839, "then every town and neighborhood will send forth a wholesome political influence, and western representatives will be, by choice, or by the constraint of a virtuous public sentiment, the advocates of righteousness."[77] These expectations were all the more important because of the "refluent wave" that would reverberate eastward. The increasing political power of the West meant not only that national issues would be skewed to reflect western interests but that such questions as "whether we should have a Sabbath, whether God shall be recognized as the Governor of nations" would also be addressed by westerners.[78]

Despite expressions of optimism about the West's future, then, Americans who traveled to the region nonetheless rehearsed the frequently expressed concerns about barbarism and irreligion, on the one hand, and the anxiety about a Catholicized region, on the other. "Our country is in danger," the *Home Missionary* continued, "and the souls of present and unborn millions are in danger" if missionaries in the West were not able to chart a middle way between the extremes of too little authority and too much.[79] In 1841, Rev. J. J. Miter

---

[76] "View of the Valley of the Mississippi," *Princeton Review* 4 (1832): 567.
[77] "The Refluent Wave," *Home Missionary* 11 (1839): 209.
[78] "Views of Rev. John Angell James," *Home Missionary* 14 (1841): 182.
[79] Ibid.

noted the myriad dangers that were coming together in what he called "this great western theatre." In this theater, minds "collected from the four winds" were "held together by no fixed principles, no homogeneous preferences, and by no long established usages." Here was a scene of "bold experiments" that included "errorists," who hoped their system would take root, and "revolutionists," who desired to begin their work of "convulsion and overthrow." Here also was a place where "mammon is the acknowledged god," to which westerners have prostrated themselves. Here was a setting where a "foreign class" was rapidly increasing, replete with a variety of beliefs. In this heterogeneous and heterodox world, "every system has its advocates," "every system has its adherents," and "every man makes proselytes."[80] A swelling of European immigrants in the 1840s and 1850s, many of whom had fled Catholic lands, only increased the concern about Catholicism in the West.

Ominous signs of a Catholicized West were everywhere. In 1839, a correspondent to the *Home Missionary* reported on a community in Illinois where almost half of the nearly two thousand inhabitants were Catholics, "who generally act together on all questions of public interest." Because others in the community were evenly divided, the unified Catholic influence was disproportionately large. The "Catholic boast" that "we have got the West" seemed to this correspondent to be realized, at least in this one instance.[81] A report from Iowa in 1842 was even more ominous. "At every important point on the Mississippi [River]," a correspondent to the *Home Missionary* reported, "the Romanists have commenced their work, and stationed their men." Supported amply by foreign resources, priests – "a little fallen creature, in a *white robe and a red sash*" – impart mistruths to followers who "eat up his words as they eat bread."[82]

Protestant observers argued that conservative European forces were interfering in this battle for the West. As Beecher among many others observed, the papacy in league with European monarchs feared that the American republic intended to use its vast resources to undermine their plan. European actors sought to destabilize the United States and would succeed through subversion rather than conquest. By relying on these secret maneuvers, the pope and his allies, moreover, not only would destroy the alarming development of republicanism but would also enrich the Church. The "valley of the Mississippi," wrote one English clergyman, "has been, no doubt, mapped as well as surveyed by the emissaries of the Vatican," and "cardinals are exulting, in hope of enriching the Papal See by accessions from the United States."[83] The West was

---

[80] Rev. J. J. Miter, "The Missionary Field in the Mississippi Valley," *Home Missionary* 14 (1841): 179.

[81] "Catholic Influence," *Home Missionary* 11 (1839): 208–9.

[82] "Romanism in Iowa," *Home Missionary* 15 (1842): 170–71. In 1845 yet another report from Iowa observed the migration of some 350 German families. Because many were wealthy, "the colony will probably be advantageous to the business part of the county, but disadvantageous, we fear, to the morals and religion of the people." "Emigrants," *Home Missionary* 17 (1845): 252–53.

[83] "Views of Rev. John Angell James," 181.

where "the battle must be fought which is to decide whether this land is *now* to be occupied for Christ, or whether it is first to be, for an indefinite period, the strong hold of Papacy [*sic*]."[84]

Protestant missionaries foresaw different outcomes if the Catholic threat was not addressed. Some missionaries held out little hope that the infant Catholic societies in the West could maintain a moral bearing because their leadership kept their minions in darkness. Any pretension of educating the people, moreover, was a ruse. Reacting to the laying of the cornerstone of a Catholic college in Wisconsin, one Protestant mocked the schooling and literacy of such Catholic lands as Mexico, Italy, and Spain. "Had the forefathers of New England but been Romanists," he concluded, "what a different aspect would that poor benighted portion of our confederacy have displayed!!"[85] Others predicted that Catholic deceit was only a part of Catholicism's design to dominate the region. Catholics' "friendliness to popular intelligence," the *Home Missionary* argued, was only an "affectation," because it was contradicted by all history. "Their apparent interest for general education," it continued "is only a temporary expedient for popular effect, to be abandoned as soon as they shall have become firmly established." The plot to gain control was such that the "thread of its influence, though now minute and unseen as the spider's web" may become "chains of iron, binding [America's children] in a bondage that will fetter both the body and the soul."[86]

These concerns endured past midcentury. Philip Schaff, lecturing in Europe in 1855, noted the continent's stormy recent history, which encouraged the Church to look to mission fields in the United States. "The last decisive engagement between Romanism and Protestantism," Schaff predicted, "will not fall in Europe ... but on the banks of the Hudson, the Susquehannah, the Mississippi, and the Sacramento."[87] In 1857, the Episcopalian theologian John Henry Hopkins expressed the fear that Protestantism would not dominate the region. "Is it at all unlikely," he asked rhetorically, "that the increasing loss of papal influence in many parts of Europe will bring to our shores a vast accession of foreign Romanists, which may give a decided preponderance to their religion in the great western valley, and finally enable them to set up their exclusive claims, in all their old intolerance?" In weakness rather than in strength, the papacy still had designs on the West. And although the federal constitution prohibited an established church, Hopkins warned that states could not be prevented from altering their constitutions to establish Catholicism. It was about developments in the "great western valley" that Protestants such as Hopkins tended to worry.[88] The political essayist Anna

---

[84] Ibid.

[85] J. C. Holbrook, "More must be done," *Home Missionary* 19 (1846): 170.

[86] "Utterances of Romanism in the West," *Home Missionary* 19 (1846): 190.

[87] Schaff, *America*, 229, 235.

[88] John Henry Hopkins, *The American Citizen: His Rights and Duties, According to the Spirit of the Constitution of the United States* (New York: Pudney and Russell, 1857), 84–85.

Ella Carroll concentrated more on the economic than on the political effect of Catholicism in the West. "It becomes a question of the first moment to the nation," she stressed, "that [the West] be occupied by Protestants, whose education tends to strengthen our liberties, while that of Romanism is designed to subvert them." The reason was simple: "The West will soon hold the balance in our national exchequer, and elect our chief ruler; and it is impossible to be too vigilant in promoting and spreading Protestant education over all that portion of our people."[89]

On the eve of the Civil War, anti-Catholics continued to utilize what had become a familiar narrative of a Catholic plot to control the West. Edward Beecher, Lyman's son, in 1855 recounted a gothic tale of deceit that linked American prelates and European reactionaries. Beginning in 1828, communiqués between Prince Metternich and the bishop of Cincinnati set in motion the plot to dominate the West.[90] Four years later, a nativist tract provocatively entitled *Pope or President?* reiterated the familiar story. A "proposed field of Papal occupancy," which included the Canadian West and states in the Old Northwest, it warned, was "being settled by a foreign Catholic population, acknowledging the Roman pontiff as their head." Because the western population would in a few years equal the present population of the United States, the "influence of the Church of Rome will be universal, and the interests of the papacy all-absorbing!" The risk was clear: "Shall the Protestant Bible and freedom be saved in the West? or shall it be reduced to the present condition of the South American States?"[91] After some two decades, a narrative that outlined a Catholic conspiracy against the West and ultimately aimed at American liberty was a story well known to vigilant Protestant Americans.

The perils just noted could be ameliorated, and perhaps solved, through conversion. On the one hand, the American born who backslid could be brought back into the spiritual fold, a movement that would aid state and society. As we have seen, Protestant religious leaders throughout the period believed that the most effective means of controlling people came from within and that the best way to achieve this end was conversion to evangelical Christianity. A widespread conversion, therefore, would benefit both the people affected and the state itself. Spokesmen for Protestant Christianity often explicitly connected the functions of church and state. A Congregationalist writing about a missionary

[89] Anna Ella Carroll, *The Star of the West; or, National Men and National Measures* (New York: Miller, Orton, 1857), 171.

[90] Edward Beecher, *Papal Conspiracy Exposed*, 401–7.

[91] *Pope, or President? Startling Disclosures of Romanism as Revealed by its Own Writers. Facts for Americans* (New York: R. L. Delisser, 1859), 252–53. This outcome was being engineered: "[S]ociety, embracing nearly all the wealthy Roman Catholics of Europe, has been organized, with the express design of establishing Roman Catholic colonies in our Western States. London is its headquarters, but it has branches in every capital in Europe."

band to the West, for example, stressed that "sacred Republicanism" would go hand in hand across the continent "with secular Republicanism."[92]

A sense of urgency surrounding conversion in the West, on the other hand, focused on the mounting Roman Catholic presence. In response, Protestant missionaries expressed optimism that a Protestant conversion would be successful provided that evangelical Protestantism did not become complaisant. As Rev. J. C. Holbrook wrote in 1846, the "tens of thousands of Roman Catholic foreigners . . . monthly landing on our American shores" would be converted only if Protestants did not "settle down into a state of indifference." Increasingly, he continued, "people are coming to feel that all the Catholics that come here will be converted as a matter of course," but the fact was that "if they are converted, it must be through the truth disseminated by Protestants." Paraphrasing Bishop George Berkeley, he observed that "westward the star of empire has taken its way and here it will soon be fixed." If this responsibility was neglected, Catholics "will swarm over our western country until they control it, and, consequently, the nation."[93] This expression of apprehension was, to be sure, part of a rhetorical strategy to win people to the evangelical cause. Warning that a dire future awaited the United States if Americans did not contribute to the objective of western conversion certainly was a useful strategy in gaining support. Yet the fervency with which it was voiced indicates that many thought the threat to be true.

Given these aspirations, the conversion of the Roman Catholic body would be transformative. It not only would restore the United States as a homogeneous Protestant nation-state, but it also would be a harbinger of change for the status of freedom in the world. The consequences, if this did not occur, were frightful. One outcome has already been discussed: the fear that Catholicism would reign supreme in the West. But a second result was also predicted. Again using Cincinnati as an example, a correspondent worried about the five thousand "backsliders from Popery" who stood "without a shepherd, waiting for some hand to help them." These backsliders would represent yet another example of "wickedness and infidelity" in the West if they were not tended to. Here was an instance of Bushnell's scenario in reverse: lapsed Catholics would become barbarian if they were not recruited by Protestants.[94]

If it was so desirable, how was the conversion of Roman Catholics to be accomplished? The obstacles were great, not least because of the control of the Catholic priesthood over the Church's followers. Yet Protestant commentators

[92] Ephraim Adams, *The Iowa Band* (Boston: Congregational Publishing Society, 1870), 11. In retrospective of the successes of the so-called Iowa Band, Adams celebrated the satisfactory results of "another Christian state" added to "the frontier, looking towards the great sea." He viewed the future, observing that "the base-line of the army of occupation for Christ is moved so much farther towards the prophesized boundary [of the Pacific]." An inculcation of a manifest destiny, Adams concluded that new bands would "meet those coming up the Pacific slope" and "then will the watchmen see eye to eye, and rejoice together; then will glory dwell in the land."

[93] J. C. Holbrook, "Romanists not to be underrated," *Home Missionary* 19 (1846): 171.

[94] "Editor's Table," *Ladies' Repository* 8 (1848): 287.

agreed that conversion could not be coerced, and they therefore tended to use an irenic tone in discussing the changes that could be effected among their Catholic counterparts. "Fear" about the West, wrote the editor of the *Ladies' Repository*, a journal of the Methodist Episcopal Church published in Cincinnati in 1845, "is mingled with hope." The increase in Catholic immigration and the "influx of money to erect Catholic churches, seminaries, and cathedrals" were a concern, but "the spread of knowledge among the people" and the "democratic tendencies of our country" were two sources of hope. In the end, "Romanism cannot resist the pressure of the truth from without; she cannot bind the mass of American mind, and she is unable to resist the progress of the age." Its believers, moreover, should not be viewed as enemies; "let us love them," the journal concluded, "gain their confidence, and endeavor to do them good."[95]

Missionaries in 1846 argued that the power of Protestant and republican truth would erode the vitality of Catholic belief. "Romanism, if broken down, and banished from our free country," they argued, "is to be broken down by the presence and influence of our free institutions." It was true that "the hardened, the stupid, the bigoted, and corrupt devotee may refuse to read" and that "his priest may burn the Bible," but life among "living, free, and devout churches" would wear away a Catholic's prejudices.[96] Bushnell agreed that Protestants "must be willing to stretch our forbearance and charity even to Romanists themselves, when we clearly find the spirit of Jesus in their life."[97] One year after Bushnell, a Presbyterian clergyman, Edward Norris Kirk, noted the bewildering array of "restless and floating" people in the West who heard "the jargon of Babel" rather than "Christ's gentle voice." If European immigrants moved to those regions of the West where American influence was weakest, Kirk argued, American Protestants should nonetheless welcome those immigrants who would accept the Protestant faith when they were encouraged to do so. The promotion of Roman Catholicism was difficult because "there is nothing here to sustain the despotic power of their priesthood." Could individuals, he asked rhetorically, born in the free air of the West and possessing free access to the Bible "remain timid slaves of men who deny them the right of thinking?"[98]

Among the most optimistic observers was Barnes. The European immigrant, Barnes wrote in 1845, "has broken away from a thousand influences in favor of a false religion, and bad principles of government, in his own land." In the immigrant's European home, all things venerable were "fitted to foster superstition; all the influence under which he grew up tending to error – in the moss-grown cathedral, the consecrated relics of the saints, the pompous ceremonial, the long train of priests, and in the sepulchral places of the dead." Significantly,

---

[95] "Perils of Popery," *Ladies' Repository* 5 (1845): 350.
[96] "The Evangelization of the West. How Shall it be Effected? And by Whom?" *New Englander and Yale Review* 4 (1846): 37.
[97] Bushnell, *Barbarism the First Danger*, 31–32.
[98] Edward Norris Kirk, "The Church Essential to the Republic" (New York: Leavitt, Trow, 1848), 16, 22.

none of these existed in the immigrant's western prairie home. And if they were to be recreated, "it will be with diminished splendor and influence," after a period of years when immigrants and especially their children "shall be open to the better influence which grows out of our Protestant and Republican institutions."[99] In America, moreover, the clergy had to be "of the people" and "have a large share of American feeling," which was something that a foreign clergy "educated with foreign notions" and "never assimilating with the American mind" could never achieve. In sum, religion was spread in the United States "not by processions, or genuflections, or pomp and show," but by those "who can do most to enlighten the public mind, diffuse farthest the word of God, [and] maintain most steadfastly the right to the free exercise of opinion."[100]

There were some encouraging signs throughout the United States. The *New Englander and Yale Review* noted in 1855 that the 3,956 Protestant churches in America could accommodate more than thirteen million persons, a sharp contrast to the nation's 1,712 Catholic churches. More significant was the seeming decline of Catholic practice in the United States. By calculating the numbers of Catholic immigrants and population changes due to natural increase, the journal reckoned that the Roman Catholic Church had lost nearly one million members in nine years. These numbers were heartening for Protestants, especially given that Protestants "have a stronger faith than ever in the steady working of their free institutions, against the despotic power of Rome."[101] The Protestant convert Nicholas Murray taunted Archbishop John Hughes from an east coast perspective about a move to Protestantism among Irish Catholics. In America, Murray wrote, "all minds are using the privilege of thinking freely" so that "where there is one Protestant who passes over to your Church, there are fifty papists who become Protestants."[102] And Lyman Beecher's son, Edward, adhered to the hopeful visions of his father. Eighteen million "free American Protestants," "if enlightened and full of moral energy," could do the necessary work for the United States and also "impart new energy to the friends of freedom in the old world." This conversion was to be accomplished with no hostility toward Catholics, but rather through "love and sympathy for them, and an earnest desire to destroy that corporation [the Church] which is their worst enemy, and which is intent only on deluding, enslaving, and plundering them."[103] Merging the hope for widespread conversion of the unwashed with the expectation of the millennium, these religious leaders and many others foresaw not only the prospects of a Protestant nation but also the fulfillment of the nation's destiny as one of singular secular and spiritual importance.

---

[99] Albert Barnes, *Plea on Behalf of Western Colleges* (Philadelphia: William Sloanaker, 1846), 13; see also Albert Barnes, *Home Missions* 17.
[100] Barnes, *Home Missions*, 29–30, 34.
[101] "The Moral of Statistics," 197.
[102] Kirwan, *Letters to the Right Rev. John Hughes*, 242.
[103] Edward Beecher, *Papal Conspiracy Exposed*, 414.

The soil of freedom would nurture a conversion to Protestantism and republicanism, but the salubrious environment needed assistance from American institutions that could encourage sympathy for the Catholic who was trapped in a web of deceit. The *New Englander and Yale Review* provides the best examples of a frequently expressed argument that outlined the ultimate defeat of Catholicism in the United States through conversion. "Under our happy government," wrote the *Review* in 1847, "the Catholic may declare himself no longer subject of the Pope, may renounce the hierarchy and superstitions of Rome, and enjoy the ordinances of the gospel, in a church of his own choice, with none to molest or make him afraid." The road to conversion might be slow because of opposition from the papal hierarchy and "from the bigotry of blind superstition," but the journal expected American successes. "The single object of all," it concluded, "should be to rescue the victims of superstition from spiritual oppression and fatal error."[104]

And the best hope for success in converting the Romanist immigrants into republican Americans was to assimilate them through kindness. The *New Englander and Yale Review* held forth in great detail on the Romanist problem in 1844. Roman Catholics, it informed its readers, are generally foreigners "marked to some extent by a distinctive physiognomy, and to a greater extent by differences in language."[105] In all nations, such foreigners were likely to become objects of prejudice and hatred. Yet this not only contradicted Mosaic law – "thou shalt neither vex a stranger, nor oppress him; for ye were strangers in the land in Egypt" – but it was unwise religious and social policy.[106] To be sure, Romanism was error ridden; it was polytheistic, idolatrous, and at war with the Bible. Yet individual Catholics were not to be treated as if they were responsible for these errors. Nor were they to be considered hostile to American political institutions. Even if a Romanist conspiracy to overturn the American republic was afoot, most of these Roman Catholic immigrants played no explicit part in it. The real danger, the journal continued, was the reinstitution of Old World religious animosities that caused Catholic immigrants to believe that Protestants intended to oppress them. Rather, if these "ignorant and priest-ridden people" could come to see that "the genius of American religion was liberty," they would in due time "feel that the genius of their religion, as they have it under the priest, is slavery."[107] It was not only naturalization or suffrage that could "convert a Bavarian or Irish peasant into an American," but kindness that would lead that individual to appreciate "American habits of thought and feeling."[108]

It was true that Romanism had for twenty years attempted to occupy the West, but the journal nonetheless counseled confidence. "Cathedrals, churches,

---

[104] E. E. T., "The American Catholic Church," *New Englander and Yale Review* 17 (1845): 138–39.
[105] "Romanists and the Roman Catholic Controversy," *New Englander and Yale Review* 2 (1844): 233.
[106] Ibid.
[107] Ibid., 239–40.
[108] Ibid., 241.

convents and colleges," it wrote, "rise on the banks of the Ohio and the Mississippi" and great effort needed to be put forth to "counteract that gigantic scheme for the extension of the papal domination."[109] Nonetheless, the rates of growth of the Catholic population were less than those of the Jewish population. Because there was no established church in the United States, "the Papist here is nothing but a sectarian among sectarians."[110] The danger was if any part of the United States, and here again the concern was with the West, was "left to the dominion of ignorance, infidelity, and fanaticism," because there "Romanism may hope to triumph."[111] And it was true that "here and there in some large town the idol cross stands as a symbol ... of the superstition that debases and enslaves." In the end, however, truth would win out and the United States would remain a land of Protestantism and religious liberty.[112]

Well into the 1850s, Thomas Harvey Skinner, a Presbyterian minister and professor of sacred rhetoric at Union Theological Seminary, optimistically predicted the triumph of Protestantism. Like most of his contemporaries, he realized that the challenge was great. The ascendancy of Romanism, he assured his readers, would "be our overthrow, as an independent people," in part because "the priests of this superstition are under an oath of allegiance to the Roman pontiff [and] could not, without perjury, stand for our country's independence, in opposition to his will." Yet Romanism could not be outlawed, and neither should the immigration of Catholics be prohibited. Immigrants came to improve their position and should be allowed "to sit down with us under the Tree of Liberty." And this was for Skinner the point: Catholics would be encouraged to come to the United States *because* they would convert. The converts from Roman Catholicism greatly outnumbered the converts to it, and Romanism will ultimately be "lost in the predominance of a nationality, civil and religious, altogether our own."[113]

The content of Beecher's narrative thus endured. The West for decades thereafter remained a flashpoint of conflict and concern. It was here, many agreed, that the destiny of the nation lay and where victory over Romanism was essential for the fulfillment of that prospect. It was here that conversion would be a powerful weapon in winning the battle for the souls of the West. Yet evangelical Protestants nonetheless had to recalibrate their aims in the decades following Beecher's plea. As the enthusiasm of the Second Great Awakening ebbed and millennial dreams began to fade, the Romanist conversion became an effort to create a homogeneous nation poised for temporal greatness. And as the war to convert the heterogeneous western populace turned into a stalemate between Catholic and Protestant forces, Protestants were forced, as we shall see in the next section, to readjust their aspirations once again.

---

[109] Ibid., 242.
[110] Ibid., 246.
[111] Ibid., 251.
[112] Ibid.
[113] Thomas H. Skinner, *Love of Country: A Discourse Delivered on Thanksgiving Day, December 12th, 1850 in the Bleeker Street Church* (New York: E. French, 1851), 20–23.

As evangelical proselytization endured, expectant hopes for the advent of the millennium waned for a variety of reasons. Not only were the disciples of the pre-millennialist William Miller disappointed in the 1840s when the predicted millennium failed to occur, but the criticism of biblical scholars such as Moses Stuart gained traction and the tendency to wed current events to biblical prophesy became less tenable. It is true, however, that close readings of apocalyptical scripture continued to appear in print. S. D. Baldwin in the 1850s, for example, used the Books of Daniel and Revelation to craft his own prediction of a coming Armageddon.[114] Dedicated to the "Friends of Bible Democracy and the Foes of Monarchy and Romanism," Baldwin's exegesis of scripture indicated that republican America, beginning in 1878, would annihilate the reconstituted kingdoms of Europe in the Ohio and Mississippi river valleys. A reflection of the climate of opinion, Baldwin utilized nativist and expansionist rhetoric to weave a story of American conquest and the destruction of the papacy and of monarchy.[115]

Yet millennial expectations ebbed, and revivalist excitement tended to give way to a greater emphasis on religious organization.[116] The new approach toward proselytization did not foreclose the hope of conversion; indeed, the problem of religious diversity endured, and the question, from a Protestant perspective, of fostering evangelical Protestantism and challenging Catholic claims persisted. The new emphasis offered a somewhat contradictory strategy of continuing to press for the conversion of Catholics and, at the same time, shoring up the institutional divisions within Protestantism to address the dual threats of Catholicism and indifferentism on either side of the confessional divide. The response, in short, was the growth of denominationalism.

The development of denominationalism is often understood in the context of the establishment of religious freedom in the United States. As we saw in Chapter 1, the establishment of freedom of belief did not undermine the assumption that the well-being of society was dependent on commonly shared religious beliefs. But, as Sidney Mead has argued, the goal of maintaining a religious substructure in the context of religious freedom forced American Protestants to relax any exclusive claims to religious truth and pressured them to pursue some higher unity that lay at the core of their beliefs. As absolute truth claims among religious groups were diminished, Americans looked for a common identity and found it, Mead continues, in the American nation. Because members of denominations were willing to

---

[114] Samuel D. Baldwin, *Armageddon; or, The Overthrow of Romanism and Monarchy; the Existence of the United States Foretold in the Bible, Its Future Greatness; Invasion by Allied Europe; Annihilation of Monarch; Expansion into the Millennial Republic; and Its Dominion Over the Whole World* (Cincinnati: Applegate, 1854).

[115] Ibid. On the Armageddon, see pp. 398, 405; on expansionism and nativism, see pp. 157, 162. Baldwin's work had the staying power to attract the attention of Mark Twain in 1861. See Edgar Marquess Branch, Michael B. Frank, Kenneth M. Sanderson, eds., *Mark Twain's Letters* (Berkeley: University of California Press, 1988), 1:120.

[116] On these developments, see James D. Bratt, "The Reorientation of American Protestantism, 1835–1845," *Church History* 67 (1998): 52–82. On Beecher specifically, see James W. Fraser, *Pedagogue for God's Kingdom*, esp. 95–101.

compromise on the inherent truth of certain confessions and ritual practices, they also disavowed a particularist position. In this way, denominationalism – as distinguished from sectarianism – forged a path of pluralism.[117]

The advance of denominationalism had a number of consequences. First, as Nathan Hatch observes, it ineluctably altered the traditional undertakings of the church, because the concept of the chosen nation replaced that of the ecclesiastical community of the redeemed.[118] Second, the essence of religious freedom and a working assumption of denominationalism was the rejection of coercion through, for example, an established state church that demanded adherence to religious persuasion and, by implication, conversion. No one put it better than Joseph Berg in a pamphlet published in 1851 on the relationship between Protestantism, Catholicism, and infidelity. "No man has a *moral* right to add to, or to take from the words of the Bible," he averred, "but all Christians do not agree in their interpretation of certain passages of Scripture." Those who prefer an episcopal form of government will be Episcopalian; those who prefer presbyterian will be Presbyterian. "So long as the regulations of the branch of the church of Christ, with which I am connected, seem to offer a more congenial communion than any other," Berg concluded, "its members will remain with it." But if they prefer another fellowship, they have the freedom to go elsewhere and "no anathemas will follow them [as among Catholics].[119]

These consequences, in turn, had implications for the nature of religious organization in the United States. First, religious freedom resulted in a multiplicity of denominations. These denominations, moreover, had to define and articulate their beliefs without coercion and through persuasion. Hence, the religious terrain in the United States did indeed resemble a marketplace of belief. Finally, these sects accepted what Hatch terms the "rationalist view" that only what all churches held and taught in common – that is, the essentials of every religion – was relevant for the well-being of state and society.

The debate between Protestants and Catholics somewhat clouds these clear distinctions. For one thing, Protestants often did not accept the notion that Catholics were engaged in a movement of persuasion so much as one of coercion. Catholics were sectarians; Protestants were denominationalists. Here was another manifestation of the perils of freedom in the American church where Catholicism could continue to coerce – to hold its believers in darkness – whereas Protestants had to play by a different set of rules based on persuasion. In contrast, the Roman Catholic leadership did not necessarily accede to the view that exclusive truth claims were relaxed and, in fact, continued to argue, as we saw in Chapter 2, that the higher unity remained the Church. Again, we revisit the logical quandaries

---

[117] Sidney Mead, *The Lively Experiment: The Shaping of Christianity in America* (New York: Harper and Row, 1963), 62–66; and Sidney Mead, "The Fact of Pluralism and the Persistence of Sectarianism," in *The Religion of the Republic*, ed. Elwyn A. Smith (Philadelphia: Fortress Press, 1971), 247–66.

[118] Hatch, *Sacred Cause of Liberty*, 142.

[119] Berg, *Trapezium; or, Law and Liberty versus Despotism and Anarchy*, 10.

encountered by both Protestants and Catholics. Because Roman Catholics wished to remain distinct, they acceded to a pluralist, rather than a unitary, structure of religion in the United States. But this pluralism was not viewed as a number of sects vying for believers so much as a particularism of the one true church set in conflict with a variety of ephemeral Protestant denominations. Likewise, Protestants continued to puzzle over an adversary that held its believers in captivity and that seemed to possess some advantages in the battle for the hearts and minds of the unwashed.

Perhaps it was Protestants who were forging a path to pluralism, as Mead suggests. Yet when we view the divide between an ostensibly unified Protestantism, which supposedly represented varieties of true Christianity, and their Catholic adversaries, Protestant denominationalism appears less pluralist. In this denominationalist structure, however, the Roman Catholic Church, as in our discussion of the millennialist expectations, played a pivotal role. The Church remained a powerful foil and organizing device for Protestants. If they continued to hope for Catholic conversions, Protestants could unite against the Roman Catholic Church, despite their own differences in church governance and theology. To be sure, theological disputes endured among Protestants, but the presence of a powerful – and potentially empowered – Church could enable common cause. In sum, if the millennium would not promise Protestant homogeneity, Protestant institutions would be formed across denominational lines to enforce it, in opposition to the Catholic threat. Catholics therefore remained a vital presence to motivate and activate the Protestant sects in terms of both coalescing into a whole and spurring its membership to action. Despite these parallels, the transition from a millennialism to denominationalism had profound implications. Millennialism was aimed at the conversion of the whole, whereas the denominationalist pattern structurally segmented Christian beliefs into Protestant and Catholic parts. One dreamed of the wholesale transformation of souls within the Kingdom of Christ, whereas the other toiled for incremental change within a visible church.

Outcomes

Is it not astonishing that, though ye all differ in opinion, yet agree in hating and maligning the church of Christ? Though ye can't "join in love," ye know well how to "join in hate." Here are unbaptized Quakers, groaning Methodists, blaspheming Presbyterians, faithless Universalists and Unitarians, and humbug spiritual rappers; and yet ye not only coincide in hating the pope, but ye are all intolerant and cruel. Hugh Quigley, 1853[120]

---

[120] A Missionary Priest [Hugh Quigley], *The Cross and the Shamrock; or, How to Defend the Faith. An Irish American Catholic Tale of Real Life, Descriptive of the Temptations, Sufferings, Trials, and Triumphs of the Children of St. Patrick in the Great Republic of Washington. A Book for the Entertainment and Special Instruction of the Catholic Male and Female Servants of the United States* (Boston: Patrick Donahoe, 1853), 156.

The stalemate of conversion is in retrospect unsurprising, in part because both Roman Catholics and Protestants had grandiose dreams and fears about the other, in part because Americans tended to hew to the faith of their parents and their community. Yet there were possible outcomes of the battle that had long-term consequences both for the crusade against Catholicism and for the efforts of Roman Catholics to become full-standing members of the state.

The most optimistic prediction, perhaps, was the anticipation of a sort of synthesis of the various faiths in the United States. As a central element of the Mercersburg theology, which originated in the German Reformed Church, Philip Schaff stressed a dialectical movement in history where the divisions between Protestantism and Catholicism were part of a divinely inspired development that would eventually result in the merger of the two parts into a whole evangelical Catholic church. His predictions are particularly fascinating because they were centered on developments in the United States and were based on the shifting sands of religious freedom. Protestantism, he argued, would continue to be weakened by what he called "growing sectarian confusion," and it would be attracted to the idea of unity in general and the imposing organization of the Roman Catholic Church in particular. To be sure, Protestantism maintained a vital energy that was impelled by both the truth of scripture and the power of evangelical freedom, but "the jejune and contracted theology" would ultimately face revolutionary change. In contrast, Catholicism would not win the confessional battle in the United States, because of its unpopularity in republican America and because its membership could not remain untouched by the "free political institutions and the thoroughly Protestant spirit of the country." Ultimately, Schaff predicted, an evangelical, rather than Roman, Catholicism would prevail. Catholicism would assume a more liberal character in the United States, and Protestantism would hunger after a more corporate, less fractious, form.[121]

An interaction between Roman Catholics and Protestants would in fact endure and it would change both faiths. In an 1868 article in the *Atlantic Monthly*, James Parton predicted that Catholicism in the United States would become Protestantized and Americanized and that "we [are] all going to be Roman Catholics, then, about the year 1945."[122] In contrast, G. K. Chesterton, some years later, expressed the belief that "in America, even the Catholics are Protestants."[123] The Protestantization of Catholicism and the Catholicization of Protestantism, if it did occur, would take some time.

Two other, less hopeful predictions – continued religious conflict, and a growing divide between a Catholic whole and a Protestant confederation – came to pass

[121] Schaff, *America*, 220–43.
[122] James Parton, "Our Roman Catholic Brethren," *Atlantic Monthly* 21 (1868): 556, cited in Susan M. Griffin, *Anti-Catholicism and Nineteenth-Century Fiction* (Cambridge: Cambridge University Press, 2004), 6.
[123] Cited in Robert N. Bellah and Steven M. Tipson, eds., *The Robert Bellah Reader* (Durham, NC: Duke University Press, 2006), 326.

more immediately and in fuller form. For one thing, violent religious conflict continued to divide Protestants from Catholics. Although the intensity of the violence modulated in the decades before the Civil War, American-born Protestants occasionally rioted out of fear of Catholic armies preparing themselves for battle. Roman Catholics, for their part, repeatedly felt the sting of what they perceived to be American Protestant intolerance. Bishop Joseph Cretin, in a letter written during the Mexican-American War, lamented the braggadocio of the Americans with whom he came into contact. "I believe that there is nothing more to expect from this Government," he wrote. "It is decidedly Protestant; above all since the war with Mexico which it regards as a war of religion." He concluded that "there are already rumors of sending 5 or 6 thousand Yankees to Mexico to civilize the country, that is to say, to Protestantize it. The Americans are becoming proud, more and more. . . . They are people whom one must handle very delicately like puffed-up persons."[124] As the Civil War loomed, the clergyman Andre Trevis wrote in a letter to France an extensive critique that merits an extended quotation:

The agitation caused here by the question of slavery and which brings confusion to the Great Republic may be followed in a few years by open war against Catholicism. . . . In fact the Protestant pulpits do not cease against the Papists and the ministers are trying by all means to raise against us hate and vengeance. Instead of preaching the Gospel, they have converted their temples into political clubs, where they spoke [*sic*] about questions of the day during the last campaign for the presidential elections. As they have contributed much to the victory of the Republican part, it is said that the chiefs of that party, either, through gratitude or to maintain themselves in power, will try to bring on questions of religion on the grounds of politics, and that under the pretext of assuring liberty, they will try to drive out of the Northern States Catholicism, the pretended enemy of the independence of the U.S. and the patron of slavery.

"Whatever is to be thought of these opinions and calculations," Trevis concluded ominously, "it may not be impossible that the palm of martyrdom, for which so many young apostles leave their country, may one day be reaped in America on the borders of the Great Lakes and the Mississippi."[125]

Conflict, verbal and theological rather than physical, also continued to characterize the relationships between Roman Catholics and Protestants. The Protestant critique continued to focus on the threats that Catholicism posed for the United States. It included the hoary accounts of Catholic abuses in Europe long before, as well as the contemporary perils posed by the growth of Catholicism in a republic, as discussed earlier in this chapter and in Chapter 1. If Protestants typically focused on the sectarian nature of the Church, Catholics stressed the follies of modern Protestantism and a decay of what they termed true belief. Freedom of religion created a subjective piety that resulted in the

[124] Letter from Bishop Joseph Cretin to Bishop Mathias Loras, 17 August 1846, cited in M. M. Hoffman, ed., "From Early Iowa to Boston, *Iowa Catholic Historical Journal* 1 (1930): 9.
[125] Letter from Fr. Andre Trevis to friends in France, cited in M. M. Hoffman, ed., "Clement Smyth: Second Bishop of Iowa," *Iowa Catholic Historical Journal* 9 (1936): 13.

proliferation of sects and the erosion of religious meaning. In an imagined exchange published by a Catholic journal between a Protestant minister and a Catholic whom he was trying to convert, the latter concluded that the Catholic Church was "the true Church of Christ," where the 666 of the Beast as cited in Daniel's prophesy represented the number of erring Protestant sects in America.[126] This escalation of church groups ended in absurdity, illogic, and ultimately indifferentism. "How contradictory the tenets of sectarianism!," wrote Hugh Quigley, referring to Protestant denominations. "You, that accuse Catholicity of teaching absurd and incredible doctrines," he continued, "are yourselves enslaved by the most incredible and contradictory creeds." Methodists, for example, followed no method but rather seemed to be intellectually the successors of the ancient bacchanalians in their "mad orgies" of religious revival that annihilated the distinctions between the sexes and legalized by custom the most indecent practices.[127] The cry of Protestantism, agreed the *Boston Pilot*, is "give us something new – no matter what it is – give us novelty." "Every cobbler and tinker who is too lazy or too stupid to work at his trade," the paper continued, "sets up for a reformer or prophet, and thus the world becomes inundated with trashing doctrines and notions." To gain adherents, these preachers speak against the Whore of Babylon and in favor of private judgment. Yet in so doing, "they have turned their guns against themselves," because "having preached so loudly against 'the false church,' their hearers begin to inquire whether there is any true one." In short, the Protestant system is "the Babel of confusion"; its "natural tendency" is to infidelity.[128]

Orestes Brownson probably put it best in his work aptly entitled *The Convert*. By focusing on the relationship between the objective (God and supernatural) and the subjective (human and natural), he contended that one could not act without the other. Yet because the supernatural was preeminent, the subjective was dependent on the objective force. From this perspective, he dismissed American Protestant theologians who emphasized subjective human action, because this diminished the motive force of the supernatural. Like other Roman Catholics described in the past two chapters, Brownson argued that Protestantism would lead to infidelity.[129]

As these intellectual lines were drawn between Catholicism and Protestantism, the structural outcome was a denominationalist Protestant establishment that posited Roman Catholicism as an oppositional force. In this way, Protestants coalesced and formed multidenominational organizations that used the Romanist threat as a quintessential adversary. To be sure, the confessional differences and rivalries among Protestant denominations, did not disappear. Presbyterians and Congregationalists sparred with Methodists and

---

[126] "Communicated for the Boston Pilot," *Boston Pilot*, 19 July 1845.
[127] A Missionary Priest [Hugh Quigley], *Cross and the Shamrock*, 233.
[128] "Grand Protestant Humbug," *Boston Pilot*, 1 May 1841.
[129] Orestes A. Brownson, *The Convert; or, Leaves from my Experience* (New York: Edward Dunigan and Brother, 1857).

Baptists throughout the period, just as they occasionally quarreled among themselves. Northern Christians argued with Christians in the South over the increasingly contentious issue of slavery. Religious offshoots outside the pale, Mormonism perhaps the best example, were often considered dangerous sects that might lead to the indifferentism and barbarism that alarmed the Protestant clergy. Nonetheless, Roman Catholicism provided a rival and sectarian force that enabled Protestants to put differences behind them and unite in some way. "How much soever," the *Boston Pilot* wrote in 1840, "the Presbyterian, the Baptist, the Methodist, and a hundred more may quarrel among themselves, they are all ready to unite in denouncing the Catholics."[130] If denominationalism fostered a willingness to jettison rituals and confessions particular to specific faiths, it also created a more unified Protestant whole, a whole that was solidified by the specter of the Roman Catholic Church.

Amid the promise of religious freedom and the threat of religious conflict, the variety of nonevangelical Protestant and Catholic immigrants had to find their place in the religious landscape.[131] Catholic immigrants were folded into the structure of the Roman Catholic Church, which in turn faced a series of conflicts between nationality groups for years to come. Many Protestant immigrant churches, on the other hand, were less concerned about the prospects of an epic battle with Roman Catholicism simply because they faced enough difficulty in creating a congregational and institutional structure that sustained their churches.[132]

Yet many Protestant denominations were drawn explicitly into alliances with American-born, evangelical Protestants. For example, the New England Society for the Promotion of Collegiate and Theological Education in the West, a Congregational and Presbyterian group, took an interest in Wittenburg College, a Lutheran institution of higher learning in Ohio.[133] Other Protestant religious bodies were in league with the American Home Missionary Society, including a variety of Lutheran and Reformed churches originating in Scandinavia, Germany, and the Netherlands. The Swedish Lutheran Augustana Synod, for example, was supported by the AHMS during the 1850s.[134] Joining the Calvinist leadership, these groups, as well as other American church organizations, labored both to convert the unwashed through their missionary efforts and to warn against the advance of Roman Catholicism.[135] As churches were swept into the maelstrom of religious conflict and were often forced to play roles in the debate about church

---

[130] "Common Schools and Catholic Children, *Boston Pilot*, 1 August 1840.

[131] Bratt, "Reorientation of American Protestantism," 75.

[132] Some churches, moreover, transplanted theological systems that fostered separation. These theological systems included the confessionalism that was fundamental to German Lutheran synods – such as the Missouri, Ohio, and Wisconsin synods – and, to a lesser degree, a variety of Scandinavian Lutheran organizations.

[133] William A. Kinnison, "German Lutherans in the Ohio Valley," *Queen City Heritage* 42 (1984): 8.

[134] Dag Blanck, *The Creation of an Ethnic Identity: Being Swedish America in the Augustana Synod, 1860–1917* (Carbondale: Southern Illinois University Press, 2006), 28.

[135] On these connections between churches, see Ray A. Billington, "Anti-Catholic Propaganda and the Home Missionary Movement, 1800–1860," *Mississippi Valley Historical Review* 22 (1935):

and nation, the predicament was less worrisome for the Protestants who ultimately exhibited their own streaks of anti-Catholicism and were able to ally with their American Protestant counterparts. Amid theological change, then, the lines between Catholicism and Protestantism were fully drawn. If there existed a spectrum of religious belief, a clear line of demarcation differentiated Protestants – of whatever stripe – from their Catholic counterparts. It was left ultimately to Catholics to contest their place in the American religious sphere.

Perhaps the most significant outcome of the battle for the conversion of the West was the failure to create a homogeneous society amid an ever more heterogeneous immigration. It became increasingly clear that missionaries would not convert the cacophonous masses that peopled the countryside and cities of America. The West, and by implication America, was not transformed into the idyllic Protestant environment of freedom and true belief; nor did it become the Catholic wasteland of Protestants' worst fears.

Edward Beecher confessed that he placed his "main dependence upon the power of God, acting through an enlightened and energetic public sentiment." Yet he also had come to realize by the mid-1850s that this was not enough. He dreaded the influence of nunneries, which he termed the "prisons of deluded and hopeless victims." He worried about the influence of the Church in the press and in politics. And he would not discount the use of the state to enact legislation that would combat the "pernicious influence of Romanism" on the American nation.[136] The conflict between the Protestant and Catholic leadership did not cease. But the power of God through conversion would have to be complemented by other more coercive forms of behavior in state and society. In short, the forging of an American homogeneity might not be a voluntary individual conversion but rather the result of pressure devised by institutions of the state, a topic to which we will next turn.

380–82. See also George M. Stephenson, "Nativism in the Forties and Fifties, with Special Reference to the Mississippi Valley," *Mississippi Valley Historical Review* 9 (1922): 185–202.
[136] Edward Beecher, *Papal Conspiracy Exposed*, 415–17.

4

Schools and the State

> Whenever we have insisted on retaining the Protestant Bible as a school-book, and making the use of it by the children of Catholic families, there has been good reason for complaining of our intolerance. But there is a much greater difficulty, I fear, and more invincible, on the other side.
>
> Horace Bushnell, 1853[1]

William Henry Seward and John Hughes, both of whom would puzzle over the place of religion in the nation's schools, had little in common before 1840. Seward, who was born in 1801 and grew to adulthood as a sickly youth in upstate New York, read the law and entered politics in 1824 as an opponent of Andrew Jackson. He became a leading member of New York's Whig Party and was elected governor of New York in 1838. In contrast, Hughes, who was four years older than Seward, emigrated at age nineteen from Ireland with his poverty-stricken family. He worked as a gardener before he was able to fulfill his aspiration of studying for the priesthood. Hughes rose rapidly to a position of influence in the American Catholic church. One year after Seward's election to the governorship, Hughes was appointed a bishop in New York City. Despite their dissimilar backgrounds, their careers crossed paths in 1840 when a crisis in public institutions evolved that laid bare both the place of Catholicism in society and the quandaries of religious belief in public venues. Each possessed his own goals; each utilized his own strategy. Yet when the dust had settled, the fate of the public school and the place of Roman Catholics within it had been clarified.

New York City was a very different place from the American West in the early nineteenth century. Although both were evolving areas with rapidly growing populations, New York was well on its way to becoming the premier urban space in the United States. A city of just under 100,000 in 1814, it was home to more than 300,000 people in 1840. In the next fifteen years, New York's population would double yet again. Brooklyn, a village of fewer than 4,000 people in 1814, grew to become a city of 200,000 in 1855. Many of these new residents

---

[1] Mary Bushnell Cheney, comp., *Life and Letters of Horace Bushnell* (New York: Harper and Brothers, 1880), 301.

arrived from Europe, and many of them had left regions dominated by Catholicism. In 1825, one-ninth of New York City's population was foreign born, a proportion that would be over one-third in 1845 and more than half in 1855. Unlike the foreign-born population in the West, immigrants from Ireland dominated the city's foreign-born population. One-quarter of the entire city in 1855 was Irish born.

Although New York resembled the West in its diversity and growth, its socio-economic structure was radically different. The city was a place of growing wealth and mounting poverty, where mansions that housed the commercial elite were located near the hovels of the poor, increasing numbers of whom had fled poor economic conditions in Europe. In such an environment, the role played by Catholicism in challenging Protestant hegemony and the resolution of this challenge differed from those in the West. As we saw in the last chapter, the West was often conceived of as a site where individuals might change themselves and where mass conversion might solve the problem of religious heterogeneity. The city, as exemplified by New York City, in contrast, required a new approach to addressing the varied religious American landscape. Here the state would play a more active role in coercing the members of society to change their behavior and belief. The aspiration of conversion, which roused the imagination of American churchmen in the West, was less viable in New York. Another path was necessary to create a sense of homogeneity in the American city. The homogenizing agent in the city, in short, would be enforced by the state rather than encouraged by religious organizations.

As a principle institution working toward this homogenizing end, the school was viewed as providing both a moral and a practical education for the youth of the city. This goal faced numerous challenges. For one, children of the poor often did not have the wherewithal to attend institutions of learning when they were forced to assist in the support of their families or were homeless themselves. The more important challenge for our purposes was the role of Catholicism in resisting these efforts to create an urban homogeneity. The schools were, in effect, overwhelmed by a growing number of immigrants who maintained at least a nominal Catholic faith and by a Church leadership that doubted the usefulness of an institution aimed at a societal homogeneity seemingly based on an imprecise Protestant Christianity.

As was true for the evangelical Protestants in the West, the outcome of this conflict was not as many of the actors had envisioned. It did not result in a unified, homogeneous institution that could tutor youth on moral citizenship in urban society as dreamt by the Protestant reformers. It did not provide for religiously separate and state-funded schools as imagined by the Catholic leadership. Rather, it ended with increasingly secularized public schools overseen by a growing educational bureaucracy that provided yet more impetus for the Catholic leadership to eschew participation in this very important public institution. And it fostered the creation of a parochial school system by members of the Roman Catholic Church that sought to separate their youth from the secular world. In the end, the Protestant leadership was able to circumvent the Catholic aim of creating a pillorized society in which civil society is structurally divided into religious groups segmented by state-run institutions. Yet the trajectory of the public school issue fostered the creation of a Catholic institutional structure around parish and school that resembled the very pillorization that the Protestant leadership had hoped to avoid. And the Protestant attempts at first aimed at the state institution of the school to enforce belief ironically ended with an outlook that expressed a preference for secularized content in education and, most important, calls for an iron wall of separation between church and state.

The Evolution of the Public Schools in the Early National Period

It may be an easy thing to make a Republic; but it is a very laborious thing to make Republicans; and woe to the republic that rests upon no better foundations than igno-rance, selfishness, and passion. Such a Republic may grow in numbers and in wealth. . . . But if such a Republic be devoid of intelligence, it will only the more closely resemble an obscene giant who has waxed strong in his youth . . . and who, therefore, is boastful of his bulk alone, and glories in the weight of his heel and in the destruction of his arm. Horace Mann, 1848[2]

The school became an increasingly relevant institution in the nineteenth century for a variety of reasons. As voting rights were expanded early in the century, an educated citizenry, so the logic went, was essential so that voters could make informed decisions. The school would also be a linchpin in spawning a knowl-edgeable population that could seize the economic opportunities in a growing economy. The school thus was a location where a moral education, which con-tributed to the creation of a virtuous citizenry in the republic, would be accom-panied by instruction in reading, writing, and ciphering. A republic was easy, the American educator Horace Mann reasoned; it was the creation of republicans that was the challenge.

Whereas education and edification in the colonial era were typically provided by church organizations or simply within households, they gradually were taken over by schools that were in turn increasingly overseen by the state. As both David Nasaw and Carl F. Kaestle point out, the earliest schools in major American cities in the early decades of the nineteenth century were based on charitable enter-prises underwritten by urban reformers and organized around an intricate system invented by the Englishman Joseph Lancaster. The Lancasterian system was based on a hierarchical structure in which older (and more skilled) students drilled the younger. Children were set in a competitive matrix where they could advance if they proved themselves proficient. This competition, in theory, engendered the motivation to succeed. Other advantages of the system were clear, not least the fact that the system was uncomplicated to implement and inexpensive to run.[3]

---

[2] Horace Mann, *Report No. 12 of the Massachusetts School Board*, in *The Republic and the School: Horace Mann on the Education of Free Men*, ed. Lawrence A. Cremin (New York: Teachers College Press, 1957), 92.

[3] Carl F. Kaestle, *Pillars of the Republic: Common Schools and American Society, 1780–1860* (New York: Hill and Wang, 1983), 40–46; David Nasaw, *Schooled to Order: A Social History of Public Schooling in the United States* (New York: Oxford University Press, 1979), 20–23.

Amid the republican spirit of the early national period, however, a group of reformers came to reject the Lancasterian system of charity as smacking of European aristocratic tradition. In its place, they worked to create the common school system, which was, Nasaw writes, "as republican and American as the charity schools were aristocratic and Old World."[4] The common schools developed differently in the major cities, but the trajectory of expansion was one where boards of volunteers increasingly oversaw the operation of the school system, which was supported by a combination of public funds and tuition paid by the children's parents. The schools themselves were to be open to all youth in the community, and the dream of the reformers was to provide a setting where the children of the poor would receive an education that would position them to succeed in the rapidly changing antebellum world.[5]

In such a situation, the moral foundation provided by educators was nearly as important as the subject matter in the classroom. To be sure, Americans had long considered moral training to be an essential component of an appropriate education. Yet the virtues of thrift, sobriety, and hard work took on greater currency in the antebellum urban economy. "The spirit of obedience and subordination," wrote the educator Charles Northend in 1853, "also tend to prepare [children] for higher spheres of usefulness and happiness."[6] More important for our purposes, the antebellum school pointedly cultivated an appreciation of the American nation and its republican foundation, in addition to a conventional Christian morality. The lessons of the virtues of republican America, moreover, were often embedded in the instruction on reading and writing.[7] The most notable case in point is the work of Horace Mann, a pioneer in the common school movement. Mann's hope was that children should be given enough religious education to be "compatible with the rights of others and with the genius of our government." He agreed that particular beliefs in politics and religion should be the purview of the family, but he also contended that when children reached adulthood they should possess "that inviolable prerogative of private judgment and of self-direction, which in a Protestant and a Republican country, is the acknowledged birthright of every human being."[8]

Some scholars have suggested that these efforts were integral to an attempt to control an increasingly heterogeneous population.[9] Social control or not, many educational efforts concerned the growing heterogeneity of American society

---

[4] Nasaw, *Schooled to Order*, 30.

[5] Kaestle, *Pillars of the Republic* 57–60; Nasaw, *Schooled to Order*, 34–39.

[6] Charles Northend, *The Teacher and the Parent* (1853), cited in Kaestle, *Pillars of the Republic*, 97.

[7] Kaestle argues that "a thoroughly American curriculum would help unify the language and culture of the new nation and wean America away from a corrupt Europe." *Pillars of the Republic*, 6, 90–103. See also Nasaw, *Schooled to Order*, 39–43.

[8] Cited in Neil G. McCluskey, S.J., ed., *Catholic Education in America: A Documentary History* (New York: Bureau of Publications, Teachers College, Columbia University, 1964), 6.

[9] See, for example, Michael B. Katz, *The Irony of Early School Reform: Educational Innovation in Mid-Nineteenth Century Massachusetts* (Cambridge, MA: Harvard University Press, 1968); and Nasaw, *Schooled to Order*, 19, 40.

and were aimed at fostering Americanization and therefore homogeneity in the republic. "Unless we educate our immigrants," Calvin Stowe, an educator and the husband of the author Harriet Beecher Stowe, argued in 1836, "they will be our ruin." It was essential, he continued, "to our national strength and peace, if not even to our national existence, that the foreigners who settle on our soil, should cease to be Europeans and become Americans."[10] The most efficient way to foster this transformation, he argued, was through the public schools.

In these circumstances, two increasingly intractable issues plagued those who directed the schools in the early nineteenth century. First, what was the basis of a moral education? Most among those in leadership roles in the early nineteenth century agreed that Protestant Christian belief undergirded American morality and therefore that instruction in elements of Christianity were essential if the minds of young Americans were to be properly shaped. Second, what was the relationship between schools and religion? Because of the establishment clause in the First Amendment, those who directed public schools were hesitant to support schools that were under the leadership of religious sects. The path taken by school leaders was to foster morality in the public schools through familiar Christian teachings but to avoid supporting schools that advocated the teaching of particularist tenets of Christian faiths. Children would therefore be edified by an overarching Protestantism that did not become mired in specific confessional difference and by an engagement with scripture that allegedly contained a basis of human truth.[11] This happy solution, many of the reformers agreed, would, in effect, educate youth in mechanical arts, as well as develop allegiance to the state, maintain proper piety, and contribute to the formation of an evolving national identity.[12]

This approach, which resembled the denominationalism that we encountered in the previous chapter, was a viable strategy when school officials and their clients could agree on the benefits of American republicanism, the English language, and Protestant Christianity. Yet many among the heterogeneous masses were not so sanguine about these efforts. In Pennsylvania, for example, parents – usually, but not always, German speakers – opposed the formation of a free school system because they wished their children to be schooled in their native tongue and according to the precepts of their faith. They maintained their localist orientation and struggled against attempts to create an overarching pan-Protestant, pan-American whole. Non-Catholic parochial schools, which were established well into the twentieth century, were potent examples of a rejection of American homogeneity.[13]

---

[10] Calvin Stowe, *Transactions of the Fifth Annual Meeting of the Western Literary Institute and College of Professional Teachers* (1836), cited in David Tyack, *Turning Points in American Educational History* (Waltham, MA: Blaisdell, 1967), 49–50.

[11] Kaestle, *Pillars of the Republic* 98–99; Nasaw, *Schooled to Order*, 42–43.

[12] See Timothy L. Smith, "Protestant Schooling and American Nationality, 1800–1850," *Journal of American History* 53 (1967): 679.

[13] Kaestle, *Pillars of the Republic*, 164–66; Nasaw, *Schooled to Order*, 54–55.

It was the protestations of a growing Catholic minority, however, that especially complicated the question of the content and approach of the American schools. Not surprisingly, the Catholic leadership, while it recognized the need for schools, rejected the conflation of Protestantism and republicanism. Likewise, this conflation was a particularly compelling example of the hazards of denominationalism within the schools because of a clear difference between the denominationalism discussed in the last chapter and the efforts at creating a homogeneous school system. If Protestant denominations used the Catholic Church as a means to highlight their theological similarities, the public school sought to incorporate Catholic children, who would be instructed on the pieties of a generic American Protestantism. The Catholic leadership opposed these undertakings, setting in motion a conflict that would have profound outcomes for the Roman Catholic Church in the United States and for state-led institutions aimed at advancing the creation of a homogeneous American whole.

This is not to say that the leaders of the Roman Catholic Church rejected the need for education. The pastoral letters of the American hierarchy, the reflections of the American bishops that were broadcast to the faithful beginning in 1829, indicate the persistent interest in education. In their first pastoral letter, the bishops noted "how important, how interesting, how awful, how responsible a charge" was the education of youth. They urged parents to educate their child, "teaching him first to seek the kingdom of God and His justice," as well as "teach him to be industrious, to be frugal, to be humble and fully resigned" to God's will.[14] It was true, the bishops continued, that securing the spiritual concerns could be "far better attained under the parent's roof." Still, when children attended proper schools that "cultivate[d] the seed which [parents] have sown," they would be edified to ensure that "by their filial piety and steady virtue, they may be to you the staff of your old age, the source of your consolation, and reward in a better world." Catholic schools were all the more necessary, the letter continued, because state schools often demeaned Catholicism. "The school-boy can scarcely find a book in which some one or more of our institutions or practices is not exhibited far otherwise than it really is," the bishops wrote, "and greatly to our disadvantage."[15]

The pastoral letter of 1840 was more belligerent about common schools and more persistent about the need for schools run by the Church. The bishops expressed doubt that reading the King James Version of the Bible, "this sacred volume as an ordinary class book," was beneficial. Parents, moreover, were warned against common schools, which offered reading material that covertly and insidiously sought "to misrepresent our principles, to distort our tenets, to vilify our practices and to bring contempt upon our Church and its members." Ultimately, it was commonly expected in the public schools "that our distinctive principles of religious belief and practice should be yielded to the demands of

[14] Peter Guilday, ed., *The National Pastorals of the American Hierarchy, 1792–1919* (Washington, DC: National Catholic Welfare Council, 1923), 24–26.
[15] Ibid., 25–26, 28.

those who thought proper to charge us with error."[16] Catholic leaders were adamant in their recognition of the role of the school but only insofar as it did not damage their religious mission. And the less irenic tone in 1840 than that offered eleven years prior was no doubt the result of the developments that year in New York City, a topic to which we will now turn.

The New York City School Controversy

If the Public Schools could have been constituted on a principle which could have secured a perfect NEUTRALITY of influence on the subject of religion, then we should have no reason to complain. But this has not been done, and we respectfully submit that it is impossible. The cold indifference with which it is required that all religions shall be treated in those schools ... form against our religion a combination of influences, prejudicial to our religion, and to whose action it would be criminal in us to expose our children at such an age. John Hughes, 1841[17]

The momentous school controversy beginning in New York City in 1840 was a controversy that would have national implications for decades to come.[18] The incident that triggered the controversy was political in nature. Seward, who assumed the governorship of New York as a Whig in the wake of the Panic of 1837, wished to attract the growing immigrant vote to his slate. His party in New York City had not accorded itself well with the immigrant population, which traditionally had been strong supporters of Democracy. As a minority party in the city tainted with connections to an aristocratic past, it had enjoyed some electoral success when it allied itself with nativist movements in the mid-1830s. Yet Seward and his principal advisor, Thurlow Reed, recognized the need to broaden the Whig appeal. When he assumed the governorship, Seward

---

[16] Ibid., 133–34.

[17] "Of the Roman Catholics, to their Fellow Citizens of the City and State of New York," *Boston Pilot*, 29 August 1840.

[18] The New York City school crisis is amply documented by William Oland Bourne, *History of the Public School Society of the City of New York. With Portraits of the Presidents of the Society* (New York: Wm. Wood, 1870). Many historians have examined the crisis from a variety of perspectives. Notable examples include Diane Ravitch, *The Great School Wars, New York City, 1805–1973* (New York: Basic Books, 1974); Ray Allen Billington, *The Protestant Crusade, 1800–1860* (New York: Macmillan, 1938); John Webb Pratt, *Religion, Politics, and Diversity: The Church-State Theme in New York History* (Ithaca, NY: Cornell University Press, 1967); Edward M. Connors, *Church-State Relationships in Education in the State of New York* (Washington, DC: Catholic University of America Press, 1951); Vincent P. Lannie, *Public Money and Parochial Education: Bishop Hughes, Governor Seward, and the New York School Controversy* (Cleveland: Press of Case Western University, 1968); Philip Hamburger, *Separation of Church and State* (Cambridge, MA: Harvard University Press, 2002); Elwyn A. Smith, *Religious Liberty in the United States: The Development of Church-State Thought Since the Revolutionary Era* (Philadelphia: Fortress Press, 1972); Timothy L. Smith, "Protestant Schooling and American Nationality, 1800–1850," *Journal of American History* 53 (1967): 679–95; and Glyndon G. Van Deusen, "Seward and the School Question Reconsidered," *Journal of American History* 52 (1965): 313–19.

attempted to cultivate the loyalty of the immigrant population by pledging to extend to them the full rights of citizenship.

This pledge fit together well with the system of common education, which was also one of Seward's principal concerns. Recognizing the importance of the schools and the fact that they failed to serve many children among the immigrant population, Seward resolved to offer a plan that would improve access to the schools and win the immigrant vote. Seward's proposal, offered in a message to the New York legislature in early 1840, observed that "the children of foreigners, found in great numbers in our populous cities and towns ... are too often deprived of the advantages of our system of public education, in consequence of prejudices arising from difference in language and religion."[19] Because "the public welfare is as deeply concerned in their education as in that of our own children," Seward recommended that schools be established in which the pupils were "instructed by teachers speaking the same language with [*sic*] themselves and professing the same faith." The United States was a land open to the "oppressed of every nation," so it followed that such generosity should be matched "by qualifying their children for the high responsibilities of citizenship."[20] A message that reflected Seward's true concern for education as a means of moral and practical training, Catholics in New York saw it as a clear signal from the governor that changes in the school system might be afoot.

Seward's message was not the first foray into the question of sectarianism in the schools. The Free School Society had been formed in 1805 principally to provide schooling opportunities to poor children who lacked church affiliation. Whereas well-to-do children attended private schools and their church-going counterparts went to religious schools, an increasingly large segment of youths was unschooled. Under this patchwork system, the lines between sectarian schools and public schools were not clear-cut. Some sectarian schools in fact were provided state support. This arrangement ended following a controversy with the Bethel Baptist Church, beginning in 1822. When the state legislature authorized this Baptist congregation to use its surplus state funds to construct additional schools, the Free School Society protested and commenced a campaign to restrict state aid to all church schools. The ensuing debate framed many of the questions that would be reignited in 1840. Spokesmen for the Free School Society contended that the clergy should not control public money and that New York State must "save untouched the sacred principle of our constitution, that church and state shall not be united."[21] The church school leadership countered that their use of state funds was not sectarian in nature but was simply an effort to educate children, an effort in the best interests of the state. In 1824, the state legislature decided to turn all of its school funds over to the city's Common Council, which one year later voted to cease allotment of these funds to religious schools.[22]

---

[19] Bourne, *History of the Public School Society of the City of New York*, 179.
[20] Ibid., 179.
[21] *Albany Argus*, 9 November 1824, cited in Pratt, *Religion, Politics, and Diversity*, 167.
[22] Bourne, *History of the Public School Society of the City of New York*, 48–75.

Significantly, if funding to religious schools ceased in 1825, the Christian content in the public schools endured, a circumstance about which Catholics were well aware. The first notable Catholic protest against the religious content in the public schools was lodged by Bishop John Dubois in 1834. In his complaint, phrased in a deferential tone, he assured the Board of Trustees of the Public School Society that "he is influenced by no sectarian motive, no views of proselytism, and that he is as much averse to encroach upon the conscience of others, as to see others encroach upon his." He even placed some blame on his flock and hoped that the changes he recommended would be "sufficient to ensure the confidence of Catholic parents, and remove the false excuses of those who cover their neglect under the false pretext of religion."[23] The suggested changes, moreover, were modest. Bishop Dubois asked that a school near his parish of St. Patrick's be staffed with a Catholic teacher; that the school might be used for religious instruction after school hours; that anti-Catholic passages in the schoolbooks be expunged, and that he be able to visit the school periodically. The Public School Society (as it was now called) rejected the proposals as "inconsistent" with the society's constitution because they provided "certain privileges for one sect" that had not been granted to others.[24] The matter was quietly dropped.

Six years later, the terrain differed not only in Albany but in New York City as well. For one thing, nativist agitation in the late 1830s roiled the waters of the city. For another, John Hughes, a much more pugnacious and insightful prelate than his predecessors, assumed the Catholic leadership. Under his guidance, a conflict erupted that would transform the school system and profoundly influence state politics for years to come. Hughes was abroad when the controversy first took form and even before he returned from his European journey, the trustees of Catholic schools in New York, taking a cue from Seward's address in Albany, submitted a petition to the Common Council of the city for monetary assistance. The Public School Society responded that such a request was both unconstitutional – "because it is utterly at variance with the letter and spirit of our chartered rights, and with the genius of our political institutions" – and inexpedient. The Democratically controlled Common Council, in a bind because it did not wish to alienate its Irish Catholic supporters, upheld the Public School Society's decision on the high ground of broad principle. "The theory and practice of our happy and equal form of government," it argued, "is to protect every religious persuasion, and support none." The United States, the council continued, was governed with a political compact that "divorced the unholy alliance between Church and State." Moreover, the schools performed an assimilative role in society. The sooner immigrants "abandon any unfavorable prejudices with which they may arrive among us," it contended, "and become familiar with our language, and reconciled to our institutions and habits, the better it will be for them, and for the country of their adoption." If this were true,

---

[23] Ibid., 160–61.
[24] Ibid., 162–63.

"the best interests of all will be alike promoted by having their children mingle with ours in the public seminaries of learning."[25]

Despite this initial setback, the Catholic leadership was undaunted. Hughes, who had by then returned from Europe, now took control and was instrumental in sparking a controversy that was far more volatile than that Seward likely had envisioned. Throughout much of the year, Hughes led protest meetings that were held every two weeks in the basement of St. James Church. He was also instrumental in writing memorials that became the bases for Catholics' complaints. In one missive, the Catholic disputants agreed with the Common Council that they were American, but argued that the public school did not have the salutary influences that its advocates supposed. On July 27, 1840, Hughes submitted a resolution that contended that the public schools tutored their children under "a system of free-thinking and practical irreligion" and that the Catholic disputants would not be worthy of their "proud distinction" as American citizens if they did not protest.[26]

One month later, the Catholics were even more combative. "We are Americans and American citizens," the "Address of the Roman Catholics to Their Fellow-Citizens" stated, and "we hold, therefore, the same ideas of our rights that you hold of yours." Perhaps the common school system had been designed to plant the principles of knowledge and virtue in youth, but it now was a dismal failure. Here the Catholic disputants utilized the dilemma that the Public School Society had created for itself: were the schools entirely secular and therefore Godless, or did they impart moral knowledge and were therefore sectarian? "Is enlightened villainy so precious in the public eye," they asked, "that science is to be cultivated, whilst virtue is neglected, and religion, its only adequate groundwork, is formally and authoritatively proscribed?"[27] The schools, by rejecting Christianity in all its forms, were "favorable to the sectarianism of infidelity, and opposed only to that of positive Christianity."[28] For Catholics, the practical problem with the schools was that they were not nonsectarian, but rather were patently anti-Catholic, both in content and in practice. The schools maintained a particularist slant in practice (the reading of scripture from the Protestant King James Version of the Bible without comment, which contradicted the "prevailing theory" of the Catholic tradition) and in content (schoolbooks that impugned Catholics in the past and present).

In their plea, the Catholic disputants suggested that the evils of infidelity could be mitigated by a sort of home rule. In contending for "*liberty of conscience and freedom of education,*" concepts that the Public School Society would have appreciated, the disputants argued that parents had the right of superintending the education of their children. The present situation in the schools, where religious rights were violated and where "the thickening ranks of infidelity"

[25] Ibid., 185.
[26] Ibid., 188.
[27] "Address of the Roman Catholics to Their Fellow-Citizens of the City and State of New York," in Bourne, *History of the Public School Society of the City of New York*, 332.
[28] Ibid., 332–33.

were rife, was unworkable. "Much as we dread ignorance," they concluded, "we dread this even more." The Catholic address finished with a warning about the erosion of rights generally. "Should the professors of some weak or unpopular religion be oppressed to-day," they wrote, "the experiment may be repeated tomorrow on some other." A process would unfold where the precepts taught in the common school would become the common religion and where all Christian sectarianism would be excluded. In this scenario, the "friends of liberty throughout the civilized world" would be aggrieved and the tyrants would celebrate as "nations from afar [beheld] with astonishment [the American flag's] bright stars faded, and its stripes turned into scorpions."[29] The school question, in Hughes's mind, was a decisive moment in the realization of American freedom.[30]

The Public School Society responded to the Catholic onslaught in a meeting held at City Hall on October 29, 1840, before the entire Common Council and a huge crowd aroused by the ongoing debate. Following an extended presentation by Hughes, which consumed over three hours, Theodore Sedgwick and Hiram Ketchum, both of whom were attorneys and members of the Public School Society, rose to speak. Sedgwick argued, in affirming the denominationalist model discussed earlier, first that the state had the right to interpose itself between child and parent because the education of youth was an outcome desired by the people of New York. Sedgwick next asked what type of education should be pursued by the schools. One possibility was a purely secular education, akin to that which a master provides his apprentice. A second option was a moral education, the instruction of "those fundamental principles of morals about which there is no dispute ... in any part of Christendom." The third type was a religious education that incorporated dogmatic and sectarian teaching. New York's public schools, Sedgwick contended, followed the second model and provided the moral grounding, including basic tenets of correct behavior, without becoming sectarian. "Mankind has never disagreed as to the propriety of robbing, or cheating, or bearing false witness," he argued, "but about these dogmas, these doctrines, the race has been cutting each other's throats for the last ten centuries" and these were the "prodigious evils that American statesmen have striven to avoid."[31] Claiming that he had no opposition to religious schools, Sedgwick stated simply that such an approach was not relevant to the mission of the public schools.

Ketchum reiterated Sedgwick's points with a sharper edge. Criticizing Hughes as "a mitred gentlemen" who descended "into the public arena," Ketchum chided the prelate for sullying himself in appealing "to the popular prejudice or passion" to influence what should be a measured decision of the "public system" of

[29] Ibid., 338.

[30] Elsewhere, Hughes made a more invidious observation that reflected his Irish past. "We are citizens when they come to gather the taxes," he contended, "but we are Roman Catholics when we look for a share of the fund just distributed." Ravitch, *Great School Wars*, 45, citing Vincent Peter Lannie's biography of Hughes. Vincent Peter Lannie, "Archbishop John Hughes and the Common School Controversy, 1840–1842" (Ph.D. diss., Teachers College, Columbia University, 1963), 150.

[31] Bourne, *History of the Public School Society of the City of New York*, 228–29, 237.

education. Neither could Bible reading in the school, he continued, be abandoned. "The institutions of liberty and the altars of piety," Ketchum averred, "have sprung up in the path of that translated Bible," and "wherever that translated Bible has gone, popular institutions have risen." Alluding to a common criticism of Catholicism, Ketchum argued that "all those glorious principles" conspicuous in the United States stemmed from the Bible and that "darkness and despotism" reigned in those realms where the Bible was forbidden the laity. Ketchum then concluded with an appeal to American homogeneity. Willing to grant an oppressed immigrant asylum in the United States, he nonetheless asked that the immigrant "give America his heart." Those who came "with an Irish heart" should "stand up by America" so that the land of his adoption is also the land of his children. And he prayed that those children, in part because of the public schools, would also be instilled with "pure American feelings," presumably replete with the assimilation of the virtues of liberty and piety.[32]

With both sides far apart, the New York media fanned the flames. Newspapers aimed at an American-born Protestant audience, such as the New York *Morning Herald*, the *Commercial Advertiser*, and the *Journal of Commerce* all doggedly opposed Hughes. Any grant of special privilege, the latter argued, would serve as "a reward for [Catholics'] bigotry and ignorance."[33] The nativist press, not surprisingly, was even more shrill. The *American Protestant Vindicator* charged that New York's ignorant and illiterate Catholic population was manipulated by a crafty clerical leadership. The broadsheet, also tapping into conventional fears of Rome, claimed that this was an attempt "to take away our children's funds and bestow them on the subjects of Rome, the creatures of a foreign hierarchy."[34] In response, Catholics waged their own war of words in print. To drum up support, the Catholic clergy launched the *Freeman's Journal* on Independence Day of 1840. In the second issue, John Power, a vicar-general under Hughes's leadership, condemned the public schools as deist, sectarian, and anti-Catholic, and argued that reading the King James Version of the Bible without comment in the schools surreptitiously privileged "Protestant principles."[35]

Even in the early stages of the debate, the principal positions of each side had been established. Hughes's argument implicitly posited a pluralist and pillorized urban society in which religious bodies possessed the power to maintain schools under the auspices of the state. At least publicly mindful of children's need of edification and learning, Hughes agreed with many Americans that religious training was an essential component of schooling the young. In this pillorized world, Hughes staked two claims. First, the family and church played essential roles, as was expressed by the pastoral letter of 1829, in tutoring the young. Second,

[32] Ibid., 240, 246, 247.
[33] *New York Journal of Commerce*, 26 February 1840, cited in Connors, *Church-State Relationships in Education*, 28.
[34] *American Protestant Vindicator*, 23 December 1840, 5 August 1840, cited in Connors, *Church-State Relationships in Education*, 28.
[35] *New York Freeman's Journal*, 11 July 1840, cited in Ravitch, *Great School Wars* 45.

the teachings of the Roman Catholic Church could not be delivered piecemeal with vague moral instruction devoid of religious guidance. His plea, and the pleas of his Catholic allies, was based on the principle of religious freedom that they claimed was denied them by the Public School Society.

In contrast, according to the Public School Society, schools provided a moral grounding without resorting to particular religious confessions. Clearly attempting to integrate Catholic children by excising objectionable material, the Public School Society nonetheless hewed to a belief that a broad pan-Christian instruction would provide children with a moral education that was not offensive to their Catholic neighbors. Theirs was a hope that the homogenizing agency that was the public school would both teach children broadly and incorporate them into a unified civil society. And a pillar of their argument was the importance of the separation of church and state in schools and elsewhere.

Yet Hughes was temporizing. The schoolbook committee earnestly attempted to correct the wrongs in the content of the school readings by meeting with the Catholic authorities and supplying them with textbooks for their evaluation. When the committee contacted Hughes in September 1840 to request passages that should be expunged, he replied that he had "many and incessant duties" that left him "insufficient leisure for the purpose" and that he had requested the schoolbooks to build his case against the public schools themselves.[36] Diane Ravitch argues, in fact, that "Hughes had no intention of making the Society's schools more tolerable for Catholic children."[37]

With both sides intransigent and with the rhetoric intensifying, the debate moved to the political realm, with profound results for all the actors involved. Seward paid a political price at the polls in the fall elections of 1840. Although he maintained the governorship, riding on the coattails of Whig presidential candidate William Henry Harrison, his margin of victory was half what it had been in 1838 before the school crisis surfaced. By all accounts, the staying power of both the nativist elements in the Whig Party and the Irish-Democratic coalition resulted in no movement favorable to Seward. To his credit, however, Seward was resolved to move ahead with school reform and he again focused on the question in his third annual message to the state on January 5, 1841. In his address, Seward pointed to divisions that increasingly cleaved society and posited a liberal solution, centered on the schools, to smooth over differences. With increased immigration, "mutual jealousies" arose, the consequences of which were seen in "the separation and alienation of classes having common interests; in the misfortunes of the weaker, in apprehensions of insecurity on the part of the stronger, and in the demoralization of portions of both." His plan of education would elevate the immigrants' social condition and lead to "the assimilation of their habits, principles, and opinions with our own." As for the different beliefs

---

[36] Bourne, *History of the Public School Society of the City of New York*, 345. The schoolbooks ultimately were revised by the schoolbook committee itself with little input from the Catholic clergy.
[37] Ravitch, *Great School Wars*, 51.

that might be taught in the schools, he fully believed that "even error may be safely tolerated where reason is left free to combat it."[38]

Because the Common Council, only six days after Seward's speech, remained steadfast and again rejected the Catholic petition, it was clear that the next chapter of the conflict would transpire in Albany and that the political stakes for both the Whigs and Democrats would increase. Despite Seward's apparent losses, his long-term strategy put the Democrats, who were in power in New York, in an untenable position vis-à-vis the schools and the Catholic voters. Hughes, who by now had allied himself with Seward, mobilized his laity. The Central Executive Committee on the Common Schools was formed, which coordinated the organization of local committees and gathered signatures on petitions protesting the state of the New York City schools. On March 29, 1841, this petition, containing some seven thousand signatures, was presented to the state senate as a "Memorial of Citizens of New York for an amendment of the common school laws." After its presentation, the senate, which was well aware of the political volatility of the issue, quickly referred the petition to John Spencer, Seward's secretary of state and the ex officio state superintendent of common schools, and requested his recommendations.

If some senators hoped that this referral would diminish the controversy, they were sadly mistaken. Spencer, who was a close ally of Seward, studied the controversy and within one month presented his recommendations replete with an extended discussion of the background of the controversy.[39] His report largely confirmed the arguments of the Catholic disputants. He asserted, first, that "in a country where the great body of our fellow-citizens recognize [*sic*] the fundamental truths of Christianity, public sentiment would be shocked by the attempt to exclude all instruction of a religious nature from the public schools." If there must be religious education in the schools, he continued, "it is impossible to conceive how [the leading principles of Christianity] can be taught ... without inculcating what is peculiar to some one or more denominations, and denied by others."[40] As Ravitch puts it, Spencer recognized the Catholics' argument that "nonsectarianism was a form of sectarianism."[41] If religion was a necessary element of education, Spencer argued that local communities should be the agents to adopt the appropriate religion in their own particular cases. With the Public School Society in control, the schools in New York City were in fact Protestant. And given the low enrollments in the city, the failure to educate large numbers of children in both moral and practical arts was an outrage.

Spencer's solution, then, was to gut the power of the Public School Society and to provide funds in each ward of the city for schools that reflected the dominant faith. If the local communities wished to maintain the schools already existent under the auspices of the Public School Society, so be it. But if they

---

[38] Bourne, *History of the Public School Society of the City of New York*, 354, 356.
[39] Ibid., 356–73.
[40] Ibid., 362, 363.
[41] Ravitch, *Great School Wars* 63.

rejected these schools, the ward-level community could establish their own schools and be provided funds from the state to administer them. In Spencer's mind, decentralization and home rule would be a much more satisfactory system than the homogeneity enforced by the rigid and centralized Public School Society.

The Public School Society and its allies, however, would not go quietly into the night. On May 8, Ketchum, speaking for the society, gave an extended speech that focused on the facts that the petitioners were dissatisfied Roman Catholics and that the issue had been fairly adjudicated by the legislative bodies of New York City. He noted the "tenacity of the Catholics" and the fact that the petition sent to Albany initially was presented by "Catholics" and that only later did they call themselves "citizens," a wry reference to the background of the complainants. He rejected the logic and evidence of Spencer's report and observed that ward school districts were also impracticable because they abused the rights of those in the religious minority within them. Imagine, he suggested, a school district where the majority affirmed the doctrines of Tom Paine or "that my Savior was an impostor." The majority would rule, he concluded, to the detriment of the minority who disagreed with these beliefs.[42] A war of words in the New York media ensued. Ketchum's speech was published in New York, which encouraged nativists to accuse a tyrannical Catholic clergy of mobilizing an ignorant laity to attempt to subjugate the state to the church. Anti-Catholic rhetoric also sullied deliberations in the state legislature, and the heated debate convinced the majority of the senate to defer the issue until after the fall elections.

The political stakes were raised once again as the November election, which would elect two state senators and thirteen assemblymen from New York City, loomed. Protestant groups mobilized on behalf of the Public School Society. The American Protestant Union, under the leadership of Samuel F. B. Morse, was formed to resist any advances in the public funding of Catholic schools. New York City's Whigs, fearful of an anti-Catholic backlash, abandoned Seward and nominated a ticket that opposed changes to the public school system. It was at this point that Hughes made a fateful decision. On October 29, four days before the election, he called a meeting at Carroll Hall, where he advocated the creation of a ticket favorable to Catholic interests. The slate included ten Democrats who were sympathetic to the Catholic cause and three independent Catholics; it had no Whigs. "Each name," reported the *Freeman's Journal*, "was received with the most deafening and uproarious applause and three terrific cheers were given at the close." Hughes then delivered a lengthy speech in which he told his Catholic listeners that "you now, for the first time, find yourselves in the position to vote ... for yourselves." When Catholics stood up for themselves, he continued, he was certain that "public men will soon come to your aid!" He asked a series of rhetorical questions – "will you be united?" – that moved his audience to "tremendous applause." When he concluded with the question, "will you not flinch?," the scene that ensued, according to the *Freeman's Journal*, was "indescribable and

---

[42] Bourne, *History of the Public School Society of the City of New York*, 373–402 (quotations from 384, 389).

exceeded all the enthusiastic and almost frenzied displays of passionate feeling we have sometimes witnessed at Irish meetings."[43]

Passionate feeling quickly was expressed beyond the Catholic community. Excepting the Catholic press, most of New York's newspapers condemned a slate of candidates based on religious confession. James Gordon Bennett, editor of the New York *Morning Herald*, was the most uncompromising. In addition to attacking Seward as a manipulator of Hughes, Bennett advised Catholics to "abandon the impudent priest and his separate ticket" and warned the city to be prepared for religious violence "of the darkest Popish ages of Roman religious tyranny."[44]

The election results were ominous for nativist New Yorkers like Bennett. Although the independent Catholic candidates garnered some two thousand votes, the ten Democratic candidates, who were victorious, received Catholic support. Those on the Democratic slate who had *not* gotten Hughes's support, moreover, lost to their Whig opponents. Despite the failure of a purely Catholic candidate to win a seat in the legislature, then, a bloc of Catholic voters seemingly held the balance of power in the city, a fact that was not lost on the Tammany Hall leadership.[45]

Democrats were swept into office throughout the state, and they now faced the school issue as the majority party. For two years, the Democrats had attacked Seward's efforts to introduce sectarianism in the schools and now some of them owed their seat in the legislature to Catholic voters who favored sectarian schools. These Catholic voters, moreover, held meetings following the election, whose upshot was to remind these Democratic lawmakers that Catholic voters would continue to agitate for Catholic schools. When Seward again called for a reorganization of the schools in an 1842 address, the Democrats responded with a proposal authored by William B. Maclay, a New York Democrat. Using antimonopoly rhetoric that appealed to his Democratic constituency, Maclay criticized the Public School Society as an "irresponsible private chartered company." He also concluded that the Public School Society "failed to accomplish the great object of its establishment – the universal education of the children in the city of New York." In effect, Maclay's bill accepted Spencer's earlier formulation by proposing that New York City's wards be considered as separate towns and that each ward should elect its own school administration. Allies of the Public School Society leapt to its defense. The Maclay report was condemned; a petition drive was begun; and the nativist and non-Catholic sectarian press denounced an imminent Catholic victory abetted by intimidation.

Events now moved quickly. On March 21, 1842, Maclay's bill passed the New York State Assembly overwhelmingly, 65–16. The bill's major hurdle,

---

[43] *Freeman's Journal,* 30 October 1841, cited in Bourne, *History of the Public School Society of the City of New York,* 373–402, 480.

[44] Cited in Ravitch, *Great School Wars,* 69.

[45] Bourne, *History of the Public School Society of the City of New York,* 479, 481 (Bourne provides the Catholic slate and election results).

however, was the more conservative New York State Senate. All the senators from New York City, two Whigs and two Democrats, opposed it. To make the bill more palatable to the senate, it was amended to prohibit grants of public funds to any district in which "any religious sectarian doctrine or tenet shall be taught, inculcated, or practiced" and it was the responsibility of all school officials to make certain that religion was not taught in the schools.[46] Unlike the Maclay version, which would have allowed religious education in public schools, this proviso prohibited sectarian instruction in any school. Because Hughes began again to mobilize his Catholic constituency with a Catholic slate for the April 12 elections, he forced the Democrats' hand and the bill passed the New York Senate on April 8, one day after Hughes's slate was announced. After the assembly approved the amended bill, Seward signed it on April 11, one day before the New York City elections.

Reaction to the new law was predictable. Election day was punctuated by street violence between groups of Catholics and groups of nativists. Hughes's home was stoned by an angry mob, which entered the house, smashed windows, and destroyed furniture. In panic, Mayor Robert Morris dispatched the militia to protect the city's Catholic churches. The mainstream New York City press mourned the passage of the bill. The *New York Observer* opined, in an editorial entitled "The Triumph of the Roman Catholics," that "the dark hour is at hand. ... People must only trust in God to be saved from the beast."[47] The *New York Tribune* detected a purely political strategy by Democrats of success- fully bringing "back the stray sheep to the fold of Tammany."[48]

The public school crisis in New York City produced a variety of outcomes, each of which was profound in its own way. For one thing, political party coalitions were shaken by the jockeying for electoral support. The Whigs in upstate New York, led by Seward, were attempting to break the hold of the Democratic Party on the Irish vote. They recognized the challenges that their party faced in the future amid a growing immigration to a growing metropolis. For their part, the leader- ship of the Democratic Party appreciated the need to incorporate Catholicism into their appeal to the Irish immigrant vote, an understanding made all the more urgent by the outcome of Hughes's ploy to create a Catholic slate of candidates. When those Democrats not endorsed as part of the Catholic slate of candidates lost the election in 1842, it became clear to political leaders, not to mention to Catholics themselves, that the Catholic voting bloc held the balance of power in New York City elections.

Perhaps the most important political outcome was Hughes's appeal itself. The specter of a political party based on religious confession promised a reorientation of American politics in profound ways. This strategy, of course, was not the first time that a religious leader had advocated religious parties. Ezra Stiles Ely made

[46] Ibid., 524.
[47] *New York Observer*, 16 April 1842, cited in Billington, *Protestant Crusade*, 154.
[48] *New York Tribune*, 11 April 1842, cited in Pratt, *Religion, Politics, and Diversity*, 188.

a similar call in 1828 to elect Christian leaders.[49] Likewise, the creation of the Catholic slate was not the only or the first change that fostered growing Catholic interest in affairs of the state. The creation of the *Freeman's Journal*, a Catholic newspaper that intervened on matters religious and political for years to come, was an earlier outgrowth of the public school controversy. Because the Catholic slate was organized by a Roman Catholic prelate, however, it was freighted with even more ominous signs to many Americans. The Catholic involvement in politics led nativists to develop political institutions that would contest the growing Catholic power in the state. Beginning with riots that saw the ransacking of Hughes's home, the nativist element would grow in power in the years to come.[50]

The consequences for the schools were equally meaningful. The sequence of events ultimately ended in the loss of power for the Public School Society and the advent of a school system run more centrally by city government. This transformation was part of a professionalization of key urban institutions – changes in the police and fire departments occurred in this era as well – that betokened the transition to the modern city. Significantly, those changes that stemmed from the efforts of Catholics regarding the schools resulted in an increasingly secularized public school system. If the Bible could not be read, morality was to be instilled at best as a system of beliefs divorced from religion. In an outcome that Protestants and Catholics alike would have resisted some decades previously, the New York schools at midcentury increasingly separated themselves from religious teaching. Ironically, the participation of Catholics in the school debate fostered both a secularization of the schools and an accelerated division of church and state. And this secularization – Hughes would call it a trend toward infidelity – only made the need greater for Catholics to develop their own system of schools that provided religious instruction.

By all appearances, Hughes's intervention in the common school debate was a failure. If the Public School Society lost power, the Catholic Church did not succeed in gaining monetary assistance from the state for its parochial schools. Rather, the Church was forced to fund an increasingly expensive system, a requirement made even more necessary because of the perception that the public schools embraced a growing infidelity. Yet despite these monetary costs, Hughes's efforts were in many ways a success. A Catholic community was fostered in which the church and the school were imposing institutions that defined the community itself. Both in the celebration of mass and in the classroom, Catholics were made aware of their distinctive position in the United States and their special responsibilities. A pillorized society, which was the intent of the Catholic leadership, in effect came into existence.

As is so often the case when a controversy roils the waters, then, there were few apparent winners as the crisis drew to a close. Seward had failed to bring

[49] Ezra Stiles Ely, *The Duty of Christian Freemen to Elect Christian Rulers: A Discourse Delivered on the Fourth of July, 1827, in the Seventh Presbyterian Church, in Philadelphia* (Philadelphia: Printed by William F. Geddes, 1828).
[50] Billington, *Protestant Crusade*, 154.

about a realignment of New York's voters. If anything, the Catholic voters were more firmly in the Democratic camp following the controversy because the Democrats pushed through the Maclay Bill. Seward personally paid an enduring political price. Not only did he soon leave the governorship of New York, but his reputation as a friend of the immigrant in many accounts diminished his viability for the Republican presidential nomination in 1860. The Public School Society lost as well. Although the new law sanctioned its power to continue operating schools in New York City, it had to solicit money from the newly formed Board of Education. In the following ten years, the popularly elected board gradually eroded the society's authority until the society in 1853 ceded its property to and merged with the board and thereafter ceased to exist. As for Hughes and the Catholic schools, the apparent victory was pyrrhic. The newly elected Board of Education was dominated by anti-Catholics; in fact, its first superintendent, William L. Stone, was a prominent nativist who was instrumental in bringing the lurid tale of Maria Monk, the escaped nun, to light. Daily Bible reading became official school policy, and the board ruled in 1844 that reading from the King James Version without comment did not constitute sectarianism.[51] If the intellectual war at heart was a contest between the religious rights of Roman Catholics and the separation of church and state advocated by Protestants, the latter clearly had won. And the public institutions increasingly hewed to the understanding that religious instruction should be excluded from them. If they were to imbue their children with religious principles, Catholics realized that they would have to do so in parochial schools, a system that they set about to create with increasing diligence in the ensuing decades.

The Pillorized Catholic World

You will, perhaps, have to live with Protestants all your lifetime. They are very numerous, you see, and we are few. Besides, we are poor and our Catholics depend on them, in most cases for a living. You will be very fortunate, more fortunate than the greater number of Catholics are, if you can get along in the world without coming in contact, at every step, with men who do not know what your religion is and who hate it. Rev. John T. Roddan, 1851[52]

The school crisis in New York City, of course, was the result of a confluence of powerful personalities in fluid circumstances striving to change the city's educational structure. All of the actors involved hoped to improve the relationships between religious organizations and state institutions and, in the end, to improve the schooling of New York's youth. These questions also were taken up in other places throughout the United States and were addressed in a variety of ways. In Philadelphia, the Roman Catholic clergy in 1843 successfully petitioned the school board to permit the reading of the Douay Bible in school, a compromise

---

[51] Ravitch, *Great School Wars*, 80.
[52] Rev. John T. Roddan, *John O'Brien; or, The Orphan of Boston: A Tale of Real Life* (Boston: Patrick Donahoe, 1851), 109.

that prompted Protestant nativists to accuse Catholics of attempting to eliminate the Bible altogether from the schools. The accusations escalated to violence, the end result being the Philadelphia riots in 1844.[53] Crises did not occur in all cities of the northeastern United States. Boston's bishop John B. Fitzpatrick, for example, had been educated in the public schools and saw little need for a competing parochial school system. In the 1840s, about one-third of Boston's schoolchildren were from Roman Catholic homes.[54] Nonetheless, the issue erupted repeatedly and controversies in Newark, Detroit, and other cities in New York State broke out over the role of religious training in the schools.[55]

Disputes such as these ignited school wars in many cities throughout the antebellum northern United States, and the question of funding private and parochial schools would recur throughout the nineteenth century and well into the twentieth. Even in New York, many issues and debates remained unresolved. The tradition of reading the Bible without comment, for example, did not vanish. Following Superintendent Stone's advice, the Board of Education ruled in 1844 that Bible reading without comment was not a sectarian practice.[56] The school controversy again erupted in New York in 1869 when "Boss" William Marcy Tweed introduced a bill that authorized the city and county of New York to give aid to nonpublic schools with enrollments of more than two hundred students, a shorthand for Catholic schools in the city. When anti-Catholic forces killed the bill, Tweed cleverly attached a school provision to the routine and cumbersome measure authorizing the city's operating funds. Only after that bill had been passed did observers notice the plan, which they perceived as a threat to the New York public school system. The outcry, which included charges that the "American doctrine of equal toleration and protection to all religious sects, but public support to none," resembled the outcome some thirty years before. Boss Tweed felt the heat and ultimately saw the school provision repealed.[57] Some years later, schemes to provide public funding for Catholic schools and to separate religious and educational instruction – known as the Poughkeepsie plan and the Faribault-Stillwater (Minnesota) plan – were developed with some amount of success.[58] The puzzle of merging the public school and particularist belief endured into the twentieth century and beyond.

Despite these geographical differences in the course of public school development and despite the continued agitation by political factions for changes in school

---

[53] Vincent P. Lannie and Bernard C. Diethorn, "For the Honor and Glory of God: The Philadelphia Bible Riots of 1840," *History of Education Quarterly* 8 (1968): 44–106; Kaestle, *Pillars of the Republic*, 169–70; Nasaw, *Schooled to Order*, 71–72.

[54] Patrick W. Carey, *Orestes Brownson: American Religious Weathervane* (Grand Rapids, MI: Wm. B. Eerdmans, 2004), 246; Kaestle, *Pillars of the Republic*, 171.

[55] Billington, *Protestant Crusade*, 156; Kaestle, *Pillars of the Republic*, 161–71; JoEllen NcNergney Vinyard, *For Faith and Fortune: The Education of Catholic Immigrants in Detroit, 1805–1925* (Urbana: University of Illinois Press, 1998), 28–47.

[56] Ravitch, *Great School Wars*, 80.

[57] Ibid., 92–99; and Pratt, *Religion, Politics, and Diversity*, 195–99.

[58] Pratt, *Religion, Politics, and Diversity*, 199–200.

policy consistent with the wishes of their constituencies, the Catholic leadership forged a clear path that fostered an institutional structure distinguished from the mainstream and, as John T. Roddan argued, aimed at separating Catholics from those who either did not understand their religion or hated it. Indeed, Catholic commentators' denunciation of the public schools, following the school controversy, became increasingly strident. James A. McMaster, editor of the *New York Freeman's Journal*, made blistering attacks at midcentury on the public school system, or what he called "state schoolism."[59] Concerned that the public schools continued to be composed mainly of Catholic children, he noted, as well, that few of the teachers shared their pupils' faith. And he suggested, foreshadowing claims that would be increasingly voiced in later decades, that education was the responsibility of the family and only secondarily of the state.[60]

The First Plenary Council of 1852, a convocation of Catholic Church leaders from across the nation, echoed McMaster's argument. Parents were urged to "give your children a Christian education, that is an education based on religious principles, accompanied by religious practices and always subordinate to religious influence." Likewise, they were counseled not to be "led astray by the false and delusive theories which are so prevalent, and which leave youth without religion, and, consequently, without anything to control the passions, promote the real happiness of the individual, and make society find in the increase of its members, a source of security and prosperity." If children were taught only human sciences without "the science of the saints," the bishops warned, "their minds will be filled with every error [and] their hearts will be receptacles of every vice" in effect "destroying the happiness of the child, embittering still more the chalice of parental disappointment, and weakening the foundations of social order." To prop up the state and maintain parental power, the bishops made explicit pleas that parents make every sacrifice to support Catholic education and pointed to the "evils of an uncatholic education, evils too multiplied and too obvious to require that we should do more than raise our voices in solemn protest against the system from which they spring."[61]

These heated disagreements had a variety of outcomes. On the one hand, they became grist for the mill of increased Protestant activism. As school crises proliferated, they only furthered the impression among nativist Protestants that the Catholic Church aimed to control public institutions and ultimately the state. How could any plan be established, asked the *New York Observer* that supported

---

[59] *New York Freeman's Journal*, 27 October 1849, cited in Connors, *Church-State Relationships in Education*, 88.

[60] *New York Freeman's Journal*, 20 July 1850, 27 July 1850, 3 August 1850, 7 September 1850, cited in Connors, *Church-State Relationships in Education*, 89.

[61] Guilday, *National Pastorals of the American Hierarchy*, 190–91. The virtues of education were stressed by Catholic writers. "Next to the blessings of religion," wrote the *Boston Pilot* on 22 November 1845, "may be ranked the advantages of Education." Adult education, moreover, was viewed as a means toward edification and economic mobility. See, for example, articles in the *Boston Pilot* on "emigrant" and adult education on 21 September 1844, 28 September 1844, 17 May 1845, 22 November 1845, and 6 December 1845.

the "teaching of the mummeries and idolatry and mariolatry of the Church of Rome"?[62] As we shall see in Chapter 6, these disputes became one very important basis for the development of political movements to oppose the seeming machinations of the Catholic hierarchy. On the other hand, the upshot of the school controversy among Catholics was the insight that they would have to fashion their own institutional structure and, in effect, foster the creation of a pillorized society, a topic to which we will now turn.

Catholics in the wake of the New York crisis realized that they had to build their own parochial school system to educate their youth. Following the Maclay Law, Hughes increasingly steered clear of public debate and until his death in 1864 labored to create a school system that would educate as many children as possible. He made explicit his change of heart in an essay in the *New York Freeman's Journal* in 1849. In answer to his own question of how best to provide Catholic education to youth, he advised that it had to be done "not by agitating the questions of the constitutionality, legality or expediency of State schools."[63] In a circular letter written one year later, Hughes expanded his argument. "I think," he observed, "the time is almost come when it will be necessary to build the school-house first, and the church afterwards." Clearly, the common schools, which mitigated religion in order to exclude sectarianism, were not suitable for Catholic children. Nor were they salutary for society at large: the school system, Hughes concluded, was not "suited to a Christian land, whether Catholic or Protestant, however admirably it might be adapted to the social condition of an enlightened paganism."[64]

In the end, New York State failed to construct a pillorized society that explicitly partitioned state institutions according to confession. Indeed, in a society that increasingly privileged a wall of separation between church and state, the possibility of developing state institutions that had confessional bases was progressively more unlikely. The school crisis both represented and fostered an explicit secularization of schools and, by implication, of other state agencies as well. In response, the Catholic leadership set about to create a separate Catholic society. It would fall to Catholics, as Hughes well recognized, to build a wall of separation that effectively as possible barred their society and especially their children from undue interaction with those about them. If an increasingly rigorous separation of church and state set up one roadblock for Catholics, the freedom of religion from state interference sustained the prospect that Catholics could remain separate from the unwashed.

The Catholic leadership's condemnation of the public schools continued following the school controversy, but its criticisms shifted from the Protestant

---

[62] *New York Observer*, 30 September 1852, cited in Connors, *Church-State Relationships in Education*, 90.

[63] *New York Freeman's Journal*, 15 December 1849, cited in Lannie, *Public Money and Parochial Education*, 255.

[64] John Hughes, *The Complete Works of the Most Rev. John Hughes, D.D., Archbishop of New York*, ed. Lawrence Kehoe (New York: American News, 1865) 2:715, cited in Lannie, *Public Money and Parochial Education*, 256

content in the schools to the schools' infidelity, a tendency ironically promoted by their own attack on the Protestant Christian domination of the schools. It was no longer the Protestant content that troubled Catholics, but the increased secularism of the schools that boded ill for America's children and society at large. Hughes, confiding in a letter, condemned public schools as one and the same with "Socialism, Red Republicanism, Universalism, Infidelity, Deism, Atheism, and Pantheism – anything, everything, except religionism and patriotism."[65]

The advantages of the parochial school system therefore were numerous. As Catholic apologists would argue, the Catholic school not only shielded children from infidelity but also provided them with a complete Catholic education. Schools, they contended, ought not to and, in fact, could not imbue children with Catholic principles and belief in a piecemeal fashion. They needed to tutor children on Catholicity in its entirety. Furthermore, the morality taught by an unadulterated Catholic education inculcated proper behavior in children, particularly when compared with the infidelity that characterized the common school. In a refrain that would become increasingly insistent in the ensuing decades, Catholics linked parental edification with the instruction provided by the school. Ever more contemptuous of a public school that both superseded the moral instruction of the home and instilled a lack of respect for parents, many Catholic leaders marveled at the success of their schools in creating a respect for authority. Finally, the segregation of children in a Catholic environment and apart from the faithless world mitigated the unpleasant influences of American Protestant society. All of these factors built one upon the other.

Morality tales were penned by Catholic authors at midcentury that aptly illustrate both the social and spiritual perils of the common school.[66] There is no better example than Mrs. James Sadlier's fictional depiction of the Blakes and Flanagans, two New York Irish families related by marriage, which not only romanticized the parochial school but reprised the New York school controversy that had occurred fifteen years before its publication.[67] The novel details the families of Tim Flanagan, "a real homespun Tipperary man, hot-blooded, blustering, and loud spoken, yet kind and generous and true-hearted," and Miles Blake, who was "more anxious for making money than anything else" (10–11). And here perhaps was the root of the problem, because the Blakes' materialism and lack of concern about religion set in motion a sequence of events that ends in

---

[65] Hughes to Anthony Blanc, 3 January 1852, cited in Lannie, *Public Money and Parochial Education* 253.

[66] See, for example, Roddan, *John O'Brien;* A Missionary Priest [Hugh Quigley], *The Cross and the Shamrock; or, How to Defend the Faith. An Irish American Catholic Tale of Real Life, Descriptive of the Temptations, Sufferings, Trials, and Triumphs of the Children of St. Patrick in the Great Republic of Washington. A Book for the Entertainment and Special Instruction of the Catholic Male and Female Servants of the United States* (Boston: Patrick Donahoe, 1853); and Mrs. J. Sadlier, *Willy Burke; or, The Irish Orphan in America* (Boston: Patrick Donahoe, 1850).

[67] Mrs. J. Sadlier, *The Blakes and Flanagans: A Tale, Illustrative of Irish Life in the United States* (New York: D. and J. Sadlier, 1855).

tragedy. In contrast, the parallel narrative of the Flanagans is one of happiness and a sense of worth.

Although the Blakes are predisposed to drift from their Catholic moorings, they compound their woes when they decided to send their children to the public schools. Young Harry Blake thrives academically in school, but he also denigrates his Irish past, on St. Patrick's Day no less. His sister, Eliza, falls under the spell of her teacher, Miss Davison, who rewarded her with a book of history that proclaimed "the hideousness and deformity of *Popery* as a system" as well as its "determined hostility to education, and, consequently, to civilization" (46). In contrast, the Flanagans' children are properly educated in the Catholic schools. Edward Flanagan learns about the greatness of Catholic Europe and, perhaps more significantly, the importance of obedience. His teacher threatens to "thrash some of that self-conceit out of" an unruly student; meanwhile, Father Power admonishes another student to remember that the acquisition of knowledge is a curse "when it is not guided and controlled by Christian principles" (78).

Not only are the Blake children not properly taught in the common schools, but there they mix with non-Catholic children, replete with the bad influences of the modern American city. Given a half dollar to buy a new dictionary, for example, Harry instead sneaks off with his Protestant friends to the Bowery and treats them to a night of entertainment. His friends salute his ingenuity at outsmarting his "old man" and observe that "you know, *he's* a Paddy" (61). The Blake elders are also pulled into the vortex of cultural change and dissonance. After his son steals the money to go to the theater, Miles Blake is advised by a Protestant father, to whom he not incidentally owes money, that the theater was fine ("boys must have amusement [and] there is a great deal to be learned there") but that corporal punishment in the family was "a barbarous practice" (92). The onset of the disintegration of the Blake family is by now clear.

The situation becomes worse when Sadlier returns to her characters after a seven-year hiatus. Harry Blake, who has taken a course in law at Columbia College and now calls himself Mr. Henry T. Blake, has turned into a fop. He has become a "tall, thin, and rather cynical-looking gentleman," whose costume resembles a "gaudy butterfly" (126). Eliza has been schooled at a fashionable academy where she "learned a something [*sic*] of everything, without obtaining a real knowledge of anything in particular." She supposedly has been schooled in history but has read no Catholic history and knows nothing about the Irish past (128). Despite their parents' efforts to act American, the Blake children are repeatedly embarrassed by their Irish customs. Ultimately, Eliza weds a Protestant, in part because she has become so tired of her parents. During her honeymoon, she immediately breaks the Catholic tradition of abstaining from meat on Friday. Her husband, moreover, shows little kindness toward his Irish in-laws. Of the Irish, he insists that "they are like certain animals I could mention – stroke them, and they will do anything, but once cross them and the game is up" (331). When Eliza reminds him that she has Irish blood, he argues "*your* Irish blood . . . has been long since refined into good American blood."

A leitmotif of the ill-effects of the lessons taught in American society in general and in public schools in particular is the deterioration of the parent-child bond. If the parents shame the children, Eliza and Henry distance themselves from their parents' reach. When Henry is betrothed to his American fiancée without asking for his parents' consent, his bemused father observes that in Ireland, "children *were* children as long as their parents lived." And when they welcome their first child into the world, the young couple is annoyed by Henry's mother, who demands that the baby be baptized immediately by a Catholic priest. But the wife demurs. "If you get Romish – I mean a Catholic priest to baptize it," Henry's wife warns him, "you and I shan't be friends" (277). As fate would have it, the baby dies before the baptism, Catholic or otherwise.

If Henry and Eliza are deracinated and Americanized, Edward Flanagan remains within the Irish Catholic community. He marries Margaret O'Callaghan, who is a stark contrast to Henry's spouse. Margaret, "Irish to the heart's core," had rejected many an admirer "because they were not of her own race" (233). Edward remains true to his faith, and his masculine self-confidence is approvingly portrayed by Sadlier. In one scene, Edward is praised by Americans when he is compared to Henry, whose cloying desire to be American is so apparent and annoying (307). To be sure, Edward and Margaret do not achieve the socioeconomic mobility of their cousins, but this is Sadlier's point: wealth does not equate with happiness in American society.

When Sadlier returns yet again to the scene ten years later, the patterns in place have only been exacerbated. The Blake children dote on their own children and ignore their parents, who are increasingly an embarrassment to them. Henry's and Eliza's spouses continue to pressure them to leave their Irish and Catholic past behind them. Henry's wife "hates Catholics as she hates soot," and her continual harping against Romanism will lead her children to grow up anti-Catholic as well (362). Although the "good obedient" Flanagan children have become "good religious fathers and mothers," the Blakes' tribulations continue. The elder Blakes "had entered on a cheerless old age," writes Sadlier, "lonely and solitary they lived together, surrounded by cold and chilling splendor, which had no longer any charms for them" (373). Eliza dies during childbirth without last rites, and her mother dies "of a broken heart ... leaving Miles lonelier and sadder than ever." Henry's wife maintains "her nervous fear of an old Catholic grandfather coming in contact with her children," so Miles can find solace only in his fellowship with the Flanagans. Clearly, his admonition that "religion didn't pay well in this country" has come to haunt him (376).

Predictably, the Flanagans' family denouement is unlike that of their relatives. Although it is not without sadness, even those moments of grief are illustrative of a correct behavior. The death of Susan, Edward's sister, is replete with didactic instruction. Susan, who predicts her own death, nonetheless feels the comfort of the sacraments and the expectation of eternal life so that "her last moments were of the most exquisite happiness" (324). Not only is the family closely knit and its members succored by the sacraments of the Church, but Edward also inherits twenty-six thousand dollars from his kind father-in-law. Living in material comfort and spiritual peace, the Flanagans are a paragon of a proper life and an exemplar of the idealized Irish American home.

Sadlier wrote some forty novels during her prolific career, but in *The Blakes and Flanagans* she has constructed a narrative that speaks especially to the importance of the school. In fact, the New York school controversy is embedded within the narrative. Not surprisingly, Bishop Hughes is a hero who, Sadlier sarcastically observes, sought to save Catholics "from the fearful abyss [of the public school] opened beneath their feet, by the *paternal kindness* of the state" (249–50). Despite Hughes's struggle with "the dogged spirit of fanaticism, leagued with infidelity," Sadlier admits the sad results of Irish children's encounters with the schools. One exemplar, of course, is Henry, who achieves fame "on the ruins of those religious principles instilled into them in childhood by Catholic mothers" (251). Indeed, it is Henry, as a cynical operative for the Democratic machine, who plays the role of a Catholic turncoat, a role that befits him well because of his training in the secularized public schools.

In contrast, Sadlier argues that the Catholic school is fundamental because it instills a morality that has implications for society's other institutions, such as church and family. She steadfastly maintains that one aspect of the early controversy has been decided: the proper school for her characters must be a Catholic institution. One character, who puzzles over "the folly of those parents who knowingly place their children in the way of acquiring false principles," argues that he would "as soon think of putting *my* child into a burning house as into a non-religious school" (163). Similarly, the parochial school undergirds the state. Sadlier uses the story of one character to disavow the necessity of public schools because they train the Irish to grow up like Americans. Although he was brought up with Irish Catholic training, he evinces a multilayered loyalty, declaring that "I am fully prepared to stand by this great Republic, the land of my birth, even to shedding the last drop of blood, were that necessary." Although he loves America, he cannot forget Ireland and "I pity the Irishman's son who can or does, for his heart must be insensible to some of the highest and holiest feelings of our nature" (164). Those Irish Americans who remain true to the Church are more apt to support the state than are the corrupt Irish American politicians embodied in characters such as Henry T. Blake.

As Sadlier attempted to demonstrate, the Catholic school was as commendable as the public school was not. Those parents who *chose* to send their children to the public schools courted disaster. Many parents, moreover, were *forced* to place their children in the public schools if they wished them to receive an education. As they built their own school system, Catholic leaders, therefore, continued to point out the dangers of the public school for youth in their confessional community and to disparage the "double taxation" they were forced to pay by having to support public schools through taxation and parochial schools through donation.

The institutional and intellectual structure created by Catholic Americans was remarkable. Between 1854 and 1862, Hughes oversaw an increase in the number of Catholic pupils in New York's public schools from ten thousand to fifteen thousand. By the early decades of the twentieth century, after the

American prelacy had called Catholic schools a necessity, the parochial school system educated more than one million students on school property valued at more than $100 million. Futhermore, the nearly one million students who attended Catholic schools in 1900 had grown to 1.8 million twenty years later.[68] This school system was the "greatest religious fact in the United States to-day," argued Archbishop Spalding in the early twentieth century, a system "maintained without any aid by the people who love it."[69]

Not every Catholic authority was enthusiastic about the parochial school system. Most notably, Orestes Brownson, in keeping with his aspiration to unite Catholicism with a larger American world, expressed some uncertainty about the merit of a system that segregated Catholic youth. Brownson's critique in part reflected his very public feud with Hughes, which began shortly after Brownson moved to New York, and Hughes's concern that Brownson was part of an "American party" that endeavored to undermine his authority in the diocese. Brownson's essay, entitled "Catholic Schools and Education," which appeared in his journal in 1862 certainly could not have mollified Hughes's concerns.[70] Arguing that "our Catholic population" was "a foreign body" and that the "civilization" of these immigrant Catholics was "a lower order than ours," Brownson saw no danger in placing Catholic and Protestant children in the same classroom. Why fear that Catholic children would become Protestant, he asked, any more than that Protestant children would see the truth of Catholicism? Writing amid the Civil War, moreover, Brownson worried that Catholics had Americanized "in a Southern rather than a Northern sense" or, put differently, that they aimed to be American not "in the sense of highest, truest, and most advanced Americanism," but in that sense that was "least remote from barbarism." Only by breaking old associations could Catholics "cease to be in this country an isolated foreign colony, or a band of emigrants encamped for the night, and ready to strike their tents, and take up their line of march on the morrow for some other place."[71] None of this, Brownson argued, contradicted his view of the relationship between church and state because he consistently maintained that religious liberty and an institutional church-state separation were required by nature.[72]

Brownson's, however, was a minority voice. A decade prior to Brownson's intervention on the public schools, the First Plenary Council resulted in a letter that cautioned against "those who would persuade you that religion can be separated from secular instruction." Parents were counseled "to watch over the

---

[68] McCluskey, Catholic Education in America, 25.

[69] Lannie, Public Money and Parochial Education, 256; "Schools," Catholic Encyclopedia (1917), http://www.newadvent.org/cathen/.

[70] Orestes Brownson, "Catholic Schools and Education," Brownson's Quarterly Review 3 (January 1862): 66–85.

[71] Ibid., 76–77, 80, 82.

[72] See also Orestes Brownson, "Public and Parochial Schools," Brownson's Quarterly Review 4 (July 1859): 324–42. For a fuller treatment of the conflict between Brownson and Hughes and Brownson's views of the relationship between church and state, see Elwyn Smith, Religious Liberty in the United States, 186–91; and Carey, Orestes Brownson, 234–49.

purity of [their children's] faith and morals with jealous vigilance." To foster this guardianship, they were urged to give their children an education based on Christian principles. And to enable this education, believers were advised to "encourage the establishment and support of Catholic schools" so that all could be spared the pain of beholding youth who have fallen into the "evils of an uncatholic education."[73]

Nearly twenty years later, Isaac Hecker echoed these sentiments in a mature exposition of the advantages of the Catholic school system.[74] The first schools in America were founded, Hecker observed, by "a religious people for a religious end." They did not dream of divorcing secular education from religion. Because no established religion presently existed in any state, he continued, American society was faced with the question of teaching morality in the schools. The solution up to that point had been a secularism based on "our common Christianity," which was practicable as long as the common denominations were Protestant. When Catholicism became an increasingly powerful religious force in the United States, however, a Christian consensus was impossible because Catholicism involved differences in principle. The impracticality of this remedy was compounded by the very nature of Catholic education. "Catholicity," Hecker contended, "must be taught as a whole, in its unity and its integrity, or it is not taught at all." Because Catholicism was "an organism, a living body, ... and is necessarily one and indivisible," any failure to recognize its distinctiveness simply excluded Catholicism itself.[75]

Catholic parents in the early republic thus were given a Hobson's choice: either send their children to the common school and thereby "violate their conscience, neglect their duty as fathers and mothers, and expose their children to the danger of losing their faith, and with it the chance of salvation" or neglect their children's education. Conversely, they were given no choice but to pay taxes to the state to fund schools that prohibited the teaching of their religion.

Secularizing the schools further through the elimination of the Bible, moreover, was worse than keeping them purely Protestant. Protestantism was better than no religion for the state, society, and morality "unless you include under its names free-lovism, free-religion, woman's rightsism, and the various other similar *isms* struggling to get themselves recognized and adopted" by Protestant elements.[76] No education, in sum, could be valued if it were divorced from religion and religious culture because "the basis of the state itself is religion."[77] The difficulty therefore lay in the religious rights recognized by the state. It was bound "equally to recognize and respect the conscience of Protestants and of Catholics, and has no right to restrain the conscience of either."

---

[73] Guilday, *National Pastorals of the American Hierarchy*, 190–91.
[74] [Isaac Hecker], "The School Question," *Catholic World* 11 (1870): 91–106.
[75] Ibid., 94.
[76] Ibid.
[77] Ibid., 98.

Not surprisingly, the logical resolution of this deadlock, Hecker concluded, was state-funded, religiously separate school systems.[78] Religion, he argued, was a central component of education. But unlike the situation in colonial America, the nineteenth-century United States was a pluralistic society. "It may be an annoyance to Protestants that Catholics are here," Hecker observed, "but they are here and here they will remain."[79] Given the multiconfessional society, the only sensible course was for Protestant and Catholic to "recognize and respect the equal rights of the other before the State."[80] Here he laid out a vision of a pillorized society, which, he argued, would not divide the citizenry so much as it would engender increased loyalty to the state. Reflecting a point made repeatedly by Brownson, Hecker asserted that "the American state is as much Catholic as it is Protestant, and really harmonizes far better with Catholicity than with Protestantism."[81] Although Catholicism was both a better agent of state loyalty and superior to Protestantism in the spiritual order, Hecker recognized that Protestants should have equal rights in the state. Yet if citizens were not able to attach loyalty to a state that sanctioned their conscience, they would be unfit citizens. And if they were forced to attend schools where "the religion of their parents is reviled as a besotted superstition," they would become "indifferent to religion, indocile to their parents, [and] disobedient to the laws."[82] The "enemy of the state" was not Catholicism, but "irreligion, pantheism, atheism and immorality, disguised as secularism."[83] Catholics and Protestants together, in the pillorized society, would maintain the state.

Hecker addressed a series of objections to his plan, most notably the place of non-Christians in his proposal. He argued that the Jews should have separate schools if they should desire them, but that Protestant denominations should be subsumed under the aegis of a Protestant system, similar to the common school system in place, which in fact *was* a Protestant system. Most notably, he rejected the rights of those who have no religion because they "have no conscience that people who have religion are bound to respect." The infidel might be guaranteed the right to his civil and political equality, Hecker maintained, but he has no guarantee of protection of his infidelity. It would be absurd to request of the state that it protect infidelity, because religion is the only basis of the state: "for the state to protect infidelity would be to cut its own throat."[84] "There is a

---

[78] Hecker also suggested two other possible solutions to the school problem. The first was the "infidel or secular solution" that excluded all religious instruction from the schools. This solution, he argued, really was "no solution at all" and made "public schools nurseries of infidelity and irreligion." The second possibility was to make education a voluntary system, as was done in religious practice. This was impracticable because it would effectively destroy the state-funded public school, an institution essential for practical and religious education.

[79] Hecker, "School Question," 100.

[80] Ibid.

[81] Ibid., 102.

[82] Ibid., 103.

[83] Ibid., 105.

[84] Ibid., 101.

recrudescence of paganism, a growth of subtle and disguised infidelity," Hecker concluded, that required attention. "Fight, therefore, Protestants, no longer us, but the public enemy."[85]

The Second Plenary Council, which met in Baltimore four years before the publication of Hecker's article and some three years after Hughes's death, confirmed the perspectives of both with regard to the need for parochial schools. The council again endorsed the development of a parochial school system, arguing that "religious teaching and religious training should form part of every system of school education." The error of developing the intellect "while the heart and its affections are left without the control of religious principle" was a blunder that not only was a "mistake [of] the nature and object of education" but also prepared the "parent and child [for] the most bitter disappointment in the future, and for society the most disastrous results."[86]

Perhaps more important, the pastoral letter both articulated the relationship between church and state in the United States and the particular role of Catholicism in the relationship that was seemingly at odds with Hecker's pronouncements. In accepting a republican state, the letter stated that "the Church ... does not proclaim the absolute and entire independence of the Civil Power because it teaches ... that the temporal magistrate is His minister, and that the power of the sword he wields is a delegated exercise of authority committed to him from on high." In short, civil power consistently had to "be exercised agreeably to God's Law" and when it was not, it had "no claim on the obedience of the citizen." Written one year after the end of the Civil War, this is a remarkable admission of the citizen's capacity to disobey civil authority. Yet the bishops explained that Catholics possessed a particular guide in the Church, "which enables [them] to discriminate between what the Law of God forbids or allows." Unlike the Protestant sects in America, the "State is bound to recognize [the authority of the Catholic Church] as supreme in its sphere – of moral, no less than dogmatic teaching." If the bishops were renouncing an active role in temporal affairs, then, they were also contending that their flock should take its signals in questions of obedience to law from the Church and that Roman Catholicism was entitled to a civil recognition denied to Protestant sects.[87]

During the New York school crisis, Hughes cited an anecdote whose moral was meant to illustrate the advantages of religious tolerance in America. When a child asked his father why so many types of churches existed in a free country, his father answered that people differ in a variety of ways. "Do they all dress alike and eat and drink alike," the father explained, "and keep the same hours, and

---

[85] Ibid., 106.

[86] Guilday, *National Pastorals of the American Hierarchy*, 215.

[87] Ibid., 205–6. Particularly helpful here is Elwyn Smith, *Religious Liberty in the United States*, 197–99. The Third Plenary Council, which convened in 1884, was even more unyielding about the public schools. The clergy – bishops and priests alike – were no longer urged, but rather required to build parochial schools. Moreover, laypeople were no longer asked to send their children to Catholic schools but were compelled to do so. Lannie, *Public Money and Parochial Education*, 257–58.

use the same diversion?" It was likewise with religion, the father concluded. People have the right to worship God as they please because "it is their own business and concerns none but themselves." Hughes contended that the child showed more sense than his father, who equated religious belief with trivial choices of food preferences and clothing styles.[88] For Hughes, the decision was not a trifling preference, but rather a choice between adhering to the one true church or to an inferior religious alternative. As in the Second Plenary Council, this anecdote illustrates the quandaries inherent in the Catholic conundrum, as discussed in Chapter 2. When Hughes and his allies envisioned a society segmented by religious confession, they did not perceive it in ways similar to politicians such as Seward. Whereas Seward offered a pluralist and liberal view, where people of different systems of belief coexisted under the aegis of state institutions, Hughes could not believe that the various confessions were all equal before God. Nonetheless, religious belief, properly embedded in a variety of denominational institutional structures, was a necessary precondition for the maintenance of state and society.

Significantly, then, the parochial school system and the pillorized societal structure of which it was a part did not deny allegiance to the state. Indeed, Catholics argued that they were better Americans than those who lived in an increasingly infidel world (and as such they co-opted much of the rhetoric of Protestants in the early national period). And leaders such as Brownson, admittedly not one of the strongest advocates of separate Catholic schools, cleaved to his view that Catholicism was necessary for the United States to fulfill its destiny because it would foster the order and attention to authority that was necessary in a republic. In this way, the Catholic viewpoint hewed to a complementary identity in which they not only claimed allegiance to state and ethnoreligious group but argued that their membership in each enriched their allegiance to both.[89] In this pillorized world, they fostered a segmented society based on a thriving institutional structure that was pluralist only insofar as it could be divorced from many Catholics' contention that their faith embraced true Christian belief.

The Move Toward Secularization in the Schools

Encourage free schools, and resolve that not one dollar appropriated to them shall be applied to the support of any sectarian school. Resolve that neither the State nor nation, nor both combined, shall support institutions of learning other than those sufficient to afford every child in the land the opportunity of a good common school education, unmixed with atheistic, pagan, or sectarian tenets. Leave the matter of religion to the

---

[88] Lannie, "Archbishop John Hughes and the Common School Controversy," 29, cited in Ravitch, *Great School Wars*, 52.

[89] On the complementary identity, see Jon Gjerde, *The Minds of the West: Ethnocultural Evolution in the Rural Middle West, 1830–1917* (Chapel Hill: University of North Carolina Press, 1997), 59–66.

family altar, the church, and the private school, supported entirely by private contribution. Keep the Church and State forever separate. Ulysses S. Grant, 1875[90]

It was a long way, both temporally and intellectually, from the speech that President Ulysses S. Grant presented in Des Moines, Iowa, in 1875 and the school crises some decades before. Grant was now uncategorically calling for the separation of religion from the school and, more broadly, of the church from the state, divisions that many Protestants decades before would have feared. Yet the crooked path that led to Grant's speech and a movement to enact an amendment that wrote the separation of church and state into the Constitution both commenced in the years of the great school debates.

As we have seen, one outcome of the school debates was reflection on the content of moral edification in the public schools. From one perspective, the Protestants had succeeded all too well. By remaining dominant in the public school enterprise, they were able to promote their particular beliefs from a far-reaching platform. Yet this dominant position almost inevitably led to compromises that would usher in a growing commitment to pluralism in the public schools. "By assuming a major part of the moral and religious instruction of the American public," writes William Kennedy, "the schools took on a responsibility which they could not easily fulfill." The result, Kennedy continues, was the emergence of a civil religion, "of [an] Americanized religion in which a national morality and a 'lowest-common-denominator' theology were mixed."[91] "In its pluralism," Kennedy concludes, "the nation seemed to be seeking a kind of secularized faith that would give it 'religious' foundation and continuity without the divisive and distinctive traditions of the various sects."[92] "While Protestantizing the culture," agrees James Fraser, "the evangelicals were also secularizing their own faith."[93] School officials, in order to exclude Catholic influence from the schools, set in motion a process that tended to proscribe Protestant influences as well. As Protestant and Catholic critics alike argued, schools instilled in children a vague morality and an allegiance to the state. But the schools increasingly lacked the governance of Protestant agencies, and they no longer taught Protestant principles utilizing the King James Version of the Bible. Ultimately, the ongoing discussion about the moral content of school instruction encouraged the move toward secularization of the public schools.

Yet these outcomes were long in coming, and many American Protestants resisted them along the way. Indeed, various antebellum Americans continued to retain their belief that it was in the interest of the state to instill in youth both knowledge and morality. And the latter, they continued, necessitated a

---

[90] *American State Papers Bearing on Sunday Legislation* (New York: National Religious Liberty Association, 1891), 203–4.

[91] William Bean Kennedy, *The Shaping of Protestant Education: An Interpretation of the Sunday School and the Development of Protestant Educational Strategy in the United States, 1789–1860*, ed. C. Ellis Nelson (New York: Association Press, 1966), 35.

[92] Ibid., 35–36.

[93] James W. Fraser, *Between Church and State: Religion and Public Education in a Multicultural America* (New York: St. Martin's Press, 1999), 46.

grounding in Protestant Christian ethics. As the editor of the *Harper's New Monthly Magazine* put it in 1853, the state not only could but it should educate its youth and promote the "highest intellectual and moral good," because the "nation owes it to itself to make good citizens" and good citizens result when they were taught ethics that in turn fostered a public morality.[94] The notion that this public morality could be cultivated only through instruction in neutral, scientific knowledge, the journal continued, was a chimera. "Under the pretense of indifference to all sects," the editor argued,

> there is a favoring of the very worst. There is a show of fairness, but in the very nature of such a state of things, every movement tends to the advantage of those who hold to negation instead of positive truth. The definite language necessarily employed in the statement or defense of the latter carried the appearance of sectarianism. It stands out clear and uncompromising. The cant of an infidel rationalism is more flexible. It assumes to be philosophical, and under this guise attacks the most precious truth without creating alarm.

The sad fact, the editor concluded, was that "it could be shown almost to a mathematical certainty" that the resolution of educational questions "must continually result in the triumph of the infidel, or negative, interest, whenever it comes in conflict with positive truth."[95]

Ultimately, advocates of Protestantism in American life were simply not willing to sacrifice their faith, and for a variety of reasons. The simplest argument was pragmatic. As the Congregational clergyman George B. Cheever argued in 1854, schools must have a moral foundation and because Protestant Christians comprised the majority of Americans, their faith should be the ethical basis of the schools. Given his premise of the ethical bedrock that was the school, he asked simply, "shall the conscience of the smaller number bind the conscience of the larger?"[96]

Cheever and others recapitulated as well arguments that the place of Protestant Christianity was at the heart of the American civilization and therefore it could be sacrificed only at the peril of surrendering the essence of the United States. Most fundamentally, they reiterated the importance of a Protestant inheritance that, as the *New Englander and Yale Review* phrased it, "hangs all the hopes and destinies of man for time and eternity on a *sound and true knowledge of God*, which fully recognizes the *inalienable right of 'private judgment*,' and which relies on *individual conviction* as the grand conservative power of society."[97] The time was drawing nigh, warned the journal, when all Americans must either adopt and act on this inheritance or alternatively "take passage on some one of the numerous railroads, which have been constructed of late, for conveying *backward towards*

[94] "Editor's Table," *Harper's New Monthly Magazine* 7 (1853): 269, 271.

[95] Ibid., 270.

[96] George B. Cheever, *Right of the Bible in Our Public Schools* (New York: Robert Carter and Brothers, 1854), 62.

[97] "Collegiate Education in the Western States," *New Englander and Yale Review* 4 (1846): 287.

Rome."[98] In the end, the journal denied that it was advocating a sectarian system of education but added that it had "no squeamishness in maintaining, that a peculiar system of religious faith furnishes, we do not say the only desirable, but the only *possible* foundation, of an educational superstructure for a free people."[99] Individual conviction and private judgment were required forces in the American commitment to liberty. Because they were a Protestant inheritance, Protestantism had to be the ethical basis for the public schools or else American liberty was imperiled.

For the philanthropist Stephen Colwell, Christian civilization fostered a "Christian tolerance" and "the worst enemy of humanity could not have devised a doctrine more dangerous to our republican institutions" than the exclusion of Protestant Christianity from the schools.[100] And although "the Catholic laymen of this country are as truly patriotic and faithful to the country as other citizens," it was also nonetheless true that the Catholic Church did not grow up "in our free atmosphere" and therefore "it neither can nor ever will adopt or concede the principle of toleration."[101] Without Protestant ethics *and* the Bible in the schools, the United States would start down a slippery slope toward intolerance.

One implication in these arguments was that because Protestant ethics exemplified freedom and tolerance, non-Protestant principles ought not to be taught because of their inherent dangers. "The conscience which commands the worship of idols," Cheever insisted, "is not to be treated with the same respect as the conscience which commands the worship of God." The conscience of those worshippers of idols, moreover, "may and does command [them] to the commission of unquestioned crime, as infanticide, or the Molochism of the sacrifice of children even in the fire." If all conscience was to be valued equally, Cheever concluded, the pagan's conscience – with all of its untoward social consequences – would be valued as much as that of the Christian. "We affirm," Cheever thundered, "that [Romanist] superstitions are not to be treated with the same respect as the Word of God" because "there is such a thing as ultimate and absolute truth and that such truth is in the Word of God."[102]

These commentators continued to stress the utility of schools that taught principles of freedom and tolerance and that furthered the development of a free conscience, principles that were Protestant in nature. Here was a continued call both to deny a religious pluralism in American education and to emphasize the utility of a particularist Protestant worldview, a call that was at obvious odds with a secularized educational system. Yet this advocacy of Protestantism in the schools nonetheless was replete with quandaries. "No man among us, whatever

---

[98] Ibid.

[99] Ibid.

[100] Stephen Colwell, *The Position of Christianity in the United States, in its Relation with our Political Institutions, and Especially with Reference to Religious Instruction in the Public Schools* (Philadelphia: Lippincott, Grambo, 1854), 98.

[101] Ibid., 99.

[102] Cheever, *Right of the Bible in Our Public Schools*, 74–75, 77.

may be his views of the desirableness," the editor of *Harper's New Monthly Magazine* argued in 1853, "maintains the practicability of a national religion." Yet in the same breath, the editor argued that education must have a moral underpinning and that the most logical ethical framework would be what he called the Protestant Evangelical model, which stood midway between the Romanist and the infidel. "The school question," the editor concluded with some exasperation, "presents a problem of the same kind, and involving the same difficulties, with that of religious liberty."[103] The *New Englander and Yale Review*, as mentioned earlier, also argued that only with Protestant Christianity could the "intellectual and moral life" of Americans be maintained. "We would gladly believe," the journal contended, "if we could, that Romanism or Puseyism would educate a free people as well as Puritanism." The fact of the matter, however, was "we can not believe it without giving the lie to history, and denying the fundamental laws both of mind and of society." Utilizing somewhat specious logic, the editors concluded that this was not a sectarian position. It was rather advocacy of "*education – universal education* – the education of *unnumbered millions of freemen* – the organization of *systems* and *institutions* of education, which shall be unfailing fountains of vital truth to a multitudinous free people."[104]

The problem, many Americans were coming to realize, was that these *were* sectarian positions that recapitulated the Protestant conundrum discussed in Chapter 1. For a variety of reasons, they were willing to restrict religious and educational liberty because not to do so would endanger the maintenance of American liberty writ large. If conscience, tolerance, and freedom were Protestant virtues, how could the nation be sustained if youth were neither instructed in them nor permitted to utilize them? Just as their Catholic counterparts were arguing that all faiths were equal but that their church was more equal than the others, Protestants maintained a particularist view based on the primacy of Protestantism in the unfolding destiny of the American nation, a destiny that purportedly included the protection of freedom and liberty for all. The Protestant conundrum, then, was not solved, but was in fact circumvented by the shift in the schools that offered an increasingly secularized morality in school instruction. In response to fears of Catholic advances in state and society, Protestants became increasingly willing to scrap their own particularistic beliefs in order to dissociate themselves from Catholic sectarianism.

The denouement at least for this element of an ongoing story, as we shall see in later chapters, was the debate in the mid-1870s when President Grant linked his support of free schools to the separation of church and state (see Fig. 5). Owing to a combination of political influences, a concerted effort was launched to alter the Constitution with an explicit prescription of a separated church and state. Known as the Blaine Amendment, it was the result of pressure from a variety of sources. On the one hand, advocates for the growing Catholic parochial school system maintained persistent pressure in promoting the public

[103] "Editor's Table," 269.
[104] "Collegiate Education in the Western States," 288.

FIGURE 5. By the 1870s, debates about the public funding of Catholic schools sharply divided Republicans and Democrats throughout the country. (Illustration by Thomas Nast, "Tilden's 'Wolf at the Door, Gaunt and Hungry.' – Don't Let Him In," *Harper's Weekly* 20 [16 September 1876]: 756–57. Prints and Photographs Division, Library of Congress, LC-USZ62-126152)

funding of nonpublic schools, which was increasingly resisted by those who advocated the separation of church and state. On the other hand, and equally important, Protestants' negative reference to Roman Catholic particularism forced them to give up their belief in the linkage between church and state so as to distance themselves from Catholic practice and belief.

The question of the role of religious training in state institutions and the relationships between state and religion would endure, as we well know, into the twenty-first century. The school wars at midcentury, however, were critical because they fractured a truce regarding conventional practice in the common schools. The strategies for those groups that came into conflict shifted, and new trajectories replaced old ones. Roman Catholics developed a model of a pillorized society in which their children were sheltered from the deleterious effects of the secular world about them. In profound ways, this strategy was a variant of their profession of a pluralist perspective. They recognized their duty to remain loyal Americans; indeed, they argued that Catholics were the most loyal to the American project. However, they made concerted efforts to remain separate as well and to maintain their particularity, efforts that became increasingly powerful as the Roman Catholic institutional structure grew in the United States.

For their part, the Protestant elite saw their domination of the public schools wane. The unmistakable religious training in the schools diminished as well. The school controversy forced Protestant leaders to accept an arrangement where the peculiarities of Protestantism were replaced with a more generic blend of Christian ethics. In short, they faced the realization that the public school, which was a central institution for the state, would become less particularistic in its orientation and increasingly secularized as a result. As such, this was, as Philip Hamburger argues, a critical moment in cementing the separation of church and state, a moment most strongly expressed in the concerted attempts to amend the Constitution to state explicitly that separation should be federally mandated.[105]

These developments are dripping with irony. As Protestants condemned Catholics for a sectarianism that was integral to their strategy of pillorization, they were forced to concede that the common schools were too particularist. Viewing the school as an institution that grounded youth in the secular merits of Protestant Christianity, Protestants saw state institutions such as the school move toward greater inclusion and pluralism. In the end, the course of events laid the foundation for an American pluralism that celebrated the diversity of the school and the overarching beneficence of the American nation. Whereas Catholics at first condemned the common schools for their particularism, the Church leadership worked resolutely to create a private system that expressed their own particularist tenets. At first faulting the common schools for their homogeneous and nonpluralist perspectives, the Catholic elite built an institutional structure based on particularist and sectarian separation. As Catholic leaders continued to maintain a pluralist perspective, it was one increasingly tinged with a particularistic flavor. As part of their strategy of pillorization, they were one group among many – rather than a group of individuals maintaining a common belief – that was part of the American nation.

The shattered consensus regarding the school continued to have immediate consequences in many arenas of American life. The political movements that

---

[105] Hamburger, *Separation of Church and State*, 10–11, 219–29.

flourished at midcentury and endured beyond the Civil War continued to grapple with the place of Roman Catholicism in American society, its state, and its institutions. Yet the question had a bearing on another crucial institution as well. As we will see in the next chapter, the role of the family, for a variety of reasons, grew in significance in relation to the school debate. Roman Catholics viewed the family as yet one more central building block of their pillorized community, and they became increasingly attentive to forces of the state that intruded on that community. If the school was one example of a perilous state institution, there were others – such as the orphanage and the poorhouse – that interfered with the family. For Protestants, who were leery of the developments in society such as the increasingly secularized school, the family came to be seen as an institution that might provide the last refuge for the development of true Christian edification. The family was for both groups a crucial institution, and for both an institution at risk because of the machinations of the other.

5

Protestant and Catholic Critiques of Family and Women

> Wherever Freedom is found, there is woman emancipated.
>
> Thomas Bangs Thorpe, 1855[1]

Amid the kaleidoscopic changes in the middle third of the nineteenth century, most Americans – Protestant and Catholic alike – could agree that the family was an institution of central importance to state and society. Edward Norris Kirk, a Presbyterian clergyman, argued in 1848 that families were building blocks of the state. "Four millions or more of these little groups are scattered from the Atlantic to the Pacific coast," he contended, and "they are the nation in miniature; for, as they are, the nation will be."[2] Those effects that rightly shaped the family, put simply, would elevate the nation. Archbishop John Hughes, writing five years before, agreed. The family, he observed, closely mirroring Kirk's phrasing, "is in itself a State," where there existed "form, dominion and order."[3]

Kirk and Hughes, using historical development as their guides, could also concur that Christianity had a felicitous influence on the family. In pagan civilizations, Kirk argued, "man was nothing; the poor were slaves ... woman was brutalized." Only with the arrival of Jesus did "true political freedom, equality and fraternity" grow forth. If Kirk believed that "rightly-influenced families elevated the nation," moreover, the state could only provide defenses in positive law against dangers to them. Even if the state, modified by republicanism, protected the family's property and secured its members' liberty, it could not "quicken the spiritual life of these families." Unlike the influences of religious

---

[1] Thomas Bangs Thorpe, *A Voice to America; or, The Model Republic, Its Glory, or Its Fall: With a Review of the Causes of the Decline and Failure of the Republics of South America, Mexico, and of the Old World; Applied to the Present Crisis in the United States* (New York: Edward Walker, 1855), 87.

[2] Edward Norris Kirk, *The Church Essential to the Republic. A Sermon in Behalf of the American Home Missionary Society* (New York: Leavitt, Trow, 1848), 8.

[3] John Hughes, "Influence of Christianity upon Civilization," January 5, 1843, in *The Complete Works of the Most Rev. John Hughes, D.D., Archbishop of New York*, ed. Lawrence Kehoe (New York: American News, 1864), 1:115.

belief, it held "no light, no promise, no word awakening hope."[4] Hughes, for his part, invoked the Roman family, which was not a "natural family," but rather a setting where the father owned his children as he did his slaves and where the wife was a slave "having no rights from the hour of her birth until she went to her grave."[5] Only with the arrival of the "Divine Author" did people begin to remonstrate against injustice and oppression, in the home as elsewhere, as they established true relations between God and humans.[6] Only through the truths of the Church could proper relationships within the home be realized.

If Kirk and Hughes could agree on these basic outlines of the historical development of the family and the role of Christianity in its reconfiguration of household power and the improvement of the condition of women, they profoundly disagreed on the particulars of the narrative. Kirk argued that American Protestantism advanced the family, whereas the papal and apostolical character of Europe and South America stamped its dangerous imprint on their societies. The cardinal principle of the Latin Church, he asserted, was "the destruction of man's individuality and manhood" so that he could not "think, judge, believe, choose, address God, or govern himself." Rather, all of these actions were performed for him "by a corporation."[7] Hughes, in contrast, celebrated the family *as* corporation and would elsewhere contribute to a Catholic argument on the importance of extra-familial institutions that contributed to the well-being of the family and its constituent members.[8]

The consensus about the importance of the family broke apart when American voices considered the reasons for the advances of the household unit. As we shall see in this chapter, the family was an institution treasured by Americans but for different reasons and in different contexts. On the one hand, for American Protestants, the family came to be seen as a haven to protect religious belief from the excesses of society. In a world that seemingly was becoming increasingly chaotic, the home was an environment that protected and edified youth. Perhaps the religious revival might encourage conversion, but it was often seen as an embodiment of turmoil. Perhaps the school would edify youth, but the home became a place of religious education when the lessons taught in school were secularized. The family thus became a refuge from the world, from the chaos of religious volatility and the desertion of the state from religious instruction. For Catholics, on the other hand, the family was part of an institutional structure that was public, particularistic, and corporate. In this context, the privatized family made little sense because it operated properly only in conjunction with other Catholic institutions of the school and the church.

---

[4] Kirk, *Church Essential to the Republic*, 17, 7, 8.

[5] Hughes, "Influence of Christianity upon Civilization," 115.

[6] John Hughes, "Influence of Christianity on Social Servitude," March 29, 1843, in Kehoe, *Complete Works of the Most Rev. John Hughes*, 1:8. Hughes likely is borrowing heavily from the work of Joseph de Maistre here. See Jack Lively, *The Works of Joseph de Maistre* (New York: Macmillan, 1965), 143–46.

[7] Kirk, *Church Essential to the Republic*, 12–13.

[8] Hughes, "Influence of Christianity upon Civilization," 115.

More broadly, Protestants and Roman Catholics used their perceptions of the family of their counterpart to critique the other group's failings. When Catholics viewed the Protestant American family, they saw not a refuge so much as a privatized realm that accentuated the excesses and individualization of larger Protestant American society. When Protestants observed the Catholic institutional structure, they perceived a systematic effort to foster the unfreedom and despotic world that allegedly characterized the Catholic worldview, an effort that was most graphically seen in the repression of women within the home and in other religious institutions.

These critiques were developed amid an era when the family was in profound flux. Historians who have listened to the voices of contemporaries likewise have underscored the transformation occurring within the American home in antebellum America.[9] Despite variations on a theme, contemporaries and historians alike identified new traits that increasingly characterized the American family, particularly the families of those Americans living outside of chattel slavery. The American home, according to many observers, was an environment that was highly individualistic, a fundamental departure from households in Europe. It was also an environment that had become increasingly mothercentered, so much so that scholars have written about the feminization of American culture.[10] The "American family" ideal, then, became naturalized as a conjugal family with an increasingly powerful female center focused on the nurturance of children. Yet it was an ideal whose virtue would be wildly contested.

If the American family endured as a powerful force in a volatile society, the debate surrounding acceptable familial behavior illustrated three fundamental issues adumbrated in the debate between Kirk and Hughes and developed in this chapter. First, Protestant critics used the debate regarding the family and especially the condition of women as yet one more example of the dangers of an authoritarian and despotic institution that *was* the Church. Catholic practices such as celibate orders corrupted familial relationships and particularly endangered women. Likewise, Roman Catholic sacraments – especially confession – contravened the proper order of familial relationships in both intergenerational and especially in conjugal terms. Second, the debate between Catholics and Protestants laid bare a contradiction in the American rhetoric about the family form. If Protestants could celebrate the American family as an institution characterized by equality and female deliverance, they did so by respecting an institution that was fundamentally unequal. The Roman Catholic family became an object

---

[9] There is a very large body of literature on this topic. See, for example, Nancy F. Cott, *The Bonds of Womanhood: "Woman's Sphere" in New England, 1780–1835* (New Haven, CT: Yale University Press, 1977); Ellen Carol DuBois, *Feminism and Suffrage: The Emergence of an Independent Women's Movement in America, 1849–1869* (Ithaca, NY: Cornell University Press, 1978); Mary P. Ryan, *Cradle of the Middle Class: The Family in Oneida County, New York, 1790–1865* (New York: Cambridge University Press, 1981); Christine Stansell, *City of Women: Sex and Class in New York, 1789–1860* (New York: Knopf, 1986); and Steven Mintz and Susan Kellogg, *Domestic Revolutions: A Social History of American Family Life* (New York: Free Press, 1988).

[10] Ann Douglas, *The Feminization of American Culture* (New York: Knopf, 1977).

to which to compare the "American" family and, as such, was seen as an example of regression and despotism. Yet a principle objection to the Roman Catholic influence was its basis for authority. If the Church instructed its followers to be obedient to authority, it was obedience to the hierarchy, and not to patriarchy. One of the most troubling aspects of the Catholic world to many Protestants was the way in which extrafamilial forces – or, put differently, the priest – invaded the sanctity of the home and competed with the patriarchal head of the household. Third, if Catholic prelates could agree on the importance of the familial institution, their interventions into the family served as a reprimand of the American household and, as such, offered a critique of an American institution. Consistent with an overarching European immigrant assessment of the American family as too individualistic, too materialistic, and too childcentered, the Catholic critique chastised Americans for the lack of authority and hierarchy in their homes. Because the family, as both Hughes and Kirk would agree, was an essential building block of state and society, this was a judgment that was damning for the American future.

The Changing Family in Antebellum America

Home! – sweet word and musical! – keytone of the heart, at whose melody, as by the harp of Orpheus, all the trees in its garden are moved, holy word! Refuge from sadness, and despair, best type of that eternal rest, for which we look, when the journey of life is ended. Lydia Sigourney, 1850[11]

Scholars in recent decades have been attentive to the vast changes in the American family in the early nineteenth century. They have marshaled an impressive array of evidence to suggest that the middle-class American home became a setting where children were nurtured and edified increasingly by a solicitous mother, who shepherded them away from a forbidding public world. They have stressed the ways in which the changing division of labor between women and men in the American city complemented these developments so that the wife became the emotional center of the home and sheltered her husband from the depredations of the hurly-burly world of commerce. And they have shown how the American family increasingly became disconnected from the patriarchal authority of the church, which in turn engendered a new sphere of influence for women or, put differently, a feminization of American culture. Certainly less maudlin than the poet and writer Lydia Sigourney, scholars today have nonetheless perceived the increased importance of the home as the emotional, feminized center of social life in antebellum America.

Contemporaries also viewed the changes in family structures in the nineteenth century. Observations about a new pattern of family from a Protestant American perspective were perhaps best expressed by Horace Bushnell in 1847 when he published his treatise on "Christian nurture."[12] Increasingly distrustful of the

---

[11] Lydia Howard Sigourney, "Home," in *Whisper to a Bride* (Hartford, CT: Wm. Jas. Hamersley, 1851), 42.

[12] Horace Bushnell, *Christian Nurture* (1847; repr., New Haven, CT: Yale University Press, 1947).

religious revival as a means of salvation, Bushnell eventually stressed the salutary influence of family life in a Christian home. He believed that if children
were nurtured in the home, they would grow up as Christians as a matter of
course. Here he rejected the notion that children would mature in sin only to
be converted in adulthood. "The Christian," he argued, "is one who has simply
begun to love what is good for its own sake, and why should it be thought
impossible for a child to have this love begotten in him?"[13]

The privatized home was central to Bushnell's aspirations for Christian
nurture. In one particularly telling passage, he contended that "the house, having
a domestic Spirit of grace dwelling in it, should become the church of childhood,
the table and hearth a holy rite, and life an element of saving power."[14] A child
steeped in a warm familial environment – "the loveliness of a good life, the
repose of faith, the confidence of righteous expectation, the sacred and cheerful
liberty of the Spirit" – would silently, almost imperceptibly, acknowledge a
spirit of duty and religious obedience to God. This, Bushnell assured his readers,
was "Christian nurture, the nurture of the Lord."[15]

In this tender and loving home, familial relationships were central and the
"organic connections" of parent and child fostered the child's development.
Young children – speculation that children were born in depravity notwithstanding – were "within the matrix of parental life," a condition that would continue
for many of their formative years. "The parental life," Bushnell argued, "will be
flowing into [the child] all that time, just as naturally, and by a law as truly
organic, as when the sap of the trunk flows into a limb."[16] This organic
connection to their parents was central to the material and spiritual sustenance
of children, and when the children became "individual creatures," they would be
inculcated with levels of good and evil depending on that sustenance.

These organic connections, Bushnell believed, were correctives for "modern
speculations" regarding the extreme individualism and doctrines of free will in
contemporary society, because "the parent exercises himself in the child, playing
his emotions and sentiments, and working a character in him, by virtue of an
organic power."[17] Yet they differed from the organicism of Roman Catholicism,
which connected the institution of the home into broader societal institutions
of church and school. As Bushnell himself admitted, the state increasingly was
focused on individual civil rights and the bonds of church authority had been
burst so that the individual was made into "a tribunal of judgment within
itself."[18] In short, if the organic form has been lost to the state and the church,
it was Bushnell's aim to restore it to the family.

[13] Ibid., 9.
[14] Ibid., 12.
[15] Ibid., 12–13.
[16] Ibid., 19.
[17] Ibid., 21.
[18] Ibid., 75.

Bushnell's vision belied the hopes and fears of the condition of the American family in the antebellum era, but it failed to address two questions. First, the *meaning* of the changes within the family has been the subject of much debate. Put simply, for example, did these modifications foster a feminism in society as well as in the home, or did the new American family create an environment that entrapped women? What, in short, did the new family morality mean for its constituent elements? Second, despite changing family norms among many Americans, it nonetheless is true that family structures varied greatly in the United States. If slave families and the kinship structures of Native Americans are obvious examples of household variability, the family structures and norms among those descended from Europe differed as well. As Kirk and Hughes were well aware, the exemplary family form that each celebrated differed from its counterpart.

These two concerns were often linked in the past because contemporaries wed the variability of family structures with an argument that posited advances for humanity and, in particular, for women.[19] Some observers averred the progress of the American family – which they attributed to its Protestant base – by belittling the European or Catholic. In 1839, a French visitor, Michel Chevalier, focused on the development of the United States when he viewed the labor of women. "It is now a universal rule among the Anglo-Americans," he wrote, "that the woman is exempt from all heavy work, and she is never seen, for instance, taking part in the labours of the field, nor in carrying burdens." As a result, Anglo-American women have "also escaped that hideous ugliness and repulsive coarseness of complexion which toil and privation every where else bring upon them." Other women, however, were not as fortunate. Canadian French and Pennsylvania German women continued to toil in the fields "at least as much as the men" and, as a result, remained "wretched objects, who are feminine only with the physiologist." "It is the glory of the *English* race," Chevalier concluded, "that they have every where, as much as possible, interpreted the superiority of the man to the woman, as reserving to the former the charge of the ruder and harder forms of toil. A country in which woman is treated according to this principle presents the aspect of a new and better world."[20]

For Chevalier, the labor differentiation among Anglo-Americans was part of a systematic shift in the distribution of power in the household. In "the earlier times," Chevalier argued, "everything was swallowed up in the father." As time

---

[19] See, for example, Jon Gjerde, "Prescriptions and Perceptions of Labor and Family among Ethnic Groups in the Nineteenth-Century American Middle West," in *German-American Immigration and Ethnicity in Comparative Perspective*, ed. Wolfgang Helbich and Walter D. Kamphoefner (Madison, WI: Max Kade Institute for German-American Studies, 2004), 117–37.

[20] Michel Chevalier, *Society, Manners and Politics in the United States: Being a Series of Letters on North America* (Boston: Weeks, Jordan, 1839), 342–43 (emphasis mine). That Chevalier understood the labor differences as at least in part related to ethnic differences is underscored in his observation that the variations could be traced to Europe. "In England," he wrote in a footnote, "a woman is never seen, as with us [in France], bearing a hamper of dung on her back, or labouring at the forge." Chevalier, *Society, Manners and Politics*, 342n.

passed, "the individuality – the rights, privileges, and duties – of the wife and children was the successive growth of ages." The United States was thus the locus of immense progress because of the American religious and political systems. It was "under the influence of Protestantism and republicanism," Chevalier stressed, that "individuality" found its fullest expression and thereby served as the driving force behind social progress. [21] Indeed, the American farmer spared his wife "all the hard work and employments unsuitable to the sex," according to Chevalier, in large part because he was "initiated" to "the series of that succession of progressive movements which have characterized our civilization ever since it quitted its cradle in the East."[22]

Intergenerational relationships were changing as well. Tocqueville, like Chevalier, utilized his French perspective to argue in the 1830s that "paternal authority, if not abolished, has at least changed form," a development that was even "more striking" in the United States. There, "the father has long anticipated the moment when his authority must come to an end, and when the time does come near, he abdicates without fuss." "The son," however, "has known in advance exactly when he will be his own master and wins his liberty without haste or effort."[23] Tocqueville noted how governmental structures informed family power. In aristocracies, the father was not only the civil head of the family but also the carrier of its traditions and customs, which were cemented with deference and "mingled with fear." In the democratic family, in contrast, "the father scarcely exercises more power than that which is granted to the affection and the experience of age." Every word "a son addresses to his father has a tang of freedom, familiarity, and affection all at once."[24] For Tocqueville, "democracy loosens social ties, but it tightens natural ones."[25]

Observations by Protestant Americans complemented those of Tocqueville. The Presbyterian Rev. J. H. McIlvaine, in a discourse that celebrated the Protestantism of the United States, cited an idealized encounter between father and son. On coming of age, the son was approached by his "good and wise father," who said, "[M]y son, you are no longer a child; you are now a man. From this time you have no master but God." As an individual freed of explicit responsibility toward kith and kin, the son nonetheless was called by God and his country "to liberty and to duty." It was the father's hope that the son would behave with honor and that social progress would accrue as a result.[26]

Roman Catholics often shared a sensibility that valued nurturance within the family. Catholic novelists' morality tales are replete with instances of parents teaching their children. Yet Roman Catholic leaders were less willing to

---

[21] Ibid., 368–69.
[22] Ibid., 428, 430.
[23] Alexis de Tocqueville, *Democracy in America*, ed. J. P. Mayer (New York: Anchor Books, 1969), 585.
[24] Ibid., 587–88.
[25] Ibid., 589.
[26] Rev. J. H. McIlvaine, *A Nation's Right to Worship God: An Address Before the American Whig and Cliosophic Societies of the College of New Jersey* (Trenton, NJ: Murphy and Bechtel, 1859), 5–6.

acknowledge the religious centrality of the home. If Protestant morality and spirituality originated in the home, argues Colleen McDannell, Catholics saw the family as an extension of the church.[27] Because of the importance of the sacraments, which were celebrated in the physical space of the church, the home was only an adjunct to public activities. This distinction waxed in the nineteenth century amid a growing devotionalism when American Catholics were building an institutional structure composed of churches and schools that reinforced, and often superseded, familial nurture.

Reflecting these changes, Catholics venerated a multifaceted religious institution and in turn developed a critique of the American Protestant family, which, they contended, suffered from too much privatization. If Bushnell's nurture was home centered and associated with psychological and spiritual links between parent and child, then, Catholic observers expressed skepticism about these privatized ambitions. Indeed, the Catholic view of societal development continued to stress the organic interrelationships of church and even the state with the family. The Catholic family ideal, in sum, disparaged the approbation of the individualized family so treasured by apologists for the American household.

Catholic critics ultimately developed an assessment of the state of the family in the United States that condemned the Protestant pattern for its tendency to privatize and individualize relationships within the home. Bereft of an appropriate authority in both the home and community institutions, the Protestant home spawned weaknesses in the family and society alike. These weaknesses, the criticism continued, had a series of ramifications. For one, Protestant practices that dominated American society had harmful consequences for Catholics, who often lived in poverty and as the social inferiors of the Protestant elite. For another, the trajectory of the Protestant home boded ill for the American future. If a growing materialism and individualism endured within the home, Catholic critics warned, the United States was in distress. Similar to their broader critique of American society outlined in Chapter 2, Catholic observers saw their contribution to the United States to be one that rescued the larger American society from misfortunes of its own making.

The conversation about the family between Protestants and Catholics illustrates the divergent worldviews fostered by religious difference *and* the inherent contradictions of their respective family ideologies. The Protestant critique of Catholicism regarding the family and the place of women within it focused on the authoritarian and regressive nature of Roman Catholic society. Women were captives of institutions that abused them. The rhetoric of slavery, so close to the surface of all things in American antebellum society, was often invoked. In contrast, the Protestant American home was a site of nurture and sustenance, a move forward from a past of mistreatment and unparalleled inequality. The Catholic experience in the United States, however, discerned its own captivities. If Protestants focused on the institutions of the Church as inherent dangers to

[27] Colleen McDannell, *The Christian Home in Victorian America, 1840–1900* (Bloomington: Indiana University Press, 1986), 104.

women and the family, Catholics perceived their own literal incarceration by the state and the privatized family as forms of captivity. The poorhouse and the orphanage were, for example, secular environments (and an extension of the common school) where people were imprisoned and denied spiritual succor. (The parallels between the state-run prison and the convent were not a coincidence.) And the Protestant family not only stifled true belief, it also allowed individuals to run amok, reveling in values of materialism and indolence detrimental to society. These forms of Catholic captivity and the destructive nature of the Protestant home served as evidence for the competing claims that a pillorized Catholic world needed support and that the Catholic family was beneficial for American society writ large.

Catholic and Protestant American paeans to their family forms, in contrast to their critiques of each other, exposed ambivalence and contradiction. This was especially so among Protestants who criticized the growing Catholic presence in America. The criticism of the captivity of women in Catholic institutions – such as the convent – might have been seen, for example, as a disparagement of authority, including patriarchal authority, within the home. Yet despite the celebration of the advance of womanhood in the new American family, one of the chief criticisms of Catholicism was the way it intruded, in the form of the confessional, on husbandly authority within the home.

The Catholic Peril to the American Family: The Convent, the Priest, and the Confessional

O, what an infernal power does the confessional give to every wicked priest! The very soul of the penitent is crushed, and virtue becomes a plaything in the hands of a bachelor monk, who has no living bond of union with his race. Rector of Oldenwold, 1857[28]

Critics of Catholicism, such as the Rector of Oldenwold, denounced Roman Catholic institutions, amid the changes occurring in antebellum America, as a threat to the American family and those living within it. Indeed, the Rector's brief condemnation contains a number of the criticisms commonly expressed by Catholicism's detractors. For one, critics argued that the Church, in its advocacy of specific family forms and in its clerical structure, was regressive. The critique of the family thus mirrored those that stressed the archaic Catholic influences in society, polity, and economy. The prisonlike convent, the celibate priest, and the secretive confessional were interlocking institutions that aptly illustrated the ravages of Catholic life on its practitioners and, more ominously for Protestants, on those who came within the Church's sphere of influence.[29]

---

[28] Rector of Oldenwold, *The Cloven Foot; or, Popery Aiming at Political Supremacy in the United States* (Boston: Wentworth, 1857), 289.

[29] One title aptly encapsulates most of the accusations against the convent: Andrew B. Cross, *Priests' Prisons for Women; or, A Consideration of the Question, Whether Unmarried Foreign Priests*

Protestant critics first fixed their gaze on the convent, where nuns lived in repression and imprisonment. In this gendered story, the depredations of the priest and the mother superior on the entrapped sister reflected the captivity of women and, as such, were common themes in the anti-Catholic literature of the antebellum era. The convent was characterized by its prisonlike building and by the secretive relationships between the clergy and their charges, both in Catholic orders and in the family itself. Secrecy complemented manipulation and regression. Yet the Church and the domestic forms it fostered affected the familial world outside of its orders, for the Church was manipulative in the ways it entered the private conjugal family and skewed relationships to its own ends. Another threat was the celibate priest, whose authoritarian posture flew in the face of the new emphasis on nurture in the American home. Church institutions intruded into the private family, an intrusion most obvious in how Catholic school students were indoctrinated to the ways of the Church and encouraged to provide it resources at the expense of aged parents. Still, the most insidious site was the confessional, where the priest encroached on the domestic scene. Like the fabled Jesuit wire-puller in political life, the priest, in another gendered narrative, was able to distort relations between husband and wife and function as a surrogate husband.

These influences, as they paralleled developments in the larger society, also reinforced the predicaments that Catholicism allegedly imposed on institutions beyond the home. Regression, particularly forms of female oppression, resembled loathsome practices – polygamy and widow burning were commonly cited – that characterized barbaric societies elsewhere in the world and seemingly were reflected in other arenas of Catholic life in the United States. Manipulative schemes were applied not only to the family but also to political institutions around the world. Concerns about authoritarianism spoke to larger anxieties about the influence of despotic figures and organizations on the individual conscience, a thriving economy, and the free exercise of political belief.

The convent was perhaps most fully explored in a series of mid-nineteenth-century exposés that allegedly were firsthand accounts of life in the religious community and escape from it. The first flurry of reports, published in the mid-1830s, coincided with the outrage surrounding the burning of the Ursuline convent in Boston in 1834.[30] They were followed by reports published at midcentury amid the growth of anti-Catholicism and the flowering of the Know Nothing

Ought To Be Permitted To Erect Prisons, Into Which, Under Pretence of Religion, To Seduce or Entrap, or by Force Compel Young Women to Enter, and After They Have Secured Their Property, Keep Them in Confinement and Compel Them, as Their Slaves, to Submit Themselves to Their Will, Under the Penalty of Flogging or the Dungeon? (Baltimore: P. B. Sherwood, 1854).

[30] Maria Monk, *Awful Disclosures of Maria Monk, As Exhibited in a Narrative of her Sufferings During a Residence of Five Years as a Novice, and Two Years as a Black Nun, in the Hotel Dieu Nunnery at Montreal* (New York: Howe and Bates, 1836); Maria Monk, *Awful Disclosures of Maria Monk, of the Hotel Dieu Nunnery of Montreal, Revised, with an Appendix* (New York: Published by Maria Monk, 1836); Rebecca Theresa Reed, *Six Months in a Convent; or, The Narrative of Rebecca Theresa Reed, who was under the influence of the Roman Catholics about Two Years, and an Inmate of the Ursuline Convent on Mount Benedict, Charlestown, Mass.,*

movement.[31] These accounts borrowed heavily from an earlier European literature on the convent and provided grist for a variety of American commentators, from political leaders to clergymen to popular novelists.[32] A form of protopornography – concerns about illicit sex in the convent – even found their way into church publications, such as the *Methodist Quarterly Review*, which in 1842 described convents as "styes of pollution."[33]

The anticonvent literature offered similar narrative structures and character development, and repeatedly expressed concern about the repressiveness of convent life. In effect, these were captivity narratives of imprisonment and escape.[34] They depicted repeated instances of claustrophobia, suffocation, imprisonment, bondage, gagging, and forced silence. Young women found themselves entering the convent as a result of either their own naïveté or the cunning of priests. Once there, they were trapped in a physical and spiritual prison from which they had little hope of escape. A sister, who was either disgruntled or mad, often befriended the narrative's protagonist, who begins to see the ruin that she faces. The event precipitating an escape usually was a rape or an attempted rape. In the case of Maria Monk, it was a pregnancy and the prospect of the infanticide of her soon-to-be-born child (see Fig. 6). Both Josephine Bunkley and Edith O'Gorman hatched plans to escape following the unwelcome advances of a priest.[35] The escape was both terrifying and liberating. Fearful of the watchful eye of obedient Catholics or of the clandestine activities of the Jesuits, the fugitive nun was at constant risk. Yet, at the same time, the escapees expressed relief at their release from what Rebecca Reed termed "the Romish yoke."[36]

---

nearly six months, in the years 1831–2 (Boston: Russell, Odiorne and Metcalf, 1835); Committee of Publication, *Supplement to "Six Months in a Convent," Confirming the Narrative of Rebecca Theresa Reed, by the Testimony of More than One Hundred Witnesses, Whose Statements Have Been Given to the Committee* (Boston: Russell, Odiorne, 1835).

[31] Josephine M. Bunkley, *The Testimony of an Escaped Novice From the Sisterhood of St. Joseph, Emmettsburg, Maryland, the Mother-house of the Sisters of Charity in the United States* (New York: Harper and Brothers, 1855); Edith O'Gorman, *Trials and Persecutions of Miss Edith O'Gorman: Otherwise Sister Theresa de Chantal, of St. Joseph's Convent, Hudson City, N.J., Written By Herself, With an Appendix by the Publisher* (Hartford: Connecticut Publishing, 1884).

[32] On the former, see, the political tract *Pope, or President? Startling Disclosures of Romanism as Revealed by its Own Writers. Facts for Americans* (New York: R. L. Delisser, 1859). On the latter, see, for example, Scipio de Ricci, *Female Convents. Secrets of Nunneries Disclosed. Compiled from the Autograph Manuscripts of Scipio de Ricci by Mr. De Potter. Edited by Thomas Roscoe. With an Introductory Essay and Appendix* (New York: D. Appleton, 1834); and Isaac Kelso, *Danger in the Dark: A Tale of Intrigue and Priestcraft* (Cincinnati: Moore Anderson, Wilstach and Keys, 1854).

[33] Cited in D. Gregory Van Dussen, "An American Response to Irish Catholic Immigration," *Methodist Quarterly Review* 29 (1990): 29.

[34] See, for example, James R. Lewis, "'Mind-Forged Manacles': Anti-Catholic Convent Narratives in the Context of the American Captivity Tale Tradition," *Mid-America* 72 (1990): 149–67; and Jenny Franchot, *Roads to Rome: The Antebellum Protestant Encounter with Catholicism* (Berkeley: University of California Press, 1994), esp. 135–61.

[35] Bunkley, *Testimony of an Escaped Novice From the Sisterhood of St. Joseph*, 143; O'Gorman, *Trials and Persecutions of Miss Edith O'Gorman*, 106–16.

[36] Committee of Publication, *Supplement to "Six Months in a Convent,"* 185.

FIGURE 6. Maria Monk was the subject of one of many nineteenth-century convent narratives that claimed to expose the repression of women within Catholic institutions. (From *Awful Disclosures of the Hotel Dieu Nunnery* [New York, 1836])

Although the convent narratives were formulaic, they laid out a consistent and powerful critique of life in a sisterhood and, by implication, of the repression of women by Catholic institutions. The convent was, basically, a site of incarceration or entombment. It was a place, wrote an author in the *Living Age* in 1856, with such "massive walls, grating, bolts, locks, and other devices" that "no felon prison [could] have a better system of securities."[37] It was a setting where women were

---

[37] "Life in Brazil," *Living Age* 50 (August 1856): 416.

crushed "within the walls of a cloister," similar to "burying the heart in a living sepulchre."[38] How could one believe that God brought humans into being, asked a character in Isaac Kelso's novel *Danger in the Dark*, "for no higher object or nobler purpose than that of filling a living grave?"[39] Given the salience of a thriving system of chattel slavery in antebellum America, perhaps the most powerful allegation pointed out the resemblance between convent inmates and slaves. Narratives repeatedly observed that women lived as captives in convents and worked tirelessly without pay for the good of the convent while the bishop and the mother superior lived in luxury.[40] Nuns continually had to cope with the threat of physical and sexual abuse; they had little hope of escape; they were, anti-Catholics observers insisted, patently unfree.

Some critics argued that convent life was *worse* than chattel slavery. Andrew B. Cross, writing in Baltimore in the 1850s, was explicit in his comparisons. "A young white women, a native born citizen of Baltimore," he insisted, "becomes *bona fide* property of the convent" after living there for one year. "The young lady," he continued, "becomes the slave, the victim of the priest." Here among families in free America, Cross lamented, existed an institution "whose object is to *kidnap* their daughters, and *imprison* them as *free white slaves*, the property of the priests." Like slaveholders, priests "gloried in tyranny" and "reveled in licentiousness" as they controlled both the body and the soul of the individual.[41] The priest's control of the soul was particularly notable because it made the slavery of the sisterhood especially repressive. As nativists contended during the Rebecca Reed controversy in 1835, "the worst and most debasing of all slavery [was] *the slavery of the mind*," which was a "mental subjection *not less effectual than external force.*"[42]

The combination of corporeal and spiritual enslavement was a powerful brew. The varieties of exploitation of the body were numerous. Most attention was of course paid to sexual abuse, which historians have equated with the pornography of the antebellum era. Perhaps the most notorious example of the powerlessness of nuns and the rapaciousness of their captors is the description in *The Awful Disclosures of Maria Monk*. Published in early 1836, with support from Arthur Tappen and Theodore Dwight among others, Maria Monk's story is set in the Black Nunnery in Montreal.[43] Receiving no religious instruction in her childhood home and with an inclination to "think well of the Catholics,"

---

[38] Bunkley, *Testimony of an Escaped Novice From the Sisterhood of St. Joseph*, 35.
[39] Kelso, *Danger in the Dark*, 179.
[40] Committee of Publication, *Supplement to "Six Months in a Convent,"* 165.
[41] Cross, *Priests' Prisons for Women*, 5.
[42] Committee of Publication, *Supplement to "Six Months in a Convent,"* 99.
[43] Maria Monk's narrative is the iconographic example of the convent captivity tale, but it was one among many. On its influence, see Ray Allen Billington, *The Protestant Crusade, 1800–1860* (New York: Macmillan, 1938), 99–108; Franchot, *Roads to Rome*, 135–61; and Susan M. Griffin, *Anti-Catholicism and Nineteenth-Century Fiction* (Cambridge: Cambridge University Press, 2004), 27–61. Other influential convent texts include Committee of Publication, *Supplement to "Six Months in a Convent"*; Rosamond Culbertson, *Rosamond; or, A Narrative of the Captivity and Sufferings of*

Maria drifts toward Catholicism and eventually takes the veil. The rite itself, which resembled ritual death, involved her lying in a coffin and covered by an incense-laden cloth that "proved almost suffocating."[44] After taking the veil, Maria learns the awful truth from the mother superior that "one of [her] duties was to obey the priests in all things," including living "in the practice of criminal intercourse with them."[45] Because celibate priests live "secluded, laborious, and self-denying lives for our salvation," the mother superior continued, this conduct "was pleasing in the sight of God."[46] Maria demurs, and then she hears further of a practice that is "scarcely less dreadful": infants born to these unions were baptized and then immediately strangled. "This secured their everlasting happiness," explained the mother superior, for they were "sent out of the world before they had time to do anything wrong" and "were at once admitted into heaven."[47]

The remainder of Maria's tale is a story of captivity, claustrophobia, and dismay. Willful nuns are smothered and crushed; a fourteen-year-old, the youngest of the nuns, is "ill-treated" by priests and lives only for a short time thereafter; babies are suffocated with callous indifference; brutal penances are assigned; and priests take "holy retreats" to be treated for attacks of disease. The combination of allusions to torture, rape, pedophilia, sadism, and sexually transmitted disease was a heady mix for antebellum readers. Moreover, like the travel literature of the era, Maria gives her reader a detailed description of the convent, a world into which few of them would ever set foot. She discovers the cellar where infants are buried, as well as the secret codes that allow priests to enter the convent via a hidden passage. She describes the convent's interiors in detail, including the "small sitting room" where the priest waits to baptize the infants before the babies are murdered. The carefully detailed account, with its series of mysterious events, closes when a pregnant Maria escapes the captivity of the convent and finds refuge with the Protestant clergyman to whom she reputedly recounts her story.

Maria Monk's tales reflected a long-standing and trans-Atlantic literature on convents and an enduring critique of Roman Catholicism in antebellum America.[48] Her narrative's structure and characters, moreover, were templates for later stories of sexual exploitation that were steeped in the gothic genre of the period and set

an American Female under the Popish Priests, in the Island of Cuba, with a full disclosure of their manners and customs, written by herself, With an Introduction and Notes, by Samuel B. Smith (New York: Leavitt, Lord, 1836); Harry Hazel, *The Nun of St. Ursula, or, the Burning of the Convent. A Romance of Mt. St. Benedict* (Boston: Gleason, 1845); Charles Frothingham, *The Convent's Doom: A Tale of Charlestown in 1834* (Boston: Graves and Weston, 1854); and Helen Dhu, *Stanhope Burleigh: The Jesuits in Our Homes* (New York: Stringer and Townsend, 1855).

44 Monk, *Awful Disclosures of Maria Monk* (New York: Published by Maria Monk, 1836), 7, 30.

45 Ibid., 30–31.

46 Ibid., 31.

47 Ibid.

48 European critics of Roman Catholicism were common, including Scipio de Ricci and Hobart Seymour. See Bunkley, *Testimony of an Escaped Novice From the Sisterhood of St. Joseph*, 141ff., which includes some European examples. Indeed, Maria Monk was accused of plagiarizing a European convent narrative. Monk, *Awful Disclosures of Maria Monk*, 208.

in a variety of subcultures in antebellum America. The convent also was a common setting in mysteries read by European immigrants. Two German American free-thinkers, Emil Klauprecht and Henry Boernstein, published novels that detailed the depredations of the Catholic threat in the United States, again with an eye to the iniquities found in the convent.[49] Klauprecht and Boernstein were certainly influenced by European traditions,[50] but their novels also contained the familiar vignettes of the incarcerated nun and the spiritual and physical abuse she encountered in the convent.

If the convent literature written by European immigrants was certainly shaped in part by European influences such as the mystery genre, the representation of convents in the English-language press was inspired for decades thereafter by themes and characters developed in the 1830s. The story of escape by Josephine Bunkley, published in 1855, for example, recounts an experience similar to Maria Monk's. Josephine's descriptions are more demure than those of Maria, perhaps a reflection of a more decorous convent literature in the 1850s. Nonetheless, she explains that she was forced to drink an "intensely biter and nauseous" liquid on becoming a nun, after which she fell into a deep slumber. The events that follow are recounted only in vague terms, but they are designed to teach the young woman that "henceforth she has no will of her own, but the will of the Superior is her law, which must be obeyed even to the slightest particular."[51] The convent remains a place of abject submission and mysterious comings and goings. Daily life there is punctuated by priestly abuse and feelings of contempt and abhorrence for the priests' behavior. It is a place, as already mentioned, from which Josephine flees following the unwelcome advances of her confessor.[52] If Bunkley's account is more reserved than that of Maria Monk, Isaac Kelso's novel, *Danger in the Dark*, portrays the lecherous priest as a comic figure. To be sure, the convent is a place of terror, but the young victims repeatedly rebuff the hapless Father Dupin's attempts at torture or abuse. In one episode, Dupin is in bed with the abbess and is wearing her clothes. When, still clad in female attire, he pursues a group of fleeing nuns, he is beaten by the nuns' male ally. "He became desperately exasperated," Kelso informs his readers, "and kindled to such a diabolical rage that he

[49] Emil Klauprecht, *Cincinnati, oder, Geheimnisse des Westens* (Cincinnati: C. F. Schmidt, 1854–55); Henry Boernstein, *The Mysteries of St. Louis, A Novel*, trans. Friedrich Münch, ed. Steven Rowan and Elizabeth Sims (Chicago: Charles H. Kerr, 1990). Klauprecht has been translated: Emil Klauprecht, *Cincinnati, or, The Mysteries of the West: Emil Klauprecht's German-American Novel*, trans. Steven Rowan, ed. Don Heinrich Tolzmann (New York: Peter Lang, 1996). Both authors, as we shall see, provide a different perspective from either Catholics or American-born Protestants on a variety of issues, including the state of women in the American family.

[50] The title of their books, both invoking an urban "mystery," clearly are taken from Eugene Sue, *Les Mysteres de Paris*, first published in 1842. Indeed, Klauprecht makes explicit reference to Sue (540). See Don Heinrich Tolzmann, "Introduction: The Great Cincinnati German Novel," in *Cincinnati; or, The Mysteries of the West*, xi-xxv, for a comprehensive introduction to the novel and mystery genre.

[51] Bunkley, *Testimony of an Escaped Novice From the Sisterhood of St. Joseph*, 55–56.

[52] Ibid., 142–43.

almost exploded."[53] Regardless of the tone of the narrative, the entrapped nun was a powerful symbol of the deficits of the Roman Catholic faith in general and, in particular, of the ravages Catholicism wrought on women in convents.

If sexual abuse was one form of bodily mistreatment, self-mortification was another. Convent narratives and anti-Catholic reports were filled with accounts of self-abnegation. Robert Anderson Wilson, in his exposé of Catholicism in Mexico, aptly summarized the physical misery of convent life. "In a cold, damp, comfortless cell, kneeling upon the pavement," wrote Wilson,

we may see a delicate woman mechanically repeating her daily-imposed penance of Latin Prayers, before the image of a favorite saint and a basin of holy water. This self-regulating, automaton praying machine, as she counts off the number of allotted prayers by the number of beads upon her rosary, beats into her bosom the sharp edge of an iron cross that rests within her shirt of sacking-cloth, until, nature and her task exhausted, she throws herself down upon a wooden bed, so ingeniously arranged as to make sleep intolerable.[54]

Physical torment could be most cruel.[55] When Rebecca Reed complains about her failing strength, she was told by her superior that she "should have left [her] feelings in the world" and ordered, as penance, "to make the sign of the cross on the floor with [her] tongue" and to eat only a crust of bread in the morning. Wilson cited a tale from Madame Calderon de la Barca in which a young woman was received into the convent because of the fineness of her voice, which ultimately proved a "fatal gift." Wishing to display the young woman's voice publicly, the abbess forced "her to sing a hymn alone, on her knees, her arms extended in the form of a cross" before a large crowd. The spectacle was dreadful, Calderon de la Barca informed her readers, because the girl's "voice faltered, and instead of singing, she seemed inclined to cry out." As the performance continued, "each note came slowly, heavily, tremblingly" until she fell forward, exhausted.[56] Maria Monk's tales of penance and torment, however, were even more graphic. She remembered that one of the most disgusting penances to which she had to submit was drinking the water used to wash her mother superior's feet. (The mad trickster in the tale, Jane Ray, comforted her by saying that it was better than drinking pure water.) Yet this was only the beginning. "Kissing the floor is a very common penance," Monk noted,

[53] Kelso, *Danger in the Dark*, 185–90 (quotation from 190).

[54] Robert A. Wilson, *Mexico and its Religion; With Incidents of Travel in That Country During Parts of Years 1851–52–53–54, and Historical Notices of Events, Connected with Places Visited* (New York: Harper and Brothers, 1855), 341.

[55] See Griffin, *Anti-Catholicism and Nineteenth-Century Fiction*, 31.

[56] Madame C[alderon] de la B[arca], *Life in Mexico, During a Residence of Two Years in That Country* (London: Chapman and Hall, 1843), cited in Wilson, *Mexico and its Religion*, 157. Madame Calderon de la Barca was born Frances Erskine Inglis in Edinburgh in 1804, grew up residing at Boston, Staten Island, and Baltimore, and married Don Angel Calderon de la Barca, who was appointed minister to Mexico in 1838. The letters she wrote were assembled into a manuscript. Despite her criticisms, Calderon de la Barca ultimately converted to Roman Catholicism.

kneeling and kissing the feet of the other nuns is another; as are kneeling on hard peas, and walking with them in the shoes. We had repeatedly to walk on our knees through the subterranean passage, and sometimes to eat our meals with a rope round our necks. Sometimes we were fed only with such things as we most disliked. . . . One of the penances was to stand for a length of time with our arms extended, in imitation of the Saviour on the Cross. . . . Sometimes we were obliged to sleep on the floor in the winter, with nothing over us but a single sheet; and sometimes to chew a piece of window glass to a fine powder, in the presence of the Superior.

Amid this torture, the more severe penances were resisted, Maria informed her readers, in which case the nuns were gagged.[57]

Convent narratives repeatedly recounted the physical costs of these practices to the author and those around her. Josephine Bunkley noted the frequency of sickness and death in the convent. She observed that she was "often sick, worn down and utterly prostrated by the services daily and uninterruptedly required of [her]." Consumption was a particularly common affliction of the sisters, many of whom died as a result. Bunkley attested that fourteen nuns had perished during her ten-month stay at St. Joseph's.[58] At times, authors contended that the physical abuse was designed to bring compliance with the aims of the Church. A character in Boernstein's novel recounted her path in becoming "a pliant tool of the Church," which resulted in "moral sorrows" that ultimately led to her premature death.[59] A political tract from the American Party in the 1850s was more succinct. "We never yet saw [a convent]," it observed, "but it was surrounded with high walls . . . as if it was the place of death itself." Moreover, it continued, "we never yet saw a nun . . . who had a good honest womanly look."[60]

In this spiritual and physical dungeon, the outcomes could not be good. According to Hobart Seymour, some nuns in England, after taking the veil, "pined, and drooped, and withered, and died," whereas others, "struggling against it for a time, in the end gave way to despair, and died of madness." Without escape, Seymour continued, the majority would die deranged before they reached their twenty-fifth birthday.[61] Edward Beecher observed a sort of Hobson's choice for nuns: those who remained in the convent "long resist temptation by a kind of living martyrdom; and of these some become insane," whereas those who escaped were often "slandered and declared insane."[62] And as a character in one antebellum novel observed, there was nothing "more iniquitous and unpardonable, than the leading of young girls, by operating on their superstitious fears, to bury themselves

---

[57] Monk, *Awful Disclosures of Maria Monk*, (New York: Howe and Bates, 1836), 72–73, 118.

[58] Bunkley, *Testimony of an Escaped Novice From the Sisterhood of St. Joseph*, 91, 216.

[59] Boernstein, *Mysteries of St. Louis*, 275.

[60] *Know Nothing Almanac and True Americans' Manual for 1855* (New York: DeWitt and Davenport, 1855), 50.

[61] Bunkley, *Testimony of an Escaped Novice From the Sisterhood of St. Joseph*, 217–18 (citing Rev. M. Hobart Seymour).

[62] Edward Beecher, *The Papal Conspiracy Exposed and Protestantism Defended, in the Light of Reason, History, and Scripture* (Boston: Stearns, 1855), 202.

in convents, where they are to pass their days in gloomy seclusion and wretchedness – torturing and attenuating their bodies to fit their souls for heaven!" This was only made worse when the "hapless victims" were made to feel that "their suffering [was] voluntary and self-inflicted."[63]

In sum, taking the veil symbolized female oppression of the body and mind, and the convent represented spiritual and physical enslavement. As such, convents were often linked with other regressive cultural forms that thrived elsewhere in the less developed world. Josephine Bunkley put it simply: Mother Seton could "rival the Hindoos in self-mortification."[64] Yet other commentators were more specific. The practice in India of burning a widow after her husband's death was repeatedly invoked as being akin to entrance into a convent. Madame Calderon de la Barca compared the woman's brave face when taking the veil with the widow's demeanor at a widow burning. "The nun kept laughing every now and then in the most unnatural and hysterical manner," she wrote, "apparently to impress us with the conviction of her perfect happiness." The feigned happiness was the same as that "which makes the Hindoo widow mount the funeral pile without a tear in her eye, or a sigh on her lips."[65] The barbarity of becoming a nun was all the worse because it took place in the United States. Perhaps, as some suggested, "the infernal process of cruelty" should be kept secret "within the walls of a dungeon," because it did not injure public morals and was really a private matter. Yet if Brahmins insisted that the widow burning in India was a custom that affected neither the property nor the happiness of others, one would rightfully interfere in private actions for the public good, just as Americans should do with regard to the scourge of convents in their midst.[66] If the convent betokened regression, the implication was that the condition of American women prefigured upward progress. And if Protestant America permitted these abuses to continue because they were none of its business, it was complicit in a barbarism toward women that existed in their own land.

Whereas nuns in convents served as one symbol in the Protestant story of familial irregularity and injustice to women among Roman Catholics, the priest played a complementary role.[67] The priest unmistakably possessed a power denied nuns, a power that was characterized by a dangerous mix of spiritual authority over his followers and a monomaniacal desire to gain temporal power for his church. Moreover, if the nun's story was one that exemplified the regressive nature of the Church, the priest's was a narrative of conspiracy.

In large part because of his celibacy, the priest, like the nun, also embodied an "unnatural" quality that violated his sex and the family and further empowered

---

[63] Kelso, *Danger in the Dark*, 61.

[64] Bunkley, *Testimony of an Escaped Novice From the Sisterhood of St. Joseph*, 207.

[65] de la B[arca], *Life in Mexico*, 155.

[66] Reed, *Six Months in a Convent*, 20.

[67] See Marie Anne Pagliarini, "The Pure American Woman and the Wicked Catholic Priest: An Analysis of Anti-Catholic Literature in Antebellum America," *Religion and American Culture* 9 (1999): 97–128.

the Church. If he remained celibate, Maria Monk explained, the priest's unnatural condition subverted "all the appointments of Jehovah in reference to the duties and usefulness of man."[68] If God implanted parental feelings in humankind, William Nevins agreed, why would God deny important elements of the knowledge of what those feelings were?[69] Celibacy, moreover, allowed the Church to have a supply of zealous men who would carry out its designs. "Men are needed," Edward Beecher mused, "fanatical, degraded, cruel, immitigable, and unprincipled, to carry such a system [as Romanism]." Celibacy served well to produce the desired results, for it "cuts off the clergy from all ties of family and home" and focused their attention on the designs of Rome.[70] If celibacy fostered a monomaniacal dedication to the Church, it did not cultivate happiness within the family. Celibate men knew nothing of the family and, in fact, harbored a hatred of conjugal love simply because it was denied them. Because the priest knew nothing of "conjugal love in its holy and chaste character," wrote one observer, "he hates it, he detests it, often with the utmost sincerity and perfect good faith."[71]

Because the priest did not remain celibate, as was often alleged in anti-Catholic literature, he also perverted the institution of the family by reproducing such regressive cultural forms as the harem or the brothel and thereby undermining the ideal of the conjugal family. Maria Monk explained that priests found it difficult to live "contrary to nature" and that they would be "great fools if they did not use and enjoy [the privilege of going into the nunneries]."[72] Yet she also portrayed the horrors that resulted. Clearly insinuating slavery and prostitution, the former priest and subsequent anti-Catholic Samuel B. Smith admitted to having "several *cages of nuns* under his sole management" during his days as a priest.[73] In contrast, nuns dreamt of a sort of fairyland called "Nun's Island," an earthly paradise that was seemingly a privilege to visit but was in reality a trip to Montreal where young women were instructed in the "mystery of iniquity."[74]

The sexual exploits of the priests were puzzling to some. Not only celibate but also typically clothed in a black, dresslike cassock and often clean shaven, priests presented an image that suggested a feminine countenance. Yet observers repeatedly marveled at the successes of priests in love. George Lippard, in *The Quaker City; or, The Monks of Monk-Hall*, provides the stock figure of Doctor Ravoni, a mysterious Jesuit who is particularly practiced in the arts of seduction.[75]

---

[68] Monk, *Awful Disclosures of Maria Monk*, 327.

[69] William Nevins, *Thoughts on Popery* (New York: American Tract Society, 1836), 102. Nevins also cited 1 Timothy 3:5 ("For if a man know not how to rule his own house, how shall he take care of the church of God") to argue against a celibate priesthood (144–46).

[70] Beecher, *Papal Conspiracy Exposed*, 148.

[71] Bunkley, *Testimony of an Escaped Novice From the Sisterhood of St. Joseph*, 306.

[72] Monk, *Awful Disclosures of Maria Monk*, 330–31.

[73] Ibid., 331.

[74] Ibid., 353.

[75] George Lippard, *The Monks of Monk Hall* (New York: Odyssey Press, 1970), 449; originally published as *The Quaker City; or, The Monks of Monk-Hall: A Romance of Philadelphia Life, Mystery, and Crime* (Philadelphia: G. B. Ziebler, 1844).

Another Jesuit, Vitelleschi, who is found in Klauprecht's mystery, is asked by a lover how it is that "the blackcoated gentlemen" are successful with women. Perhaps, she suggests, "there must be a secret spiritual magic which is your monopoly, and which makes it possible for you to turn the imagination of girls and women in such a way so that they prefer those dried-out abbes to handsome rosy cheeked Seladons." In fact, Vitelleschi explains, "our magic potion and talisman with which we entice [women] is religion, which is a surrogate for the incomparable beauty which was lost to the world in Greek myth."[76] In these narratives, the power of priestly authority transformed the earthbound human and entranced the women under his control.

If the convent and rectory were two sites of aberrant behavior, the iniquity of Catholicism was perhaps best exemplified in a third site, the confessional, where priests used their power both to seduce women and to subvert the conjugal family.[77] The convent narratives, of course, focused on the dreadful consequences stemming from the interaction between nun and priest in the confessional, where the former became ever more docile as the influence of the latter became all the more powerful.

The confessional, however, was also a site of indecent interaction between the priest and women in the world. Edward Beecher's imagination appears almost overwrought as he sought to describe the depravity of confession. "Here, now," he wrote, "is an unmarried priest surrounded by hundreds or thousands of females." These women had "their frailties, their impure thoughts, their temptations," which no man could easily discover. But the confessional provided the priest with a secret weapon. "It spreads before him," Beecher continued, "a perfect map of every female heart in his whole flock," because all women disclosed to him "their most secret thought as to God." If "the natural laws of female modesty" could operate and if the priest had "no religious pretext for introducing sensual ideas," all would be well. But the confessional intervened and "under a pretence of religion, introduces a regular conversation at stated intervals between the priest and every female of his flock on all topics involved in the violation of chastity, in thought, word and deed."[78] Bunkley's sexual imagery was even more explicit. Here the priest, "armed with the assumed authority of God," officiated "to the suppliant slaves prostrate before him." He dispensed absolution to the "faithful and submissive" and assigned penance to expiate sin. "Seated at the confessional," she continued,

he is empowered, by virtue of his self-arrogated position, to propound queries which, for the lips of others, would be deemed flagrant insults. Kneeling there, the young maiden answers questions calculated to eradicate every feeling of modesty, woman's highest charm, and lays bare to the inquisitive search of her "spiritual director" every secret

[76] Klauprecht, *Cincinnati; or, The Mysteries of the West*, 593.
[77] For the British perspective on this issue, see Susan David Bernstein, *Confessional Subjects: Revelations of Gender and Power in Victorian Literature and Culture* (Chapel Hill: University of North Carolina Press, 1997).
[78] Beecher, *Papal Conspiracy Exposed*, 184, 187.

thought, every incipient emotion, every impulse of her being. How easy, then for an evil-disposed confessor stealthily to infuse into the innocent and trusting heart, taught to consider blind obedience a virtue, thoughts, whose growth, cherished by his daily care, shall soon fill it with a diseased vegetation.

It was no surprise, Bunkley concluded, that those who were raised in such an environment of total surveillance would yield themselves to priestly control and "see no danger in their abject submissiveness, nor evil purpose in [the priest's] exercise of unlimited power."[79] Because female penitents often gave answers that "should shame a demon," wrote another, it was not surprising that the confessional was the "parent of prostitution and crime."[80]

Confession symbolized to many Protestants the inherent failing of Catholicism. For some, it encouraged rather than absolved sin. Kirwan, a convert to Protestantism, contended that confession made "the bosom of the priest the repository of all the sins of all the sinners of his parish." And the rite resulted in even further sin because after confession "the load of guilt was gone," so that Kirwan felt he could commit sin with impunity.[81]

Perhaps more significantly, the confessional both amplified the power of the priest and impaired an individual's freedom of conscience. Josephine Bunkley made the connection between churchly power and loss of individual thought explicit. "Confession," she pointed out, "is the chief and most potent appliance by which the Church of Rome gains ascendancy over individual minds and bodies." Without the confessional, the Church was "a powerless mechanism, a huge, inert mass, deprived of its motive power and ruling energy." The confessional was the root of the "grand secret of her [the Church's] success"; it solved "the mystery of that tenacious fortitude with which she has endured the countless attacks that have threatened her stability."[82]

Confession, critics continued, enabled a priestly despotism that had dire consequences for state and society. The extraordinary opportunity of the priest to learn the deepest secrets of his parishioners and suggest avenues to address their weaknesses gave him immense power over their lives, a power that allegedly could be utilized for secular ends.[83] In the confessionals, the Church seized the conscience of its subjects and exterminated their every sentiment of freedom,

---

[79] Bunkley, *Testimony of an Escaped Novice From the Sisterhood of St. Joseph*, 140–41.

[80] Rector of Oldenwold, *Cloven Foot*, 276.

[81] Kirwan [pseudonym of Nicholas Murray], *Letters to the Right Rev. John Hughes, Roman Catholic Bishop of New York* (New York: Harper and Brothers, 1855), 49.

[82] Bunkley, *Testimony of an Escaped Novice From the Sisterhood of St. Joseph*, 24–25.

[83] Observers repeatedly noticed not only the ways the priest in confession heard individuals' innermost secrets, but also how he directed their actions. Bunkley recounted an instance when she confessed that she intended to marry a Protestant. The priest became threatening and "continued for some time in this angry manner to scold and threaten me." She burst into tears, she remembered, and assured the priest that she would not marry the Protestant, which assuaged his anger and he allowed her to depart. Bunkley, *Testimony of an Escaped Novice From the Sisterhood of St. Joseph*, 38.

and "through the agency of its sacred spiritual police," it could influence patterns of suffrage among its believers.[84] Joseph Berg argued that the confessional was "the hiding place of Rome's power" and " the secret source of her despotism." As long as the Church could maintain a hold on the conscience of men and women, he concluded, "they are enslaved, without the aid and without the need of fetters and manacles of iron, or any appliances of chains, or dungeons of darkness."[85] Never known to mince words, William G. Brownlow, a Methodist minister, newspaper editor, and politician, was even more provocative some years later. The confessional was "a secret tribunal" where every Catholic had to make known "not only *immoral* actions, but every thought and purpose of the heart" or else suffer the pain of eternal damnation, a practice that strengthened the hand of "a talented, designing, and villainous HIERARCHY absolutely controlled by an *anti*-Republican Priesthood."[86]

The power of the priest to manipulate the most private thoughts of the laity through confession, however, did not only enable the Church to control public events. It also destroyed an individual's capacity to think freely and nurture his or her individual relationship with God. This was particularly true, according to the European Scipio de Ricci, of a nun, whose "will [was] subdued" by confession and who "surrendered herself" to the priest and mother superior, "two unspeakably artful profligates, who have her reputation entirely at their disposal."[87] Yet this was also the situation among the laity. The confessional, warned Kirwan, was "a priestly device to gain an absolute authority over your consciences." By telling the priest everything you do, he continued, "you put your peace and liberty in his hands."[88] As political nativists phrased it in the late 1850s, the confessional was "destructive to the liberties of the nation, and incompatible with the morals of a people," whereas the consecration of nuns was "a polluting marriage ceremony with the bishop" in which its victims could not escape and where "they are often doomed to a life of gross licentiousness or the severest inflictions of bodily torture."[89] H. A. Boardman put it simply: the confessional allowed priests to "exercise a more thorough despotism than that of any Asiatic sovereign."[90]

If the confessional allegedly empowered the priesthood, the *rhetoric* about confession – and about alleged Catholic abuse of women more generally – sanctioned the authority of evolving norms about the American family in a

---

[84] *Pope, or President? Startling Disclosures of Romanism as Revealed by its Own Writers. Facts for Americans* (New York: R. L. Delisser, 1859), 281–82.

[85] Joseph F. Berg, *Trapezium; or, Law and Liberty versus Despotism and Anarchy. A Vindication of Protestantism from Papal Assailants, and Infidel Advocates* (Philadelphia: E. S. Jones, 1851), 7.

[86] William G. Brownlow, *Americanism Contrasted with Foreignism, Romanism, and Bogus Democracy, in the Light of Reason, History, and Scripture; in Which Certain Demagogues in Tennessee and Elsewhere, Are Shown Up in Their True Colors* (Nashville, TN: Published by the Author, 1856), 34.

[87] de Ricci, *Female Convents*, xxii.

[88] Kirwan, *Letters to the Right Rev. John Hughes*, 96.

[89] *Pope, or President? Startling Disclosures of Romanism as Revealed by its Own Writers*, 348.

[90] H. A. Boardman, *A Lecture Delivered in the Walnut Street Presbyterian Church, Philadelphia, on Sunday Evening, December 28th, 1840* (Philadelphia: Hooker and Agnew, 1841), 17.

number of ways. Most simply, many Americans, as avid readers of contemporary anti-Catholic literature, derived illicit pleasure in reading about sexual
deviation in the convent and the confessional; yet, at the same time,
American readers adjusted their own sexual practices in opposition to those
described in the anti-Catholic narratives. In other words, drawing on Michel
Foucault's observations regarding the history of sexuality, discourses of sexual
aberration worked to establish normative standards of sexual behavior.[91] Yet
the practices in the convent and the alternative paths for women outside of
the family also provided challenges to a developing ideology that glorified the
privatized home. As Marie Anne Pagliarini notes, a celibate and child-
less sisterhood implied an independence of women that contradicted the
notion that females were subject to a domestic world. These alternative institutional structures and ritual practices, as Jenny Franchot points out, seemingly
checked individual autonomy, simultaneously oppressed and liberated
women, and complicated the distinctions between the private and the public.[92]
Nowhere was this ambivalence more apparent than in the confessional,
which was deemed dangerous in the Protestant mind because it epitomized
the regressiveness, despotism, and secrecy of the Church and also because it
clearly represented a violation of the design of the family in antebellum
America. Here was a specific instance of the Roman Catholic hierarchy intrud-
ing upon and seemingly manipulating a Protestant patriarchal family. As such,
as we will observe in the next section, the confessional both exemplified the
challenges to Christian nurture and provided a concrete example around
which Protestants could create a sense of religious difference and so criticize
the "Romanist system."[93]

The Catholic System and the American Family

It has usually been supposed that for a marriage two persons sufficed. This has changed.
In the new system, as it has been propounded, there are three constituent elements: First,
the Man, strong and violent; second, the Woman, by nature feeble; and third, the Priest,
born a strong man, but studying to render himself woman-like, that he may resemble the
wife, and thus, partaking of the nature of both, may interpose himself between them –
between those who should become one! Jules Michelet, 1851[94]

---

[91] Pagliarini, "Pure American Woman and the Wicked Catholic Priest," 99, 117; Michel Foucault,
      The History of Sexuality, trans. Robert Hurley, vol. 1 (New York: Vintage Books, 1990), 44–49,
      105–7, 77–131; David Bennett, "Women and the Nativist Movement," in *"Remember the
      Ladies": New Perspectives on Women in American History*, ed. Carol V. George (Syracuse,
      NY: Syracuse University Press, 1975), 79.

[92] Pagliarini, "Pure American Woman and the Wicked Catholic Priest," 116; Franchot, *Roads to
      Rome*, 117.

[93] Franchot, *Roads to Rome*, 117, 120, 142; David Bennett, "Women and the Nativist
      Movement," 78.

[94] Michelet, Appendix, "Preface to the Third Edition," *Romish Confessional*, 211. Translated from
      Du Pretre, De La Femme, et De La Famille (1845).

The deficits of the Catholic system that were condemned by critics of the Church as regressive forces for women's well-being in society – principally the practice of celibacy among clerics and the rite of confession – were also utilized to stress the failings of Catholicism in relation to developing norms about the conjugal family in antebellum America. The practice of celibacy reflected a disparagement of motherhood; a devotion to the Church hierarchy weakened faithfulness to parents; and Roman Catholic rites impaired the growth of conjugal love. In sum, the developing bourgeois values regarding the family as a haven in the world were endangered by the Church. Significantly, however, the dreadful outcomes that Catholicism forced on the family were focused not entirely on the regression of the Church. Rather, as the influential French historian Jules Michelet implied, Catholicism's forms and practices weakened the family and impaired the power of the household head.

The first component of the critique of the Catholic system was that its celebration of celibacy simply did not honor the family or the role the family played in reproducing society. Alexander Campbell, for example, focused on celibate women when he condemned the obituary of a nun in 1833 as a "luminous exposition ... of the inanity, inutility, and folly of the whole Catholic religion." Campbell suggested that, rather than an obituary celebrating a life of celibacy, had the woman "given her hand to some help meet, and performed to him faithfully and fully all relative duties," she would have lived and died "usefully, happily, and honorably." She would have left behind not only memories of her virtues but also children, "living and efficient models of her influences, and active representatives of her virtues." Nothing, Campbell concluded, was "more useful, more honorable, more acceptable to God, than that which adorns the wife and the mother!"[95] And the male priest, because he was forced to remain celibate, was, according to Edward Beecher, "degraded, polluted, and defiled" by the confessional "and at the same time rendered a hardened and cruel hypocrite and villain, fit for any deed of infamy which the system demands."[96]

The Catholic system not only maligned marriage, critics argued, but it also devalued marriage spiritually. Robert Wilson, writing about the Mexican past, mused on the outcomes of matrimony. Marriage, he observed sarcastically, made a woman unfit for sainthood. Even if a woman had been "the best of mothers and the best of wives" and had "performed scrupulously the duties that God had assigned to her upon earth," she lacked the romance that fostered sainthood. Rather, Wilson continued, saints derived from "damp, cold prison-cells" where women fabricated visions amid self-inflicted misery.[97] Bunkley, citing the work of St. Alphonsus Liguori, made similar observations. Married persons, because they were of the world, could think of nothing but worldly affairs. "Poor worldlings,"

---

[95] A. Campbell, "Catholic Superstition," *Millennial Harbinger* (December 1833): 604–5.
[96] Beecher, *Papal Conspiracy Exposed*, 148.
[97] Wilson, *Mexico and its Religion*, 93. In this passage, Wilson is writing about Marianna, the mistress of Hernán Cortés.

Liguori assured his listeners, faced insurmountable difficulties in being virtuous and sanctified. To find sainthood, a married woman would have to make insuperable efforts – through acts of mortification, humiliation, and poverty – to please God. "But how," Liguori asked rhetorically, "can a married person find the time?" A married woman had to provide for her family, educate her children, and please her husband. "Oh!" Liguori concluded, "how unhappy is the life of . . . married persons!"[98]

In addition to endangering motherhood and a woman's deference to patriarchy, Catholicism imperiled the filial obligation of children to parents. The most frequently cited instance of parental neglect occurred when Church authorities were able to wrest property from aging parents by deluding their children, usually their daughters. If this narrative encompassed variations on a theme, one instance will suffice.[99] An aged couple sends their only daughter to a convent to receive an education. The school is noted for its quality, scholarships enable the young woman to attend, and the nuns promise that the daughter's religious faith will not be modified. When she graduates, her parents "[welcome] her back to their humble home with every demonstration of love." Yet they soon see "wondrous changes" in their daughter. Not only does she reject them, but they discover that she has been indoctrinated to popery and educated as "a dazzling simpleton, a showy bigot." Eventually, she "basely" deserts her father and mother for the city, where she can enjoy "those things she had been taught to love in a convent." The cautionary tale was clear enough: do not let your daughters be educated in convents. In this instance of convent education and conversion, however, the reader was also instructed about the dangers of the desertion of parents by children – especially daughters – who neglect their filial duties and live a self-absorbed life.[100] In this way, the convent narrative swung away from women's self-abnegation to their self-actualization, which, not coincidentally, threatened customary obligations within the nuclear family.

If celibacy demeaned married women and convent education endangered loving parents, then, the celibate convent life also tended to empower women

---

98 Bunkley, *Testimony of an Escaped Novice From the Sisterhood of St. Joseph*, 36–37. Bunkley repeatedly noted the pressure she encountered to remain unmarried. "Another priest once asked me if I were married," she wrote, "to which I answered in the negative. Then, he asked me if I thought of marrying, which I also answered in the negative. 'Well, my child,' said he, 'it is infinitely better to live a life of celibacy, and escape all those ills, etc.,' and proceeded to enumerate in detail what he called the ills of married life" (38).

99 For other examples of the Church's amassing property at the expense of the aged in the family, see Cross, *Priests' Prisons for Women*, 34–35; William Earle Binder, *Viola; or, The Triumphs of Love and Faith: A Tale of Plots and Counterplots* (New York: Evans, 1858), 29–30; Hazel, *Nun of St. Ursula*, 17; and Charles Frothingham, *Six Hours in a Convent; or, Stolen Nuns! A Tale of Charlestown in 1834*, 8th ed. (Boston: Graves and Weston, 1855), 19.

100 *Know Nothing Almanac and True Americans' Manual for 1855*, 50; Griffin, *Anti-Catholicism and Nineteenth-Century Fiction*, 49–55. Griffin notes that a major element of convent narratives is the issue of loss of property resulting from the convent education and conversion of Protestant girls.

in religious orders.[101] Wilson, in his critique of Catholicism in Mexico, noted a woman's "important place which God has assigned her in the world." And he argued that when a woman joins a convent "and shuts herself up within high stone walls to avoid the society of the other sex, she equally sins against her own nature, and not only brings misery upon herself, but inflicts upon society the evils of a pernicious example, and furnishes a theme for all kinds of scandal." Yet sisterhood also provided societal power. Wilson concluded, "When [a woman] separates herself from the family circle, and elbows her way to the rostrum, where, with a semi-masculine attire, and with a voice not intended for oratory, she harangues a tittering crowd upon the rights of women to perform the duties of men.[102] Bunkley, in contrast, again used Liguori to chronicle the travails of a woman's life as a wife and mother. Regardless of their standing in society, married women were not contented. "The bad treatment of husbands, the disaffection of children, the wants of the family, the control of relatives, the pains of childbirth," Liguouri contended, "which are always accompanied with danger of death," all contributed to a life of unhappiness. Far better to live free from the dangers of the world, where "affections are not fixed on their families, nor on men of the world, nor on goods of the earth, nor on the dress and vanities of women."[103] As the bourgeois family became an increasingly privatized and mothercentered institution, Protestant critics were sensitive to Catholic celebrations of the convent, celibacy, and the contemplative life. Curiously, as we shall see, Catholics would criticize the Protestant home for its materialism and individualism and its empowerment of women, precisely those characteristics for which Protestants were condemning the Church and its orders. Or, as Andrew B. Cross put it in 1854, "if a woman wants to retire from the world, let her stay at home with her parents."[104]

Yet again, however, the confessional was a decisive site of the power of the Church in assaulting the sanctity of the family and fragmenting its unity. Perhaps the most influential voice in this discussion was that of Jules Michelet, whose work on Catholicism in Europe had a profound effect on the American debate.[105] Michelet, who engaged in a prolonged invective against Roman Catholicism after a controversy stemming from a series of lectures he delivered in 1824, provided a historical lesson on the development of the Church in France, with particular emphasis on its ill effects in the nineteenth century.[106] In Michelet's view, the priest used a variety of strategies to destroy the sanctity of the family and to disrupt the

---

[101] Catholic apologists for the convent and a celibate sisterhood stressed the advantages of the contemplative life. See below and Mary Ewens, "Removing the Veil: The Liberated American Nun in the 19th Century" (working paper, 1978), which argues that American nuns enjoyed greater access to education and "non-sexist" relationships than other American women did (32).

[102] Wilson, *Mexico and its Religion*, 335–36.

[103] Bunkley, *Testimony of an Escaped Novice From the Sisterhood of St. Joseph*, 36–37.

[104] Cross, *Priests' Prisons for Women*, 47.

[105] Michelet, *Romish Confessional*.

[106] On Michelet's lectures, see "The Priest – the Wife – the Family," *United States Democratic Review* (1845): 127.

patriarchal order that governed family life. One strategy was the priest's recognition that he could utilize performance to amplify his influence. Michelet observed that the priest "has adorned himself with his own church, he has re-enveloped himself in this glorious mantle, he places himself there triumphantly." Moreover, "phantasmagoria adds still to its grandeur." In the church, "the deceived eye deceives itself – sublime lights, deep shadows – everything favors the illusion." As a result, a man who one might think was the village schoolmaster "is here a prophet ... transfigured by this gilded frame." Compared with this splendor, on returning home from church, a woman saw only the prosaic and the commonplace. The attraction of the home and the husband's power within it is diluted.[107]

The power stemming from the confessional was the critical element in the family's ruin. If the priest in his robes of purple and gold was a powerful presence during mass, his influence only increased when he descended to hear the wife's confession. Through the confessional the priest also gained a twofold advantage over the husband. On the one hand, he heard a woman's deepest secrets. "This man now knows of this woman, what the husband has never known," Michelet observed, "in the long out-pouring of the heart by night and day." On the other hand, the priest held a power over the wife not possessed by the husband. "Every one ... knows very well," Michelet contended, "that thought is in a person that which most controls him" and that "the master of the thoughts is he to whom the person belongs." And it was the priest who grasped the woman's deepest thoughts and, in effect, possessed her soul. "An entire division is made between the spouse," he continued, "for now there are two; the one has the soul, the other body." Yet this division was clearly not an equal one because the priest, with his possession of the soul, in truth controlled everything, whereas the husband, "if he keeps anything, keeps it by grace."[108]

Children as well as wives fell under the influence of the priest and thereby contributed to the harm of the family. Sons and, especially, daughters, educated in Catholic schools were, like their mothers, seduced by the teachings of the priests and nuns. In the schools, the celibate Catholic teacher "is the absolute master," Michelet assured his readers, and "the little trembling and believing creature just from her mother's arms, receives the words, which are impressed upon her gentle mind, and fastened there as with the rivets of brass."[109] The indelible imprint of the priest's teaching will manifest itself in the young woman when she takes a husband. "These girls will presently be women," Michelet continued, "mothers who will deliver to the priests, as far as in their power, their daughters and their sons."[110] The cycle of family destruction thus endured.

In these many ways, then, the competition for dominance in the home between the priest and the patriarch was not a fair fight. "We may converse with our mothers, our wives, our daughters," Michelet observed in his preface,

---

[107] Michelet, *Romish Confessional*, 130.
[108] Ibid., 140.
[109] Ibid., 180.
[110] Ibid., 178.

on the common-place themes upon which we converse with mere acquaintances. We may speak upon business – upon the news of the day – but we may not open our lips in relation to the subjects nearest the heart – the moral life, the things of eternity, religion, the soul, the Deity. Take the hour when one would fain unite with his family circle, in sympathetic communion – the hour of repose around the evening board. There, in your own house, at your own fire-side, venture a work on the these subjects. Your mother sadly shakes her head – your wife contradicts you – your daughter, though she remain silent, disapproves. It would seem as if, in the midst of your household, there sat an invisible man to contradict what you may utter. And why should we be astonished at this state of the domestic relations? Our wives and daughters are educated and governed by our enemies.

These enemies were "enemies of the modern mind, enemies of liberty and of the future." They not only fostered an "old dead system," but they were "naturally envious of marriage and domestic life." Shut out of the comfort of the family, the priest could console himself only by "tormenting us in the household."[111]

Priestly designs were made even worse by the changing worlds of home and work in which people now lived.[112] Husband and wife were separated during the day as the former engaged in his work. "In this time of sharp competition, when the day is full of efforts," Michelet wrote, "from which one returns home less wearied and broken with labor than with disappointments, a man needs at his family hearth a woman to cool and refresh his burning temples." But such was unfortunately not the case. Because the husbands' professions were becoming more and more specialized, wives had difficulty following their spouses' increasingly complex lives, which fostered discord. He became annoyed at her, and she became resentful of him.[113]

The outcome of this dismal domestic scene only makes the intrusions of the priest more effective. Women are forlorn even with a husband and children, as they are often absent from the home. When her children leave for school, there follows the wretched destiny of the now half-forgotten mother. She falls victim to ennui, which "fastens on and gnaws at its prey" and then, perchance, to superstition. Step by step, her prospects of happiness in life are destroyed, or her mind is overtaken with inanity and adjusted to the idle and profitless duties that are left to her to perform. And whoever suspends the torment for a moment is considered a savior.[114] Enter the priest. Cunningly playing the role of confessor, he conscientiously isolates the woman still further. Now it is the husband who is alone. His enemy holds the upper hand. "The husband finds his house larger and

---

[111] Ibid., vii–viii.

[112] Michelet, as a historian, was well aware of historical change. In addition to viewing changes within the family, his work also detailed Catholic practices prior to the nineteenth century and argued that contemporary priests no longer lived a life of self-mortification, but rather lived a soft and worldly life that fostered a tendency to destroy the family. Indeed, Michelet argued that it was now members of the laity who suffered from self-mortification. Michelet, *Romish Confessional*, 189–90.

[113] Ibid., 184–86 (quotation from 185).

[114] Ibid., 186–87 (quotation from 187).

emptier," Michelet continues, "his wife has become entirely altered." Although she is physically present, "she is absent in mind; she acts as if not acting; she speaks as if not speaking. . . . There are in this sad house fewer friends; but there is one more person, and he most assiduous": the habitual confessor.[115] Aware of the hazards of the increasingly privatized bourgeois family, Michelet focused his apprehension on institutional forces outside of it that imperiled household arrangements and fostered the power of the Roman Catholic Church in France.

Michelet's work caused a stir upon its translation into English in 1845, and American observers repeatedly reiterated Michelet's concerns, even when they did not cite his work.[116] Joseph Berg, who argued that Catholicism changed the human condition from "gospel liberty" to one of "abject slavery," surveyed the influence of the confessional on young women. The confessional "demands of the young maiden," he argued, "that she tell every thought that has passed through her mind, and every word that has been whispered in the ear of her betrothed!"[117] Bunkley also cited the work of one Dr. Desantis, a convert to Protestantism, who reflected on the hostility toward marriage and on what Bunkley called "conjugal love in its holy and chaste character." Because the Roman Catholic priest knew only a "sensual and bestial passion" and was not acquainted with conjugal love, he hated love between husbands and wives. Therefore, he condemned it from the pulpit and confessional. The convent, however, again exemplified the most horrible example of the eradication of both conjugal love and filial respect. Attempts by parents to foster a marital match for a daughter who was affiliated with a convent, for example, were dashed by authorities who spread rumors about children rendered miserable by acceding to their parents' will. Domestic life was extinguished, for "there is no father but the confessor, no mother but the 'mistress mother.'" In the end, parents were ignored and marriages were not contracted. Instead, the willful young woman descended into a life of unfreedom and became "a blind instrument in the hands of the Jesuits."[118] The circle is complete: the enterprises of the Church have destroyed the lineaments of family and tied its victims to institutions of authority that further its dastardly designs and enslave those – women, in particular – under its thrall. In so doing, it illustrated the ways in which external forces could invade the family and erode the power and influence of

---

[115] Ibid., 142.

[116] Those who did cite his work included M. J. Spalding, *Miscellanea: Comprising Reviews, Lectures, and Essays, on Historical, Theological, and Miscellaneous Subjects*, 4th ed. (Baltimore: John Murphy, 1866), 436ff.; "The Priest – the Wife – the Family," *United States Democratic Review* (1845): 127–35; and *Living Age* 5 (1845): 336–40. Given these observers' very different perspectives on the text, their portraits of Michelet varied dramatically. Spalding and Brownson were so livid at the text that they engaged in ad hominem arguments against Michelet; the *United States Democratic Review*, reflecting the Catholic constituency of its party, argued that Protestant ministers were equally guilty of meddling in family affairs; and the *Living Age* spoke approvingly of Michelet's work.

[117] Berg, *Trapezium; or, Law and Liberty versus Despotism and Anarchy*, 6.

[118] Bunkley, *Testimony of an Escaped Novice From the Sisterhood of St. Joseph*, 306, 318–20.

the patriarch and thus was an apt reflection of many Protestants' concerns about what indeed was an ideal domestic design.

The Catholic Response

Yes, dominies, you are responsible for all the extravagance of modern times, for the irreparable loss to virtue and society of the noble youth of your country. You hate the church of God because she is a witness against you. The priest, the nun, and the recluse are objects of your malice; for they are living examples of what you call impossible morals, and refuters of the code of low virtue you practice and preach. Hugh Quigley, 1853[119]

Catholic commentators did not sit by idly in the face of these accusations. Like Hugh Quigley, they swiftly began to pen critiques of the anti-Catholic literature that not only demonstrated its inherent viciousness but also illustrated the Protestants' tendencies to fanaticism in both word and deed.[120] In *The Chronicles of Mount Benedict*, Norwood Damon, writing under the pseudonym "Mary Magdalen," parodied the convent narrative two years after the publication of the Maria Monk and Rebecca Reed accounts. Damon wrote of a plan by a long-gone pope to send a nun to a convent in Charlestown, Massachusetts, where the rituals satirize those described by the Protestant convent narratives. Each week, "Mary Magdalen" observed, the nuns watched as the priest broiled beef or chicken on the altar and were "obliged to lick off the gravy that ran down the sides of the altar, less it should soil the carpet."[121] Extreme penance, detestable disease, and the gothic dungeon all found their place in this parody, which, according to Damon, was "nothing more nor less than a faithful representation of the ignorant prejudices and narrow-minded belief of thousands of New Englanders; those who pretend to be charitable men."

Other authors provided literal rebuttals of the anti-Catholic literature. Father John T. Roddan, in his novel of a Boston orphan entitled *John O'Brien*, for example, devoted some fifteen pages to condemning the canards of the anti-Catholic literature. Not only were these writers ignorant, Roddan contended, but they were also "foul mouthed." "They cannot speak of confession, priests, or nuns," he observed, "without vomiting obscenities which would disgrace hogs." This was simply because "their minds are incurably filthy, and any thing that can be twisted into their uncleanness is eagerly seized, and used

---

[119] A Missionary Priest [Hugh Quigley], *The Cross and the Shamrock; or, How to Defend the Faith, An Irish American Catholic Tale of Real Life, Descriptive of the Temptations, Sufferings, Trials, and Triumphs of the Children of St. Patrick in the Great Republic of Washington. A Book for the Entertainment and Special Instruction of the Catholic Male and Female Servants of the United States* (Boston: Patrick Donahoe, 1853), 10.

[120] Catholic writers of fiction included immigrants, largely from Ireland and many of whom were clerics, and American-born converts. The Catholic press was also active in forging a response to anti-Catholicism and presenting the Catholic family to counter these nativist views.

[121] "Mary Magdalen" [Norwood Damon], *The Chronicles of Mount Benedict: A Tale of the Ursuline Convent. The Quasi Production of Mary Magdalen* (Boston: Printed for the Publisher, 1837), 136.

accordingly." The lesson was simple: "Just as all things are pure to the pure, so all things are filthy to the impure."[122] Roddan rehearsed the tales of Maria Monk and Rebecca Reed, but he reserved particular venom for Samuel Smith, a former priest who edited the anti-Catholic periodical the *Downfall of Babylon* and sponsored the publication of *Rosamond* in 1835. After citing a passage from *Rosamond*, Roddan concluded that "Protestantism must be dying when it gives such very desperate kicks."[123] Father Hugh Quigley concurred. His story about Catholic America, he explained, was an antidote to "the corruption of the cheap trash literature, that is now ordinarily supplied for the amusement and instruction of the American people, – and that threatens to uproot and annihilate all the notions of virtues and morals that remain." A clear connection existed, he lectured Protestant America, between these "abominable publications" and "the *roués* of your cities, your Bloomer women, your spiritual rappers, and other countless extravagances of the diseased public mind."[124]

The falsehoods about American Roman Catholicism, moreover, had real human consequences, and Catholic writers condemned the violence – both verbal and physical – that ensued. The burning of the Ursuline convent in Charlestown, Massachusetts, in 1834 remained a benchmark of Protestant extremism for years. The question of an indemnity from the state to replace the convent that persisted into the 1840s no doubt kept the issue alive in the Catholic mind.[125] But novelists continued for long thereafter to use the convent burning as a marker of Protestant intolerance. Roddan memorialized the burning and approvingly cited Bishop Fenwick's sermon about it in *John O'Brien*.[126] And J. V. Huntington cited the move of the Ursulines to Canada following the fire along with his very human portrayal of the life of a nun in his 1852 novel *The Forest*.[127] Not only were these events symbols of Protestant intolerance in

---

[122] Rev. John T. Roddan, *John O'Brien; or, The Orphan of Boston: A Tale of Real Life* (Boston: Patrick Donahoe, 1851), 188.

[123] Ibid., 201. The full title of Smith's work is *Rosamond; or, A Narrative of the Captivity and Sufferings of an American Female under the Popish Priests, in the Island of Cuba, with a full disclosure of their manners and customs, written by herself, With an Introduction and Notes, by Samuel B. Smith*. See also Willard Thorp, "Catholic Novelists in Defense of Their Faith, 1829–1865," *Proceedings of the American Antiquarian Society* 78 (1968): 46–49.

[124] A Missionary Priest [Hugh Quigley], *Cross and the Shamrock*, 6.

[125] The *Boston Pilot*, a Catholic newspaper, repeatedly reported on the "Convent Indemnity" question, specifically the failed attempts to gain restitution for the destruction of the convent. See, for example, 20 February 1841, 17 April 1841, 6 January 1844, 27 January 1844, 17 February 1844, 9 March 1844, and 17 August 1844. See also Nancy Lusigan Schultz, *Fire and Roses: The Burning of the Charlestown Convent, 1834* (New York: Free Press, 2000), for a comprehensive study of the Ursuline convent story. Attempts to gain compensation from the Massachusetts legislature persisted until 1854 (275).

[126] Roddan, *John O'Brien*, 196, 208.

[127] J. V. Huntington, *The Forest* (New York: Redfield, 1852), 108–9. In particular, a character in *The Forest* explains how the "convent agreed so well with [the nuns'] mental, as well as [their] bodily health" (108). Huntington, a Catholic convert, was widely read by Catholic and non-Catholic readers alike and was among the most talented antebellum Catholic novelists. See Thorp, "Catholic Novelists in Defense of Their Faith, 1829–1865," 70–86.

Catholic America, but they often were connected to issues of family organization and sexual propriety. In the celebrated tarring and feathering of Father John Bapst in Maine in 1851, for example, the Protestant ruffians mocked him by asking if the Virgin Mary would save him and how many wives and children he had, inquiries that many Catholic observers condemned as evidence of the excesses of Protestant intolerance.[128] The Bapst episode too was commemorated by Charles Cannon in his novel *Bickerton*, which recounts a riot led by the "Order of United Americans" in the Little Dublin section of the fictional city of Bickerton.[129]

The burning of the convent was a sign to many Catholics of a Protestant fanaticism that violated manly norms toward women. The *Boston Pilot* in 1844 (ten years after the convent fire) admonished the rioters and, especially, those elites who had abetted the attack on the convent. After the "horrible deed," those who had countenanced the "attack on women, skulked in shame." Yet once public opinion had cooled, the "Reverend hunters of the helpless women whom they caused to be driven from house and home" advanced arguments "teeming with the most filthy abuse and most infamous fabrications about nunneries and monasteries." Editors of the *Boston Pilot*, a Catholic periodical, wondered if there existed a spark of manhood to redress this "ferocious pillage of the home of women and children."[130]

Defenders of Roman Catholicism made another – and more important – argument, however, regarding characterizations of the Catholic *and* the Protestant home. Rather than merely criticize the Protestant account of their home and family, Catholicism's defenders wrote a story that celebrated the robustness of the Catholic family *because* of the Roman Catholic system. On the one hand, they assiduously explained the benefits of practices among adherents and institutions in the Church. Celibacy was a condition well suited to clerics.[131] (Catholics often griped about "families" of clergy, and one asked with tongue in cheek how successful St. Paul might have been among the Greeks with six "squealing" children in tow.[132]) Priests were consistently portrayed as wise leaders of their flock who gently maintained discipline and adherence to the faith.[133] Sisterhood was a happy existence in which the nun lived secluded from

---

[128] See, for example, Spalding, *Miscellanea*, xxi.

[129] Charles James Cannon, *Bickerton; or, The Immigrant's Daughter* (New York: P. O'Shea, 1855), 79.

[130] "Sectarian Opposition to Indemnity," *Boston Pilot*, 27 January 1844.

[131] Commentators occasionally attempted to show the hypocrisy of Protestant views on celibacy. For example, Quigley describes a pious "old maid" who reproaches the Church for celibate orders. "There is no part of the wicked Popish system I regard so much contrary to God's holy word as celibacy," she argued, which was a clear "doctrine of devils." A Missionary Priest [Hugh Quigley], *Cross and the Shamrock*, 90.

[132] Bishop John B. Purcell made this observation in his debate with Alexander Campbell in 1835. See "Debates on the Roman Catholic Religion," *Christian Examiner* 23 (1838): 60.

[133] One example among many is Charles Cannon, *Father Felix: A Tale* (New York: Edward Dunigan, 1845).

the world and "her life was passed in divine meditation and worship of her Divine Spouse." Hers was also a devotion that served society.[134] The convent was not a prison. Rather, it was a place of contentment, where one rested in "a chaste and narrow cell, with no companion but the crucifix" or knelt "daily in a retired and silent convent-chapel safe behind its lofty grille."[135] The convent, was, to be sure, a place of discipline, but it was a salubrious discipline in an environment where nuns were able to perform their religious duties free from the burdens of family life. Inmates of the convent, moreover, were there of their own accord and their wealth was not appropriated by avaricious officials of the Church as was so frequently alleged.[136]

Catholics also justified their conjugal family and developed their own critique of the American family and the place of women within it. They began with a celebration of the triumph of American Roman Catholics in the face of immense obstacles. Migration from Europe and toil in America posed many challenges for the Catholic family. In some respects, Catholic critics recognized a domestic ideology that privileged succor and nurture within the home. The *Boston Pilot* extolled the role of mothers, whose "vigilance, and care, and affection" was "consecrated to the blessed work of sowing the seeds of piety in childhood's heart."[137] It asked for gratitude to parents – "there is nothing on earth [that] can equal or should equal, the love and gratitude of a child for its parents" – because of their nurture and sacrifice.[138]

Yet the Catholic narrative also incorporated a watchfulness about the privatized family because ties of family and kinship endured for reasons connected to external institutions, most notably the Church. Put differently, the Catholic family deviated from the norm of the privatized family *because* of Church authority. The solidity of Church doctrine, in contrast to the Protestant penchant for moving freely from religious affiliation to religious affiliation, in fact provided a structure that was not detrimental to society. And the institutional forms of the Church – the parochial school, the communal mass, the confessional – enforced the extrafamilial discipline that was lacking in the homes of many Americans. If Protestants detected the costs of celibacy, confession, and self-abnegation among Catholics, then, their Catholic counterparts saw the

---

[134] Catholic periodicals stressed the service of sisterhoods to society. In copying a report from the *London Tablet* on the Charlestown convent fire, the *Boston Pilot* described the role of nuns, priests, and prelates in caring for victims of the 1832 cholera epidemic. "When the cholera had ended its ravages," the report noted, "the Protestant parsons returned, and . . . 'soon succeeded by their blasphemous and licentious preaching and praying, in driving the Sisters away from the Almshouse,'" 17 August 1844.

[135] J. V. Huntington, *Rosemary; or, Life and Death* (New York: D. and J. Sadlier, 1860), 224.

[136] See, for example, Huntington, *Rosemary*, 239.

[137] "Parents and Children," *Boston Pilot*, 1 December 1849. It also argued that "pious mothers have done more to people heaven than any other class of persons, next to preachers of the gospel." Moreover, it also memorialized sisters, who provided cheer to the home, and daughters, who were a "steady light of her father's house." Note the gendered portrayal of parents and children.

[138] "Gratitude to Parents," *Boston Pilot*, 4 January 1840.

Protestant family as individualized and without authority. Unlike the Catholic home, the Protestant home was distinguished by a penchant for materialism and self-indulgence, especially among the women and children. These behaviors had deleterious outcomes for the American family and, by implication, for society as a whole.

It is difficult to overemphasize the challenges faced by poor immigrants in the antebellum era, especially those fleeing the Irish famine beginning in the late 1840s. Protestant and Catholic organizations were formed to aid the hungry, the homeless, and the parentless. Founded in 1847, the Philadelphia Society for the Employment and Instruction of the Poor distributed food and clothing, and provided medical aid. In 1852 nearly two-thirds of the white people receiving lodging in Philadelphia had been born in Ireland. More than two-thirds of those who received outdoor relief between 1854 and 1860 from the New York Association for Improving the Condition of the Poor were Irish immigrants. Many of the poverty stricken were women, in part because poor households were disproportionately female headed. Nearly one-fifth of Irish homes in Buffalo, New York, in 1855 were headed by a woman. And orphanhood was increasingly common. By the early 1850s, the Catholic orphanages in Philadelphia were full, accommodating 350 children.[139]

Because these ills racked the Irish Catholic community, Catholic American social critics consistently noted these burdens and provided prescriptions to alleviate them. Catholic organizations also strove to address these shortcomings. The Irish Emigrant Association, for example, was active even before the famine influx in acclimating immigrants who might be "ignorant of the customs, habits, and localities of the country" and in shielding them from unsavory and un-Catholic influences that would endanger their "moral worth and social respectability."[140] Charitable institutions under the aegis of the Roman Catholic Church grew thereafter. In Buffalo, the Sisters of Charity operated a charity kitchen that in 1848 fed up to one thousand of the hungry per day, a benevolence that, according to the historian David A. Gerber, was the only thing that separated many from starvation during the depression in the late 1850s.[141]

In the face of such want, antebellum Catholic writers also used these ills as a salve for the actual state of contemporary society and to critique Protestant America. Perhaps they idealized the Irish family *because* of the reality of social disorganization, but these writers did not ignore the trials of the Irish immigrant. To the contrary, their fictional depictions recounted many instances of loss and

---

[139] See J. Matthew Gallman, *Receiving Erin's Children: Philadelphia, Liverpool, and the Irish Famine Migration, 1845–1855* (Chapel Hill: University of North Carolina Press, 2000), 76–77, 79; and Hasia R. Diner, *Erin's Daughter in America: Irish Immigrant Women in the Nineteenth Century* (Baltimore: Johns Hopkins University Press, 1983), 61, 107–8.

[140] "Irish Emigrant Association," *Boston Pilot*, 17 April 1841.

[141] David A. Gerber, *The Making of an American Pluralism: Buffalo, New York, 1825–1860* (Urbana: University of Illinois Press, 1989), 153–54, 313–15.

separation during the migration and the early stages of immigrant life and labor in the United States. The orphan, a child who had lost his or her parents and who was consigned to wander in the wilderness of a Protestant world, was an especially common and rhetorically useful character.[142] In Quigley's *The Cross and the Shamrock*, the characters' difficulties begin in Ireland, where a widower with four children is dispossessed by an evil landlord. Moving to America ("'a free country,' where there were no landlords or tyrants") against the advice of his brother, who is also a priest, the father is stricken with cholera and leaves his children orphaned. The stage is now set for Quigley to tell a tale of the virtuous orphans, separated from one another and forced to dwell among Protestants, who exemplify the virtue and righteousness of the Catholic faith.[143] Likewise, Charles Cannon's *Bickerton* describes the travails of a Catholic family making their way to America. The family is robbed and both parents die, leaving their daughter to fend for herself. Only later do we discover that the daughter has been adopted by the family of an abusive and somber minister, where she is "condemned to live in an atmosphere of cant and hypocrisy that was almost stifling."[144] In John T. Roddan's *John O'Brien*, the protagonist is also an orphan, one who is left parentless at age eight. His story, which relates the orphan's encounters with a Protestant world of fanaticism and wrongdoing, is a cautionary tale for Catholics to remain true to the faith. Indeed, the protagonist's exposure to the Protestant world, even before his father's death renders him an orphan, fosters his foolish conviction that he is better than "Paddies" and ultimately weakens his Catholic faith.[145]

As these writers suggest, the ravages of poverty inflicted on orphans and the homeless were symbols for Catholics, who found themselves constantly at risk of losing their freedom of religion and their connections to their kin. In effect, the orphan could represent two forms of captivity that rebutted the Protestant captivity narratives of Catholic institutions. The first and most obvious – indeed, a literal – form of captivity was in a state institution, which Catholics often framed as a type of imprisonment that deprives inmates of their religious and familial rights. And the most apt settings for this captivity were the poorhouses and the houses of correction where inmates encountered the Protestant ministry and the King James Version of the Bible. A report in the *Boston Pilot* in 1844, for example, condemned the chaplain of the Massachusetts state prison, who had

---

[142] Two novels are representative of the orphan story: Mrs. J. Sadlier, *Willy Burke; or, The Irish Orphan in America* (Boston: Patrick Donahoe, 1850); and Roddan, *John O'Brien*. *Willy Burke* is a didactic story meant for children. When Willy's brother Peter strays from Roman Catholicism, Willy remains true to the faith. See also, A Missionary Priest [Hugh Quigley], *Cross and the Shamrock*.

[143] A Missionary Priest [Hugh Quigley], *Cross and the Shamrock*, 26.

[144] Cannon, *Bickerton*, 67.

[145] Roddan, *John O'Brien*, 58–61. John's father recognized his error on his deathbed. "Mind your religion," he said as his last words, "Never go near Protestant meetings and Sunday schools. Associate, as far as possible, only with good Catholics" (65). Alas, John did not immediately heed his dying father's advice.

forbidden inmates to read any literature from the Catholic or Unitarian churches.[146] And in *The Cross and the Shamrock*, the orphaned children find themselves in a poorhouse, an institution historically of great repugnance to the Irish. On their way to the prisonlike structure, one orphan is told that he "must live here in this free country, and learn to be a man and a Christian – a thing he could not be at home, in the old country."[147] Catholic children are thus entrapped in this land of freedom.

The tale of Dorah Mahony also encapsulates the misfortunes that befall the Irish in America, but it focuses more on the prison than on the poorhouse.[148] Although she is better off in Ireland than she will find herself in the United States, Dorah leaves for America with her lover, who perishes on the journey. Alone and in a country where "the people here don't like our folk, at all," she falls in with Protestants only to be framed for the crime of drunkenness.[149] Although Dorah proclaims her innocence, the judge believes that "a little confinement will be of advantage both to you and to society."[150] In the House of Correction, Dorah faces six months of hard labor. She is subjected to "heretical preachers" and is told that she will "lead a virtuous and holy life" in prison, away from the devil in the world.[151] The parallels between the convent and the prison are clear, but the latter is a state institution that deprives the Catholic devout of their priesthood. Once she escapes from the House of Correction, Dorah vows never again to interact with Protestants, either black or white, and to warn other Catholics against consorting with heretics lest a similar fate befall them.

John O'Brien also is framed – this time for theft – and he too finds himself in a prison, the Boston House of Correction.[152] He, too, is constantly surrounded by Protestant influences that cause many Catholic boys to forget that they had been anything but Protestant. In this matter-of-fact narrative, the author, John Roddan, provides intricate details about prison life and presents the many complaints about its conditions. Roddan concludes that the house of correction is only one of the cunning traps set for "Catholic souls" and that the state's reform schools and farm schools are also "no places for Catholic children."[153] Perhaps worse, however, are the Protestant families to whom former inmates of the poorhouse and reformatory are next assigned. Roddan complains that the Catholic boys, after their stay in the reformatory, are rarely returned to their

---

[146] "Intolerance in the State Prison," *Boston Pilot*, 27 January 1844.

[147] A Missionary Priest [Hugh Quigley], *Cross and the Shamrock*, 46–47. The boy replies that "the very best Christians are in Ireland, which was once called the 'Isle of Saints,' when all the people were Catholics."

[148] *Six Months in a House of Correction; or, The Narrative of Dorah Mahony, who was under the Influence of the Protestants about a Year, and an Inmate of the House of Correction in Leverett St., Boston* (Boston: Benjamin B. Mussey, 1835).

[149] Ibid., 31.

[150] Ibid., 74.

[151] Ibid., 95.

[152] Roddan, *John O'Brien*, 142–54.

[153] Ibid., 158.

parents; more often, they are farmed out to Protestant families where their indoctrination continues. And he also asks sympathy for the poor widow whose only child is surrounded by "people who are sworn to crush Popery in every possible way, and more especially by teaching Catholic boys to trample upon the cross."[154] Quigley makes similar observations about the outcome of poorhouse life where the great delight of the poormaster is to convert Catholic children and where adopting parents view poorhouse children with the aim of further altering the youths' identities.[155] One parson's wife, eying an orphan in the poorhouse, speculates that the child would make an elegant preacher, especially if his name is changed from "Patrick, which is too Irish, to Ebenezer, Zerubabbel, or some Scripture name."[156]

The second kind of Protestant captivity inflicted on orphans, the privatized American home, was also described by Catholic authors in two ways. Here the most obvious was the adoption and deculturalization of Catholic youth freed from public state institutions. Roddan and Quigley are especially attentive to the travails of Catholic youth sequestered in the Protestant home. Indeed, Quigley's is a captivity narrative – he actually calls the experience of one child a "captivity within the gates of strangers" – in which siblings are separated but never lose their faith in their religion or in one another. The children repeatedly refuse to eat meat on Friday or to have their rosaries taken from them, and they decline invitations to go to Protestant meetings; all the while, they face punishment for their fidelity to the Church. The tragedies that ensue allow Quigley to denounce Protestant hypocrisy. "O ye mock philanthropists, ye lovers, on the lip of freedom of conscience," he keens,

where was your voice, where your sympathy, where your indignation, where your meetings, speeches, and resolutions, when this Catholic child, this destitute orphan, this noble son of Catholic Ireland, this spotless confessor and glorious martyr of Christ, was being sacrificed, like his divine Master, to the demon of cruel sectarianism?[157]

In the end, Quigley's version of the family captivity narrative results in religious apostasy and ultimately in death for Catholic youth.

The second type of family captivity is more subtle. Because many Catholic novelists were themselves converts, conversion to Roman Catholicism is a recurring theme in antebellum Catholic literature. Yet conversion in these narratives is often curbed because kinship relations impede the access to true belief. In *Father Felix*, for example, Protestants come to know the truth of the Catholic faith, but they remain enmeshed in their family networks and so live as "a Protestant, to the eye of the world, but a coward and hypocrite to [their] own heart."[158] Father Felix

[154] Ibid., 154.
[155] Ibid., 27.
[156] A Missionary Priest [Hugh Quigley], *Cross and the Shamrock*, 63.
[157] Ibid., 97, 210. For examples of religious abuse of the adopted children, see 81, 194.
[158] Cannon, *Father Felix*, 42.

himself grows up in a Protestant home where attacks on Catholics are both unsparing and misinformed. Only a severe illness leads him to seek the truth. His father disowns Father Felix, who never reconciles with his kin.[159] In sum, the closed, privatized family became a unit impenetrable to religious change. Horace Bushnell's "Christian nurture" in the home did not just guard against the sectarian divisions and rigid orthodoxy of Protestantism.[160] It also protected the religious status quo and subverted the possibility of religious conversion and, therefore, the free will of its members. If anti-Catholic novels bemoaned that people were forced into convents against their will, their Catholic counterparts viewed the family as an environment where individuals were coerced to remain faithful to an erroneous religious outlook. The closed family led to the captivity of the mind. Put differently, if Protestants emphasized the institutional religious captivities of the convent and the confessional, the captivities for Catholics were that of the state and the privatized family itself.

If one prong of the Catholic family narrative was the perils of the American world for those cut away from ties of kith and kin, a second theme was the varying patterns of behavior inherent in the American home. As the ideal of the private, female-centered family became increasingly normalized in antebellum America, the Catholic response was both to underscore the role of extrafamilial and religious institutions – such as celibate orders and the confessional – and to criticize the outcomes of this new American ideal. Despite the social disorganization that resulted from dislocation and poverty, the Catholic press stressed the salutary influences of kinship and the family in addressing these challenges and argued that members of the Catholic household fared better than their American counterparts and, especially, better than those who forsook the faith. Catholic children respected authority, were less materialistic than children in Protestant families, and were not opposed to labor; nor did they resemble the idling set of youth that characterized the American city. In sum, the story told was of the value of those institutions of authority and discipline that characterized the Catholic past, which boded well for their contributions to an American future.

It bears emphasizing that European immigrants frequently voiced disapprobation of the American family throughout much of the nineteenth century.[161]

---

[159] Ibid., 156–63.

[160] Again, see Bushnell, *Christian Nurture*; Douglas, *Feminization of American Culture*; Colleen McDannell, *The Christian Home in Victorian America, 1840–1900* (Bloomington: Indiana University Press, 1986), esp. chap. 2; and Maxine van de Wetering, "The Popular Concept of 'Home' in Nineteenth-Century America," *Journal of American Studies* 18 (1984): 5–28.

[161] It should be noted that this is an immigrant story well into the twentieth century and that non-Catholics also employed it. The Norwegian Lutheran Herman Preus, for example, argued in 1867 that Americans showed a "glaring lack of external discipline, obedience and order" that "inculcated in the children" the "principles of a false freedom and independence . . . that in time cannot but bear its tragic fruits in domestic relations with parents and masters and in civil relations with the authorities." H. A. Preus, *Syv Foredrag over de kirkelige Forholde blandt de Norske i Amerika* (Christiana: Jac Dybwad, 1867), in *Vivacious Daughter: Seven Lectures on the Religious Situation Among Norwegians in America*, trans. and ed. Todd W. Nichol (Northfield,

Even those immigrants who expressed a clear anti-Catholic agenda evinced an antagonism toward the families of the American born. In Emil Klauprecht's mystery set in Cincinnati, for example, a German American who treasures Americanization is portrayed as materialistic and uncultured. His American wife has been "dulled in the lazy indolence of life in a rocking chair."[162] Boernstein's St. Louis mystery likewise castigates the materialism of the Yankee as well as the scheming of the Jesuits so that German Americans represent a happy medium.[163]

Yet these criticisms were particularly germane to Catholic America, and they were voiced, not coincidentally, by Catholic Americans. One basis for condemnation was the Protestant influence underlying the American family. The household in this assessment was distant and unloving as well as dogmatic and lacking in piety. When Father Felix describes his conversion to Roman Catholicism, for example, he depicts his mother as a Methodist "with all the enthusiasm, and much of the straitness and illiberality, of the sect to which she belonged," and his father as a "Unitarian, or rather, a free-thinker."[164] His family is cold and is made colder when news of Father Felix's conversion comes to light because his father "with words of liberality forever on his lips, was a man of narrow views and most violent prejudices."[165] Quigley, never one to mince words, points to the malice and hypocrisy of all sectarian Protestants citing "the 'spiritual rappers,' 'women's rights,' 'Mormonism,' 'gold hunting' and other manias," all of which he attributes to their teachings.[166] In contrast, we observe the salutary influence of a Catholic governess on the indifferent Protestant home in George H. Miles's *The Governess*.[167] With a father thinking only in monetary terms and

---

MN: Norwegian-American Historical Association, 1990), 127–28, 64. For their part, German Lutheran pastors in the early nineteenth century advised their flocks to scrutinize the *Eirishdeutsch*, who lacked farms that were as well kept, families as happy, or children as loyal as their own. When children ceased "going to church – to the church where they are taught to honor mother and father" and "to esteem honest toil," they are transformed. "They won't get up in the morning, but will loll in bed like ladies and gentlemen," the argument continued. "Neither will they be ordered about; with their new self esteem they will be an independent, mincing set." Enervated by a materialism and a shiftlessness, "what a tearful thing when wayward children do not honor father and mother but squander the fruit of their toil." Summarized from *Evangelisches Magazin* in Heinrich H. Maurer, "Studies in the Sociology of Religion: II. Religion and American Sectionalism, The Pennsylvania German," *American Journal of Sociology* 30 (1924): 425. Note that this summary indicates that Germans who had become Irish Germans – that is, Germans who had begun to speak English – were associated with sloth and materialism. Jon Gjerde, "Prescriptions and Perceptions of Labor and Family among Ethnic Groups in the Nineteenth-Century American Middle West," in *German-American Immigration and Ethnicity in Comparative Perspective*, eds. Wolfgang Helbich and Walter D. Kamphoefner, (Madison, WI: Max Kade Institute for German-American Studies, 2004), 117–37.

[162] Klauprecht, *Cincinnati; or, The Mysteries of the West*, 193ff.
[163] Boernstein, *Mysteries of St. Louis*.
[164] Cannon, *Father Felix*, 156.
[165] Ibid., 160–61.
[166] A Missionary Priest [Hugh Quigley], *Cross and the Shamrock*, 239.
[167] George H. Miles, *The Governess; or, The Effects of Good Example* (Baltimore: Hedian and O'Brien, 1851).

children treated as individuals and not as part of a corporate whole, the once insensitive family becomes increasingly hospitable under the governess's watch. Despite the family's intentions to convert the governess to Protestantism at the outset of the novel, the denouement is an abundance of conversions to Catholicism because of her examples of good behavior.

Not only cold and unloving, the Protestant American family also manifested the social ills of materialism, excess, and languor. The thirst for worldly goods and social mobility was a common criticism of the American home.[168] Characters in J. V. Huntington's novels repeatedly confirmed the Protestant materialist tendencies. One "hearty, genial character," writes Huntington, is "devoted to the world, particularly to the increase of his fortune."[169] Two youth in *Blonde and Brunette* exhibit their habits in dissimilar ways: one "would never earn money, the latter would spend all the money he got."[170] Huntington, moreover, comments generally in another novel that "the rich in America are fond of ostentation in their dwellings, dress, equipage."[171] Quigley in *The Cross and the Shamrock* was more blunt. He chastised Protestants who are "blinded by love of money, impurity, and the hatred that the ministers excite against the church in the minds of the hearers."[172] And he censures, in particular, "the Yankee" who, while not having a discerning eye for nature or art, "when *dimes* and *dollars* are in prospective, none is more penetrating or sharpsighted than he."[173] All that is beautiful – art, architecture, and landscape – has as much attraction for his attention as it can be used "'for making money,' and no more."[174] When Quigley contends that the "cross of Christ" is continually dishonored by the "scramble for money and pleasures," he connects Protestant materialism with the excesses of comfort.

Members of the family, because of the household's manifest ills, were set on a course of bad behavior. The materialism, excess, and loneliness of Protestant life were a dangerous brew, as suggested by common allusions to drug abuse and suicide. Roddan used his orphan as a mouthpiece to explain that the "diseases" of suicide and religious insanity are common among Protestants, who have no remedy – such as confession – to grapple with human pride and foster human sacrifice.[175] These temptations were exemplified in the governess's employer, a man who fought against opium, alcohol, insanity, and suicide and whose nightly companions were "a loaded pistol, a little golden box, and . . . a liquor case." By confessing to the governess, he admitted to being "a blighted, cursed, corrupted clod, hoping nothing, loving nothing, and fearing nothing but immortality."

[168] McDannell, *Christian Home in Victorian America*, makes a similar point (63).
[169] J. V. Huntington, *Alban: A Tale of the New World* (New York: George P. Putnam, 1851), 32.
[170] J. V. Huntington, *Blonde and Brunette; or, The Gothamite Arcady* (New York: D. Appleton, 1858), 75.
[171] Huntington, *Rosemary*, 181.
[172] A Missionary Priest [Hugh Quigley], *Cross and the Shamrock*, 29.
[173] Ibid., 226.
[174] Ibid., 266.
[175] Roddan, *John O'Brien*, 164–66.

Witnessing his despair, the governess urged him to confess to God and not to her, which inaugurates his decision to convert.[176]

The behavior of children, characterized by materialism, laziness, and self-indulgence, was the most often cited criticism of the Protestant family. The theater – Roddan called it "a school for scandal" – and the ball were constant temptations for the urban Catholics living in a Protestant world.[177] Huntington stressed the perils of the city and the tendency of young women to engage in reading rather than in housework.[178] Far better was the humility and virtue exhibited in the church-centered Catholic tradition. It was, after all, the governess who through the force of her example became a "humble mission in the hands of God" and converted her employers.[179] And while the poor, again exemplified most frequently in the orphan's story, suffered from dissolution in the Protestant world, threats of Protestant influence on the Catholic family were equally profound, threats cleverly described in Mrs. Sadlier's *The Blakes and Flanagans*, outlined in the previous chapter.[180]

Recall that Sadlier juxtaposes two Irish American families to illustrate the perils of American life and the benefits of the Catholic Church for its adherents.[181] The root of the problem is the public school where the Blake children, Eliza and Harry, become secularized and fall into bad company. As youngsters, Eliza is deracinated (she has no interest in Ireland) and loses her faith, while Harry sneaks off with Protestant boys to the Bowery and all its attendant evils. Eventually, both children marry American Protestants and increasingly turn away from their parents. The Flanagans, by contrast, remain true to the Church and its institutions. Most importantly, the youth attend the Catholic school, which sets them on a course that fosters internal discipline and encourages friendships with other Catholic children. In the Catholic school, the male teacher (as opposed to the woman who is the instructor in the public school) is a disciplinarian who edifies his students on the greatness of the Catholic past. Edward Flanagan, Harry Blake's counterpart, is the voice of the author in explaining the benefits of Catholicity and the authority of the priest, defending the catechism and confession, and illuminating the meaning of meatless Fridays.[182] Even his Protestant interlocutors, who attest to being "free-born

---

[176] Miles, *Governess*, 124.
[177] See, for example, Miles, *Governess*, 96–109, on a ball; and Roddan, *John O'Brien*, 229–30, on the theater. See also Mrs. J. Sadlier, *The Blakes and Flanagans: A Tale, Illustrative of Irish Life in the United States* (New York: D. and J. Sadlier, 1855).
[178] Huntington, *Alban*, 39, 54.
[179] Miles, *Governess*, 5.
[180] See both Miles, *Governess*; and Roddan, *John O'Brien*, especially 114–32. The governess herself was an orphan.
[181] Sadlier, *Blakes and Flanagans*. Sadlier was concerned with the ways in which fashion and appearance suggested the content of people's character. See, for example, Mrs. J. Sadlier, *Old and New; or, Taste Versus Fashion* (New York: D. and J. Sadlier & Co., 1863), which, while focused solely on Irish American families, comments on the ill effects of materialism and competition.
[182] Sadlier, *Blakes and Flanagans*, 303, 310, 336.

Americans," come to see the virtue of staying true to faith as opposed to Harry Blake's denial of it.[183]

If institutions are central in shoring up religious belief among American Catholics, the family supports and is sustained by them. The denouement is a morality tale that juxtaposes the fate of the Blakes and the Flanagans. The elder Blakes "entered on a cheerless old age; lonely and solitary they lived together, surrounded by cold and chilling splendor."[184] In contrast, the Flanagans remain contented and happy – their "good obedient children" are now "good religious mothers and fathers" – and become prosperous, the result of a somewhat implausible narrative turn regarding the expansion of their business.[185]

Recall that Sadlier's story is set amid the great New York City school debates of the 1840s. Sadlier's project clearly is to write a paean to the Catholic schools, a celebration of Archbishop John Hughes, and a critique of what she sarcastically derides as "the paternal kindness of the state." It excoriates Catholic parents who turn their back on the Church, a folly that is as inhuman as "the heathens of China and of Madagascar who destroy their helpless infants."[186] For our purposes, the book thus nicely illustrates two central factors of the Catholic critique in antebellum America. First, it demonstrates that the family that hewed to the Catholic tradition and educated its children in the Catholic schools raised hardworking children loyal to their parents and their faith. In contrast, the family of mindless Americanization and secularization maintained a materialism and selfishness that belied any corporate ideal. Second, Sadlier plainly believes that the Catholic institutions – the parochial school and the parish church – are linchpins in fostering enduring family life and religious belief. This latter contention was complemented by a series of articles in the *Boston Pilot* on the evils of the public schools in 1840. Catholic children in the public schools, the newspaper wrote with tongue in cheek, will "speedily acquire a gentility of address, a smartness of manner and a quickness of idea altogether fashionable and extraordinary." Indeed, it continued, they would acquire them with a vengeance:

"gentility of address," which prompts them heartily to despise the homely manners and honest simplicity of their parents and kindred; "smartness of manner" in turning into ridicule every thing Irish and any thing Catholic; and "quickness of idea" in exposing to mockery all the imaginary defects of the moral and religious obligations, to which they had hitherto been accustomed.

Clearly, Catholic families need to avoid the seduction of the "evil genius of a Paganized Rational Pantheistic Protestantism."[187]

---

[183] Ibid., 307.
[184] Ibid., 373.
[185] Ibid., 376.
[186] Ibid., 390.
[187] "Common Schools and Catholic Children," *Boston Pilot*, 1 August 1840, 8 August 1840.

The cautionary tale of the Protestant captivities for Catholics, then, offered two outcomes. On the one hand, the insularity of the privatized family, working in conjunction with the ills of a modernizing society, resulted in ill-bred children and cultural disorder. Thankfully, the authority of the Church mitigated these failings. On the other hand, the state enforced captivities that forced the weak from their homes and indoctrinated them in the very faults of American society. The resolution for these authors was clear: a shoring up of Catholic institutions independent of the state and the cultivation of intra-Catholic fellowship through these institutions. In the end, the family was embedded in a web of Catholic institutions – including the parish church and the parochial school – that fostered a pillorized society.

Conclusion

Ultimately, both anti-Catholic and Catholic critics focused on the deleterious effects that the other system had on the health of the family and, not coincidentally, on the power of the male household head. If Protestants, following Michelet's argument, perceived a weakened family because of the intrusions of priestly power enabled by confession, Catholics fretted over the increased power that women possessed in contemporary society. If both rued the state of the patriarchal family, however, their distinct concerns are perhaps more noteworthy because they illustrate larger critiques about the society in which the family was embedded. For Protestants, the Catholic menace was focused on institutions and practices that violated the increasingly private home. Priests during confession were able to weaken the ties between husband and wife. The institutions of the Church paradoxically tightened the screws of authoritarianism in society as they undermined the authority of the husband at home.

These challenges were all the more daunting in the volatile world in which Americans lived. The lack of an established church, which many saw as a boon to religion and society, also destabilized religious authority and fostered revivals that others, such as Bushnell, found unbecoming. The public school itself was increasingly secularized and, one might argue, underwent a process akin to the disestablishment of religion. The family, which might serve as an institution to temper these changes, itself was seemingly under siege from within and without. Yet again, individual freedoms had their costs.

Catholic critics regarded this instability to be at the root of their condemnation of American society. They focused on the inroads of American civilization – its individualism, materialism, and fanaticism – that increasingly characterized the American home, the erosion of parental power, and the need to foster Catholic institutions that would impede a Protestant advance. The outcome of these efforts is notable for at least two reasons. First, it provided a further justification for a strategy of pillorization and the development of a Catholic institutional structure, including the parochial school and the religious orphanage, that shielded its members from the troublesome influences of Protestant society and thus was a linchpin in the argument in the school wars discussed in the previous chapter.[188] By separating children from their Protestant peers, the family was shielded from the deleterious influences at the same time that it could sustain itself as a central component in the Roman Catholic institutional structure.

Second, it offered an explanation of the costs of the Christian nurture in the privatized family that would lead to the excesses so discernible in contemporary American society. Whereas the trajectory of American religion seemingly led toward an anything-goes view of churches that contributed to the growth of inane sects, the American family also was subject to centrifugal tendencies that were destabilizing society and perhaps leading to what Brownson lamented in 1849 would result in "a petticoat civilization."[189] As such, the Catholic critique of the state of religion and the family was part of a larger alternative view of society. As Isaac Hecker confided to himself in his diary in 1843, "Catholicism is solidarity" whereas "Protestantism is individuality."[190] If the Catholic model of family stressed the idea of solidarity in opposition to the individual Protestant household, then, questions about labor and the American economy and even about the ethics of slavery were also grist for the mill of debate in the antebellum world, a topic to which we will now turn.

[188] McDannell argues that Catholic homes by the late nineteenth century had accepted many of the Victorian domestic norms that had flourished earlier in Protestant homes. Yet the view of a multi-institutional society that included the church and its organizations and increasingly also encompassed the state nonetheless endured. See McDannell, *Christian Home in Victorian America*, 72–76; Jon Gjerde, *The Minds of the West: Ethnocultural Evolution in the Rural Middle West, 1830–1917* (Chapel Hill: University of North Carolina Press, 1997), 283–318.

[189] Orestes A. Brownson, "Socialism and the Church," *Brownson's Quarterly Review* 3 (January 1849): 72.

[190] Hecker diary, 28 April 1843, in *Isaac T. Hecker: The Diary*, ed. John Farina (New York: Paulist Press, 1988), 98.

6

The American Economy and Social Justice

> That Catholicity gives full scope and freedom to individual action, is seen on a broader scale in the characteristics of Catholic nations. For though she makes all men Catholic, yet at the same time they lose nothing of their individual or national virtues. Italy, Spain, Germany, France, Ireland, Belgium, are all Catholic nations, yet how widely different in their personal and national character! . . . The Catholic Religion is the only religion which preserves the individuality of persons as well as the characters of nations. Alas! there was a time when England had a national character, and that was when she was under the healthful influences of Catholicity; – England then was merry, renowned for her piety and religious institutions. What is England renowned for now? Sadness, impiety, ginshops, workhouses, and factories.
>
> Isaac Thomas Hecker, 1857[1]

In 1843, Madame Calderon de la Barca painted a discerning picture of life when she compared village life in New England and in Mexico. The wife of the Spanish ambassador to Mexico, she had fond memories of home when she took her readers on a tour of an archetypal "small and flourishing" New England town. There, the four new churches – each representing a different sect – symbolized a "religion suited to all customers." Elsewhere, neat stores and dwelling houses – all new, wooden, clean, and ornamented with slight Grecian pillars – proclaimed "prosperity, equality, consistency" and an eye toward the future. Implicitly, she suggested that a happy marketplace existed both in commerce and religion. In contrast, the Mexican village was dominated by two images. One included the "Indian huts, with their half-naked inmates," and the other included the church, "grey and ancient, but strong as if designed for eternity," with saints and virgins and gold, silver, and precious stones, "whose value would buy up all the spare lots in the New England village." Everything there was reminiscent of a distant past, whereas all in the present was "decaying and growing fainter" as humans seemed to trust "to some unknown future which they may never

---

[1] I[saac] Hecker, *Aspirations of Nature*, 4th ed. (New York: J. B. Kirker, 1857; New York: Catholic Publication House, 1869), 274–75.

see."[2] The garish, backward-looking church complemented an economy of lethargy, and a society divided between haves and have-nots.

Orestes Brownson, at the same time, wrote another story of spatial difference, only he compared circumstances in England and the United States.[3] Written shortly before his conversion to Catholicism, Brownson's account was less a paean to American progress and prosperity than a dystopic vision of what America could become. Brownson began with a reference by Thomas Carlyle to Irish parents who, in a plot to defraud a burial society, poisoned their own children. Whereas some might indict "the depravity, savagery and degraded Irishism" for this act, Brownson saw a more fundamental cause: they were driven to it by starvation and misery. In contrast to the variation Calderon de la Barca found between her Mexican and New England villages, Brownson focused on the similarities between England and New England. For it was in the "wealthy, charitable, industrious, Christian city of Boston" that able-bodied men and women trod, "with tears in their eyes," begging for work and seeking alms.[4] If such was the state of affairs in the United States – in this "blessed land of America, of universal suffrage, universal education, under the blessed light of the Gospel, dotted all over with industrial establishments" – the question that must be asked, Brownson concluded, was "is this God's world, or a devil's world?"[5]

Calderon de la Barca and Brownson each used a spatial comparison to write a historical narrative, yet their conclusions were profoundly different. For the former, the United States was, by virtue of its Protestant religious foundation, a nation of industry, prosperity, and progress. In Brownson's reading, a thoughtful critique to which we will return later in this chapter, the injustices of Europe could move to the United States, a movement that would betoken regression and dystopia and whose underlying cause was also religious or, put differently, was the result of religious decay. The problem, as Brownson voiced it, was that "men have substituted the worship of Mammon for the worship of God" so that "Mammonism has become the religion of Saxondom."[6] As such, Calderon de la Barca and Brownson adumbrated views about economic development that placed religious belief and practice at their core.

The relationship between Christianity and the acquisition of wealth has been ambiguous since its origins when Jesus warned against the ease with which the

---

[2] Madame (Calderon) de la B[arca], *Life in Mexico, During a Residence of Two Years in That Country* (London: Chapman and Hall, 1843), cited in Robert A. Wilson, *Mexico and its Religion; with Incidents of Travel in That Country During Parts of Years 1851–52–53–54, and Historical Notices of Events, Connected with Places Visited* (New York: Harper and Brothers, 1855), 288.

[3] Orestes A. Brownson, "Present State of Society," *United States Magazine and Democratic Review* 13 (July 1843): 17–38.

[4] Ibid., 20, 28.

[5] Ibid., 30.

[6] Ibid., 32.

wealthy would find the Kingdom of God (Matthew 19:24).[7] The connections between religious organization and economic change, however, created exceptional challenges in the antebellum era, a period of growing denominationalization and individualism, not to mention vast economic change and escalating inequalities of wealth. To be sure, Protestants did not speak as one voice about the opportunities and consequences of economic change in antebellum America. Protestant sects focused on revivalism and the restoration of primitive Christianity, for example, were leery of the accumulation of capital to foster religious projects.[8] Even those who were active in missionary societies were apprehensive about the consequences of the church's role in the market.

Yet there did develop a clear differentiation between Protestants and Catholics on the "present state of society" with regard to economic change. Again, they tended to use the other group as an exemplar of the nation's social problems and therefore assert the superiority of their own system of belief. Those among the articulate Protestant voices perceived the possibility of the market in bringing about religious and moral change and economic betterment. Indeed, many sensed the parallels between a marketplace of goods and of souls, the latter of which could be won for Christianity. As such, these spokesmen were missionaries not only for religious change but also for ways to use the accoutrements of the new economy – such as a burgeoning print culture and charitable donations by the wealthy – to promote the growth of Christianity. Not coincidentally, they often favored alliances between Christianity, as they perceived it, and institutions that fostered the nation-building project. All of these undertakings knit well with their concerns about a growing Catholicism, which they saw as a threat not only to economic growth but also in the national religious marketplace. If Catholicism emerged triumphant, the American village would come to resemble the Mexican, mired in a past shackled to the Church.

In contrast, many leading Catholics wrote insightful critiques of the economic developments in antebellum America. Deeply influenced by neo-Aristotelian and neo-Thomistic thought, theologians and prelates such as Brownson, John Hughes, and Isaac Hecker foresaw the costs of economic change stemming from a destructive individualism that festered in the post-Reformation West.[9]

---

[7] This verse's admonition that it was simpler for a camel to go through the eye of a needle than for a rich man to enter the kingdom of God was complemented by warnings that love of money was the root of all evil (Timothy 6:10).

[8] View Curtis Johnson's distinction between the "formalists" and "antiformalists." The former represented those of greater wealth and common allegiance to Congregationalism, Presbyterianism, and low-church Episcopalianism who were willing to attach large-scale projects to wealth. The latter were early Methodists and Restorationists who were suspicious of voluntary societies and their use of money raised for the advancement of Christianity. See Curtis Johnson, *Redeeming America: Evangelicals and the Road to Civil War* (Chicago: Ivan R. Dee, 1993), 7–8, cited in *God and Mammon: Protestants, Money, and the Market, 1790–1860*, ed. Mark Noll (New York: Oxford University Press, 2001), 12.

[9] John T. McGreevy, *Catholicism and American Freedom: A History* (New York: W. W. Norton, 2003), 25–37.

Moreover, they argued that American society, because of its social deficits, did not have adequate capabilities to address these challenges. For them, the American garden could become a dystopic factory of exploitation that mirrored the British industrial world. And for them, Roman Catholicism was the last best hope for faith and justice.

If economic change and justice for labor were critical issues for Protestants and Catholics alike, then, they forged very different remedies. Catholics often pointed to a condition of wage slavery among free laborers and argued that a corporate society would work to ameliorate their plight. Protestants in turn condemned Catholicism as a system that stifled progress and initiative and doomed labor to reap fewer fruits from the sweat of its toil. The differences between the two views were profound. The corporatism in the Catholic view was based on conceptions of justice and was relational. It was often deeply conservative, and not a few observers noted its compatibility with arguments justifying slavery. The Protestant view celebrated a dynamic society that fostered individual rights and individual initiative. It admitted the possibility that inequalities might result, but it considered the combination of a free labor system that fostered mobility and Protestant religious organization that would ameliorate suffering as beneficial for the whole. As in many arenas of life, Protestant and Catholic leaders intensely disagreed on the benefits and harmful outcomes of their respective faiths. This debate would have a bearing on other vital issues; questions about the accumulation of wealth and the ownership of one's labor would ultimately converge on the issue of slavery, the burning question of the day.

The Protestant Market of Goods and Souls

Protestantism found the world in medieval barbarism; feudalism and tyranny triumphant; mankind in slavery and ignorance. She has disenthralled the people, blessed them with literature and science, raised them to the virtue and dignity of MEN. ... She has invented railroads, telegraphs, steam-engines, and countless appliances to benefit humanity. Her myriad presses carry heaven-born thought into far-off climes; she commands the ocean, and commerce is obedient to her. Man, disenchained man, stands forth as sovereign of the universe, a being after the image of God. Frederick Saunders and Thomas Bangs Thorpe, 1855[10]

For many, the engine of economic growth in antebellum America was a wondrous development. In the half century after 1810, the value of manufacturing in the United States rose tenfold, more than twice as rapidly as population growth.[11] These increases, which accelerated after 1840, dramatically altered

---

[10] Frederick Saunders and Thomas Bangs Thorpe, *The Progress and Prospects of America; or, The Model Republic, Its Glory, Its Fall; with a Review of the Causes of the Decline and Failure of the Republics of South America, Mexico, and of the Old World; Applied to the Present Crisis in the United States* (New York: Edward Walker, 1855), 166–67.

[11] Douglass Cecil North, *The Economic Growth of the United States* (Englewood Cliffs, NJ: Prentice Hall, 1961), 165.

the processes of production as manufacturing was more and more concentrated in large factories.[12] Commodity production grew as well, as cotton in the South and food in the West were produced in growing quantities.[13] If the factory and farm were nodes of production, the transportation networks provided the tendrils that linked producers together. Total railroad mileage, for example, quadrupled to thirty thousand miles in the 1850s.[14] Anna Ella Carroll called the railway and the canal "the true conquerors of the world" around which the "industry and energy of the Anglo-Saxon race" would be centered. The railroad provided "the medium which circulates and regulates commerce"; it enlightened and expanded the energies of humankind and "dissipate[d] that very darkness, under which men have been deluded, and their means squandered, to grow rich without labor, or wise without learning."[15] Significantly for our purposes, as Frederick Saunders and Thomas Thorpe made clear at midcentury, many Americans linked Protestantism to the virtues of human freedom and economic growth.

This economic growth, in turn, encouraged a growing marketplace of goods that was not infrequently also connected to a marketplace of souls.[16] The prospect of economic growth, in other words, was explicitly connected with that of spiritual improvement both in the causes of these improvements and in the ways in which they would develop over time. The causes of moral progress and economic growth for many Protestant Americans were clear: their faith reflected an advancement of individual pursuits in both secular and spiritual terms. Religious belief and economic betterment also had a common currency because similar strategies could be employed to promote each. Put differently, if there were parallels between the market of goods and that of souls, so was there also the belief that the market itself created the possibility not only for economic growth but for spiritual improvement as well.

European visitors to America offered particularly useful observations on these developments. The Frenchman Michel Chevalier, for example, differentiated the Catholic and Protestant characters in 1839. "Protestantism," he argued, "is republican," and under the influence of these two forces, "the social progress has been effected by the medium of the spirit of individuality." In contrast,

---

[12] On the increasing scale of manufacturing, see Jeremy Atack, "Economies of Scale and Efficiency Gains in the Rise of the Factory in America, 1820–1900," in *Quantity and Quiddity: Essays in U.S. Economic History*, ed. Peter Kilby (Middletown, MA: Wesleyan University Press, 1987), 286. See also North, *Economic Growth of the United States* 166.

[13] Robert Gallman, "Commodity Output, 1839–1899," *Trends in the American Economy in the Nineteenth Century* (Princeton, NJ: Princeton University Press, 1960), 215.

[14] Lance E. Davis, Richard A. Easterlin, William N. Parker, et al., *American Economic Growth: An Economist's History of the United States* (New York: Harper and Row, 1972), 493.

[15] Anna Ella Carroll, *The Star of the West; or, National Men and National Measures* (New York: Miller, Orton, 1857), 181, 172.

[16] R. Laurence Moore, *Selling God: American Religion in the Marketplace of Culture* (New York: Oxford University Press, 1995).

Catholicism was "essentially monarchical."[17] For Chevalier, republicanism, Protestantism, and individuality were imbricated as sources of economic development and social change. Count Adam Gurowski, two decades later, reprised the argument that American society fostered freedom and economic growth whereas Romanism stifled it. "Freedom and social equality," as well as "the increasing demand for labor, skill, industry," Gurowski, argued, constituted "the magical attractions exercised by America over the old world." Romanism, in contrast, "fatally affected and degraded the nations submitted to its sway" by combating with prejudice and passion "primordial conditions of social and political liberty" such as self-judgment, self-consciousness, and "thought and mental emancipation."[18]

As in other arenas of Protestant American life, then, the specter of a growing Catholic presence in the United States was an ominous change. There were two reasons. For one thing, the culture of Catholicism inhibited commercial improvement, a fact of which Calderon de la Barca was well aware. As Carroll put it, "[T]he endless holidays of the Catholic church have always checked industry."[19] Richard Henry Dana, Jr., agreed. An attorney who was best known for writing a travel narrative about his experiences as a sailor, Dana recounted the Easter observance among Catholic sailors during his sea voyages. He wrote that there was "no danger of Catholicism's spreading in New England" because "Yankees can't afford the time" to be Catholics.[20] If Americans were "a time and money saving people," he observed elsewhere, Californians – in reference to Mexican Catholics – were "an idle, thriftless people" who could make nothing for themselves.[21] These criticisms of Catholicism were part of the larger Protestant critique discussed in Chapter 1. Given the authoritarian – some termed it despotic – nature of Catholic society, the individual could not be free from its constraints. The outcome was not only the absence of civil and religious liberty but also of economic and social freedom. Catholicism, so the argument went, bred sloth and a lack of ingenuity. Recall that Protestant critics mapped Europe according to confession and concluded that Catholic Europe was not only a site of ecclesiastical despotism but also a setting for poverty, torpor, and lack of intellectual or scientific improvement. Protestant Europe, by contrast, bred industry and economic growth. Carroll herself stressed that most exports from Europe came from the "skill and ingenuity" of its Protestants, despite their being a minority on the continent.[22]

---

[17] Michel Chevalier, *Society, Manners and Politics in the United States: Being a Series of Letters on North America* (Boston: Weeks, Jordan, 1839), 368.
[18] Adam G. De Gurowski, *America and Europe* (New York: D. Appleton, 1857), 259, 263.
[19] Carroll, *Star of the West*, 171.
[20] Richard Henry Dana, Jr., *Two Years before the Mast: A Personal Narrative of Life at Sea*, (New York: Harper and Bros., 1840; repr. Boston: Houghton Mifflin, 1911), 166.
[21] Ibid., 168, 94.
[22] Carroll, *Star of the West*, 171.

Given these geopolitics of faith, the threat of a growing Catholicism on American soil was daunting. Again an emergent Catholicism in the West raised special concerns. Because the region would soon be dominant both politically and economically, the West, Carroll argued, must be Protestantized, a process that would strengthen American liberty and economic growth. This Protestantization would be aided by the railroad and the canal, transportation systems that would transform both the industrial and religious landscapes of the nation and the world.[23]

Catholicism, moreover, reinscribed differences of social class in the United States that were readily apparent in Europe. It fostered a favoritism toward the wealthy just as it siphoned off the wealth of the working class to finance its institutional structure. Edward Beecher argued that the Church's exclusive power to confer salvation turned it into a "trading company," which enabled it to accumulate immense wealth in exchange for the grace of God.[24] Scipio de Ricci, from a European viewpoint, agreed. Whereas Catholicism decreed "that ignorance [was] the mother of devotion," he wrote, Protestantism claimed the power of knowledge. As a result, the superiority of Protestantism with reference to "mercantile enterprise [was] so palpable." In contrast, the indolent life of monks and nuns was a barrier to national improvement because "their example . . . of poverty, wretchedness, debasement, and pillage characterize the whole community."[25]

In addition to its negative effect on the American economy, Catholicism was a system of religious extortion that tended to impoverish nations.[26] In contrast, Protestantism favored the poor. William Nevins made this point explicitly in 1836. "Christianity [and again, he was writing about Protestantism] inclines to the poor," he wrote, while Catholicism favored the affluent. The Church of Rome, he continued, "preaches better tidings to the rich than to the poor," a message that was not imparted by Jesus.[27] This criticism was especially common among converts from Catholicism such as Nicholas Murray. Writing under the pseudonym of Kirwan, Murray argued that "Romanism fosters a law of caste unfriendly to all the great interests of society."[28] Conversely, Protestantism was vastly superior "in wealth, in enterprise, in rational liberty, in literature, in commerce, in all the elements of political and moral power." Protestant nations were to Catholic ones "as the sun and moon in the heavens are to the fixed

---

[23] Ibid., 171, 181.

[24] Edward Beecher, *The Papal Conspiracy Exposed, and Protestantism Defended in the Light of Reason, History, and Scripture* (Boston: Stearns, 1855), 134–37.

[25] Scipio de Ricci, *Female Convents. Secrets of Nunneries Disclosed. Compiled from the Autograph Manuscripts of Scipio de Ricci by Mr. Dr. Potter.* Edited by Thomas Roscoe. With an Introductory Essay and Appendix (New York: D. Appleton, 1834), xiv–xvii.

[26] Beecher, *Papal Conspiracy Exposed*, 145.

[27] William Nevins, *Thoughts on Popery* (New York: American Tract Society, 1836), 196–97.

[28] Kirwin [pseudonym of Nicholas Murray], *Letters to the Right Rev. John Hughes, Roman Catholic Bishop of New York* (New York: Harper and Brothers, 1855), 30–35.

stars."[29] Catholics were exploited and degraded because they funded the pomp of church ritual and fed the enormous appetites of their priesthood. And, ultimately, the American Catholics, although they were "freemen in a land of freedom," were "yet the veriest slaves that tread the soil."[30]

The growth of class division would in turn endanger the reality and, certainly, the rhetoric of the social mobility that many Americans believed existed in the United States. The ideology of free soil has long been associated with a segment of American society, most notably the nascent Republican Party at midcentury.[31] Yet it bears emphasizing that it not only crossed the political spectrum but also linked together differences in social class and religio-ethnic affiliation. Consider the thoughts of Samuel F. B. Morse, who already in 1835 perceived the destruction of the American republic from within by a Roman Catholic Trojan horse. Morse celebrated an equality in condition that put no "*artificial* obstacles in the way of any man's becoming the richest or most learned in the state." Yet "true Christian [and here he certainly meant Protestant] republicanism" tempered inequality of outcomes. Its "benevolent and ennobling principles" obliged the wealthy and educated to use their talents for the benefit of the whole community and thereby "to lessen the natural obstacles in the way of the poor and uneducated." This benevolence caused the poor to strive for improvement and to be reluctant to resist the wealthy. The society was thus "knit together by a mutual confidence, and a mutual interest." How different it was in European society where "the *poor* and *illiterate* are considered as the natural slaves of the *wealthy* and *learned*." Arbitrary power begat condescension and hopelessness. Sadly for Morse, European elements were moving to the United States where they remained in "mental darkness" surrounded by "a police of priests." The "sober, orderly body of *native* mechanics" in turn would be infected by "a rude set of priest-governed foreigners" that would alienate one class from another. And it would be the poor who would suffer. "In a moral and intelligent Democracy," Morse concluded, "the rich and poor are friends and equals," whereas "in a Popish despotism the poor are in abject servitude to the rich."[32]

Some twenty years later, spokesmen for the American (Know Nothing) Party echoed Morse's view that a heterogeneous dystopia was in the offing. As the "low population of Europe" was carried to America, the United States would come to reflect a religious and linguistic diversity. The newcomers, who would "adhere to their former government, laws, manners, customs, and religion," would be joined by some Americans. Discord and civil war would result and the

---

[29] N[icholas]. Murray, *The Decline of Popery and Its Cause: An Address Delivered in the Broadway Tabernacle, on Wednesday Evening, January 15, 1851* (New York, 1851), 364.

[30] Kirwan, *Letters to the Right Rev. John Hughes*, 219–20.

[31] Eric Foner, *Free Soil, Free Labor, Free Men: The Ideology of the Republican Party Before the Civil War* (New York: Oxford University Press, 1970).

[32] [Samuel Finley Breese Morse], *Foreign Conspiracy Against the Liberties of the United States. The Numbers of Brutus* (New York: Leavitt, Lord, 1835; New York: Arno Press, 1977), 158–63.

American republican spirit would be subverted, an upheaval that would delight the conservative forces of Europe.[33] Like Morse, these Know Nothings tied economic improvement to political tranquility.

Protestantism, then, not only fostered economic enterprise and commercial improvement, but it was also a force that promoted the well-being of all Americans, rich and poor alike. Catholic countries, in contrast, lived in poverty and sloth. This confidence in Protestantism's sponsorship of believers' individual pursuits, the conviction that America's resources were an engine of economic growth, and the belief that Protestantism tended to distribute wealth more fairly and thereby improved the well-being of the whole encouraged many Protestants to accept liberal views of economic and moral change. In many ways, these perspectives fused with secular ideologies that applied beliefs in American exceptionalism to expectations of economic growth and opportunity.[34]

Yet if Protestantism both laid the foundation for economic growth and provided for a more equitable distribution of that wealth, its believers nonetheless had to confront the fact that economic inequality would continue to exist. Some among them rejected a laissez-faire approach to the distribution of wealth, and they repeatedly expressed apprehension that escalating levels of wealth inequality might result in societal degeneration. A few observers tied the growth in wealth explicitly to the rise of Catholicism in American society. H. A. Boardman, for example, worried that Americans – and here he meant Protestants – were too engrossed in business and politics to worry about the dangers of popery.[35] Others offered a solution that religion – and again they meant Protestant Christianity – was a necessary element because it bridled the state and economy.

Most Protestant commentators, however, expressed the belief that the role of religion was one that only ameliorated the contemporary economic structure. Put differently, they accepted the certainty of the market economy and argued that it was their responsibility to adapt to it in one way or another. Mark A. Noll, after investigating a number of Protestant texts, agrees with this characterization. "Protestants regularly, consistently, and without sense of contradiction," he writes, "both enunciated traditional Christian exhortations about careful financial stewardship and simply took for granted the workings of an expanding commercial society."[36] To be sure, Noll continues, if there existed significant differences in attitudes held by Protestants regarding money and commerce, there remained "an uncomplicated acceptance of commercial society alongside an extraordinary elaboration of scruples concerning how the wealth engendered

[33] *The Know Nothing Almanac and True Americans' Manual for 1855* (New York: DeWitt and Davenport, 1855), 29.

[34] See, for example, Daniel Walker Howe, *The Political Culture of the American Whigs* (Chicago: University of Chicago Press, 1979), 96–122; and Foner, *Free Soil, Free Labor, Free Men*, 11–39.

[35] H. A. Boardman, *A Lecture Delivered in the Walnut Street Presbyterian Church, Philadelphia, on Sunday Evening, December 28th, 1840* (Philadelphia: Hooker and Agnew, 1841), 47.

[36] Mark A. Noll, "Protestant Reasoning about Money and the Economy, 1790–1860: A Preliminary Probe," in Noll, *God and Mammon*, 271.

by modern commerce should be used."[37] The following sermons suggest this outlook: Protestant clergy frequently fostered the belief that Christian charity should be built into market activities so that the marketplaces, of souls and goods were complementary and self-reinforcing. Yet they did not reject the market itself.

In 1837, for example, John Harris rued the human tendency of covetousness, which he defined as "a state of a mind from which the Supreme Good has been lost." Possession of wealth and even the desire to enjoy it were not sinful, he assured his readers, but the temptation to possess it inordinately or desire it for its own sake was.[38] This covetousness could take a variety of forms, varying from all-consuming prodigality to parsimony and avarice. The miser, Harris argued, did not possess wealth; rather, it possessed him "like a fever which burns and consumes him as if molten gold were circulating in his veins."[39] Indeed, covetousness was "native to our fallen nature"; gold was universally worshipped, and it was the source of such evils as war and slavery.[40] Taught to respect wealth, humans accorded it the status of a virtue, the consequence of which was that to be rich was a merit and to be poor, an offense. A false standard of morality was thus created where wealth was of greater consequence than wisdom.[41] What was Harris's solution to these developments? Bring Christian charity into the equation, he answered, in effect making it a budget item on a business ledger.[42] If Harris was promoting a business model, he also argued that "the Bible appeals to *a principle of well-regulated self interest.*"[43] The "signal blessings" of earthly as well as spiritual prosperity have often been merged with Christian liberality. In effect, it was in one's self-interest to be charitable or, put differently and citing Proverbs 11:25, "the liberal soul shall be made fat, and he that watereth shall be watered also himself."[44]

H. A. Boardman, an influential Presbyterian minister in Philadelphia, some years later agreed. In an 1863 treatise on the Bible in the countinghouse, Boardman argued that "society [in the United States] must be virtually what the merchants are."[45] In fact, American society had a stake in merchants' characters, Boardman contended, because it is they "who regulate in a great measure the current morality of our cities."[46] Every commercial nation will be

---

[37] Ibid., 273.
[38] John Harris, *Mammon; or, Covetousness the sin of the Christian church* (New York: American Tract Society, 1837), 55.
[39] Ibid., 59.
[40] Ibid., 77–78.
[41] Ibid., 88.
[42] Ibid., 229–30.
[43] Ibid., 260 (emphasis in original).
[44] Ibid., 263.
[45] H. A. Boardman, *The Bible and the Counting-House: A Course of Lectures to Merchants* (Philadelphia: Lippincott, Orambo, 1853).
[46] Ibid., 31.

judged by its merchants because "the world is ruled by money."[47] If Boardman was preaching to a choir of merchants in his lectures, he not only noted the importance of commerce but also of the ways in which it aided Christianity. Commerce was a "friend and ally of true religion" because it contributed "even while contemplating only pecuniary gain" to supplying the means for the diffusion of religious belief.[48] It enabled missionary work – "commerce has conveyed the Book of Life to many a pagan land, the harbinger of peace and freedom to the benighted nations" – and it could provide monetary resources at home as well.[49]

Conversely, Boardman assured his listeners, Protestant Christianity improved commerce as well. In the amoral commercial world where "MONEY is everything," true Christian integrity created a framework that rejects fraud and falsehood in economic interchange and facilitates improved character among workers and capitalists alike.[50] The "ethics of the Word of God," in short, was a safe and reliable guide that met all the exigencies of the merchant's profession.[51] "Enthrone the BIBLE in your COUNTING-HOUSES," Boardman counseled his readers, "and God of the Bible will bless you and make you a blessing."[52] Commerce – as "one of GOD's agencies for governing and blessing the world," could be salutary.[53] "Dignified and controlled by religious principle," he argued, "[business] is one of the most beneficent institutions which adorn the globe." If business was divorced from this principle, however, "it was surcharged with mischief" because, among other things, it nourished "inferior appetites" and weakened a sense of moral responsibility.[54] All of this was to say that commerce and religion were complementary *and* that the former could not be rejected but only improved. Put differently, the inevitable growth of the countinghouses posed a great challenge for those contemporary Americans who were without religious principles to master human passions.

An 1853 sermon by the philosopher and Congregational theologian Laurens P. Hickok entitled *A Nation Saved from its Prosperity Only by the Gospel* reaffirmed Boardman's concerns.[55] The natural course both for rich people and wealthy nations, Hickok argued, was destruction. Because the latter "will trust in its prosperity, and boast of its destiny, and lose its integrity," it will bring ruin on itself.[56] Yet God alone had the power, he continued, to save affluent nations and wealthy people from the consequences of their own prosperity.

---

[47] Ibid., 34.
[48] Ibid., 81.
[49] Ibid., 82.
[50] Ibid., 95.
[51] Ibid., 97.
[52] Ibid., 98.
[53] Ibid., 358.
[54] Ibid., 359.
[55] Laurens P. Hickok, *A Nation Saved from its Prosperity Only by the Gospel* (New York: Home Missionary Society, 1853).
[56] Ibid., 3.

Because of humankind's depravity, "the possession of wealth stimulates avarice; the presence of power kindles ambition; the allurement of pleasure induces voluptuousness."[57] The same was true for nations, which as they grew populous, powerful, and prosperous became corrupt and ultimately perished.

Conditions in the United States were particularly troubling to Hickok because his nation had accumulated wealth and power beyond all precedent and was therefore particularly vulnerable to collapse. And, in addition to common dangers – "an increase of luxury, dissipation, prodigality, inducing popular effeminacy and frivolity; a growth of ambition, ostentation, vain-glory ... destroying the very life of all patriotism and public liberty" – were specific American perils, many of which were related directly to immigration in some way.[58] Amid growing prosperity, for example, was the increase in crime abetted by the influx of foreign paupers. More important, immigrants themselves created a heterogeneous mass that would not allow for "the preservation of our free institutions, except under an influence which shall assimilate the discordant parts."[59] Not only did "national habits and prejudices work themselves out very tardily from the exotic, and assimilate it very gradually to the indigenous stock," but these peculiarities became ever more troublesome with the "perpetual collision" of varying religious creeds and especially with the increasing power of Romanism, which was "constantly receiving fresh vigor from new infusions of its native spirit."[60] "Romanism cannot naturally become republicanism," Hickok averred, reiterating a claim we have seen often in these pages, and the degree to which "American political liberty and free institutions" can be maintained "is truly a problem of vital importance to American freedom."[61] In sum, immigration and ethnic diversity were the natural result of American national prosperity; the massive influx of Europeans would continue as long as the United States remained wealthy. Left to its own devices, American heterogeneity would completely revolutionize the civil polity. Some force, therefore, was needed to assimilate the discordant elements and create harmony. And that force was the power of the Gospel, which would "ultimately assimilate all on the right basis."[62]

A founder of Unitarian Christianity, Theodore Parker too was fearful of the dangers that threatened the young American republic, which included both a "devotion to Riches" and the Roman Catholic Church.[63] In a sermon delivered in 1854, Parker rued Romanism, which, because it "denies Spiritual Freedom,

---

[57] Ibid., 5.
[58] The other dangers were slavery, which we will discuss later, and annexation. Hickok, *Nation Saved from its Prosperity Only by the Gospel*, 9.
[59] Ibid., 11.
[60] Ibid., 12.
[61] Ibid.
[62] Ibid., 13.
[63] Theodore Parker, "A Sermon of the Dangers which Threaten the Rights of Man in America. Preached at the Music Hall, on Sunday, July 2, 1854," in *Additional Speeches, Addresses, and Occasional Sermons* (Boston: Little, Brown, 1855), 2:215–93. In addition to the dangers of

Liberty of Mind or Conscience, to it members," is "the foe to all progress."[64] He echoed complaints among Protestant critics of the Church at midcentury. Roman Catholicism, he averred, was not American, free, or individual. Rather, it was a despotic organization owing its allegiance to a foreign leader. It opposed "everything which favors Democracy and the natural rights of man" and hated "our free churches, free press, and above all our free schools" and loved instead "violence, force, and blood." "No owl," Parker concluded, "more shuns the light."[65] Curiously, Parker, unlike Hickok, welcomed the arrival of Catholics. "Let America be an asylum for the poor and down-trodden of all lands," he rejoiced, "let the Jew, the Chinese Buddhist, the savage Indian, the Mormon, the Protestant, and the Catholic have free opportunity to be faithful each to his own conscience."[66] Armed with "Truth and Justice," Parker was convinced of Protestant victory, yet another instance of the Protestant conundrum discussed in Chapter 1.

The devotion to wealth, Parker continued, was particularly troublesome in the United States because "gold is most powerful" in democratic states. Because possessors of wealth controlled the church, society, and government, "money is the great object of desire and wealth."[67] And because manufacturing created wealth, the United States suffered slavery in the South and "the rapid immigration of the most ignorant Irishmen to the North."[68] The outcome not only endangered the nation, but it produced "a great love for vulgar finery" measured by the standard of money. "Mammon," Parker concluded confidently, "is a profitable god to worship."[69] Yet again, however, Parker exuded hopefulness. Humans would eventually discover that riches were not the only thing in life. Wealth, moreover, was indispensable, "the material pulp around the Spiritual seed." As people forged a power over the material world, they laid the basis for a higher development in their spiritual faculties. "No nation," Parker reckoned, "was ever too rich, too well fed, clad, housed, and comforted."[70]

These jeremiads are noteworthy because whereas they adumbrate the challenges of prosperity, they do not focus on the victims of economic change so much as on the improvements necessary to maintain societal harmony, improvements that were made possible through an assimilation of Protestant Christianity by a heterogeneous people. Despite these cautions, mainstream Protestants simultaneously tended to maintain their trust in a liberal market, which, as they often remarked, was at best surcharged with mischief and at worst, as Boardman put it, amoral. Parker, who told harrowing tales of the

---

Roman Catholicism and "devotion to riches," Parker cited the danger from the idea that there is no higher law above human statutes and slavery.

[64] Ibid., 241.
[65] Ibid., 243.
[66] Ibid., 245.
[67] Ibid., 232–33.
[68] Ibid., 235.
[69] Ibid., 239.
[70] Ibid., 240.

effects of wealth and Roman Catholicism, nonetheless exuded a confidence that these challenges would be routinely surmounted.

Indeed, some critics – consciously or not – conflated secular business enterprises with the commerce of Christian belief. Samuel Harris, for example, argued that *"the aim of all business must be to glorify God"* and that the acquisition of property was to be sought not as an end but as a means of doing good.[71] "Benevolence," he continued, "must be not only systematic, but systemizing, pervading and regulating the whole business."[72] Yet benevolence could promote prosperity and seemingly engender greater benevolence. By encouraging industry, energy, and enterprise, sobriety and economy were advanced and worldliness was moderated as a result. In the end, "doing business is not necessarily serving mammon" and "therefore not necessarily the antagonist of serving God." Systematic benevolence, in fact, was indispensable in causing business to be a helper and not a foe of religious growth. When this occurred, a place of business became a Bethel; money became "fragrant with the memory of the cross," and "divine love" was fastened to every material possession.[73] Business could be integrated into Christianity, which served all concerned, not least the industrious benefactor of the church.

There was occasional dissonance in these arguments. Three years after Boardman and Hickok published their treatises, Thomas Dick, a Scottish clergyman, reflected on covetousness in American society and offered a somewhat different prescription.[74] In 1856, Dick provided an historical lesson that demonstrated the "revolting detail of the operations of covetousness and ambition."[75] Examples such as New World slavery illustrated "the wretched and degraded condition to which avarice reduces the soul of man."[76] Indeed, he continued, "the service to God and mammon are absolutely irreconcilable" and the man who devotes himself to the latter is the most pitiful example "of human depravity and degradation."[77] Covetousness, in short, which displays itself in a variety of arenas in human life including commerce and even the ministry, slows the progress of Christianity. Despite their successes, Christian missionaries could observe vast tracts of land, including Catholic Europe, that still lay within the confines of "Pagan darkness."[78] The solution to covetousness and these failures among missionaries was simple: a consecration of wealth and influence toward efforts at proselytization. Differing from many of his peers, Dick argued that acquired wealth was not "exclusively your own, and that you may do with it as

---

[71] Samuel Harris, *Zaccheus; or, The Scriptural Plan of Benevolence* (New York: American Tract Society, 1850), 13.

[72] Ibid., 14.

[73] Ibid., 66–68.

[74] Thomas Dick, "Essay on Covetousness, or the Love of Money," in *The Complete Works of Thomas Dick* (Cincinnati: Applegate, 1856), 98.

[75] Ibid., 12.

[76] Ibid., 21.

[77] Ibid.

[78] Ibid., 49, 70.

you please."[79] Rather, all Christians had a duty to contribute large sums "without a murmur, nay with the utmost cheerfulness" toward the missionary effort. Dick stressed that these were voluntary contributions, but he went further in arguing that the possession of wealth was not strictly an individual ownership but was part of a Christian whole.[80]

Yet even Dick, who hedged the degree to which wealth was absolutely the possession of the individual, saw voluntary charity to be the remedy for inequality. The clergyman Parsons Cooke agreed. Believing that "the poor will always be with us" and that "every holder of property [was] a steward, not an individual owner," Cooke saw charity, which should be bequeathed by rich and poor alike, to be a salve to society and a benefit to the individual.[81] When the accumulation of money came to rule the mind, he contended, it "*takes possession and spreads and fortifies itself, and leaves no place in the heart for homage to God.*"[82] Using the primitive Christians as his model because "*their kindness to the poor was boundless,*" Cooke viewed the salutary outcomes of a voluntary philanthropy.[83]

Broadly speaking, Protestant apologists argued that their faith created wealth whereas Romanism retarded its acquisition. On an individual level, moreover, they believed that Protestantism fostered individual ambition and that people living under the thrall of Roman Catholicism were remarkable for their lassitude. Given this perspective, one can understand how the Protestant leadership could stake its claim on the attractiveness of an evolving marketplace that through philanthropy and individual enterprise would be responsive to the emerging poor in the growing antebellum economy.

The Catholic Response

[The New Englander] is smart, seldom great; educated, but seldom learned; active in mind, but rarely a profound thinker; religious, but thoroughly materialistic: his worship is rendered in a temple founded on Mammon, and he expects to be carried to heaven in a soflty-cushioned railway car, with his sins carefully checked and deposited in the baggage crate with his other luggage, to be duly delivered when he has reached his destination. Orestes Brownson, 1864[84]

Roman Catholics had a very different view of the American economy from their Protestant counterparts. This perspective was nested in a broader European

---

[79] Ibid., 90.

[80] Ibid.

[81] Rev. Parsons Cooke, *The Divine Law of Beneficence* (New York: American Tract Society, 1850), 6–7, 24, 45–46.

[82] Ibid., 61.

[83] Ibid., 97. Early Christians were often cited as exemplars of charity. See Rev. Edward A. Lawrence, *The Mission of the Church; or, Systematic Beneficence* (New York: American Tract Society, 1850), 66–67.

[84] Orestes Brownson, "Note on 'Liberalism and Progress,'" *Brownson's Quarterly Review* (October 1864): 166–67.

immigrant criticism of their American neighbors. Immigrants to the United States of many religious backgrounds disparaged the seeming proclivity of the native born to take undue pleasure in their nation's economic opportunities. Americans, so the critique went, were overly materialistic and excessively interested in amassing wealth to feed their acquisitive instincts. Their materialism fed their thirst for goods as well as for leisure, which was often expressed in gendered terms. Scandinavian immigrant men, for example, were known to deprecate the materialism that they characterized as a trait of American women, a trait that was spreading among women of their own ethnic group. Germans and Scandinavians likewise often denigrated the propensity of women to disdain heavy labor.[85] German freethinkers could belittle both their Catholic compatriots and their American neighbors. Woe to the good German freethinker who married an American woman who had been "dulled in the lazy indolence of life in a rocking chair."[86] To be sure, many of these expressions were part of an attempt to romanticize life in the homeland in the face of economic realities in the United States, but they also linked American materialism and ennui to economic growth.

If the American Catholic response to the economy mirrored a critique often voiced by European immigrants generally, it also set the appraisal of American materialism in a religious context. Father Hugh Quigley, for example, maintained that the American pursuit of worldly goods and pastimes dishonored Christian principles.[87] Quigley's larger point was more complex. By romanticizing Ireland and condemning the materialism of the United States from the perspective of Irish American poverty, he fostered a view among Roman Catholics that celebrated not only the Irish nation but also the fact that Catholic poverty in and of itself led to greater spirituality and less avarice.

Clearly, Catholics, many of whom were immigrants or children of immigrants, often lived in poverty in antebellum America. In New York City and Buffalo, for example, Irish immigrants accounted for between half and two-thirds of the

---

[85] See, for example, Jon Gjerde, *The Minds of the West: Ethnocultural Evolution in the Rural Middle West, 1830–1917* (Chapel Hill: University of North Carolina Press, 1997), 171–74, 256–57. See Jon Gjerde, "Prescriptions and Perceptions of Labor and Family, among Ethnic Groups in the Nineteenth-Century American Middle West," in *German-American Immigration and Ethnicity in Comparative Perspective*, ed. Wolfgang Helbich and Walter D. Kamphoefner (Madison, WI: Max Kade Institute for German-American Studies, 2004), 128–29.

[86] Emil Klauprecht, *Cincinnati; or, The Mysteries of the West: Emil Klauprecht's German-American Novel*, trans. Steven Rowan, ed. Don Heinrich Tolzmann (New York: Peter Lang, 1966); Henry Boernstein, *Mysteries of St. Louis, A Novel*, trans. Friedrich Münch, ed. Steven Rowan and Elizabeth Sims (Chicago: Clark H. Kerr, 1990). The allusion to the idle American woman in the rocking chair was a common trope. See Gjerde, "Prescriptions and Perceptions of Labor and Family," 128–29.

[87] A Missionary Priest [Hugh Quigley], *The Cross and the Shamrock; or, How to Defend the Faith. An Irish American Catholic Tale of Real Life, Descriptive of the Temptations, Sufferings, Trials, and Triumph of the children of St. Patrick in the Great Republic of Washington. A Book for the Entertainment and Special Instruction of the Catholic Male and Female Servants of the United States* (Boston: Patrick Donahoe, 1953), 7–8.

poorhouse population.[88] Among those in the workforce, roughly half the Irish-born men in New York City in the 1850s worked in unskilled and service jobs whereas half of the Irish-born women toiled as domestic servants.[89] Unlike those who criticized the Irish poor, spokespeople for Catholic America focused less on the slothfulness of Roman Catholics than on the disadvantageous circumstances and the inequalities that Catholics suffered in American society. And if it went without saying that many immigrants – especially those who crossed the Atlantic from Ireland under duress during the Great Famine – were poor, then Catholics faced a dual-pronged discrimination as a result of their poverty and their confession. As a Protestant character in a George H. Miles's novel argued, being Catholic "hurts one in getting along in the world."[90] Archbishop John Hughes was more explicit in an 1842 letter to newspaper editors. Religious freedom, he noted, permitted Americans to forsake the Catholic communion. If they did so, Hughes continued, their salvation would be in doubt, but there was little uncertainty that it would "tend to an improvement of their worldly circumstances, considering the ignorance and prejudices of a vast portion of the public."[91] When Catholics did cite the thirst for economic betterment among Americans, they comprehended its spiritual costs as well as its material benefits. In its condemnation of the common schools in 1840, the *Boston Pilot* argued that "like the degenerate Romans in the decline of their glory, too many Catholic parents seem to regard the acquisition of wealth as the one thing needful."[92] Indeed, a common incident of tragedy in Roman Catholic antebellum fiction was when members of the Church became infected with the American infatuation with material betterment.[93] *Because* Americans were so intent on making a fortune, Quigley concluded, they did not have the inclination or the time to pay attention to religious training.[94]

A more fundamental and systemic critique developed by leading American Catholics – indeed, the core of the Catholic critique – was that the current economic system was not only inherently unequal but intrinsically evil *because* of its inequality. And the remedy for economic inequality and immorality was

---

[88] Kevin Kenny, *The American Irish: A History* (New York: Pearson Education, 2000), 107–8.

[89] Ibid., 109–11.

[90] George H. Miles, *Governess; or, The Effects of Good Example* (Baltimore: Hedian and O'Brien, 1851), 11. Another Protestant character, in Charles James Cannon's novel, evinced her "cant and hypocrisy" by arguing that all street beggars were merely impostors who needed no real help. Charles James Cannon, *Bickerton; or, The Immigrant's Daughter: A Tale* (New York: P. O'Shea, 1855), 67.

[91] John Hughes, in *Complete Works of the Most Rev. John Hughes, D.D., Archbishop of New York. Comprising His Sermons, Letters, Lectures, Speeches, Etc.*, ed. Lawrence Kehoe (New York: American News Company, 1865), 1:328–29.

[92] *Boston, Pilot* 8 August 1840.

[93] These cautionary tales of the perils of wealth were complemented by warnings against the rejection of family and kinship discussed in Chapter 4. On the hazards of affluence, see, for example, Mrs. J. Sadlier, *The Blakes and Flanagans: A Tale, Illustrative of Irish Life in the United States* (New York: D. and J. Sadlier, 1855).

[94] A Missionary Priest [Hugh Quigley], *Cross and the Shamrock*, 119.

the Roman Catholic Church. The unchecked freedom that was so celebrated by American Protestants, so the argument went, had deleterious effects if it was unrestrained. The modern self, the autonomous individual, the voluntarist free agent were examples of momentous changes that were commonly celebrated by many, but Catholics often expressed apprehension about the consequences of these changes. Liberty, as many noted, could lead to license. Much better was a society based on institutions – such as the family, the school, and the church – that cultivated communitarian outlooks and established connections between individual action and the community. This society provided the stability and unity of the church and tempered the excesses of individualism.[95] It provided for orderly progress. "I have no doubt," the convert Isaac Hecker confided to Orestes Brownson in an 1844 letter, "and believe the Church the center from which flows all progress in art[,] science and industry, and the best methods for to labour for the good of the Race is in the cause and advancement of the reign of the Church."[96] And it fostered a relational societal perspective that tempered excess and advanced justice in the economy.

The most trenchant critic of economic developments from a Catholic perspective was Orestes Brownson, who championed the economic rights of the laboring classes throughout his long and varied career and whose observations about the dystopic political economy in contemporary America framed the introduction to this section. Indeed, his 1840 essay *The Laboring Classes* was so radical that it possibly contributed to the defeat of the Democratic incumbent, Martin van Buren, in the presidential election and certainly encouraged Brownson to move toward Catholic conversion.[97] Following his conversion in 1844, Brownson continued to excoriate the costs of growing economic inequality. Although he had been criticizing Protestantism for its individualism beginning in 1836, his prescriptions to address these problems increasingly took on a Catholic cast. Brownson was joined by others – John Hughes, Isaac Hecker, Martin J. Spalding – who together rued the condition of labor in Europe and the United States and advocated for the centrality of Roman Catholicism in the amelioration of its horrors.

These Roman Catholic critics began their assessment of contemporary society by identifying the problem of the growing inequality in American society.

[95] See McGreevy, *Catholicism and American Freedom*, 36–37. See also O. A. Brownson, *The Convert; or, Leaves from my Experience* (New York: Edward Dunigan and Brother, 1857), which addresses the significance of institutions in creating an objective piety.

[96] Letter from Isaac Hecker to Orestes Brownson, 15 July 1844, cited in *The Brownson-Hecker Correspondence*, ed. Joseph F. Gower and Richard M. Leliaert (Notre Dame, IN: University of Notre Dame Press, 1979), 108.

[97] Anonymous [Orestes Brownson], "Art. IV – Chartism, by Thomas Carlyle," *Boston Quarterly Review* 3, no. 3 (July 1840): 358–95 (republished as Orestes Brownson, *The Laboring Classes. An Article from the Boston Quarterly Review* [Boston: Benjamin H. Greene, 1840]). Brownson, as he decried the increasing hardship faced by the working classes, argued that chattel slavery, which was waning, would be replaced by wage slavery. Most radically, he advocated an end to the intergenerational inheritance of property to address these increasing inequalities.

Brownson argued that inequality was inextricably bound up in the modern economic system and the disequilibrium between production and consumption. When a surplus of goods was created, the opportunity to labor was reduced until those goods were consumed. Unemployment or underemployment created want and growing inequality. For Brownson, the "great evil" was not the tyranny or oppression of the state, but the industrial order itself, whose evil was inherent.[98] Hughes, for his part, used the Irish famine to illustrate the malicious outcomes of what he called "the invisible but all pervading divinity of the Fiscal, the unseen ruler of the temporal affairs of the world," to which "we are all its slaves, without any power to emancipate ourselves."[99] It was pure selfishness that set this "vast and intricate machinery in motion" and that, unfortunately, "leaves us at liberty to forget the interest of others."[100] Winners were clearly winners in this system, but their enjoyment would be "disturbed if [they] could only hear the cries of the wounded and the dying who have fallen in the battle."[101] In the end, the fault of this system was that it valued wealth too much and people too little or, put differently, that it did not take "a large comprehensive view of self-interest" because it did "not embrace within its protecting sphere the whole entire people, weak and strong, rich and poor, and see, as its first and primary care, that no member of the social body, no man shall be allowed to suffer or perish from want, except by the agency of his own crime."[102]

If Brownson and Hughes implicitly condemned Protestantism for the growing inequality in the modern world, M. J. Spalding was unequivocal. In a manifesto decrying the "spirit of the age," Spalding argued that "avarice is the besetting sin of the age." The "fever of avarice" caused everything to be measured in dollars and cents and practitioners of almost every intellectual enterprise "all worship in the temple of mammon."[103] Spalding then moved in another essay to rebut the widespread claim that Protestant lands were freer, more enlightened, more moral, and happier than Catholic ones. In so doing, he noted the different approaches to the poor in Protestant and Catholics countries. In the former, they were viewed as "state criminals" and treated accordingly, whereas in Catholic

---

[98] Orestes A. Brownson, "Present State of Society," 33.

[99] John Hughes, "A Lecture on the Antecedent Cause of the Irish Famine in 1847," in Kehoe, *Complete Works of the Most Rev. John Hughes*, 2:554.

[100] Ibid., 2:555.

[101] Ibid., 2:554.

[102] Hughes's criticism was all encompassing, but he ultimately set it in the context of the Irish famine. "The fault that I find with it is," he said, "that it guarantees the right of the rich man to enter on the fields cultivated by the poor man whom he calls his tenant, and carry away the harvest of his labour, and this, whilst it imposes on him no duty to leave behind at least food enough to keep that poor man alive, until the earth shall again yield its fruits." Hughes, "A Lecture on the Antecedent Cause of the Irish Famine in 1847," 2:555.

[103] M. J. Spalding, "The Spirit of the Age," in *Miscellanea: Comprising Reviews, Lectures, and Essays, on Historical, Theological, and Miscellaneous Subjects*, 4th ed. (Baltimore: John Murphy, 1866), 393–94.

lands, the poor were "objects of compassion, and are almost always accosted with kindness, and treated with tenderness."[104] England, for example, was a land of "boldest social contrasts" of rich and poor, of "speculators amassing enormous wealth in the manufacturing district, and a mass of wretched operatives worked almost to death," of "immense profits realized by avaricious capitalists, while the price of labor is cut down to the very starving point."[105] Perhaps, Spalding concluded with tongue in cheek, England's success as a nation was that, like all Protestant lands, "she was emancipated by the reformation from the harassing thralldom of a conscience."[106]

Spalding in fact was suggesting that the disparagement of the poor in Protestant lands was one piece of a larger societal malaise. Because Protestantism fostered "a spirit of isolation, of individualism, of selfishness, of pride," only it could have invented the maxim "every man for himself, and God for us all!"[107] Thrift, self-interest, and acquisition of wealth, from one perspective, could be seen as virtues in a society that fostered economic opportunity for the individual. But that was the problem in Spalding's mind: "the Protestant principle of private judgment tends to isolate from the rest of society those who profess it, and to foster in them a spirit of individualism, of pride, of avarice." The result might be greater individual wealth and greater devotion to the world, but this principle did not render people "more amicable, more charitable, or better members of society."[108] In sum, Catholic countries, where the "social feeling" was greater, were societies that were "the real friends of the poor and the true champions of human liberty."[109]

Spalding was not the only critic who focused on the problem of individualism in Protestant American society. Brownson blamed the growth of individualism on the increase in print materials that encouraged Americans to read. Because they read, Brownson argued, Americans "fancy themselves competent to sit in judgment on all matters human and divine" and this, then, "serves to foster the spirit of individualism, which is only one form of the supreme selfishness." Americans, who did not have the "meekness to obey, who feel they were as good as you," soon decided that they owed no duty but to themselves and that "the true morality in [their] case is to take care of Number One." For Hughes, the watchword was "every man for himself."[110] Hughes argued that a premise of individualism created a political economy where the prejudices of a nation, like the principles of science, viewed "individual interest as the lifespring of society" and did not allow the possibility that conditions could be

[104] Spalding, "Catholic and Protestant Countries," in *Miscellanea*, 467.
[105] Ibid., 461.
[106] Ibid., 460.
[107] Ibid., 467.
[108] Ibid., 473.
[109] Ibid., 471.
[110] John Hughes, "A Lecture on the Importance of a Christian Basis for the Science of Political Economy, and its Application to the Affairs of Life," 17–18 January 1844, in Kehoe, *Complete Works of the Most Rev. John Hughes*, 1:525.

different.[111] With this faith in the naturalness of individual self-interest, poverty and inequality were themselves also natural. When the regulator of economic life was self-interest, Hughes concluded, "it was perfectly natural for those who were at once landlords and lawmakers, to secure for themselves the largest amount of rents; and to throw off, on others, the weight of every public burthen."[112]

Hecker confided similar concerns in his diary. As he struggled with the possibility of conversion to Catholicism, he observed that the Catholic Church "alone seems to satisfy my want my faith life soul [*sic*]." "I have not wished to make myself catholic," he continued, "but answer to the wants of my soul," in large part because "Catholicism is solidarity" and "Protestansm [*sic*] is individuality."[113] Some months later, Hecker was more expansive. Protestantism, he wrote, "is the spirit of individualism antagonism selfishness competition definitiveness [*sic*]," and no good would come to humanity if the Protestant spirit prevailed. If humans were inherently selfish, Hecker inquired, would not "the doctrine of private judgment ... tend necessarily to selfishness?" Thankfully for Hecker, Catholicism was destined to become the sole faith in Christendom. "Its progress is progressive," he wrote, "silent and permanent," whereas Protestantism was "unprogressive and must eventually become extinct."[114] Hecker put these ideas in print with the publication in 1857 of *Aspirations of Nature*. Practically speaking, Hecker argued, Protestantism was "the exaggeration of the authority of private judgment to the entire exclusion of all other authorities," a fact illustrated by history. Beginning with the Reformation, Protestantism's growth was a march in the denial of authority, a march that culminated in the deification of private judgment. For Hecker, the watchword was *Homo sibi Deus*, "Man is his own God."[115]

This Protestant self-interest and solipsism wrought evils in economics and politics. A character in Quigley's didactic novel, for example, noted the American proclivity to make money. "The Yankee is not remarkable for having an eye for the beautiful in nature or art," he declared, "but when *dimes* and *dollars* are in prospective, none is more penetrating or sharpsighted than he."[116] This materialism not only destroyed a love of beauty and art (unless money was to be made), but it wrought harmful consequences in society. Hughes detected a disequilibrium in what he called "the social machine" due to "a vicious displacement of its essential weights and balances." In the epic societal transitions from slavery to serfdom to the modern freedperson, the conditions of the worker had in some respects become even less tolerable because the latter now had fallen

---

[111] Ibid.
[112] Ibid., 1:524, 523.
[113] Isaac Hecker, 24 April 1843, 28 April 1843, *Diary* 97–98.
[114] Isaac Hecker, 18 December 1844, *Diary* 282.
[115] Hecker, *Aspirations of Nature* 307–8.
[116] A Missionary Priest [Hugh Quigley], *Cross and the Shamrock* 226.

under "a new and undefined power, called capital."[117] Economically, Protestant American society was condemned not only by the inequality generated by its increasingly self-centered worldview but also by its materialism. Children in the public schools of civil society, Spalding argued, were instructed "to make money – honestly if they can, but at all events to make money." To be sure, ethics were given lip service, Spalding concluded again with tongue in cheek, but they should not "sit too heavily on us, much less clog our progress toward wealth and worldly eminence."[118]

The political sins of self-interest were suggested in what Brownson called the "democratic principle."[119] Although Brownson took pains to celebrate the republican form of government for his readers, he traced the evolution of the democratic principle in American life, the doctrine that "the people" were the "origin and source of all authority and all law, that they are absolutely supreme, and bound by no law or authority that does not emanate from themselves."[120] Brownson argued that this principle had a number of destructive tendencies. First, because it derived its power from the government, it tended to make the governed superior to the government itself. The result was that the will of the majority was subject to no authority and bound by no law. Rather, simply put, it was "political atheism."[121] The tyranny of the majority, in such a situation, became an especially knotty problem. Protestants, for example, could venerate their toleration of Roman Catholics, but they knew that they had the power as a majority to enact prohibitions if they wished.[122] Perhaps more troubling was the government's lack of moral authority. A government's authority to rule, Brownson believed, had to be sanctioned by an authority superior to itself. Laws that originated in the people or that "emanate from any human source alone ... bind no conscience, and restrain, except by force, no will."[123] With no authority to bind the conscience, the state had no moral support and was "impotent to govern, except by sheer force."[124]

In the end, Brownson argued, if the people were the source of all legitimate authority and all law was of purely human origin, the "divine order" that possessed the authority of conscience was excluded, ethics were divorced from politics; and utility was substituted for right and made the measure of justice. This was "either no government at all, but a mere agency of the controlling private interests of the people, or a government of mere force."[125] Although it

---

[117] John Hughes, "The Influence of Christianity on Social Servitude," 29 March 1843, in Kehoe, *Complete Works of the Most Rev. John Hughes*, 1:385.
[118] Spalding, "Common-Schools," in *Miscellanea*, 654–55.
[119] Orestes Brownson, "The Democratic Principle," *Brownson's Quarterly Review* 27 (April 1873): 235–59.
[120] Ibid., 256.
[121] Ibid., 239.
[122] Ibid., 240.
[123] Ibid., 238.
[124] Ibid., 245.
[125] Ibid., 255.

might be argued that democracy maintained equality, Brownson concluded that it did the reverse. Because it operated "in favor of those who command and employ capital or credit in business, and against the poorer and more numerous classes," the rich were becoming richer and more materialistic, while the poor simply became poorer.[126] An individualized polity, like an individualistic economy, only fostered oligarchy and exacerbated inequality.

Given this decline in economic justice, how could the problems of inequality, materialism, and individualism be addressed? These Catholic commentators clearly argued that a liberal answer, an answer they associated with the deficits of individualism in Protestant America, would not work. Indeed, a liberal answer was the root of these evils that it was meant to address. Brownson allowed that the revolutionary age in Europe had "a philanthropic origin" that was aimed at redressing political and social grievances; he agreed that the working class was right to assert natural equality.[127] The error, however, was to address these grievances and inequality through political action because the state could only proscribe behavior. Many desirable outcomes, in short, were beyond the ability and competency of the state.[128] As we will see, Brownson would appeal to a higher law that was affected only by the Catholicity of his church with its "supernatural virtue of charity."[129]

Nor did a socialist approach yield any solutions. Indeed, Hecker condemned the "evil of the prot. Heresy [*sic*]" as responsible for the rise of socialism.[130] Brownson's reflections on socialism, as on most other matters, were both extensive and voluble.[131] It was true, he wrote, that although most people saw socialism as "undeserving of a moment's attention," it had in some forms already taken possession of the age. This success stemmed from political revolutions aimed at political equality. Once political equality became an asset, humankind realized that it was meaningless without social equality. And once it was conceded that political equality was an object worth seeking, it followed that social equality was also a positive good. With these premises, the end result was a slippery slope where all human institutions – religion, government, property, family – were annihilated by the quest for equality.[132]

---

[126] Ibid., 207, 216.

[127] Orestes Brownson, "Liberalism and Socialism," *Brownson's Quarterly Review* 17 (April 1855): 135, 146.

[128] Ibid., 146–47.

[129] Ibid., 157–59.

[130] Letter from Isaac Hecker to Orestes Brownson, 7 April 1855, cited in *Gower and Leliart, Brownson-Hecker Correspondence*, 179.

[131] Orestes A. Brownson, "Socialism and the Church," *Brownson's Quarterly Review* 3, no. 1 (January 1849): 91–127.

[132] Brownson also responded to notions of Christian socialism or notions of equality in Christian doctrine. It had been suggested that no discrepancy existed between Catholicism and liberty because all humans were equal before God and therefore equal to one another. Christian law in this reading was everywhere violated because all societies were stamped with examples of privilege and authority. Yet this precluded the role of the Church. If socialists were correct to

Brownson conceded that evil existed in the world – "far more heart-rending, far more terrific, than socialists depict" – but the evil stemmed from the sins of humankind.[133] The creation of human institutions to address the immorality of inherently sinful humans, then, was folly, especially when it ignored the Church, the one institution that offered comfort from the world's wickedness. Perhaps not surprisingly, the solution to the social problem for Brownson and the other Catholic critics was the succor provided by the Roman Catholic Church.

The comfort that Roman Catholicism provided humankind in response to the evils of the contemporary economy was many faceted. For one thing, the Church provided an extrinsic force that tempered the ravages of the modern economy. Hughes, for example, argued that the true cause of the problems of class division that stemmed from industrializing societies was the "absence of a religious power which should be able to extend the obligation of *duties* in exact proportion with the extension of *rights*." Because "the social machine" could be adjusted only through the machinations of individuals seeking their self-interest, it was clear that a stable equilibrium could not be maintained and that political economy as a science was "inadequate and defective."[134] Only through the invocation of an outside power, such as found in "practical Christianity," could a proper equilibrium be maintained. For Hughes, the only way to correct the root of the evil of self-interest was to "bring temporal interests into harmony with *spiritual* – infuse some portion of the attributes of God, justice and mercy into the minds and hearts of princes, of legislators, of nobles, of landlords; yea, if possible of capitalists."[135] The system that now prevailed, Hughes concluded in yet another essay, has lost sight of Cicero's and John Locke's admonition *Salus populi suprema lex*, that the welfare of the people should be the supreme law. In its place was a system of competition in which the people's well-being was ignored.[136]

Brownson's own conversion to Roman Catholicism illustrates, perhaps more clearly than Hughes's prose, the need for an external force. An 1844 essay by Brownson, written shortly after his conversion, traced the origins of his beliefs to his own personal journey toward Roman Catholicism.[137] As a young man, he wrote, he was struck by the economic inequality in American society and specifically by the advantages that capital held over labor. His initial solution

equate Christian law with liberty, they were not always right to assume that human movements for liberty were Christian. Brownson recognized that Christian law was the law of liberty because the coming of Jesus freed those who believed in his word. Yet his order was entirely independent of the world. Those who sought liberty in the secular realm represented not Christian liberty but a world that actually enslaved humans to nature and society. Brownson, "Socialism and the Church," 91–127.

[133] Ibid., 105.
[134] Hughes, "A Lecture on the Importance of a Christian Basis for the Science of Political Economy," 1:525.
[135] Ibid., 1:533.
[136] Hughes, "A Lecture on the Antecedent Cause of the Irish Famine in 1847," 2:553.
[137] Orestes A. Brownson, "No Church, No Reform. Addressed especially to the Fourierists," *Brownson's Quarterly Review* 6 (April 1844): 175–94.

was to accept a principle of selfishness in humankind and create a social system that harmonized the interests of each with the interests of all. But here he realized that "the community, organized on selfish principles, can be nothing but a community of inherently repellant and antagonistic forces."[138] The fundamental predicament of modern reform was the assumption that a human was sufficient for his or her own redemption. The solution to this problem, Brownson soon discovered, was a force external to humankind. That force, not surprisingly, was the Church. Society could be protected only if human law rested on spiritual law. Put differently, because reform was possible only through some superhuman aid, the truest such aid was the rock of Catholicism.[139]

The moral economy of the Church, these Catholic critics continued, fostered a corporate ideal that mitigated against individual excesses in the polity and economy. Hecker distinguished what he considered the universality of the Roman Church from Protestantism, which triggered "countless dissensions, endless disputes, and perfect isolation, making a void in the heart."[140] Catholicism linked peoples' identities together into the unity that was the Church. It was also a visible organic body that taught divine truths, and this organicism played a role in providing comfort to society's weakest members. Brownson, for his part, stressed the unity and universality of the Church.[141] The Church created a harmonious and synthetic order to replace the disunited society created by Protestantism and therefore would rejuvenate society. This worldview was a relational rather than an individual one. Justice and mercy, rather than mere rights, were what motivated their Church.

In writing this story, Catholic critics often fell back on a romantic portrayal of the Middle Ages as a golden age of peace and justice. Brownson was fully convinced that class relations in medieval Europe were preferable to what existed at the time in which he wrote. Tapping into a proslavery argument, he maintained that the connection between a slave owner and a slave was "more generous and touching" than that between a capitalist employer and an employee because of the corporate relationship between the former. Again, in the medieval world a corporate societal organization, according to Brownson, was fostered by a belief in God and justice, whereas people in the present day were "free" to advance the "Gospel of the cotton mill, *laissez-faire*, save who can, and the devil take the hindmost."[142] The foremost feature that Brownson appreciated in the Middle Ages was that humans believed both in God and "in some kind of justice" and that whatever their conditions, people "owe[d] some

[138] Ibid., 179.
[139] Patrick W. Carey, *Orestes A. Brownson: American Religious Weathervane* (Grand Rapids, MI: Wm. B. Eerdmans, 2004), 355–58.
[140] Hecker, *Aspirations of Nature* 279.
[141] See Orestes A. Brownson, "The Church Question," *Brownson's Quarterly Review* 6 (January 1844): 57–84; and Brownson, "No Church, No Reform," 175–94.
[142] Brownson, "Present State of Society," 28.

kind of duty to [their] fellow man."[143] Hughes agreed. Because of the disequilibrium in the modern social machine, class relations were now less tolerant than they were for feudal serfs in a time when the true relation between rights and duties was understood.[144]

As they looked back to the halcyon medieval world, however, these critics also promoted the belief that Catholicism permitted the advancement of humankind and therefore was at the vanguard of providing for an enlightened future (as discussed in Chapter 2). Brownson, well after the conclusion of the Civil War, continued to muse about the increasing inequalities engendered by the modern economy, and he continued to believe that a spiritual solution was the only viable resolution of economic inequality.[145]

These arguments conform to the Catholic American narrative that we have discussed in the preceding pages. On the one hand, proponents of American Catholicity believed that the comfort of the Church provided a justice that permitted humankind to survive the ravages of the new economic age. Catholicism in the modern world was therefore central to the progression not only of American society but of the entire industrializing world. On the other hand, the Catholic conundrum, discussed in Chapter 2, again reared its head. If Roman Catholicism was the sole force that could ameliorate the challenges faced by labor in the world's developing economies, could it be integrated into a pluralist landscape of American religion?

There was, however, a more immediate problem for Catholics in antebellum America. In his condemnation of socialism in 1849, Brownson observed that none of the conditions that socialists denounced – "monarchy, aristocracy, inequalities of rank, inequalities of riches, poverty, want, distress, hunger, starvation even" – was in and of itself necessarily evil. None could harm the just human or prevent humans from the fulfillment of their destiny.[146] Brownson in this condemnation did not mention chattel slavery as a condition that was not necessarily evil. Perhaps this was his conscious decision in an essay he wrote during a high point in the debates over slavery in the late 1840s. Yet it is clear that slavery was an issue that cleaved American society and profoundly divided spokesmen from the various branches of Christianity, a topic to which we now turn.

The Slavery Question

I am told there is not in all America a single Catholic newspaper hostile to Slavery; not one opposed to tyranny in general; not one that takes sides with the oppressed in Europe.

---

[143] Ibid., 41.
[144] Hughes, "Influence of Christianity on Social Servitude," 1:385. On Catholic converts' fascination with medievalism in the nineteenth century, see Patrick Allitt, *Catholic Converts: British and American Intellectuals Turn to Rome* (Ithaca, NY: Cornell University Press, 1997), 43–51.
[145] Carey, *Orestes A. Brownson*, 355–58.
[146] Brownson, "Socialism and the Church," 103.

There is not in America a man born and bred in the Catholic Church who is eminent for Philosophy, Science, Literature, or Art; none distinguished for Philanthropy! The water tastes of the fountain. Theodore Parker, 1854[147]

The questions of slavery and race were touchstones for many antebellum Americans, informing their perception of their place in society and the place of others. Scholars in recent years have discerned the disquieting intensity of the slavery debate among America's immigrants and white workers in the northern United States. They have noted the acute racism that emanated from working-class neighborhoods in antebellum America and that immigrants in the United States were much less sensitive to the evils of slavery than their counterparts who had remained in Europe. Specifically, they have observed that the pleas for the abolition of slavery by Irish nationalists, such as Daniel O'Connell, fell on deaf ears among his compatriots in the United States.[148]

African Americans witnessed and commented on both the changes wrought on European immigrants on their arrival in America and the slights they themselves endured from whites in the North. The abolitionist Frederick Douglass, for example, famously wrote that the Irish people, who were "warm-hearted, generous, and sympathizing with the oppressed everywhere, when they stand upon their own green island," were taught at once "to hate and despise the colored people" when they arrived "in this christian country." They were taught "to believe that we eat the bread which of right belongs to them" and that African American "adversity is essential to their prosperity" (see Fig. 7).[149] In her *Incidents in the Life of a Slave Girl*, a memoir of her life as a slave in the South and a fugitive slave in the North, Harriet Jacobs recounted the transformation among urban laborers in New York when one among them was discovered to be colored. "This at once transformed him into a different being," she wrote, and native-born Americans and Irish Americans alike, who found it to be "offensive to their dignity to have a 'nigger' among them," began to treat him "with silent scorn."[150] Frederick Douglass too faced disparagement when he worked among white carpenters in Baltimore. Claiming that "poor white men would be thrown out of employment" if additional blacks were hired, the white carpenters began "to put on airs, and talk about the 'niggers' taking the country, saying we all ought to be killed." Rhetoric escalated into violence, and a bloody row pitted Douglass against his tormenters. For Douglass, the

---

[147] Parker, "A Sermon of the Dangers which Threaten the Rights of Man in America," 2:244.

[148] Noel Ignatiev, *How the Irish Became White* (New York: Routledge, 1995); McGreevy, *Catholicism and American Freedom*, 43–67; Charles P. Connor, "The Northern Catholic Position on Slavery and the Civil War: Archbishop Hughes as a Test Case," *Records of the American Catholic Historical Society of Philadelphia* 95 (1985): 35–48; Vincent A. Lapomarda, *Mid-America* 53 (1971): 160–69; John C. Murphy, *An Analysis of the Attitudes of American Catholics toward the Immigrant and the Negro, 1825–1925* (Washington, DC: Catholic University of America Press, 1940).

[149] Frederick Douglass, *My Bondage and My Freedom* (New York and Auburn: Miller, Orton, 1857), 454.

[150] [Harriet Jacobs], *Incidents in the Life of a Slave Girl* (Boston: Published for the Author, 1861), 279.

FIGURE 7. African Americans such as Frederick Douglass observed how recent immigrants, who were once oppressed in their own European homelands, quickly discovered that they could gain social acceptance in America by denigrating African Americans on the basis of their race. (Prints and Photographs Division, Library of Congress, LC-USZ62-15887)

"watchwords of the bloody-minded" were "Damn the abolitionists!" and "Damn the niggers!" which encapsulated "the state of things in the Christian city of Baltimore."[151]

[151] Frederick Douglass, *Narrative of the Life of Frederick Douglass, An American Slave* (Boston: Published at the Anti-Slavery Office, 1845), 91–93.

Yet Catholics also faced expressions of intolerance. Catholic immigrants from Ireland and elsewhere often encountered derisive sneers about their racial character, religious beliefs, and inherent abilities, sneers that were often suggested by abolitionists. As early as 1838, the attorney George Templeton Strong recorded his observations on immigrants in America in his diary, specifically condemning the naturalization of European immigrants, whose male populace would then enjoy the rights of suffrage. "It was enough," he confessed in his diary on November 6, "to turn a man's stomach – to make a man adjure republicanism forever – to see the way they were naturalizing this morning." Here, "wretched, filthy, bestial-looking Italians and Irish ... the very scum and dregs of human nature filled the clerk of C[ommon] P[leas] office so completely that I was almost afraid of being poisoned by going in."[152] Adam Gurowski observed that Americans in the cities, when comparing the "Hibernians" with the "colored population," "almost unanimously give the palm for intelligence, honesty, cleanliness, aptitude to work, and good-breeding" to the latter.[153] As the slavery question heated up, Theodore Parker at midcentury also noted the moral inadequacy of the Irish, which had repercussions for their New England home. "The Irish," he wrote, "had the vices of their condition. ... Dirt and rum, with pestilence and blows, follow their steps." Their voices, he added, "debauched the politics of the city," and the Irish press inhibited "humanity, education, freedom, progress."[154]

African Americans, who felt the sting of white working-class racism, offered their own denigrations of the Irish and their Catholic beliefs. Douglass, for example, mentioned in passing the "cunning illusions" of the Church of Rome, a trope widely held by Protestant America, both black and white.[155] Indeed Douglass and the abolitionist James McCune Smith, according to Robert Ernst, believed that the Romanism carried from Europe by Irish and German immigrants threatened the integrity of American institutions.[156] African Americans often saw themselves as harbingers of the advances of Protestantism and antislavery, which they tended to link together. "A Colored Female of Philadelphia," writing in the *Liberator* in 1832, saw an African American migration to Mexico as a means of securing the fortunes of black people but also as a vehicle for religious regeneration. Because Mexico was a "Papist" country, she wrote, "perhaps we may be made the honored instruments in the hand of an all-wise God, in establishing the holy religion of the Protestant

---

[152] Allan Nevins and Milton Halsey Thomas, *The Diary of George Templeton Strong: Young Man in New York, 1835–1849* (New York: Macmillan, 1952) 94.
[153] Adam G. De Gurowski, *America and Europe* (New York: D. Appleton, 1857), 270.
[154] Theodore Parker, *Condition of the People of Massachusetts*, 191, cited in William G. Bean, "Puritan versus Celt: 1850–1860," *New England Quarterly* 7 (1934): 71.
[155] Frederick Douglass, "Pictures and Progress: An Address Delivered in Boston, Massachusetts, on 3 December 1861," in *The Frederick Douglass Papers*, Series 1, *Speeches, Debates, and Interviews, vol. 3, 1855–1863*, ed. John W. Blassingame and John R. Mckivigan (New Haven, CT: Yale University Press, 1985), 462.
[156] Robert Ernst, "Negro Concepts of Americanism," *Journal of Negro History* 39 (1954): 208.

Church in that country."[157] The black nationalist Martin Delany, according to Wilson Jeremiah Moses, considered Protestantism to be the highest form of civilization and disparaged Roman Catholicism in part because "slavery was its legitimate successor."[158] These expressions of scorn certainly were a function of the social environment in which ethnoracial groups competed for scarce economic resources. Yet they also illustrate the ways in which political allegiances among antislavery advocates *and* Protestants were forged using Roman Catholicism as a negative reference in contemporary America.

This racial and religious denigration clearly was linked to socioeconomic disputes between members of disadvantaged groups vying for political power and economic resources. Indeed, Roman Catholics in Europe exhibited a much more diverse view toward slavery and some offered opinions that condemned slavery itself.[159] So if we censure immigrant racism, we can understand it as one element in their repertoire to increase their social and psychological standing in society. And if we criticize native-born Americans for vilifying the Irish Catholic, this too was related to fears of the growing political influence of citizens who allied with what their detractors considered authoritarian regimes, fears that I have recounted throughout this book. Yet these disputes were overlaid with intellectual debates about economic rights and justice and ultimately the place of slavery in human society that distressed Northerners and Southerners, black and white, immigrant and native-born in the decades leading up to civil war. And it should not be surprising that the views of a moral economy discussed earlier informed the slavery debate.

The question of the morality of slavery and the advisability of its abolition was often nested in larger questions of economic principles and scriptural interpretation. Regarding the latter, antislavery advocates often criticized the inactivity of church leaders in the United States in part because of the leaders' beliefs that the Bible did not explicitly condemn slavery and on occasion sanctioned it. The radical abolitionist Parker Pillsbury, for example, aptly joined the Christian religion and the institution of slavery when he condemned churches as *"spiritual and ecclesiastical plantations."*[160] Abolitionists often focused too on Roman Catholic authorities who seemingly shared a similar perspective with proslavery advocates. This common outlook offered an antimodern perspective that condemned what they considered an objectionable drift toward a liberal society, which in turn had implications for the question of free labor and slavery. This perspective was manifested in a variety of forms. For one thing, both Roman Catholic leaders and proslavery advocates in the South agreed on the

[157] *Liberator* 2 (28 January 1832): 14, cited in Wilson Jeremiah Moses, *The Golden Age of Black Nationalism, 1850–1925* (Hamden, CT: Archon Press, 1978), 277.
[158] Moses, *Golden Age of Black Nationalism*, 48. Moses also notes that David Walker's *Appeal* condemned Bartholomew de las Casas as "that very, very avaricious Catholic priest" (48).
[159] Mark A. Noll, *The Civil War as a Theological Crisis* (Chapel Hill: University of North Carolina Press, 2006), 132–59.
[160] Parker Pillsbury, *Acts of the Anti-Slavery Apostles* (Concord, NH: Clague, Wegman, Schlicht, 1883), 323.

ways in which the slavery debate symbolized negative theological, social, and intellectual developments that characterized modern society. Most basically, because they did not share the urgent need to abolish slavery, Roman Catholic leaders and proslavery advocates argued that the Bible sanctioned slavery or, at the very least, did not condemn it.[161] For example, James H. Hammond who served as both a U.S. Senator and governor of South Carolina, contended that "American slavery is not only not a sin, but especially commanded by God through Moses, and approved by Christ through his apostles."[162]

As the scriptural debate between proponents and opponents of slavery spread, arguments often became ad hominem. Abolitionists, for their part, often freely mocked Christian proslavery advocates and occasionally ridiculed the Christian religion.[163] In response, antiabolitionists began to condemn those who advocated for the end of slavery as fanatics or worse. Elizabeth Fox-Genovese and Eugene Genovese provide ample examples of proslavery Southerners condemning Northern Christian radicals as "baptized infidels," practitioners of "Protestant Jesuitry," or wayward souls in conflict with truth, "of the Bible [in conflict] with Northern infidelity – of a pure Christianity with Northern fanaticism – of liberty with despotism – of right with might."[164] Archbishop John Hughes was more succinct. "Sometimes it has appeared to us that abolitionism," he observed, "stands in need of a strait jacket and the humane protection of a lunatic asylum."[165]

For apologists of slavery, the abolitionists embodied a dangerous drift in modern society, a tendency that was both fanatical and scheming. From a Roman Catholic viewpoint, the growth of fanatical religious movements – as varied as Unitarians, freethinkers, spirit rappers, and Mormons – was evidence of an increasingly subjective and human-centered spirituality that allegedly eroded the authority of the church and boded ill for the future. Rev. J. Henry Smith of North Carolina condemned these developments and remarked that the South was "exempt from the radicalism, infidelity, fanaticism, ultraism and the

---

[161] See, for example, Elizabeth Fox-Genovese and Eugene D. Genovese, *The Mind of the Master Class: History and Faith in the Southern Slaveholders' World View* (New York: Cambridge University Press, 2005), 473–565; Noll, *Civil War as a Theological Crisis*, 31–50; and Molly Oshatz, "Accidental Liberalism: The Slavery Debates and the Rise of Protestant Liberalism in America, 1830–1890" (Ph.D. diss., University of California at Berkeley, 2007).

[162] Letter to Thomas Clarkson, esq., *Selections from the Letters and Speeches of the Hon. James H. Hammond, of South Carolina* (New York: John F. Trow, 1866), 124. See also Thorton Stringfellow, "The Bible Argument; or, Slavery in the Light of Divine Revelation," in E. N. Elliott, *Cotton is King, and Pro-Slavery Arguments Comprising the Writings of Hammond, Harper, Christy, Stringfellow, Hodge, Bledsoe, and Cartwright, on this Important Subject* (Augusta, GA: Abbott and Loomis, 1860; New York: Negro Universities Press, 1969), 459–92. Citations are to the Negro Universities Press edition.

[163] Fox-Genovese and Genovese, *Mind of the Master Class*, 485.

[164] Ibid., 482.

[165] John Hughes, "Abolition Views Brownson Overthrown," reported from the *Metropolitan Record* in the *Catholic Mirror*, Baltimore, 12 October 1861, cited in Rena M. Andrews, "Slavery Views of a Northern Prelate," *Church History* 3 (1934): 65.

countless forms of error, lawlessness and riot that blind and madden so many communities."[166] Many among these religious factions were associated with growing social movements, discussed in the previous chapter, that included women's rights as well as the abolition of slavery. In sum, a fanaticism connected to the abolitionist movement was linked with other modern impulses and all were evidence of a world careening out of control. Proslavery advocates, in contrast, were prone to castigate the "cold, calculating, ambitious" modern world and to celebrate the "more heart-felt" influence that bound together master and slave in a mutually dependent relationship.[167] These beliefs accorded well with the Roman Catholic argument that Catholicism was a culture of justice and charity, as opposed to the grasping and avaricious Protestant world discussed in the previous section and in Chapter 2.

These observations were related to another and probably more important similarity between proslavery advocates and Roman Catholic leaders: a common appreciation of a corporatism that embraced the organic relationships within society and challenged modern developments that were allegedly eroding them. As we have observed in this and in the previous chapter, Roman Catholic authorities were leery of celebrating the advance of an individualistic and liberal society in which a market economy mindlessly created growing wealth. Catholic leaders and proslavery advocates alike linked the relationship between master and slave to other bonds in family and society that were unequal and reciprocal. Archbishop Hughes, following a visit to Cuba, celebrated the mutuality of the master-slave relationship and dreamt that it could be extended throughout human society. If the "master has a right to claim obedience" of the slave, he is charged with a responsibility to extend "every means by which they shall be enabled also to fulfill the purposes of their being towards Him who created and redeemed them." If Christian parents and employers did likewise, "how would the whole order of society begin to be renovated by the practice of primitive virtues!" Indeed, he continued, "let us all endeavor to imitate the pastorship of the good Shepherd – for we are all shepherds, each in his own sphere." Then, "every family become a church, its head the high-priest and king, protecting, guarding, and instructing those who constitute the objects of his affection as well as his authority."[168] Such organic mutuality clearly buttressed core human institutions – the family, the church, the school – that strengthened human life. And it complemented the arguments of proslavery ideologues who set the master-slave relationship in a context of other societal arrangements of reciprocal inequality.

As proslavery advocates and Roman Catholic leaders romanticized an organic, relational world, they fretted over the outcomes of wage labor in a

[166] James Henry Smith, *Sermon at Greensboro* (Charleston, SC, 1863), cited in Fox-Genovese and Genovese, *Mind of the Master Class*, 503.

[167] Elliott, *Cotton Is King*, 411.

[168] John Hughes, "Sermon on the Occasion of his Return from Cuba," in Kehoe, *Complete Works of the Most Rev. John Hughes*, 2:221, 223.

growing capitalist system. The educator and author George Frederick Holmes, who flirted with conversion to Roman Catholicism, for example, condemned the Reformation, which initiated a spirit of individualism that not coincidentally departed from a corporatism that in his mind supported chattel slavery.[169] Even more famous is the stark argument of Virginia attorney and author George Fitzhugh, who claimed that it was "the duty of society to enslave the weak," a duty that varied according to the labor systems that dominated in each society. Even in Europe, the protection provided the poor in the form of poor relief was "enslavement of some sort."[170] This was natural because inequality and reciprocity was inherent in all human society. "Parents, husbands, guardians, teachers, committees, &c., are but masters under another name," masters who protected the weak "and whose right it is to control them." Given this human condition, slavery was the most just labor system. "Your freedmen at the North," he continued, "do the same work and fill the same offices." But there was a difference: "we love our slaves, and we are ready to defend, assist and protect them; you hate and fear your white servants, and never fail, as a moral duty, to screw down their wages to the lowest and starve their families, if possible as evidence of your thrift, economy and management – the only English and Yankee virtues."[171] The "cruelty and suffering" of free labor, with its "severe, heartless, grinding employers and miserable starving hirelings," William John Grayson, a politician and writer from South Carolina, asserted was not less than that of a slave system.[172] The dystopic vision of wage (or "white") slavery posited by proslavery advocates resonated with those of Roman Catholic critics such as Brownson and the others cited throughout this chapter.[173]

The combination of a social dynamic that pitted actors on the ground – African Americans, Irish Catholic immigrants, native-born abolitionists – against one another, then, was linked to a compatibility of views between the Roman Catholic leadership and Southern proslavery advocates about the state of the modern economy and about vehicles to address the economy's ills. It is probably too much to say that the Roman Catholic leadership mirrored the Southern proslavery advocates in their opposition to abolitionism, their steadfast racism, and their "slavery as a positive good" philosophy. But they did evince a clear tendency to take a less forbidding view toward slavery. Indeed,

[169] Fox-Genovese and Genovese, *Mind of the Master Class*, 650.
[170] George Fitzhugh, *Cannibals All! or, Slaves without Masters* (Richmond, VA: A. Morris, 1857; repr., Cambridge: Harvard University Press, 1960), 187.
[171] Ibid., 220.
[172] W. J. Gray [William John Grayson], "The Hireling and the Slave," *DeBow's Review* 19 (August 1855): 209.
[173] The term "white slavery" was forcefully articulated again by Orestes Brownson in "White Slavery," *United States Democratic Review* 11, no. 51 (September 1842): 260–70. In describing the young laborers in England who died prematurely from their toil, Brownson wrote, "[I]t is common to hear people say, 'work like a negro – like a galley slave.' But this is mere child's play compared with the working of a Lancashire weaver. ... American slaves ... are fat and happy compared with many free-born Englishmen!" (263).

many opponents of slavery such as Theodore Parker argued that Roman Catholicism was a bulwark that opposed abolitionism throughout the United States. Parker had good reason to make this observation. Few Roman Catholic leaders condemned slavery before the onset of the Civil War. It is true that Pope Gregory XVI reproved the slave trade in an apostolic letter in 1839, a few years before Daniel O'Connell called for Irish Americans to join the antislavery crusade. Yet it was not until 1862, one year after the outset of the Civil War and shortly before Lincoln's Emancipation Proclamation, that Orestes Brownson and Archbishop John Purcell called for freedom for slaves.[174] In the meantime, Catholic condemnation of slavery and slaveholders was tepid at best. John Hughes, approving of Pope Gregory's letter, argued that it was wrong to enslave a free person. But where slavery already existed, he continued, the Church did not require that it be abolished nor assert that masters or slaves were "individually responsible for the condition which they respectively occupy toward one another."[175] If slavery was an evil, "it was not an absolute and unmitigated evil." Indeed, it was "infinitely better than the conditions in which this people would have been had they not been seized to gratify the avarice and cupidity of the white man."[176] Bishop John England, moreover, argued that Pope Gregory's 1839 encyclical condemned merely the slave trade, not the institution of chattel slavery itself. Although he personally did not support the institution, he wrote elsewhere, England confessed that it could not be abolished.[177] His editor was even more adamant. "There is no danger," he wrote, "no possibility, on our principles – that Catholic theology should ever be tinctured with the fanaticism of abolition." Although Catholics might disagree about slavery, he concluded, "our theology is fixed, and is, and must be the same now as it was for the first eight or nine centuries of Christianity."[178] England certainly was influenced by living in fire-eating Charleston, but Bishop Francis Patrick Kenrick of Philadelphia tended to agree. Although Kenrick rued the ill effects of slavery on its victims, he argued nonetheless that "it does not seem unjust to hold the descendants of these slaves in slavery."[179]

---

[174] Noll, *Civil War as a Theological Crisis*, 126–27.

[175] Andrews, "Slavery Views of a Northern Prelate," 61–63.

[176] Hughes, "Sermon on the Occasion of his Return from Cuba," 2:222.

[177] Bishop John England, first and second letters to Hon. John Forsyth, Secretary of State, United States 29 September and 7 October 1840, *Works* (1849), 3:115–19, cited in John Francis Maxwell, *Slavery and the Catholic Church: The History of Catholic Teaching Concerning the Moral Legitimacy of the Institution of Slavery* (Chichester: Barry Rose, 1975), 111.

[178] Reynolds (I. A.) in Bishop John England's *Works* (1849), 3:107–8, cited in Maxwell, *Slavery and the Catholic Church*, 112.

[179] Hugh J. Nolan, *The Most Reverend Francis Patrick Kenrick, Third Bishop of Philadelphia, 1830–1851* (Washington, DC: Catholic University of America Press, 1948), 242. On the definitions of slavery as intrinsically and accidentally evil among Roman Catholics, see John T. Noonan, Jr., *A Church That Can and Cannot Change: The Development of Catholic Moral Teaching* (Notre Dame, IN: University of Notre Dame Press, 2005).

The debate about slavery ultimately had a bearing on the political coalitions that were formed in an era when the immigration and slavery questions were burning issues of the day. As such, the increasing urgency of the slavery issue in ante-bellum America had a number of political consequences for the economic debate, to which it was related. First, it might not be too much to suggest that the Catholic critique, which was more fundamental than that which accepted commerce and a money economy, was made vulnerable by its association with slavery. After the union had been torn apart in civil war, some noted Catholic leaders such as Brownson began to call for abolition. But it was too little, too late. In the end, calls for corporatist solutions to economic inequality became a minority resolution for a minority community, an antimodernist joust toward the seeming inexorable march of capitalist civilization. It marginalized an already marginal critique. Although it would find expression in the Roman Catholic community in the United States and beyond, it would have little impact other than in the pillorized Catholic American community.[180]

The second consequence was political. If the more fundamental and trenchant elements of the economic critique were diminished, they were replaced by a tendency among Roman Catholics to join political movements that reinforced their social, class, and racial positions in the United States. In the end, they found a political home in the Democratic Party, whose leaders worked assiduously to school them on, among other issues, the racial politics in antebellum America. Catholic leaders and its press favored the enforcement of fugitive slave laws and the extension of slavery into the territories through popular sovereignty. The response by Boston's residents during the Anthony Burns affair in 1854, when Burns, a fugitive slave, was sent back to Southern slavery is telling. Irish immi-grants would mimic the expressions of the white South when they noted that the Fugitive Slave Law of 1850 had been "openly violated and resisted" only by "the descendents of the Puritans." No Irish immigrants joined these Puritans because they "have taken a solemn oath to sustain the Constitution and law of this glorious Union."[181] In this way, the Irish could simultaneously offer allegiance to their adopted party and nation, assert with self-confidence their virtue as law-abiding citizens, and denigrate other ethnoreligious groups – such as the "Puritans" – who represented the ill-effects of a modernizing world, and object to antislavery movements.

This allegiance among many Roman Catholics to Democracy *and* racist ideologies only further infuriated their political adversaries, reinforcing their

---

[180] To illustrate the ways in which the debate about economic justice among Roman Catholics endured after the abolition of slavery and indeed well into the twentieth century, see Katherine Healan Gaston, "The Genesis of America's Judeo-Christian Moment: Secularism, Totalitarianism, and Redefinition of Democracy" (Ph.D. diss., University of California, 2008), 369–484.

[181] *Boston Slave Riot, and Trial of Anthony Burns. Containing the Report of the Faneuil Hall Meeting; the Murder of Batchelder; Theodore Parker's Lesson for the Day; Speeches of Counsel on Both Sides, Corrected by Themselves; a Verbatim Report of Judge Loring's Decision; and Detailed Account of the Embarkation* (Boston: Fetridge, 1854), 41.

conviction that Catholicism was a regressive force that supported despotic institutions such as slavery and the Church itself. Roman Catholics were ridiculed for the seeming endorsement of slavery by both their leadership and the rank and file, an allegation that became increasingly fraught as the slavery debate grew more heated in the decade before civil war. During the Burns controversy, Theodore Parker, an exemplar of a descendant of the "Puritans" castigated by his Irish neighbors, condemned the collusion of Irish Catholics with advocates of slavery. Parker, the prominent minister from Massachusetts, put it simply: "the Catholic clergy are on the side of slavery," in part because "they like slavery itself." Slavery, it seems, was "an institution thoroughly congenial to them, consistent with the first principles of their church."[182] Moreover, the views of the Catholic clergy reinforced those of the Catholic print media. The *Commonwealth* argued in 1854 that "the Catholic press upholds the slave power and seeks to annihilate those who resist its atrocious doctrines and doings."[183] Parker argued that "the Catholic clergy are on the side of slavery." These tendencies were reflected, according to Parker, in Catholic practice; "the Catholic worshiper is not to think, but to believe and obey; the priest not to reason and consider, but to proclaim and command; the voter is not to inquire and examine, but to deposit his ballot as the ecclesiastical authority directs."[184] The deficiencies of Roman Catholicism, in Parker's mind, were related not only to a sympathy for tyranny but also to an explicit support of chattel slavery in the United States.

In the decade before the firing on Fort Sumter, then, the association between Romanism and slavery only became more entrenched in many Americans' minds. The *Chicago Daily Tribune*, for example, dated the descent from the 1852 election, after which "ninety-nine one-hundredths" of Catholics took the side of "Despotism." The United States, the newspaper continued, saw renewal of "the contest [between] Freedom and Despotism," and the Roman Catholic Church clearly sided with the latter. "There is not a Catholic journal ... that is not intensely Pro-Slavery. ... There is not ... a priest of the Church who would dare to call himself an Anti-Slavery man."[185] The linkages between the Church and slavery, the *Chicago Daily Tribune* observed elsewhere, were due to common sentiments. "The sentiment that impels men to wink at the buying and selling of human beings," it contended, "makes them lenient toward the assumed power of the Church that enslaves the conscience and cramps the reason of its adherents." Both Catholicism and slavery had "their root in the ignorance and abasement of human kind. Both fear discussion; both court power for the few, while they tread down and oppress the many."[186] Condemnations used for decades to disparage Roman Catholicism now were explicitly linked to the Slave Power.

---

[182] *Boston Evening Telegraph*, 2 July 1854, cited in Bean, "Puritan versus Celt," 82.
[183] *Commonwealth* 31 May 1854, cited in Bean, "Puritan versus Celt," 82.
[184] Parker, "Sermon of the Dangers which Threaten the Rights of Man in America," 2:244.
[185] "Catholics and Slavery," *Chicago Daily Tribune*, 11 February 1856, 2.
[186] "Popery and Slavery," *Chicago Daily Tribune*, 8 February 1856, 2.

To be sure, not all who opposed slavery were hostile to Roman Catholicism, nor were proslavery advocates the universal supporters of Roman Catholicism. Abraham Lincoln, for example, famously wrote that "I do not perceive how anyone professing to be sensitive to the wrong to the Negro can join in a league to degrade a class of White men."[187] Moreover, views about the abolition of slavery shifted over time. Orestes Brownson, who published a scathing essay on "white slavery" in 1842 and who rued the dystopic future of an industrializing America a year later, for example, was calling for the abolition of slavery twenty years later as the Civil War grew more bloody. However, a political dynamic nonetheless created an inclination among Roman Catholics to favor political movements that were in accord with their worldview and were seemingly less hostile to their faith and racial class position. Anti-Catholics, in turn, viewed the laity as pawns of a proslavery priesthood and duplicitous Democratic politicians, which only increased the venom with which they attacked the benighted immigrant. These criticisms consequently only pushed them further into the Democratic fold. A vicious circle exacerbated already conspicuous political cleavages that grew increasingly divisive as the United States careened toward civil war. A political crisis erupted that attempted to solve the questions of slavery and religious diversity in American society. One question was solved. The other was not.

---

[187] Letter to Owen Lovejoy, 11 August 1855, in *The Collected Works of Abraham Lincoln*, ed. Roy B. Basler (New Brunswick, NJ: Rutgers University Press, 1953), 2:316.

Editor's Epilogue

Jon Gjerde saw the nation's encounter with Catholicism in the nineteenth century as the first of many encounters with religious minorities, particularly with those groups that arrived in the massive waves of migration in the early and late twentieth century. Indeed, one could easily substitute "Judaism," "Hinduism," "Buddhism," or "Islam" for "Catholicism" and advance the century in his title. Moreover, the many conflicts that have emerged between minority and majority faiths, like the debates between nineteenth-century Catholics and Protestants, have rarely come to any clear resolution but instead play a profound role in shaping the economy, society, and politics of the United States. In short, religion continues to constitute a vital component, both divisive and constitutive, of American life in the modern age.[1]

To reinforce this point, Gjerde, in an unfinished epilogue to *Catholicism and the Shaping of Nineteenth-Century America*, wrote about the ongoing tensions between Protestants and Catholics after the Civil War. Strikingly, very little had changed in the relationship between these two groups before and after the war; but this, I believe, was exactly the point Gjerde meant to convey. It was Gjerde's aim to demonstrate the ways in which the antebellum era dialectic between Protestants and Catholics created the framework for analogous debates from the late nineteenth century to the present. Postbellum Protestants and Catholics recapitulated their conundrums regarding the relationship between faith and American freedom. On the one hand, Gjerde describes how a German immigrant Catholic celebrated the "freedoms of religion that strengthened their allegiance to the United States."[2] On the other hand, this orator "remind[ed] his German

---

[1] Gjerde, *Catholicism and the Shaping of Nineteenth-Century America* (New York: Cambridge University Press, 2011), 16.

[2] Here Gjerde emphasizes that race served as a prerequisite to political freedom. He writes, "The United States exemplified an ideological environment that enabled these immigrants defined as 'white' to develop loyalty to American traditions *because* they had access to citizenship and the right to reroot traditions of language and belief in the American landscape." Jon Gjerde, "Epilogue" (unpublished manuscript, n.d.), 1.

friends of the Biblical injunction to remain distinct from others who did not share his faith."[3] Late nineteenth-century Catholics, in other words, continued to face the dilemma of how to reconcile their appreciation for American freedom, which enabled their own integration into American society, with their own insistence on the distinctiveness of the Catholic faith.

Gjerde continues his unfinished epilogue with a second anecdote about the Protestant conundrum, or the Protestant effort to reconcile assumptions about the Protestant character of the American nation with their own commitment to religious freedom. The Protestant theologian Philip Schaff articulated this tension when he celebrated the religious freedoms afforded by the Constitution. As Gjerde writes, Schaff praised "the 'American theory' of church and state, which offered religious liberty and thereby precluded religious persecution."[4] Yet Schaff simultaneously "cautioned that the separation of church and state, which had become cemented in American practice, did not separate the nation from Christianity."[5] Gjerde continues,

In fact, [Schaff] assured his readers, the religious rights encoded in the First Amendment could not have originated in a pagan or "Mohammedan country," [but instead] presuppose[d] "Christian civilization." The question of course is begged: if religious liberty was guaranteed and religious persecution precluded to all, how would these rights and conditions be transferred to non-Christians? And what might happen if people of these religious persuasions gained political power and altered the genius of the "American theory"?[6]

Despite his paean to American religious liberty, Schaff raised profound questions about the rights and roles of non-Christians in American society. As Gjerde concludes, "The fact that many Protestants in the nineteenth century questioned whether Roman Catholicism was a part of the Christian tradition calls into question whether [non-Christians], like the Muslims that Schaff ... cited, could really contribute to the march of religious progress in the nation."[7] Ultimately, Schaff's declaration served as a harbinger of the animosities and conflicts that emerged in response to the growth of the Muslim, Hindu, Sikh, Buddhist, Jewish, and Catholic immigrant communities, among others, in modern America.

It was not Gjerde's intent to offer a complete account of how religious minorities transformed the nation in the twentieth and twenty-first centuries. Yet, it is clear that he would have wanted scholars to take his work as a starting point for thinking about how religion shaped the contours of American life. For Gjerde, this was particularly important given the ongoing salience of religious observance, broadly defined, to Americans in the

---

[3] Ibid.
[4] Ibid., 2.
[5] Ibid., 3.
[6] Ibid., 3 (citing Philip Schaff, *Church and State in the United States; or, The American Idea of Religious Liberty and Its Practical Effects* [New York: G. P. Putnam's Sons, 1888], 9, 10, 53, 40).
[7] Gjerde, "Epilogue," 3.

twentieth century.[8] As he notes in the Introduction: "Those who expect that the residents in modern America have rejected mysterious and arcane religious elements, moreover, are sadly mistaken. Among Americans as a whole, 86 percent of them in the recent Gallup poll affirmed that they believed in God; 70 percent in the devil; 75 percent in angels; 81 percent in heaven; and 69 percent in hell."[9] And while Christianity continues to be the dominant religious practice in America, non-Christian and non-Western faiths (such as Buddhism, Taoism, Confucianism, Islam, and Hinduism, among many others) have proliferated, particularly as a result of the demographic transformation wrought by the Immigration and Nationality Act of 1965.[10] At the same time, these new waves of immigrants often transplanted their own distinct versions of Christianity from abroad; as Edwin Gaustad and Leigh Schmidt write, "Christianity in America is no longer just European, African, and Hispanic but increasingly Asian as well."[11]

Gjerde also understood that, when construed as a cultural phenomenon, religion remained a powerful force in modern American society. He certainly concurred with Robert Bellah's famous account of an American civil religion, that is, the ways in which conceptions of religion lent a sense of coherence to ideas of the American nation.[12] Yet unlike Bellah, Gjerde stressed that religion divided as well as unified the nation, creating highly disparate conceptions of American society, the state, and the nation. Hence Gjerde found it intriguing that late twentieth-century religious and political conservatives, like nineteenth-century Protestants, used religious language to express a distinct vision of the American nation. For instance, Samuel Huntington famously warns that the growth of the non-Anglo-Saxon Protestant population in America will lead to a "crisis of national identity."[13] Meanwhile, evangelical and fundamentalist

---

[8] For sociologists of religion, the prevalence of religious observance in an ostensibly secular state presents an intriguing anomaly, especially in light of the increasing secularization within more spiritually oriented European states. The political scientist Ted Jelen provides one widely circulated explanation for this phenomenon, arguing that the very secularization of the state bolstered the growth of religious devotion in the United States. He writes, "The Establishment and Free Exercise Clauses of the First Amendment may provide a legal and political environment in which a competitive religious market can flourish." Ted Jelen, "The Constitutional Basis of Religious Pluralism in the United States: Causes and Consequences," *Annals of the American Academy of Political and Social Science* 612 (July 2007): 26–29, 39.

[9] Gjerde, *Catholicism*, 11 (citing http://www.gallup.com/poll/1690/religion.aspx).

[10] On contemporary Christianity, Gjerde notes, "Over four-fifths of Americans informed interviewers in a 2007 Gallup poll that they identified with a Christian religion. Of those who identified with any religious faith, moreover, well over 90% are Christian." Gjerde, *Catholicism*, 11 (citing http://www.gallup.com/poll/1690/religion.aspx).

[11] Edwin S. Gaustad and Leigh E. Schmidt, *The Religious History of America*, rev. ed. (New York: Harper One, 2002), 413.

[12] Robert Bellah, "Civil Religion in America," *Daedalus* 96, n. 1 (1967): 1–21. For a discussion of the changes in Bellah's own view of the notion of an American civil religion, see Richard D. Hecht, "Active versus Passive Pluralism: A Changing Style of Civil Religion?" *Annals of the American Academy of Political and Social Science* 612 (July 2007): 133–51.

[13] Samuel P. Huntington, *Who Are We? The Challenges to America's National Identity* (New York: Simon and Schuster, 2004).

Christians, as the sociologist Wade Clark Roof explains, "remind multiculturalists emphasizing the rights of religious and secular minorities that in this
country white Christians are still in the majority. Evangelical and fundamentalist
Christians see themselves as embroiled in nothing less than a struggle for
America's soul."[14]

Gjerde undoubtedly would have explored the responses of religious and
ethnic minorities to these exclusionary conceptions of national identity. In his
unfinished final chapter and epilogue, he suggests that Catholics continued
to articulate a bifurcated notion of national identity, albeit in a new political
context created by the Civil War and Reconstruction. As he writes, "The
American Constitution and traditions that developed from it in the next century
provided an ideological space for individuals simultaneously to recognize a
national allegiance and more local and particularist loyalties."[15] In the twentieth
century, the Supreme Court's interpretation of the free exercise and establishment clauses certainly provided an expanded juridical space for religious minorities to assert their rights.[16] Hearing more cases on the separation of church and
state in the 1970s (and again in the 1980s) than it had from 1790 to 1940, the
Court has become a key arbiter in religious debates.[17] Moreover, by the late
twentieth century, as Gaustad and Schmidt observe,

it appeared that religion in America was something that one took to court. ... By the
1980s, with local confrontations mounting over the public display of such Christian
symbols as nativity scenes, even the baby Jesus, the three wise men, and the reindeer
pulling Santa's sleigh had made it to the Supreme Court in the case of *Lynch v. Donnelly*
in Pawtucket, Rhode Island.[18]

In short, late twentieth-century legal developments have only reinforced the
political freedoms that enabled religious minorities to sustain their particularist
faiths in a pluralist society.[19]

---

[14] Wade Clark Roof, "Introduction," *Annals of the American Academy of Political and Social
Science* 612 (July 2007): 6. At the same time, Gjerde reminds us that the religious right does not
hold a monopoly on this notion of America as a Christian nation; poll data from the late
twentieth century report that over half of Americans believe that the United States
Constitution is a Christian document. Gjerde, *Catholicism*, 11 (citing http://www.christian-
post.com/pages/print.htm?aid=29297).

[15] Ibid., 2.

[16] Gaustad and Schmidt offer several explanations for the growing role of the Supreme Court in
mediating the relationship between church and state. These include the application of the First
Amendment to the states; the increasing organization and political activism of religious minorities
who possess the resources to bring religious cases to the Court; and mounting pressures from a
diverse society for a more secular state, especially by the 1960s. Gaustad and Schmidt, *Religious
History of America*, 349–50.

[17] Ibid., 350.

[18] Ibid., 349.

[19] The literature on religious minorities in modern America is voluminous. As a result, I hesitate to
draw firm conclusions as to how disparate religious groups responded to, in Gjerde's words, the
expanded "ideological space" afforded by the twentieth-century legal developments regarding

Finally, Gjerde was keenly aware that contemporary religious debates are not simply academic; they also continue to manifest themselves in countless instances of violence, further attesting to the centrality of religion in American life. As Diana L. Eck, director of the Pluralism Project and professor of comparative religion and Indian studies at Harvard University, reminds us, pluralism and extremism are the two defining features of the contemporary and global religious landscape.[20] Given that responses to the arrival of these new immigrant groups often resemble the nativism directed toward nineteenth-century Catholics, some contemporary observers such as Rhys H. Williams have asked whether "the current cultural conflict over diversity is really anything new."[21] In light of the internecine debates in 2010 over the construction of an Islamic center near Ground Zero in Manhattan, numerous commentators have hearkened back to the nineteenth-century Catholic experience as a model for the contemporary Muslim experience in America.[22] While I strongly suspect that Gjerde would not have created a perfect equation between the history of American Catholics and the histories of Mormons, Jews, Muslims, and freed blacks, among others, he would have drawn our attention to the parallels and then demanded that we offer nuanced explanations for the recurrence of religious conflict in American life. At the same time, he would have asked us to consider how the religious debates of the twentieth and twenty-first centuries differ from those of previous eras.[23] And, I am certain that he would have explored

the establishment and free exercise clauses. It would, however, be safe to say that the responses varied between and even within groups. Sulayman S. Nyang, for example, has identified at least three different orientations among Muslims with respect to the separation of church and state. Nyang's nuanced study serves as an important reminder to scholars to explicate the differences both within and between religious communities, particularly regarding their relationship to the American state. Sulayman S. Nyang, "Seeking the Religious Roots of Pluralism in the United States of America: An American Muslim Perspective," *Journal of Ecumenical Studies* 34, n. 3 (1997): 402–18.

[20] Diana L. Eck, "Prospects for Pluralism: Voice and Vision in the Study of Religion," *Journal of the American Academy of Religion* 75 (December 2007): 743.

[21] Rhys H. Williams, "The Languages of the Public Sphere: Religious Pluralism, Institutional Logics, and Civil Society," *Annals of the American Academy of Political and Social Science* 612 (July 2007): 44 (citing John Higham, "Cultural Responses to Immigration," in *Diversity and Its Discontents: Cultural Conflict and Common Ground in Contemporary American Society,* ed. N. Smelser and J. Alexander [Princeton, NJ: Princeton University Press, 1999], 39–61; and Jose Casanova, "Civil Society and Religion: Retrospective Reflections on Catholicism and Prospective Reflections on Islam," *Social Research* 68, n. 4 [2001]: 1041–80.)

[22] Religious historians as well as journalists and pundits have drawn parallels between the Catholic and Muslim experiences. One eloquent example is a recent essay by R. Scott Appleby and John T. McGreevy that exhorts Americans to learn from the past so that they may ameliorate the discrimination faced by Muslims in the present. R. Scott Appleby and John T. McGreevy, "Catholics, Muslims, and the Mosque," *New York Review of Books,* September 30, 2010.

[23] In this vein, the historian Christopher Beneke offers several fruitful points of comparison between nineteenth-century Catholic history and the twentieth-century Muslim experience. Christopher Beneke, "Non-Papists," *Religion in American History: Group Blog on American Religious History and Culture,* August 28, 2010, http://usreligion.blogspot.com/2010/08/non-papists. html (accessed 27 November 2010).

the larger implications of these disputes by reminding us of the paradox that has characterized American religious history from the founding to the present – that is, the ways in which contemporary religious conflicts have continued to build a nation.

S. Deborah Kang
Berkeley, California

Index